ADIRONDACK CANOE WATERS
NORTH FLOW

by
Paul Jamieson and Donald Morris

with a chapter on camping
by Robert N. Bliss

The Adirondack Mountain Club, Inc.
Lake George, New York

Published by the Adirondack Mountain Club, Inc.
RR3, Box 3055, Lake George, NY 12845-9523

First Edition published 1975, revised 1977.
Second Edition 1981, revised 1984 and 1986.
Third Edition 1988, revised 1991, 1993, and 1994.

Quotations from John Kauffmann's *Flow East* appearing on pp. 46 and 216 are from *Flow East: A Look at Our North Atlantic Rivers,* © 1973 by John M. Kauffmann; used with permission of McGraw-Hill Book Company. The chapters on the AWA Safety Code and Classification of Difficulty are from the American Whitewater Affiliation and are used with permission. Map on p. 58 courtesy of *Adirondack Life:* Vaughan Gray.

Library of Congress Cataloging-in-Publication Data

Jamieson, Paul F.
    Adirondack canoe waters, north flow / Paul Jamieson, Donald Morris; with a chapter on camping by Robert N. Bliss.—3rd ed.
        p.   cm.
    Includes index.
    ISBN 0–935272–43–7 (pbk.)
    1. Canoes and canoeing—New York (State)—Adirondack Mountains Region—Guidebooks. 2. Adirondack Mountains Region (N.Y.)—Description and travel—Guidebooks.   I. Morris, Donald, 1950–
II. Title.
GV776.N72A344 1988
917.47'53—dc19   87–33378
                                                                                                          CIP

Printed and bound in the United States of America

A note about this printing:

This 1994 printing of the Third Edition of North Flow *has several changes from the 1991 printing. The most significant of these is an update on p. 3 regarding the status of the public's right to carry around rapids and other obstructions when the carry is on private land. Other noteworthy changes include new information about points of access to the Raquette River below Piercefield (pp. 88 and 91), a revision of the sketch map showing the carry trail to the Jordan River (p. 94), and a new description of Hatchery Brook, which connects Little Clear Pond with Upper Saranac Lake (p. 210). Other changes in the text are relatively minor and reflect either new information that has come to light since 1991 or refined descriptions of certain rapids.*

This printing continues to include two addenda from the 1991 printing. These cover the Middle Branch of the Oswegatchie from Long Pond Road to Bryants Bridge and a North Flow Voyageur *trip from Newton Falls to Meacham Lake.*

Further changes and additions are anticipated for the Fourth Edition. It is hoped that legal rulings will soon allow descriptions of those canoe routes that are presently restricted.

Donald Morris, August 1994

CONTENTS

PREFACE

A century ago the Adirondacks were the nation's favorite resort for small-boat tripping. The region was a paradise of waters for W. H. H. Murray and the many disciples of his *Adventures in the Wilderness* (1869). "The novel and romantic peculiarity of this wilderness," he wrote, "is its marvelous water communication. . . . One can travel in a canoe or light boat for hundreds of miles in all directions through the forest."

The sport of modern canoeing began about the time of Murray's book. For the next few decades the Adirondacks were the principal scene of activity. Among the first and best craftsmen to meet the new market for canoes was J. Henry Rushton, who had grown up on an Adirondack river, the Oswegatchie. In the 1870s he founded his Boat Shop in Canton, just north of the present park boundary. Here he designed and built many prize-winning models for cruising, sailing, and racing. Among them were the *Sairy Gamp* and other lightweight canoes that George Washington Sears, known as Nessmuk, made famous in stories of three Adirondack cruises in the early 1880s. And when the American Canoe Association was founded in 1880, there was little hesitation over the site. The founders' encampment and the next two annual meets were held on Lake George.

Adirondack canoe waters gradually lost their primacy with the increasing mobility of Americans on vacation. The motorcar and interstate highways made distant regions accessible. New highways in the Adirondack Park itself, where few roads existed a century ago, diverted travel from the waters. Many traditional canoe routes were neglected and then forgotten.

But the network of waters is still there. The past can be recovered. Many Adirondack rivers are authentically wild. Most of them are also clean, to the relief of paddlers accustomed to the discolored, smelly waters and littered banks of many Eastern rivers.

In re-exploring this network, I have often felt like the city dweller who began a new life in the sticks: I have seen the past and it works.

True, the past might work better. Some of the old canoe and guide-boat routes, both river courses and chains of lakes and ponds, are now partly or wholly closed to the public by posting in private parks and corporate timberlands. Yet this guidebook describes nearly 800 miles of open canoe waters in two of the five major drainage basins of the park: the St. Lawrence River and the Lake Champlain basins. North Flow, as the two watersheds are called here, looks on the map like a lopsided lady's fan three-quarters open. At the left tip is the West Branch of the Oswegatchie; at the right, the Boquet River, from which hangs the tassel of Lakes Champlain and George. The fan consists of 26 navigable rivers, including branches; several naviga-ble brooks; and about 1,400 lakes and ponds.

Enamored of the High Peaks, outdoorsmen in recent times have slighted other areas of the Adirondacks. This is easy to do in a park slightly larger than the state of New Hampshire. The consequence has been overuse and deterioration of trails and summits in the High Peaks of the northeast and underuse of canoe waters and foot trails in other sectors. A canoe goes gently through the wilds. Wakes are sooner wiped out than footprints. Canoeing waters, moreover, lead the hiker to areas where foot trails are little eroded and bushwhacking is an act of discovery.

The Adirondacks are once again beckoning canoeists who seek a wild forest environment. Negative as well as positive factors are bring-ing this about: dam building for irrigation or power in the Southwest and elsewhere; the overuse plaguing such popular waterways as the Allagash, the Everglades, and many a Western river; quota systems in the Boundary Waters and the Okefenokee Swamp; and, in some of the river canyons of the national parks, reservation systems that favor commercial tour operators at the expense of the free-lance paddler.

"Overuse" is a subjective term. In the Adirondacks the Raquette may be approaching overuse. The white water of the Upper Hudson is attracting some whose temerity exceeds their skill, as broken canoes in the Hudson Gorge testify. But as yet no regimentation exists on these or other Adirondack streams. Time and place are at the will of the paddler.

There are other positive factors. The Adirondack forest is, paradoxi-cally, more beautiful today than it was a century ago. The photographs of S. R. Stoddard and some of the watercolors of Winslow Homer show river corridors, hillsides, and lake shores devastated by fire, clear-cutting, or flooding through the building of dams to float logs. The last two practices have come to an end, and there have been no large-scale forest fires since early in this century. State-owned lands (now over forty percent of the park's six million acres and growing as new acquisitions are made) are a forest preserve protected by the "forever wild" state constitutional amendment of 1894.

"Forever wild," like "overuse," is a subjective term. Since 1894 successive conservation commissioners have interpreted it variously. Some have sought to domesticate the woods for the tenderfoot. This tendency, along with uncontrolled development on private lands, prompted John M. Kauffmann to remark in his fine book *Flow East:* "Without a vast rollback to wild status, most of the famed Adirondack waterways which captured the heart and imagination of eastern America in the last century are destined to be forever only partly wild."

Even as Kauffmann wrote, his plea for a rollback was being met in the work of the Temporary Study Commission on the Future of the Adirondacks. And in 1972 a master plan for the state lands of the park at last established precise standards for "forever wild" and regulations for realizing these standards. It designated sixteen wilderness and canoe areas for the greatest degree of protection, as well as primitive, wild forest, and intensive use zones. In 1973 a zoning plan for the private land within the park was also adopted. Its purpose is to prevent overdevelopment and to safeguard the open-forest appearance of vast areas.

The Adirondack Park Agency, which prepared the two plans, was also charged with making a survey of Adirondack rivers and devising protective regulations. The Rivers Act became law in 1972; it provides that designated rivers "shall be preserved in free-flowing condition and that they and their immediate environs shall be protected for the benefit and enjoyment of present and future generations." By 1986, 1,238 miles of Adirondack rivers were brought under the system and classified as wild, scenic, or recreational. Future impoundments (except for log fishery dams) are prohibited in all three categories. Motor vehicles of all kinds and new structures are prohibited on rivers classified as wild, and development on privately owned scenic and recreational river corridors is controlled in density, setback, sewage disposal, timber cutting, and other respects. This comprehensive legislation is a model for the nation.

In his autobiography Bertrand Russell says that the few moments of peace he experienced in life were in the presence of moving water. Peace could hardly come more beguilingly than on a balsam-spired river bend in the Adirondacks, with only the song of the whitethroat, spirit of the north woods, breaking the silence. In their brawling moods these upland rivers also offer challenge and exhilaration. Most of all they invite awareness. Land forms, sky patterns, and the community of plant, animal, and bird life are on display in river corridors as nowhere else in the forest. Wild rivers are the museums of the natural world. They are as different one from another as art galleries are likely to be.

In an attempt to convey the distinctive qualities of each river, tabular presentation is rejected. Directives and statistics are woven into connected discourse. This method may turn off some paddlers used to quick summations. The risk is taken in the hope of enriching the experience of river running by addressing not only the paddler but also the amateur geologist, geographer, historian, folklorist, and naturalist.

The Carry. By history and design the canoe is an amphibious craft. Two positions natural for it are bottomside down in the water and upside down on the shoulders of a single carrier. For portages of over 200 yards, the latter way is generally less awkward and tiring than the two-person, at-the-side carry. The lone kayaker has an advantage in the light weight of his craft. But today many lightweight single and tandem canoes are available and serve well enough for the Adirondacks, where one is seldom more than two or three days from a supply source.

In the Adirondacks the portage has always been known as the carry. Saranac guides of the last century were capable of prodigious carries, one of which was a rough five-mile affair over a shoulder of Ampersand Mountain from Middle Saranac Lake to Ampersand Lake. But the lengthy carry is an aspect of the past not recommended for revival; modern highways are good for something. Most carries today range from a few yards to one mile. In ten minutes of practice in the backyard, one can learn the knack of grasping the center thwart at opposite sides, rolling the canoe bottom over a bent knee, thrusting upward with the knee as the arms swing the craft over head and shoulders, and then balancing it with outspread arms grasping the gunwales and the bow slightly uptilted for visibility. The center thwart can be padded for comfort, or a yoke (supplied by many canoe factories) can be clamped to it.

Side Excursions. Beached or hidden in the bush is a third position natural for canoes. It is a pleasant variation in mode of travel to climb a mountain for the view or follow the windings of an esker crest or a cascading brook. The fullest enjoyment comes from a combination of canoeing, hiking, and overnight camping. The following pages describe side trips on foot—some on trails, others through untracked woods with the aid of compass and topographical map—which amount to a comprehensive guide for walks in the northwest sector of the park. For hiking trails in the High Peak region of the northeast, one should consult the Adirondack Mountain Club's *Guide to Adirondack Trails: High Peaks Region,* hereafter called *Guide to Adirondack Trails.*

Maps. Most of the routes described in the text are represented in forty sketch maps. Some readers of the first edition complained of difficulty in finding certain put-in sites from verbal directions. My explanation in the preface to that edition was: "Sketch maps were rejected in favor of indicating U.S. Geological Survey maps needed for each tour. No sketch or reproduction possible in book form is as richly informative as detailed topographic maps. They contribute greatly to understanding and enjoyment of an area. They are of course essential . . . for side excursions where trails do not exist."

That statement is still valid, and the practice of naming USGS maps for each tour is continued in this edition. In the meantime, however, the price of topographic maps has risen. Over sixty of them would be necessary for all the tours described herein. This number increases by three each time a new 7.5-minute map (one inch equals 2,000 feet) replaces a 15-minute quadrangle (one inch equals approximately one mile). Maps of the 7.5-minute series are now available for much of the Adirondack Park. The larger scale makes greater detail possible. Perhaps their most valuable feature is that, unlike the 15-minute series, they show the boundaries of state-owned forest preserve. The United States Geological Survey also issues metric maps for some areas, especially in the northeast sector of the park. These cover 7.5 minutes of latitude and 15 minutes of longitude, twice the area of the 7.5 series and half that of the 15-minute one.

Care has been taken to make the sketch maps as satisfactory a substitute as possible. But canoeists on camping trips who want to combine some hiking with paddling are advised to supplement them with USGS maps. The latter are available at sporting goods stores and some book stores in most Adirondack villages. They can also be ordered directly from the U.S. Geological Survey's Map Distribution Center (Bldg. 41, Box 25286, Denver, CO 80225). Allow three weeks for delivery. Orders must specify state, map title, and series. An index map of New York State is available, without charge; it shows the outlines of quadrangles and lists local dealers. To avoid wetting and tearing, insert the maps needed for each trip in a clear plastic case.

Rental and Transportation. Canoes can be rented throughout the Adirondacks. Many marinas provide hauling service, at least for large parties. A small party of one or two canoes should be equipped with a cartop carrier. Reservations can be made by calling one of the following centrally located marinas: *In area code 315,* Old Forge, Rivett's, 369-3123; Raquette Lake, Burke's, 354-4623; Cranberry Lake, Trout's, 848-3698. *In area code 518,* Blue Mountain Lake Outfitters, 352-7306 or 7675; Long Lake Marina, 624-2266; Moody, McDonald's 359-9060; Tupper Lake, Raquette River Bike and Boat Livery, 359-3228; Fish Creek Ponds, Hickok Boat Livery, 891-0480 or 3328; Hoel Pond, St. Regis Canoe Outfitters, 891-1838; Lower Saranac Lake, Crescent Bay, Inc., 891-2060; Saranac Lake (village), Swiss Marine, 891-2130.

When only one car is used, a shuttle problem arises. Walking back from the end of the float trip may be too time consuming. Some canoeists use a bike for the shuttle, hiding or padlocking it at the take-out site. Where there is only one access to a stream, the shuttle problem does not arise. The current is moderate enough on many Adirondack rivers to make upstream paddling easy. Where it is not, a canoeist who has acquired poling techniques enjoys an independence denied to others. He drives to put-in, poles upstream, and floats back with paddle. If experienced, he can ascend rapids of paddle-breaking force. He also enjoys an advantage in small, shallow creeks and the upper reaches of rivers.

Classification of Difficulty and Safety. This guide is intended for the canoe or kayak traveler who may range in skill from novice to expert. The novice never goes alone. He does not take chances in wild regions where help is not quickly available. He is chary even of Class II rapids and doesn't attempt them until, after examination from shore, he feels certain of success. The rating of rapids as Class I, II, III, etc., is based on the international classification system quoted in the appendix, along with the safety code of the American Whitewater Affiliation. The ratings are useful as approximate indications of risk and difficulty. But they have limitations. Estimates are subjective to some extent. Nature resists reduction to six neat categories. There is latitude within a class. And different water levels may mean different degrees of risk and difficulty. An easy Class II at medium level may turn into a torrent after a downpour; conversely, a rock garden requiring close maneuvering at low water may be, at high level, as smooth as a lake. For these reasons, even the instructed and practiced beginner should reconnoiter a rapid designated as Class II if it bends or drops out of sight; and then, if in doubt, cheerfully carry (or wade or line the canoe) around the rough stretch, as he would for a Class III or higher. In the northwest sector of the Adirondacks especially, there are several cruising routes with no rapids or only mild ones. Even on the whitewater streams of the northeast, there are smooth reaches to which a tour can be limited.

Training with a group under competent instruction is the best preparation for river running. If this is not practicable, the following paperback manuals are helpful:

Canoeing, American National Red Cross, 452 pp., softbound. A complete manual, well illustrated.
Basic River Canoeing, Robert E. McNair, 102 pp., softbound.
The Complete Wilderness Paddler, James West Davidson and John Rugge, 260 pp., softbound.
The White Water Handbook, John T. Urban, 198 pp., softbound.
The Kayaking Book, Jay Evans, 275 pp., softbound.

Abbreviations, Symbols, Names. Unless the context indicates otherwise, R and L (right and left) refer to positions in downstream travel. Small m. stands for mile or miles; km. for kilometers. DEC is the New York State Department of Environmental Conservation and APA the Adirondack Park Agency. N, S, E, and W stand for north, south, east and west.

"Blue Line" refers to the boundary of the Adirondack Park. A four-section wall map of the park published by the DEC shows the boundary as a heavy blue line, with state lands shaded in red.

Adirondack naming is haphazard. Many "ponds" are of lake size and several "lakes" are ponds. Some lakes have two names, plain and fancy. Variant spellings are common. The 19th century trappers, guides, and lumberjacks who dropped names on the land were shy of the apostrophe. "Paul Smiths," the post office address, would never do for a college; so it is Paul Smith's College, Paul Smiths, N.Y. "Sols Rapids," "Hulls Falls," etc., are still honored by the U.S. Geological Survey; tradition must be kept up. In general, names appear here as they are on USGS maps, with apologies to sticklers for "Racquette" or "Racket," "Grasse" or "Degrasse," etc.

Changes and Corrections. With each new printing or edition of this guide at intervals averaging three years, numerous revisions are necessary. One might assume that, in wilderness areas at least, change could be reckoned in geologic time. But even here the DEC can intervene with alterations in management policy. Change is endemic in other areas of the Forest Preserve and in the private lands of the park. Canoe routes can be opened or closed as property is exchanged between private owners or between a private party and the state. Readers are invited to report errors or changed conditions to Paul Jamieson at 13 Jay Street, Canton, N.Y. 13617, or to Donald Morris at 166 Park Avenue, Saranac Lake, N.Y. 12983.

Third Edition. In this edition a co-author comes on board. Henceforth Donald Morris will keep *North Flow* current, with diminishing assistance from Paul Jamieson. Even paddlers must eventually retire. Of a younger generation, Don is an experienced kayaker at home in technical waters beyond the skill of the original writer. Readers will note a principal difference between this and earlier editions in the new or considerably more detailed descriptions of whitewater routes. For the convenience of advanced paddlers in canoe or kayak, segments of sustained rapids are indexed under "whitewater routes."

Paul Jamieson

PREFACE TO THIRD EDITION

Readers of this edition will note a number of additions. At Paul Jamieson's request, I have expanded certain portions of this book. First and foremost, I have added a number of completely new descriptions. These typically cover sections of extended whitewater not generally regarded as cruising sections but nonetheless interesting and challenging for those with the requisite skills. Secondly, I have modified earlier descriptions by providing additional elaborations of particular rapids or sections of rapids. In some cases the elaborations are minimal, whereas in others they are extensive. Finally, I have included updated information about a number of pertinent developments such as land acquisitions, dam proposals, etc.

As the major focus of my additions has been the description of whitewater runs, it is increasingly important for readers, particularly less experienced paddlers, to take note of the Safety Code and International Scale of Difficulty in the appendix of this book. North Flow contains numerous rapids of each difficulty level. Some are bound to think that I have overrated the difficulty level of certain rapids, while others will think the difficulty levels are underrated. I have tried diligently to assume a middle-of-the-road attitude that would portray difficulty levels accurately to the majority of paddlers. This is understandably difficult in a sport where water levels change so drastically and where there is so much reliance upon a subjective rating system. Remember that ratings are only general guidelines and cannot substitute for experience, good judgment, and careful preparation. Keep this in mind when determining which rapids can be safely run with your current skill level, the strength and size of your party, air and water temperature, remoteness, and other pertinent factors.

Readers will note that I frequently "split the difference" in assigning difficulty levels. For example, many rapids are rated Class II-III or Class IV-V. My rationale for this is that many experienced paddlers prefer a finer discrimination than that allowed by a six-point scale. It is also important to note that the actual difficulty of a rapid can easily vary from the assigned rating by as much as one degree of difficulty in either direction because of changes in water conditions. For example, a Class III rapid in late spring can easily fade to a Class II by early summer or be a powerful Class IV during early spring snowmelts. Extreme conditions can lead to even greater variations. Experience and good judgment must be used.

As a general rule throughout the book I have avoided the use of first person pronouns in order to avoid confusions with references to Paul's experiences or feelings. I have clearly indicated those few exceptions to this rule. Also, I have generally preferred to use the term "paddler" rather than canoeist or kayaker. This is because decked and open canoes are increasingly seen on whitewater runs.

Acknowledgements. First and foremost I would like to extend my utmost appreciation to Paul Jamieson for inviting me to partake in this venture and for all the assistance he has given. This includes careful review of manuscripts, sharing of pertinent information, and general guidance throughout the several years that it took me to run these rivers and prepare the manuscripts. It is an honor to be able to contribute to a book which has justifiably been considered a classic. Secondly, I would like to thank my wife, Karen, who helped immensely in the editing and preparation of countless draft and final manuscripts. I would also like to thank her for her support and understanding during the long periods of time it took to paddle these rivers. Finally, I would like to thank all those who have provided assistance in one form or another. This includes fellow paddlers Bill Schoch, Gary Marchuk, Dave Nettles, David Butler, Tom Dodd, and Tom Kligerman. Their presence not only made these trips possible but much more enjoyable as well. I would also like to thank those who provided additional information that proved most valuable in correcting or updating information about various rivers: Gary Koch, Ron Canter, Henry Kirchner, Robert Bliss, Gordon Tharrett, David Trithart, Paul Capone, and Tom Windt.

Donald Morris

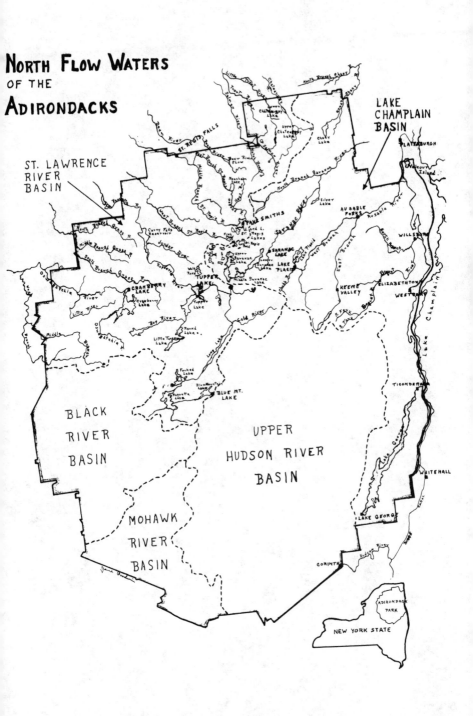

NORTH FLOW WATERS
OF THE
ADIRONDACKS

LAKE
CHAMPLAIN
BASIN

ST. LAWRENCE
RIVER
BASIN

BLACK
RIVER
BASIN

UPPER
HUDSON RIVER
BASIN

MOHAWK
RIVER
BASIN

ADIRONDACK
PARK

NEW YORK STATE

NORTHWEST WATERSHED

The St. Lawrence River Basin is the largest of the five major drainage systems in the park. It consists of streams that rise in the central or northern highlands and empty into the parent river in St. Lawrence and Franklin counties or in Quebec Province. The westernmost is the West Branch of the Oswegatchie; the easternmost, the Chateaugay.

Geologists call these rivers "young" because their courses were altered during the ice age, perhaps as recently as ten thousand years ago. Some preglacial channels were filled, and drainage was deflected into new courses according to the slope and position of glacial deposits.

There are exciting whitewater runs in the northwest sector of the park. But it is in opportunities for river cruising that this basin excels. The tilt of the plateau is gentlest on the northwest, and cruising reaches are longer and more numerous. Nineteen rivers and several navigable brooks beckon the paddler interested in exploring wild country. They are for the most part unpolluted and little marred by development. They are much as Frederic Remington found one of them during a canoe trip in August 1892: "The dark woods tower on either side, and the clean banks, full to their fat sides, fringed with trailing vines and drooping ferns, have not the impoverished look of civilized rivers. The dark water wells along, and the branches droop to kiss it. In front the gray sky is answered back by the water reflection, and the trees lie out as though hung in air, forming a gateway, always receding."

The canoeing season is prolonged in the northwest. In late spring and summer water levels drop less than in most areas of the state. Chain lakes, marshes which release their water slowly, and spongy conifer-forested soils have a regulating effect on runoff and help maintain a steady flow. Between headwaters and the rim of the plateau, streams of the St. Lawrence Basin have long flatwater stretches deep enough to float a small boat throughout the summer. These levels are interrupted by rough gradients which may be canoeable till late spring but in summer are sometimes shallow enough to require carrying, wading, or lining for short to moderate distances.

In physical characteristics the northwest watershed is ideal for canoe cruising. The river valleys are heavily wooded and rich in wildlife. No barbed fences plague the paddler as in farmlands. Logging is rotational, but there is little deforestation. Though the peaks are modest ones in this sector, the ground is fascinatingly uneven, gouged and molded by the last ice sheet into such landforms as eskers, kames, and kettles. On many rivers and chain lakes and ponds the sense of being in a primitive, timeless realm is easy to come by.

Since Eve ate that unlucky apple, however, no paradise has been quite without flaw. The relatively high proportion of private land in the northwest imposes a limitation on boating. Where land ownership is fragmented in small holdings, right of passage is pretty well established by traditional use. Challenges to passage come mostly from large landowners, corporations, clubs, and individual owners of private parks ranging up to the tens of thousands of acres. Restrictions on passage began in the late 1880's with the posting of private parks and later of the timberlands of forestry companies.

For a half century from the arrival of the first tourists about 1840, all waterways were open to travel. Presumably this situation could have continued indefinitely if some authority had invoked prescription (the establishment of a claim by virtue of long use and enjoyment). But this did not happen. On the contrary, the digest of the posting law distributed to landowners declares that "both lands and waters" can be posted. This unqualified statement encourages landowners to assume that they own the waters flowing through their lands. Actually there is no title to running water.

Inland navigation and riparian rights are controlled by a mixture of common law, statutory law, and court interpretations. If the bed of a stream or lake is state owned, it is of course open to public use. But in New York the courts have ruled that title to the beds of ponds, lakes, and non-tidal streams may be vested in private owners. In the northwest sector, where corporate and individual owners have title to hundreds of thousands of acres, the custom has grown up of excluding the public from the banks and beds of navigable streams as well as other bodies surrounded by private land.

Although interpretations have differed on the use of privately owned stream beds, a landowner's right to prohibit the use of the shore for lining or carrying around obstructions has had tacit recognition for the last hundred years in the Adirondacks. And this is Catch 22. It is ironic to affirm the public's right to travel on streams navigable in fact and yet withhold a necessary condition of travel. Few streams are free, for any great distance, from obstructions such as shoals, rapids, falls, dams (including the works of beavers), and deadfalls. Some states have recognized this contradiction by enacting a statute. The Idaho code, for instance, provides: "Where irrigation dams or other obstructions interfere with the navigability of a stream, members of the public may remove themselves and their boats, floats, canoes, or other floating crafts from the stream and walk or portage such crafts around said obstruction at the nearest point where it is safe to do so."

In New York State public rights in this respect are not categorically spelled out as yet. Access is legal at most bridges on public roads and on state land, but right of passage is a different matter. Care has been taken to ascertain the attitudes of landowners and lessees and to report them in this guide. Changes in ownership make revisions necessary with each reprinting. Some owners, while posting against other kinds of trespass, are willing to allow paddlers to use the shore for the sole purpose of transporting a boat. Most have refused this concession, citing such reasons as suspicion that boaters would hunt, fish, camp, leave litter, or damage property; desire for privacy; interference with an ongoing fisheries experiment; and possible liability for injury. The last reason is no longer valid. In 1977 an amendment to section 9-103 of the General Obligations Law added canoeing to the recreational activities a landowner can permit without incurring liability for injury to person or property. He has no duty to keep his premises safe for such use or to give warning of dangerous conditions. He can be held liable only if "willful or malicious failure to warn" can be proved.

We may be entering a new era that restores the freedom of water travel enjoyed in the last century. A pending case in state Supreme Court will likely result in a modern interpretation of the public's common law right of passage on navigable streams. Since the last edition, a landowner brought a five million dollar trespass suit against a party of canoeists who paddled down the South Branch of the Moose River in 1991. The state Attorney General and ADK intervened in the case on the test of navigability issues. By the summer of 1994, both the trial court and a middle level appellate court have ruled that recreational use of a stream can establish that a waterway is navigable in fact and thus open for public use. Once a stream is established to be navigable in fact, both courts concluded that the public's right to navigate includes the right to use the bed of the river or stream below the mean high water mark to detour around natural obstructions, to line, and to portage below the mean high water mark if necessary. However, the Moose River case is likely to be appealed to the state's highest court, the Court of Appeals and so it cannot yet be considered a final decision. Until there is a final decision, ADK members should not attempt to paddle this river.

Similarly, until the navigability issues involved in the Moose River case are finally resolved, paddlers wishing to avoid similar litigation should confine their travel to rivers and streams where there are no posted carries or contested issues of navigability.

OSWEGATCHIE RIVER

People wonder about the name *Oswegatchie*. Lewis Morgan's early warning that the meaning is lost has not prevented several reputed authorities from trying to satisfy this curiosity. According to Onondaga tradition, *Oswegatchie* means *black river*. Beachamp says that *black water* may be authentic if you add the idea of *flowing out* or *draining a great region*. According to the famous guide Sabattis, whose credentials are questioned because he was an Algonquin, it means *long* or *slow*. E. R. Wallace elaborates: *"Os-we-gatchie* or *Ogh-swa-gatchie . . .* signifies *going or coming round a hill. . . .* An Indian tribe, bearing the name of the river, once lived upon its banks; but its fate, like that of many sister tribes, has been to melt away before the progressive step of the Anglo-Saxon."

Indian names have also tended to melt away before the Anglo-Saxon. But the Vermonters who settled northern New York after the Revolution were progressive enough to invent another interpretation, now established in North Country folklore. According to this, a party of horseback riders originated the name when they caught a runaway on the river bank and chortled, " 'Oss, we got ye!"

This guide has now discharged its obligation to Adirondack etymology. It is more at home with the intricacies of a braided Adirondack river.

The Oswegatchie is a major drainage system of the NW sector with a length of about 135 m. All three branches rise in northern Herkimer or northwestern Hamilton County. The main or East Branch flows through one of the largest of Adirondack lakes, Cranberry. Buck Pond, a source of the West Branch, is separated from a loop in the Middle Branch only by a quarter-mile ridge. The separation widens to about 6 m. as these two branches flow W into Lewis County and then swing N. The West Branch absorbs the Middle near Harrisville and enters St. Lawrence County to join the East Branch below

Talcville. The main stem then runs a circuitous course to the St. Lawrence at Ogdensburg. A tributary, the Indian River, joins it below Black Lake. The Indian is not considered here because it is a mere unnavigable brook inside the Blue Line. Outside, it has a long cruising reach through woodlots and farmlands.

The lower Oswegatchie was a boundary between the easternmost of the Iroquois nations, the Mohawks and the Oneidas. It was an artery for their canoes in beaver hunts and raids on the Hurons of Canada. Probably it was known to nameless French trappers in the early 17th century. But the first white man of record to travel on the river was a captive of the Mohawks—the French Jesuit priest Joseph Poncet. In 1653 he was released and returned to New France under Indian escort. Poncet made the eight-day foot journey up a trail along West Canada Creek and through mountain passes of the western Adirondacks in a daze of exhaustion. Finally taking to canoe, the party then descended the lower Oswegatchie for two days to its mouth and thence through the rapids of the St. Lawrence to Montreal.

For more than a century the Oswegatchie had close associations with the French empire in America. On a 1664 map in *The Jesuit Relations* it appears as the only southern tributary of the St. Lawrence between Lake Ontario and the Richelieu River. Poncet's journey eleven years earlier had made it known to the French as a travel route to the Iroquois nations in central New York. Its course is shown at exaggerated length and bears the inscription in French: "River that comes from the direction of the Mohawks," as Poncet himself had come.

Nearly a century later, in 1749, another French priest, François Picquet, founded a settlement for Christian converts among the Iroquois at the mouth of the Oswegatchie, where modern Ogdensburg stands. La Présentation, as Picquet called his mission, was also a fortified post. It figured in skirmishes of the French and Indian Wars until it was abandoned in 1760 after Wolfe's conquest of Quebec.

Today the lower Oswegatchie flows through dairy country. But on its upper branches remnants of the wilderness Father Poncet traversed three centuries ago are still to be found. Best known to canoeists is the East Branch with its long reach of flatwater and its corridor of virgin timber in Herkimer County. The West and Middle branches, on the other hand, are steep and difficult of access near their headwaters. But within the Adirondack Park, the West Branch offers several miles of choice cruising; recent acquisitions along the Middle Branch now allow a remote and lengthy combination of flatwater and whitewater.

WEST BRANCH

Long Pond Area, 8 m. (12.9 km.)
USGS: Number Four 15, Belfort 7.5

The big surprise is the azaleas. You don't have to go to the Carolinas in April to see them. In these days of energy shortage, just wait two months for the spring to come up this way and then wheel your canoe to the Long Pond area of the West Branch. Everything about this trip, on a sunny day in early June when the wild azaleas are at their height, is sheer joy. Everything except the blackflies, at the height of *their* season too. Never mind them. Concentrate on the varied waters—chain ponds connected by narrow corridors of stream with riffles dancing in shafts of sunlight, marshy floodplains, waterfalls in sculptured granite; and on the sudden splashes of color amid dark evergreens and the spicy scent in the air. Azaleas in the North Woods? Yes. Not the range of colors you see in the April gardens of Charleston, but the pure, glowing pink of the wild variety.

The drive from Belfort in Lewis County is a pleasure in itself. This hamlet is a trim relic of the past. Its streets are forest lanes, with a dozen or so houses under canopies of maple leaves, a balconied general store, and a neat churchyard of weathered headstones and immaculate white-steepled church. St. Vincent de Paul's is said to be the oldest Catholic church still standing between Utica and Canada. The Long Pond Road bears east on the north side of the Beaver River in Belfort. It is a shady lane 10 m. long and blacktopped most of the way (at road junctions, follow the blacktop). It climbs the plateau by stages, flat pastures alternating with ascents through woodlots of maples and finally unbroken wild forest.

At 6.5 m. the road makes the first of three crossings of the West Branch, where the stream describes a series of wide loops through chain ponds. (The three bridges will hereafter be referred to as lower, middle, and upper.) A low density summer colony is clustered around and between the bridges. The outlying loops of the river are undeveloped.

In early June few summer people are in residence. The river is at medium level or better so that little or no tracking through shoals should be ncessary. The white of bunchberry bracts, Canada mayflower, and false Solomon's seal gives a clean, tidy look to the forest floor. Pink lady's slipper is also common. But the unique feature of the West Branch among north-flow waters is the wild azalea.

All land to the Herkimer County line is private. But the state, which stocks the Buck Pond headwater with speckled trout, has acquired easements for public fishing on river and pond shores. Trails open to the public are indicated by yellow state signs and include the put-in sites mentioned below. At the north end of Long Pond are camp buildings of the Future Farmers of America, a summer extension school. The school has a few lean-tos on the river below the upper road bridge, but these are of course private and must not be used for camping unless permission is obtained from a caretaker or manager. It is possible to sample the two canoeable levels within the Blue Line in one long day. Parties that want to fish, hike, or linger in the area might consider an overnight camp on state land at the head of the upper level, just over the county line. If time is limited to a half day, only the lower level should be attempted.

Upper Level. There are no developments except footbridges in this two-mile stretch, consisting mostly of marshy floodplains. In the state Rivers System it is classified as scenic. Put-in is at the lower end, and a round trip is necessary.

Drive to the end of town maintenance on the Long Pond Road,

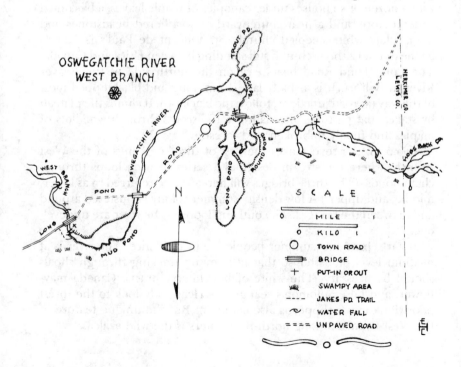

about 0.7 m. beyond the upper bridge. Here, at the edge of a clearing, turn R on the Jakes Pond Trail, which may or may not have a sign and DEC trail disc (sometimes vandalized) at this junction. Drive 0.1 m. downgrade to parking space, close to a splash pool in the West Branch. Carry the canoe 0.2 m. up an easy grade over bedrock, following trail markers. Instead of crossing the footbridge at the head of a waterfall, stay on the N side of the river among lady's slippers and pines and look for a put-in on shelving rock.

For the next 1.25 m. upstream the river winds through a marshy basin between hardwood slopes. Widths vary from 30 to 100 feet. Around a bend at about 1 m. two boulders mark the site of a beautiful azalea bush, the only one in this first stretch. Not far above this is a rift 100 yards long where the stream bed rises a few feet to a beaver dam and a footbridge on the Jakes Pond Trail. There is no carry trail around the rift, and the banks are bushy. The easiest ascent of the rapids is made by tracking in water from ankle to knee depth.

Above the footbridge another, more scenic floodplain opens. Narrower and deeper, the river first winds among standing dead trees, drowned in the flooding caused by the beaver dam. It then circles a grove of fine tall tamaracks and continues between low banks of marsh grass enclosed by wooded hills. The canoe can easily be lifted over any of the beaver dams that may have survived spring floods. Halfway through this stretch of .75 m., on your L headed upstream, is a splash of azalea bloom on the hillside——the finest display of all if your trip is properly timed (late May, if the spring is an early one, to June 10). Elsewhere the shrubs appear singly or in small clusters; here they are massed.

Once past the prominent mouth of Hogs Back Creek (on your L headed upstream), you are across the Herkimer County line and will soon reach the head of navigation at a narrow, bouldery gorge. This is state land where camping is permitted. A patch of sward on the N bank makes a fair campsite. Maximum defense against blackflies and mosquitoes is essential here, including a tent with floor. The Jakes Pond Trail is a short distance up the N bank. If you are not camping, retrace the route to put-in.

Jakes Pond Trail, 4.2 m. This trail, which begins at the Long Pond Road, is varied and scenic. For the first 1.6 m. it is an easement through private land. At the Herkimer County line (marked on the trail) it enters Forest Preserve, crosses the West Branch for the third time, and then bears SE to Jakes Pond, passing a waterfall en route. A good place for canoeists to pick up the trail and shorten the distance by 1 m. is at the second footbridge. Take care to lead E from the bridge. This will take you through the splendid patch of azaleas seen earlier from the river.

Lower Level, 6 m. This cruise would logically begin at the pool below the waterfall where the car was parked for the Upper Level, but this is not advised. Below the pool the stream enters a narrow, unnavigable gorge of cascades and boulders. Carries over rough ground in bug season should be avoided if possible. An inverted canoe shelters hordes of head-hunting insects. A June canoeist soon learns to stay on water as much as possible, relying on breezes to disperse blackflies or on a speed of 3 to 4 miles an hour to leave them trailing. So skip a half-mile section of the West Branch. Drive back 0.5 m. on the Long Pond Road to a jeep track on the S side of the road (0.2 m. E of the upper bridge if coming from the other direction). Park on the town road near the jeep track and carry your canoe 0.2 m. downgrade to a covered footbridge, a quixotic creation of the Future Farmers of America. Put in here for a short float down-stream to Round Pond. This section of the West Branch to the park boundary has been classified as recreational by the APA.

Cross Round Pond to a narrow strait spanned by a footbridge on the W shore. Head for the outlet at the NE bay of Long Pond. Here the West Branch is a narrow shady lane between densely wooded banks. In the next 0.5 m. to Rock Pond there are two or three shoals. The boys of the FFA canoe the river all summer, prepared to wade. In June wading is usually avoidable by keeping in the main current. The bottom of my ABS plastic canoe ripples flexibly as it slides over the cobbles; an aluminum canoe might stick to them in places. Near Rock Pond there is a carry of 15 feet, R, around a low dam.

Rock Pond is apparently named for a large boulder on the W shore. The tawny cliffs of Trout Pond are more impressive and justify a side trip through a narrow strait at the N end of Rock. Returning, paddle S into the outlet of Rock, which is wide for the first 0.6 m. Floating logs may block the channel at a log bridge, requiring a short carry on the R.

The current quickens as the West Branch narrows again, winds down a gentle incline, and dances over the cobbles. The next 0.6 m. is the loveliest part of the river, secretive and gay. Moss and ferns line the banks; arching trees admit glancing shafts of sunlight, making the ripples sparkle. At wide intervals azalea bloom lights up a dark background of evergreens. The canoe moves easily with the current without paddling; just keep it in the deepest part of the channel and relax.

Azalea bushes become more numerous and taller as the stream widens and flattens again, backed up now by a dam 2 m. downstream. The middle bridge on the town road and a cluster of summer camps are passed on entering Mud Pond. The outlet of this pond is a wide submerged marsh ending at a dam just above the lower bridge on the Long Pond Road. The carry, R, is a well-defined trail of 70 yards to the road, passing camps.

The route continues on the other side of the road, where there is a public parking lot. From this a carry trail descends alongside a picturesque waterfall, best seen from the footbridge at its head. The river drops about 30 feet here. At the foot of the carry is a sheltered spring of very cold drinking water.

Launch in the pool below the fall. In the next 0.7 m. the West Branch winds sluggishly through a marshy basin and crosses the Blue Line or park boundary. Where the channel divides around a small island, the roar of a second and more spectacular waterfall can be heard. Either the R or the L channel can be taken and the canoe beached at either end of the footbridge over the head of the fall. In a grove of pines on the R a fringe of shoreline is marked by yellow state fishing-rights posters, and a trail descends steeply to the foot of the fall. A longer trail on the L bank skirts around an outlying part of the fall and the secluded pool below it, to a point, which commands a view of the entire bedrock structure over which the river pours in angular sheets.

The 2.25-m. flatwater reach below this second waterfall would be an anti-climax to the cruise and would create a shuttle problem. Return to the parking lot on the Long Pond Road. If there are two cars in your party, you will have parked one here. Or you could have chained a bike to a tree for shuttle use. Light traffic on the Long Pond Road in June reduces the chance of a pick-up. Never mind. It is a pleasant walk of 3 m. back to your parked car.

MIDDLE BRANCH

Bryants Bridge is the highest point on the Middle Branch which can be reached on a well-maintained road. Above are 31 m. of the most tantalizingly remote watercourse in the NW Adirondacks. It is steep too, with an average drop of 35 feet per mile, much of it in scenic waterfalls. The headwaters lie in the roadless Five Ponds Wilderness of NE Herkimer County, which miraculously escaped logging before the state acquired it from W. Seward Webb in 1896.

Access to the headwaters through the Five Ponds Wilderness Area
is difficult indeed. The June 1987 issue of *Adirondac* describes this
route. Paddle up the East Branch of the Oswegatchie from Inlet,
carry 7.2 m. over the Five Ponds Trail to Sand Lake, float down the
outlet into the Middle Branch and continue 14 m. to the Streeter
Lake trail, an overgrown road, which is gated about 3 miles from the
river. Canoeists can use boat carts to ease the carry. Access to the trail
is by the Streeter Lake Road from Aldrich (see map on p. 41), which
is gated during the off-season, usually until mid-May.

The practicality of visiting this remote area has improved notably
in the past several years because of improved road access and state
purchase of fee title or easement rights. In 1986 a slight improvement in accessibility took place with state purchase of over 16,000
acres in the NW corner of Herkimer County. This opened to the
public a logging road (USGS: *Number Four 15; Oswegatchie SW,
Oswegatchie SE 7.5*) that is an extension eastward of the Long Pond
Road from Belfort described in the previous section and shown on
the sketch maps on pp. 8 and 348.

The second event making the headwater section a more practical
trip occurred in 1989 when Lassiter Properties sold easement rights
to the Nature Conservancy, which in turn transferred them to the
state. These rights are limited to canoe-related activities and cover a
4-mile stretch beginning at the Lewis County line. The easement
thus provides paddlers with a legal means to carry and camp and to
take out at Bryants Bridge. Prior to this easement paddlers were
legally obliged to leave the river further upstream and to utilize
either the Streeter Lake or Pins Creek trail.

Probably the most dramatic story connected with the Middle
Branch is Verplanck Colvin's account of his search for the northwest corner of the Totten and Crossfield Purchase (southern corner
of St. Lawrence County). As state surveyors, Colvin and his men
attempted to trace a line marked in the original survey of 1772. To
find the corner—searching for blazes over a century old, some
hardly distinguishable from minor contortions in the bark, others
on fallen and rotting trees—was the proverbial search for a needle
in a haystack. The terrain was so rough, says Colvin, that his
pedometer recorded nearly 9 m. in going 2 m. of direct distance.
They crossed the Middle Branch at Alder Bed Flow. Finally, on the
fourth day, July 16, 1878, the blazes pointed toward the center of a

glade, and Colvin realized that he stood on the "long sought-for corner, the great pivotal point on which all the land titles of nearly five millions of acres depended" (*Seventh Annual Report of the Topographical Survey . . . to the Year 1879*). He erected a stone monument to mark the corner, a quarter mile E of the Middle Branch.

The Middle Branch reaches a scenic climax in an 8.5-m. stretch half above and half below Bryants Bridge, where it drops from the 1360-foot level to the 850. This is a staircase in pink granite. Each of the nine waterfalls has a unique character. Straight or angular gorges with walls up to 80 feet or more alternate with quiet pools and marshy hollows. A geologist has pointed out that the Middle Branch here, in its descent from the plateau, is at odds with the structural grain of the land. Its many sharp bends are "not true meanders but deflections around bedrock hills" in a channel that is largely postglacial.

The Middle Branch is a small river. Its sculpturings in pink granite gneiss are on a miniature scale. Though it is no match in grandeur for the Ausable Chasm in the eastern Adirondacks, neither is it commercialized as that tourist attraction is. Its fantasies lie hidden in the woods to be discovered by the canoeist who happens to pass that way.

The entire stretch of 8.5 m. is in private land and seems to be little known today except by members of game clubs. The situation was different in the last century when there was a rustic hotel at downstream end. A guidebook writer of the 1880s called this part of the stream "the Elysian Fields of the sportsman." Ninety years later an APA survey team was also impressed. In its report to the Legislature it commented: These "falls and gorge areas are notably scenic and impressive; more so than some of the better known falls and gorges on some of the other rivers of the Park." It gave the classification "scenic" to this part of the river.

For the section from Long Pond Road to Bryants Bridge, see addendum at the back of this book (1991).

Bryants Bridge to Middle Branch Corners Bridge, 6.8 m. (10.9 km.)
USGS: Oswegatchie SW, Remington Corners 7.5

The 4 m. below Bryants Bridge match the dramatic scenery above the bridge, although the average gradient is only half. With a 2.8-m. smooth-water continuation to the bridge near Middle Branch

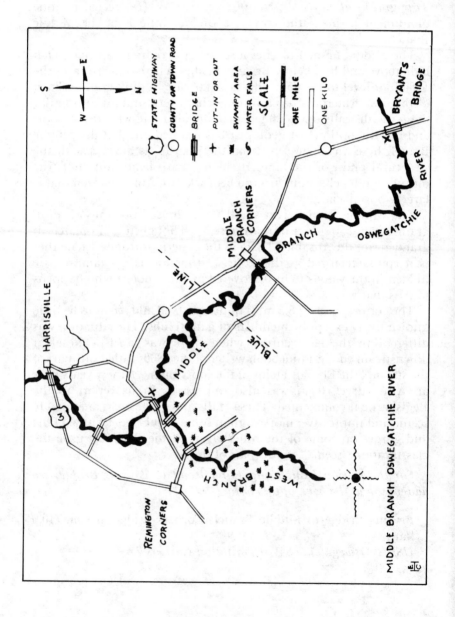

Corners, this lower stretch makes a strenuous but delightful cruise. If carry routes are well chosen, none exceeds 0.25 m. and most are very short.

There are posters around the put-in site at Bryants Bridge. The town right of way extends to the line of trees on both sides of the bridge, however—ample space for launching a canoe. And talks with owners and lessees confirm that posters are directed against hunters and abusers of private property. In the first edition of this guide I was obliged to call this a restricted route after a talk with a deputy sheriff who was then caretaker for the camp at the head of the run and other properties below. But a favorable change has taken place. The new owner of the camp on the R bank below the bridge and members of a game club downstream agree that local use has made this an established route. They assent to public canoeing access and use of the carries to the extent necessary for navigation (no camping of course). I had not anticipated this cordial response. It is rare among private owners and lessees. And it should be encouraged by the most scrupulous behavior on the part of canoeists. The men I approached named four restrictions: no hunting, no camping, no littering, and no canoeing during the big game hunting season, normally from the last week in October through the first weekend in December. It is no hardship to obey these reasonable demands. Scenery is the big attraction of this route, and there is no restriction on enjoying that.

The sound of fast water ahead is a warning to be taken seriously. A young man whose canoe approached too closely the lip of Sluice Falls was swept a quarter mile downstream to his death in July 1980.

For medium to medium-high water levels, May-June and September are ordinarily the best months for this route. The shallowest part is the first quarter mile below Bryants Bridge. If the depth here is adequate to float a canoe, you will find plenty of water in the rest of the run. The river averages about 60 feet wide in flatwater sections but narrows to an amazing 6 to 12 feet in two flume-like gorges.

The two points of access are the road bridge 0.1 m. W of Middle Branch Corners and Bryants Bridge 8.5 m. SE of Harrisville. The two bridges are 4 m. apart by road, 6.8 m. by river. A lightweight canoe and a strong back are desirable. The run can be made in three hours by those familiar with the carries, but for full enjoyment on an initial trip, five hours should be allowed.

The best launching site at the head of the run is the far side of Bryants Bridge. There is a shallow, rocky section of 0.3 m. to thread below the bridge. These mild rapids are followed, below the mouth of Palmer Creek, by a 2-foot pitch over a ledge and a boulder-strewn channel around a bend. You should reconnoiter this Class II-III pitch from the carry trail on the R before attempting it.

The carry trail ends at a pool below the rapids. Halfway across the pool a roar ahead can be distinguished from the chatter behind, and in 0.15 m. the float ends above an 8-foot fall in a split channel around a small island. The framework of the double falls is pink to tawny granite. The carry, R, is 200 feet.

At the next bend, where the river swings N, a short rapid is easily run at medium water level. In another 0.25 m. the river begins to swing a little E of N alongside a ridge on the L shore. This is the first of three transverse fingers of bedrock which deflect the channel in its descent and cause it to double back on itself at elbow bends of 140 degrees or more. Below all three elbows the river plunges down a steep staircase. At the first two you have the choice of proceeding around the elbow and making several short carries or of making a single carry across the ridge to smooth water below the turbulence.

If you choose the single carry at the first elbow, look for a dip in the ridge on the L about 0.1 m. above the sharp bend. The carry is about 0.15 m. in a NWerly direction. Before resuming your float downriver, you might find it worthwhile to reclimb the ridge and follow it out to its point, where the river begins a drop of about 28 feet in sculptured pink granite. There is a rickety footbridge at this point to a hunting camp on the opposite shore.

At the second corner of this zigzag course, reached after 0.4 m. of flat water, the drop is 50 feet in three cascades and a waterfall. Here again a single rough carry can skirt all the turbulence. It begins on the R bank 0.1 m. above the first cascade (no trail) and proceeds WNW to a flat rock beneath the big waterfall. But it would be a shame to miss one of the most scenic segments of this picturesque river. The cost is three short carries or linings over smooth granite buttresses and a slightly longer one in woods around the big waterfall, a spectacular pitch of 25 feet over a wide cliff. A flat rock below the falls on the R bank is a likely spot for a lunch break. You have now descended 90 vertical feet from the put-in site 2 m. back.

The next reach of smooth water is a gratifying 0.8 m., though a strong current hurries you over it. On approaching the third and sharpest elbow and hearing fast water ahead, pull to the L bank where the stream begins a R bend as it is deflected by a ridge. Paddlers in open canoes really have no choice here; they must make the single carry through a saddle in the ridge over a faint trail and slide their craft down a very steep slope. At the foot of the slope, shoulder the canoe again and carry over boulders in a low drainage basin, WNW from the base of the ridge to a smooth-water put-in. This bottom land should be scouted first without a load to determine the shortest distance. The whole carry is 0.25 m. if the route is well chosen.

This is the most spectacular flight on the route. Don't leave before walking on top of the ridge to its point. From the crest you look down on a switchback gorge far below. An opening in the trees gives a stunning view of a quarter-mile stretch of twisting, tumultuous chasm where the river drops nearly 60 feet. At the point of the ridge is a swirling trough of water only 12 feet wide (6 feet at one point!) around a 150-degree bend. A 19th century guidebook calls this Sluice Falls; another local name is Elbow Falls. It has only one peer among the waterfalls of the Middle Branch—Rainbow Falls a mile above Bryants Bridge. Whitewater paddlers with lightweight craft may wish to follow Sluice Falls all the way around the R bank, putting in wherever possible on the lower section. Runnable rapids in this stretch are generally Class II-III.

A 0.7-m. reach of smooth water follows, between high, densely wooded banks. Then comes a mild rapid at a bend. In another quarter mile the last of the carries is reached at a rapid and cascade with a total drop of about 12 feet. Land on the L bank for a carry of 0.1 m. (the R bank is posted here).

The remainder of the trip is a restful float of 2.8 m. in moderate current with no carries. At the bend below the mouth of Fish Creek is a short Class I rapid which may have to be waded at low water but at high levels manifests itself only in a quickening of current. Bedrock now disappears under a deep, fertile cushion of alluvium. The hardwood forest, mixed with hemlock and an occasional pine, is of almost tropical luxuriance. Eroding banks undercut several big trees that lean over the amber water. During May and June these woods are full of birdsong. Sapsuckers hammer out a rhythmic territorial code on metal no-trespassing signs. At the beginning of the last mile there is a house on a bluff at the R. Take-out is either at the upper end of a rock-fill embankment 100 feet above the bridge at Middle Branch Corners or just below the bridge on the L bank.

Middle Branch Corners to the Remington Road, 6 m. (9.6 km.)
USGS: Remington Corners, Harrisville 7.5

Canoeists with a full day at their disposal need not take out at the Middle Branch Corners bridge. The cruise can be extended 6 m.

farther to the next bridge at the Remington Road crossing, 2 m. S
of Harrisville. This is a trouble-free reach of flatwater with a drop
of only 10 feet. Most of it is outside the Blue Line, which crosses
the river about a mile below Middle Branch Corners. A second car
should be available for the 8-m. shuttle by road back to Bryants Bridge.

Shuttle distance is only 4 m. if this lap is done separately, a pleasant
walk unless one has left a bike at the lower bridge. Put-in is about
100 feet upstream from the bridge at the Corners. Cruising time is
about one hour and three-quarters. The river meanders through a
floodplain which averages about a third of a mile wide between lines
of low hills. Marsh and woodland alternate in these bottom lands.
Oaks, which rarely appear above the 1200-foot level on the Adirondack
plateau, are here intermixed with the northern hardwoods. There
are also scattered conifers—spruce, hemlock, and pine. I cruised this
reach in October of an exceptionally wet fall. The river was at flood
stage, sprawling out through red and silver maple groves and making
cut-off lanes at the bends. Yellow leaves still clung to some of the
hardwoods. Leaning trees hung out over the river in the misty light
of a thin overcast. A certain bend reminded my companion of a
Corot painting. This seemed apt, and for the rest of the trip we
floated through a succession of Corots as if in an art gallery.

Confluence of the Middle and West branches is reached near the
end of this stretch. Below the junction, the West Branch, though a
smaller stream, gives its name to the river till it in turn enters the
East or Main Branch. If one turns up the West Branch from its
mouth, he soon reaches a bridge on the French Settlement Road.
Continuing downstream from confluence, however, one reaches the
take-out bridge on the Remington Road in 0.4 m. The L bank provides
dense cover for hiding a canoe during the shuttle.

EAST BRANCH

A hydrologist accounts for the fascination rivers have for him by
saying, "They are so different from one another and so different in
their several parts." The three branches of the Oswegatchie are good
examples. Each has a distinct personality. At Long Pond the West
Branch is gentle and blithe, with a whisper of the South in its wild
azaleas. The Middle Branch is stern but full of creative energy in
the sculpturing it has done in pink granite since the Ice Age. The
East Branch has no azaleas, no pink granite. Where exposed, its rock

is a somber gray. Its brown waters meander through boreal swamp and marsh and conifer forest. You associate it only with things northern, like the song of the white-throated sparrow and the witchhobble bloom of a slow spring awakening in late May. Its beauty is more subtle than that of its siblings. It puts distance between you and the civilized world you have left behind.

That distance increases as you paddle up the East Branch from Inlet amid riverscapes little changed since Indian times. For the stream leads eventually into the most considerable stands of virgin timber left in the Northeast—the Five Ponds Wilderness Area S of the Herkimer County line.

Steep at their headwaters, the West and Middle branches take the short way off the plateau, to the W. The East Branch (hereafter referred to as the Oswegatchie) flows N, the long way off the plateau, before turning W and NW for its sharp descent. Hence it has a long flatwater section beginning near the headwaters. In this it resembles most rivers of the NW watershed. And like them, it is canoeable all summer because of the gradual release of ground water in wooded, swampy basins.

To do justice to the Oswegatchie, canoeists should be prepared for a camping trip of three days to a week. The minimal trip is two days upstream from Inlet and one down. A network of trails leading off the river makes possible a more intimate acquaintance with this region of tall pines, glacial ponds, eskers, swamps, and rounded hills than one gets from the river alone. Plans could well include a night of camping on one of the islands of Cranberry Lake. There is a scattering of lean-tos, but the one you want may be fully occupied. It is wise to bring a tent as well as backpack and hiking shoes. Rain is frequent, and the numerous streams and wetlands are breeding grounds for blackflies and mosquitoes. The insect plague abates in late summer and fall. Provisions are available in Wanakena and Cranberry Lake.

The Oswegatchie above Cranberry Lake, or the Inlet as it is also called, has been a favorite stream with sportsmen since the 1860s. No angler of the 19th century was complete until his initiation on the Oswegatchie. The Inlet's reputation as one of the best trout streams in the state has long outlasted the reality. But in spring many fishermen still go up to High Falls in hope of catching a big one. They need luck or persistence to catch the limit of small ones. The DEC blames this condition on the introduction of perch into Cranberry Lake. Old-time guides blame it on the over-fishing prevalent since the 1920s, when a state highway penetrated the area and drew growing numbers of fishermen in cars and powerboats.

But the Oswegatchie does not need trout to attract canoeists. It wanders through a picture gallery of the North Woods. Here there are no problems created by private ownership. Above Wanakena all the Oswegatchie is in the Forest Preserve except a small inholding on the S bank at Inlet and a few of the remotest headwaters. Red disks mark over forty sites for tent camping, often on piny knolls. The state maintains lean-tos and trails, which are described and mapped in *Guide to Adirondack Trails: Northern Region,* published by the Adirondack Mountain Club. An entertaining book of local history and guide lore is Herbert Keith's *Man of the Woods,* published by the Adirondack Museum and Syracuse University Press.

The *State Land Master Plan* of 1972 recommended that the Oswegatchie above Inlet be closed to motorboats. The classification of this section as a wild river in 1975 was a further step toward this goal. And finally, in January 1978, the order became effective: no more powerboats on the Oswegatchie above Inlet. Motor vehicles of all kinds are banned in the area the river drains.

Above Inlet, 40 m. (64.4 km.) round trip
USGS: Newton Falls, Five Ponds, Wolf Mountain 7.5

The river is canoeable for about 20 m. above Inlet. The head of this stretch is deep in a wilderness area and cannot be reached by road. The tour necessarily begins with upstream paddling. If one goes as far as he can at medium high water, the round trip is 40 m. or more, depending on one's degree of patience in lifting over fallen trees and beaver dams in the narrower part of the river above High Falls. The current is slow to moderate. In 13.2 m. from the foot of High Falls to Inlet, the drop is barely one foot a mile. Above the confluence of the Robinson River, the grade steepens a little and the current is stronger. The downstream trip can be made in about two-thirds of the time taken for an upstream one. At low water it is necessary to wade or line short distances through shallow rock beds. At medium to high water most of the rapids are easy to navigate in both directions. Like other meandering streams of the NW watershed, the upper Oswegatchie has a deep and narrow channel. Near the headwaters at Partlow Milldam it is about 10 feet wide; it broadens to an average of about 75 feet near Inlet.

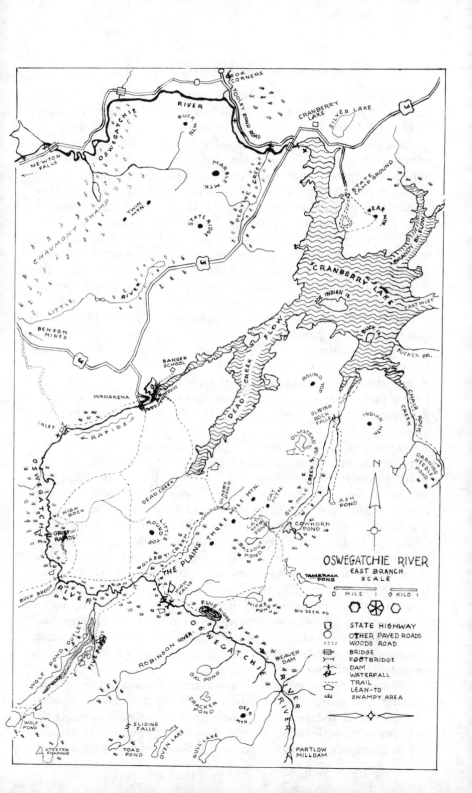

OSWEGATCHIE RIVER
EAST BRANCH
SCALE

0 MILE 1   0 KILO 1

STATE HIGHWAY
OTHER PAVED ROADS
WOODS ROAD
BRIDGE
FOOTBRIDGE
DAM
WATERFALL
TRAIL
LEAN-TO
SWAMPY AREA

N

Access to the river is a dirt road (Sunny Lake Road) S off Route 3 one mile E of the junction of the Benson Mines-Newton Falls road. Take the L fork, where a recessed sign reads "Inlet." This road, 3.2 m. long and partially rerouted, used to be part of the Albany Trail, which continued S through the wilderness to Fish House, Sir William Johnson's sporting lodge near Broadalbin, where it joined a road to Albany. The Albany Trail is one of the likely routes taken by Sir John Johnson and his Loyalist followers and Indian guides in their escape to Canada during the Revolution. During the War of 1812, the state legislature aughorized a road to be built over the route. It was partially constructed, but no wheeled vehicle ever made the whole trip from Fish House to Russell all at one time. Today the northern end is a road only as far S as Inlet; across the river here the continuation is an overgrown hunter's trail.

Inlet is a clearing and boat launching site on the N bank. A graceful rustic suspension footbridge crosses the river to camps in a small private inholding. Inlet has been a natural rendezvous and campground from Indian times to the present. Where the footbridge is now, the river was shallow enough to be forded by men and horses. Heavy rapids prevented navigation downstream, while upstream were many miles of unexcelled trout waters and beaver-hunting grounds.

On maps of the 1890s and early 1900s Inlet was named Sternberg's after George Sternberg and his son, who ran a hotel for sportsmen. River guides foregathered there. Loren and Mary Moore succeeded the Sternbergs. The most recent proprietors, a husband and wife named Smith and their 16 cats, rented boats, served meals and snacks, and took lodgers until, in the 1960s, the state bought the 28-acre inholding and razed the buildings. Nothing remains now but a parking lot, some picnic tables, and a privy. State ownership of Inlet means fewer conveniences for sportsmen but protects the fragile ecology of the little river.

In recent years vandalism and theft have been occasional problems in the parking lot. Minimum precautions are locking car doors and leaving no valuables in sight to lure lock-pickers. A surer precaution is to engage someone to drive you in and come back for you at an agreed date and hour.

The landing is a small sand beach at the upstream end of the Inlet clearing. For the first mile the banks are high and densely wooded with balsam fir and spruce that have grown to moderate size since the last lumbering early in the century. Toward the end of this reach are two small rapids, where caution is needed to avoid scraping submerged rocks. All rapids on the upper Oswegatchie are short, mild ones of Class I, but one or two can be more successfully ascended by poles than by paddles at medium to high water. At low water rocky shoals may require tracking for a few yards.

The river now weaves through a swamp. Otter Pond Outlet comes in on the W and Dorsey Creek on the E; their mouths, choked with alders, are hard to detect. After a few more bends an extraordinary change takes place in this twisty stream. A long straight corridor opens up between canyon-like walls of spiry balsam and an occasional pine. The river widens over a shallow bed covered with eelgrass waving in the current. Naturally this is called the Straight of the Woods.

Above the Straight the river resumes its meandering through a wide swamp, inching by a series of lazy maneuvers toward high ground first on the E and then on the W. Your shadow circles around the boat. If you take the bends fast enough, the saying is, you can see the back of your neck. Don't argue with the Oswegatchie. You came to get away from assembly lines. A meander is the pleasantest distance between two points.

At close to 4 m. you slide into a niche of High Rock, an outcropping with a flattish top 25 feet above the water. It is a good place for leg-stretching and a panoramic view over the swamp. Riverwise people plan on reaching it in time for lunch. Below the rock is a small clearing used by campers who get a late start from Inlet and carry their own shelter. A spur road connects the rock with the fire trail (an old logging railroad grade) from Wanakena to High Falls.

The river now makes a series of coy gestures toward the W edge of the swamp, stretching less than one air mile to 2 m. in reaching Griffin Rapids. This section has been productive in guide lore. In *Man of the Woods* Herbert Keith tells how the following places got their names: the Seven Sisters, the Battleground, the Cherry Hole, Hair Bottle Cove, Steve Ward Cutacross, the Pork Barrel Fish Hole. Today the Seven Sisters (standing dead pines), once the eye-catcher of these flats, are gone, and you can no longer count the seven times the river headed for them and then turned away. The most colorful time here is late October and early November when the tamaracks turn gold and red berries hang in clusters from the winterberry holly.

First-time canoeists on the Oswegatchie wonder why the name Griffin Rapids is on the topo map. At medium high water you notice nothing except a slight quickening of current. Only at low water is the rock bed visible. But the thing to look for here, as the river emerges from the swamp to wash the base of a high bank, is the fine trees. A trail up the bank leads to a lean-to (usually occupied). The original lean-to, which was closer to the spring, burned and was replaced with spruce logs cut on the spot. This site is the center of a tract of 4,500 acres that was part of the original Forest Preserve of 1885. The river enters this tract about 3 m. above Inlet, but because of marshy shores—except at the Straight of the Woods—few tall trees are seen before Griffin Rapids. The big hardwoods and conifers are worth a landing. This rectangular tract runs S to the county line, but the river turns E above Griffin Rapids and soon reenters second-growth for the rest of its course in St. Lawrence County.

For the next quarter mile the river continues to hug high ground, passing good tent sites; then it bears SE into the swamp again. The next lean-to, 1.7 m. above Griffin Rapids, occupies a pretty site amidst tall pines at a spring hole, where the outlet of Cage Lake and Buck Pond enters the Oswegatchie. Formerly there was a footbridge here on the yellow-marked trail to Cage Lake. But the bridge is out, and under the new management plan for the Five Ponds Wilderness Area, it will not be replaced. Hikers on the trail can often secure ferry service from canoe-campers at the lean-to.

The river now follows a twisting easterly course between low banks for the next 1.5 m. and passes two large boulders. Watch for submerged logs. The banks begin to rise again, the current quickens, and the woods close in. The next 2.5 m. are the most beautiful reach below High Falls, with tall tamaracks on the lower banks and straight, high-crowned white pines on the ridges. The pines were of merchantable size prior to 1912, when the Rich Lumber Company was cutting in the township, but were purposefully left standing near the river as a concession to the guides who operated sportsmen's camps here-abouts.

At Ross Rapids the river approaches the fire trail, which can be used for a carry if necessary. Aluminized rocks just below the surface are a warning to steer carefully. Strong paddling is necessary to top the upper part of the 200-foot long rapid at high water. Oswegatchie guides used to discard paddles here and use poles for surer control of their vulnerable all-cedar Rushtons and Peterboroughs. Just above Ross Rapids the river makes a V-shaped bend to the N and then pulls away from the fire trail at Straight Rapids. Beyond a few more bends is the Root Hole, where an enormous pine stump was washed out of the bank at floodwater several decades ago. Trundling down-stream, it made the long journey in stages, often moored in one place for several years until a mighty spring flood pried it loose again.

In the 1960s it was firmly lodged on the beach at Inlet, where three or four picnickers could perch in its crooks. Then in the spring of 1971 or 1972 it lost its hold again, and by now it is probably hung up in the rapids below Inlet or flushed into Cranberry Lake.

Beyond the Root Hole is a creek mouth with a riffled bottom of white sand. This is Wolf Creek (called Wolf Pond Outlet on the topo map), which drains a chain of ponds in the virgin timber S of the St. Lawrence-Herkimer County line. Beyond the next horseshoe bend the old footbridge on the Five Ponds Trail used to cross the river. In 1972 spring floods washed it out. A flat clearing on the S bank is a popular campground.

The Five Ponds Trail now crosses the river at a new footbridge about 0.3 m. above the old one. The present location, less susceptible to bank erosion, is at the head of Round Hill Rapids. About 200 yards upstream on the S bank is a fine campground on the site of an old guide camp. Canoeists whose schedule allows time for hiking and who have ascended the river thus far the first day (11.2 m.) can camp here or hike to one of the four lean-tos on the Five Ponds Trail: at Big Shallow Pond, Little Shallow, Wolf Pond, and Sand Lake.

For wilderness enthusiasts the Five Ponds Trail (blue markers) is likely to be the most interesting in the Cranberry Lake region. Before reaching the ponds, the trail crosses the St. Lawrence County Line, which divides second growth timber from virgin forest. Fifty thousand acres in NE Herkimer County had never been logged before the state acquired them in 1896 as part of the Webb Purchase. In listing selected natural areas throughout the United States—areas not likely to be disturbed by man—the Society of American Foresters designated three stands of virgin timber in this tract, notable for white pine, red spruce, yellow birch, and sugar maple. There are several features of special interest on or near the Five Ponds Trail. The ridge that bisects the five ponds is a classic among Adirondack eskers, reaching a height of 150 feet and supporting a stand of tall white pine. With interruptions the esker continues 6 m. in a SW direction to divide Rock and Sand lakes, where Colvin happened on it in 1878 and found it "far more entrancing than the choicest ramble of guarded park." But today the pines at the northern end have withstood hurricanes better than those on the ridge between Rock and Sand.

Other attractions of the trail are the splendid hardwoods between Five Ponds and Wolf Pond, the 10-acre grove of uniform-aged white pines on the N shore of Wolf Pond which succeeded a fire in the area over a century ago, the high-crowned red spruce on the trail S of Wolf Pond, and the end-of-the line twin lakes, Rock and Sand. To local woodsmen, Sand Lake had always been a place inviolate. No longer. When a man from Wanakena hiked there on a recent summer day, anticipating a lonesome swim, he saw a mixed party of nude bathers cavorting on the fine natural beach. The news spread like wildfire among the fraternity of woodsmen in Wanakena. Nothing had so violated their sensibilities since the incident early in the century, when a lumber jobber worked off a spite by cutting the big pines at High Falls. The sand beach sometimes suffers submergence as well as disgrace when a beaver dam on Sand Lake Outlet raises the water level.

From the footbridge at Round Hill Rapids the river distance to High Falls is 1.8 m. Half way along a fairly straight NE stretch, Carlson's Creek enters from the N. Below its mouth a faint trail leads up the bank to a hidden campground on the W side of the creek, a former guide's camp. At Crooked Rapids a narrow ribbon of main current leads one successfully through an S curve except for a possible scratch at the head.

At the end of its NE stretch, the river approaches the fire trail at Carter's Landing. There are campsites on high ground here. A small feeder called Moses Rock Spring (not shown on the topo map), beside a large flattish rock between the fire trail and the river, has been a source of cold drinking water from early times but looked polluted the last time I saw it.

About 100 yards above, Glasby Creek enters on the outer side of a sharp bend to the S. The reach between the two feeders, known as Carter's Spring Hole, was once celebrated for its brook trout. Cornelius Carter was a teacher-lawyer who retired to be a woodsman-poet and who had a guide camp nearby before 1900. To the E of Carter's Landing lies The Plains, a nearly treeless flat bewteen two mountains, the origin of which is unknown—probably a severe ground fire— and has given rise to much speculation.

Above Carter's Landing the river meanders through a swamp. A big boulder, Moss Rock, which keeps a record of water levels, is the last prominent feature before High Falls.

How high is high? The vertical drop at High Falls is little over 15 feet. But since this is about half of the total drop between the head of the fall and Inlet, perhaps the name is justified. At any rate, viewed from below, the volume of water and the ledges and walls of gray rock are impressive enough. The carry is on the E side. Before the state acquired Rich Lumber Company lands, ther was a popular rustic lodge here known as Dobson's Camps. Sportsmen were drawn by the excellent hunting and fishing and naturalists, including Ernest Thompson Seton, by the spectacle of the three-to-four pound brook trout trying, always unsuccessfully, to jump the falls. Today there are no trout big enough to try. But High Falls is still popular with campers. In summer there is ordinarily an overflow at the two lean-tos, one on each side of the falls. A footbridge which used to connect these lean-tos has been removed.

An interesting circular day's hike from High Falls is as follows: Pine Ridge, 1.5 m. SE; Nicks, Cowhorn, and Cat Mountain ponds; Cat Mountain on a spur trail (the fire tower has been removed since this area was classified as wilderness, but the view is good without it); Glasby Pond, Glasby Creek, and The Plains back to High Falls. If the season is late May, the mass of witchhobble bloom at Cat Mountain Pond is a memorable sight.

Above High Falls the Oswegatchie is a winding black ribbon with a width tapering from about 25 feet to brook size near its sources. It is canoeable for 4 to 7 m., depending on water levels and the canoeist's patience in dragging his craft over beaver dams and windfalls. There are no lean-tos above High Falls but several inviting camping sites, some with nearby springs. The DEC tries to maintain signs pointing to springs, but vandals often remove them.

The first tributary on the L, Red Horn Creek, is close to the county line. Nicks Pond Outlet, also on the L, is well inside Herkimer County. Look on the L for the big white pines and hemlocks that have made this area famous. A few can be seen from the river, but the biggest are on the crest of Pine Ridge. To see them, you must climb the hill on the E shore. The best place to do this is at Camp Johnny, about 0.5 m. above Nicks Pond Outlet (2.5 m. above High Falls). An otherwise ideal campsite—a flat clearing large enough for several tents—is often messy. Canoeists can help the local ranger by policing the area as they head downstream and leaving plastic bags of trash at Inlet. This is as much a courtesy to the next party of campers as leaving a supply of dry wood used to be.

Behind Camp Johnny, across 200 feet of grassy swale, is a cold spring, located at the base of Pine Ridge on the R side of an old, much overgrown logging grade which was bulldozed up the ridge after the hurricane of November 1950 by a salvage crew permitted to remove windfalls. This spring is sometimes flooded in wet seasons and therefore unusable. Campers should use purification tablets for water from the river or feeding streams.

The logging grade leads up the hill past a grove of tall pines on the L and intersects the Nicks Pond Trail. To see other virgin pines of large size, follow the trail downgrade toward the E for 0.2 m., or better still, bushwhack SE on the crest of the ridge till the pines give way to red spruce. Though Pine Ridge is not so glorious as it was before the Big Blow of 1950, which toppled about half of the pines, it is still a memorable sight. Virgin pines appear at intervals along the next 2.5 m. upstream.

Less than a mile above Camp Johnny, the Robinson River comes in on the R. Its first mile is too steep for canoeing, with a gradient of 100 feet, and the fishermen's trail along it is too rough for a carry. There is a good campsite at the confluence. From here on, progress on the Oswegatchie is slowed increasingly by deadfalls, rocks, sharp bends, and beaver dams. The beaver are busy in the main stream as well as on feeders. A patient observer at dusk should be able to see the workers, particularly if he removes portions of an active dam in advance.

The Robinson River Rapids on the main stream are a pretty stretch of fast water where a pole is helpful. Shortly thereafter is another rapid with slalom-placed rocks—much more fun to run down than to pole up—and a fine campsite on the R, with a spring close by for cold, clear water, contrasting with the tea-like stain of the river water.

The Oswegatchie now winds like ribbon candy through what seem like interminable alder thickets. It is deep but narrow, and those who use 15-foot canoes find the job of maneuvering easier than those with longer craft. On this stretch one can spend a half hour paddling a half mile as the crow flies.

Finally, a look ahead shows tall trees on both sides of the stream, and the Oswegatchie enters a ravine bordered with hemlock, cedar, pine, and spruce. A natural bridge (a huge dead tree) forces one to duck; it is followed by an even larger white pine leaning over the river. A big rock on the L seems to stand as sentinel for those who enter the upper river. A campsite appears on the L, and behind it is a crude but well-marked trail.

The banks now revert to the earlier swampy alder-thicket character. Several brooks enter in a fan-shaped pattern. From here on, it is up to each party to determine its head of navigation. In an abnormally wet summer Robert Bliss led a party of boys and girls in four canoes above the place where the Oswegatchie assembles its headwater brooks, choosing at each fork the largest flow and the longest vista of smooth water. Once more the hills and the big timber closed in as they ran out of time and ended their five-hour push above Camp Johnny. There was still an ample supply of water. They had dragged their boats over 19 beaver dams. Penetration thus far (about 7 m. above High Falls) takes a high degree of enthusiasm as well as high water levels. But the feeling that you share these wilds only with the bear and the beaver may be reward enough.

In downstream perspective the river looks different enough to hold interest. Once the obstacles of the upper reaches have been passed, the return trip is fast and easy. The bends unwind like thread off a spool.

Postscript for pathfinders (November Four, Big Moose 15; Five Ponds 7.5). My lasting regret is that, when much younger, I failed to penetrate the Five Ponds Wilderness Area southward from the end of the High Falls trail over the divide between Oswegatchie and Beaver River drainage. Before his death A. T. Shorey sent me a detailed description and a map of the route as planned in 1919 by R. K. Jessup, one of the founders of the Adirondack Mountain Club. The Red Horse-Oswegatchie Trail, as it was called, was actually constructed under Conservation Department direction with Jessup's aid. A very few people tramped over it in the early 1920s until enlargement of the Stillwater Reservoir in 1924 or 1925 made access at the S end more difficult and the trail as a whole was abandoned. But 5.5 m. at the S end are still maintained. The 6.5 air miles from the N end of that trail to High Falls on the Oswegatchie stretch to 8 or 9 on the ground as one skirts blowdowns, elevations, and beaver floodings. Progress in some areas may be less than a mile an hour. Crisscrossing hunters' trails may lead the unwary astray. As A. T. Shorey put it, this trip today would be "an adventure in pioneer woodcraft and pathfinding."

The logistics are complicated. The trip is best attempted by two parties headed in opposite directions on a synchronized schedule. The N-bound party must use canoes to reach the trail head, and it is essential for the S-bound party to find those canoes waiting for them at Trout Pond, where the Red Horse Trail begins, so that they can cross the reservoir to a public road at Stillwater. The N-bound party would either pick up canoes left for them at High Falls or take the trail to Wanakena. Each party should have one sacrificial member (an ardent fisherman?) willing to guard the canoes. The

time has passed when you could leave any valuable but whiskey in
the woods for days and count absolutely on recovering it.

Terry Perkins, ranger at Stillwater in the 1970s, '80s, and '90s, has
made the round trip between the two rivers several times. He and
his successors can give helpful advice. The rangers maintain the
Red Horse Trail, so named for the creek along which it is routed.

A few hardy skiers have made this traverse in late winter when
snows are firmly packed down and deep enough to cover debris on
the forest floor. Attempting this trip along, however, ad did the
writer of the article in the January-February 1983 issue of *Adirondack
Life*, is an unacceptable risk.

Canoeists put in at Stillwater (little more than a sportsman's inn)
and paddle up the Stillwater Reservoir 7 m. to Trout Pond, where
the Red Horse Trail begins. This trail, which is marked on the Big
Moose map, passes Salmon and Witchhopple lakes. Maintenance ends
on the S shore of Clear Lake and bushwhacking begins. Skirting
Clear Lake on the W side, the N-bound party ascends to the W side
of Summit Pond (2067 feet in elevation), headwater of Red Horse
Creek. The route then bears NW around the E tip of Crooked Lake,
which drains into the Oswegatchie through the Robinson River. After
rounding a narrow bay of Crooked Lake, it heads NNE into a notch
and follows the lower contours of a hill around to Pettis Pond (unnamed on the Five Ponds map, at the bottom), another headwater
of the Robinson. Continuing N and NW on a downgrade, it crosses
to the W side of the Robinson River and skirts the S shore of Toad
Pond toward the NE. It then bears NNW along the W side of the
Robinson past Sliding Falls. About 1 m. S of the easterly bend of
the Robinson the abandoned trail passed directly through a swamp,
but extensive beaver flooding now makes necessary a wide detour to
the W on higher ground, circling back to the river near its E bend.
The old trail then followed a NE bearing through a notch of Partlow
Mountain and down the northern slopes, finally crossing a swamp
before reaching High Falls.

The S-bound party, having reached High Falls either by trail or
canoe, looks for an unmaintained hunters' trail marked by yellow
blazes on the L bank above the falls. It bears W a little way and
then swings S through a swamp, reaching a fork on the county line
in about 0.6 m. The L fork is the old Albany Road, now overgrown
except for a thread of trail used by sportsmen bound for Gal Pond
and Gull Lake. Our S-bound party takes the R fork here. Paint blazes
continue up the slopes of Partlow Mountain in a S to SW direction.

The condition of the "trail" deteriorates as one continues S, reversing the route described above. Somewhere the two parties should cross as ships that pass in the night.

Some random tips. Terry Perkins suggests a bushwhacking detour off the Red Horse Trail at the S tip of Witchhopple Lake on an upgrade to Little Rock Pond, which is deep, clear, pretty; its bottom can be seen through 60 feet of water. Second, an alternative route is use of the Five Ponds Trail. In this case, the northern rendezvous would be the footbridge at Round Hill Rapids, which can be reached either by trail from Wanakena or by canoe from Inlet. The S-bound party would take the Five Ponds Trail from that footbridge and, on reaching Little Shallow Pond, bushwhack one mile ESE to the bend in the Robinson River. The N-bound party would reverse this route, bearing W below Partlow Mountain at the easterly bend of the Robinson. Third, the obsolete Cranberry Lake 15-minute topo map, if a copy is obtainable, marks the course followed by the old Red Horse-Oswegatchie Trail in its northern half from Crooked Lake to High Falls.

These directions are not guaranteed. Let no one undertake this trip until he is an accomplished map and compass reader and an old hand at bushwhacking. The S-bound party should notify the ranger at Wanakena of its intentions, and the N-bound party the ranger at Stillwater. For qualified persons the tramp should be an unforgettable adventure. For the inexperienced, a nightmare.

Cranberry Lake, 9 m.+ (14.5 km.+)
USGS: Newton Falls, Cranberry Lake 7.5

The Oswegatchie tour can end where it began, at Inlet, or continue through Cranberry Lake. A week's camping trip in the region should, however, include two or three days on Cranberry Lake—the third largest body of water in the Adirondacks (after Lake George and the Sacandaga Reservoir) and the only large lake to be nearly surrounded by Forest Preserve. The Five Ponds Wilderness Area to the south is penetrated by trails accessible by boat. The lake is shaped like a giant starfish. The central body has seven radially extended arms of varying width where inlets enter and a large arm on the N where the Oswegatchie makes its exit. This irregularity makes the lake fascinating to explore. The central part should be avoided on windy days, especially in the afternoon. But refuge can be found at all hours in the arms or "flows."

The villages of Wanakena and Cranberry Lake are the principal access points. Canoeists who intend to explore the lake only and not the river should put in at the State Boat Launching Site in Cranberry Lake (across the outlet). Canoes can be rented in the village and provisions obtained at the general store, which is also an information center. The proprietor is knowledgeable about the region. A Chamber of Commerce map shows the location of campsites around the lake and on the islands. The lake is an ideal playground for all kinds of outdoor recreation. Even fishermen have cause to rejoice in recent reports that brook trout are returning to a lake that once had an abundance of them.

The description that follows is intended for parties entering the lake as part of a cruise down the river. The 2.2 m. of rapids between Inlet and Wanakena may present a problem. This section can be avoided altogether by arranging a shuttle between Inlet and Wanakena. Alternatively, this section can be paddled. Cruising paddlers can paddle the first 0.7 m. of this section with no difficulty and thereby shorten the carry to 1.5 m. The Rapids Trail is on the L bank and, although tiring, is a pleasant walk and provides frequent glimpses of the river. The remainder of this section consists of nearly continuous whitewater. Intermediate level paddlers can paddle most of this section at high water levels with no problems. The most notable difficulty is a Class III-IV rapid requiring more advanced skills. Total drop is 80 feet.

Paddlers wishing to attempt these rapids are advised to check the water level at the road bridge at Wanakena. No more than three feet of bridge abutment should be visible. From Inlet, the current begins to quicken at 0.7 m., just before a small stream enters on the L. Rapids build to Class II in the next 0.25 m. At a moderate turn to the R is the Class III-IV rapid. There is a jagged, knife-shaped island dividing the current into two channels. The river drops 8 feet in a series of pitches over 20 yards. Bear far L until the foot of the island. Class II-III rapids continue for approximately 0.3 m. before tapering to Class I-II rapids, which persist until the road bridge at Wanakena. There are several scratchy sections toward the bottom, even at spring time water levels. Take out on the L just before the bridge or continue on to Cranberry Lake.

Wanakena is a pretty hamlet in deep woods at the foot of the rapids where the Oswegatchie enters Cranberry Lake in a long flow. The story of how it started as a lumber camp in 1892 and was kept going through sheer love and grit after the logging ended is told in

Herbert Keith's *Man of the Woods.* The dam at the foot of Cranberry Lake, first built in 1867, nearly doubled the size of the natural lake by raising the level over marshy floodplains of numerous inlets, including the Oswegatchie. The original channel, marked by buoys, winds through Inlet Flow. At low water the buoys should be heeded by canoeists, as well as by motorboat operators, to avoid rocks and snags. Early dam builders were not required to clear flooded land. Most of the old stumps have rotted, but there are still some close enough to the surface to be treacherous.

The distance from Wanakena to the foot of the lake is 9 m. Most of it is in protected waters or has the advantage of the prevailing SW winds of summer. At the end of the Narrows, 1.5 m. below Wanakena, is the New York State Ranger School, where forestry students get training in an experimental forest of 2,330 acres. Beyond the school, on both sides of Inlet Flow, are stands of virgin timber. By taking a trail a little way downstream from the school on the opposite shore, one can hike in 10 minutes to a stand where the white pines range up to 52 inches in diameter.

There is a state lean-to on a point on the L shore nearly a mile below the Ranger School. A half mile farther, on the R, is Flatiron Point, where Inlet and Dead Creek flows merge. (From here it is 3.25 m. up Dead Creek Flow to another lean-to at Janack's Landing and the pleasant 2.25 m. trail to the open summit of Cat Mountain, elevation 2,261, where a golden eagle has been spotted.

Continuing toward the main part of the lake, one bears E and NE around a peninsula called the Hawk's Nest. Ahead, in the center of the flow, are two islets known as Fred's Islands. The outermost has a good bathing beach on the E side. Like most of the islands, it is state owned. Camping is permitted for three days without a permit. The few privately owned islands of the lake are posted, as is about one-fourth of the mainland shore; all the rest is a vast playground of woods and waters. There are enough private camps, however, to make motorboat traffic fairly lively in summer.

Summits up to 2,600 feet ring the main lake on the E and S and give it a skyline of rounded or flat-topped ridges. Foot trails lead into passes or up the mountains, as described in *Guide to Adirondack Trails: Northern Region* (ADK). One of the most attractive is Six-Mile Creek Trail. To reach it, go through the channel between Joe Indian Island (the largest, with many campsites) and the W shore, paddling 2.7 m. SW and S into West Flow. Objects of interest are Sliding Rock Falls at 0.7 m. and Cranberry

Lake Esker, the crest of which the trail follows for 1.5 m. before
reaching Cowhorn Junction at 4.2 m. This narrow ridge of glacial
outwash supports a flourishing second-growth forest. One looks
down into treetops on both sides. The esker is a long sinuous one
stretching from the S shore of the lake past the E end of Nicks Pond.
Side trails lead to other trout ponds.

Canoeists going to the foot of the lake (N end) keep Joe Indian
Island well on their R and head N along the shore. Cranberry is
large enough to attract many gulls. They can usually be seen around
Norway Island and acorn-shaped Gull Rock.

The Cranberry Lake Public Campground is located on the E shore
at Dog Island Flow. A circular trail from the campground goes over
Bear Mountain to an open lookout on ledges on the S ridge and
then down to the S end of the campground.

Just above the dam at the foot of the lake, on the opposite shore
from the village, is a state-owned launching site with a large parking
lot. Most canoeists on the Oswegatchie end their trip here, if not at
Inlet. Cranberry Lake was the first storage reservoir constructed in
the state to regulate the flow of a river for downstream industry.
The original dam of 1867 has been rebuilt several times.

A shuttle between Cranberry Lake and Wanakena is an opportunity
to drive on dirt roads over a self-guiding tour of the second-growth
forests and plantations of the Ranger School. Pamphlets are available
at the start of the tour about 1.5 m. E of the Wanakena turnoff on
the S side of Route 3.

Cranberry Lake to Newton Falls, 8.7 m. (14 km.)
USGS: Newton Falls 7.5

The segment between the dams at Cranberry Lake and Newton
Falls is especially enjoyable at the height of fall color in late September.
The river is wide now and winds through hardwood slopes that gradually flatten as Chaumont Swamp is approached. Hunting camps are
visible through the trees, and the road to Newton Falls is often within
sight and hearing. This stretch is classified recreational. It is stocked
with speckled and brown trout.

Immediately below the dam is a brief stretch of mild Class I rapids.
Class II rapids begin just below the bridge on Route 3 and continue
for about 0.25 m. before tapering to flatwater. These rapids are likely
to be scratchy at all but high water levels. About a half mile W on
the Tooley Pond Road from its junction with Route 3 are two or

three good put-in sites in a quiet pool across from the village dump. Those wishing to avoid intermittent rapids and a low footbridge in the next 1.3 m. can make use of a lower put-in on the same road, 1.8 m. from its junction with Route 3 where it approaches the river's edge in a hollow. Below this, two short rifts are easily run at medium water level or higher. The remaining 6.7 m. are all smooth water.

The river widens to a half mile above the Newton Falls dam. At Chaumont Swamp the channel threads through the islands and stumps of an extensive flooded area. The view to the S is a dreary prospect of dead and dying trees. As the channel bends W (the road from Cook Corners to Newton Falls is occasionally in sight), keep close to the N shore, but not so close as to mistake a deep narrow bay for the main channel. The river narrows as it bends SW between peninsulas and then NW to the highway bridge. The trip can end here or continue 0.6 m. to the Newton Falls bathing beach or 1.3 m. to the dam.

Newton Falls to South Edwards, discontinuous, 12.9 m. (20.6 km.)
USGS: Newton Falls, Oswegatchie, Fine, South Edwards 7.5

Below Newton Falls the Oswegatchie drops 675 feet in about 18 m. to the Adirondack Park boundary. Arduous carries are necessary around the many falls, dams, penstocks, and heavy rapids that separate smooth-water stretches. This section is not recommended for cruising, though it is scenic in many places. The artist Frederic Remington, a native of St. Lawrence County, gives a vivid account of this part of the river as it was in the 1890s, before engineers restructured it, in his book *Pony Tracks*. In his canoe *Necoochee* he descended the Oswegatchie from Cranberry Lake with his guide, Has Rasbeck. To suffer like an anchorite, he says, was part of the program. A true sportsman exults in "fighting a game with the elements," which are "remorseless." The trip put him in "a conflagration of ecstacy." Not so his guide. Has was ready to take hardship in stride in killing deer and catching trout, but to court it for its own sake was beyond his understanding.

In the July-August 1983 *Conservationist* Eileen Stegemann describes a canoe cruise on the Oswegatchie from Newton Falls to the mouth in Ogdensburg.

It is not possible to paddle downstream continuously below Newton Falls. Because of interruptions by numerous dams and penstocks this section will be described in three parts. The first two are suitable for brief cruising trips; the third is suitable as a whitewater run for expert level decked boats or as an extended cruising trip for those willing to carry numerous difficult rapids.

I. Level 1. Access to the East Branch in the village of Newton Falls is very difficult because of the buildings of the Newton Falls Paper Company. About 0.3 m. W of the hamlet on a gravel road there is a 20-foot dam. You can put in on the L bank shortly after this dam. The downstream paddle continues for 2.2 m., with the last half of the river gradually widening into an impoundment behind Browns Falls Dam. Most paddlers will prefer to return to the put-in for a round trip. The alternative is a 0.9 m. carry on a dirt road beginning at the L side of the dam. This road ends at a double intersection with Browns Falls Road and Schuyler Road. Access to the dirt road is blocked by a Niagara Mohawk Chain, preventing automobile travel; foot travel is generally allowed.

II. Level 2. Those wishing to continue downstream can put in at the end of the NIMO access road to the power plant or at the Browns Falls Road bridge over the Little River. Mild Class II rapids last for several hundred yards before the river flows into a second impoundment of the East Branch by the dam at Flat Rock power plant. This dam is approximately 1.5 m. below the Browns Falls Road bridge. It is possible to paddle up a small bay to the R at the head of the impoundment to the power plant. There the aqueduct from the earlier impoundment empties after a 1.2 m. journey, dropping almost 270 feet along the way. Cruising paddlers can also paddle NE from the dam underneath Skate Creek Road and proceed up Skate Creek for an exploratory trip. Skate Creek Road also serves as a put-in for paddlers desiring a round trip in this impoundment. For those choosing to continue to Flat Rock, take-out for this section is on the L bank just before the dam. Niagara Mohawk maintains a boat launch and small parking area here. The short access road may be chained, but Niagara Mohawk allows boaters to carry on this road. This dirt access road may be reached by proceeding NW on Route 3 for 2 m. after it crosses the Little River. Note that there are several other access roads at this point, but they are heavily posted.

III. Level 3. There is no easy access to the East Branch directly below Flat Rock power plant, and paddlers are advised that water levels in this section can rise and fall rapidly depending upon releases at Flat Rock. Niagara Mohawk posts the several access roads and also posts the area between the boat launch site and the dam. The best alternative is to put in 0.25 m. further downstream where the river approaches the highway. Enterprising paddlers can then bushwhack up the L bank for 300 yards and put in just above a 50 yard long Class III rapid, which consists of a set of ledges and is best run on the far L. Below this are several hundred yards of Class II rapids which begin to dissipate at the foot of an island. The river then flattens for the next several miles. The East Branch approaches a parking lot off Route 3 at 0.8 m. and flows beneath Scotts Bridge on the Degrasse Road at 1.6 m. A mile and a half below Scotts Bridge the East Branch comes to within 30 feet of Skate Creek Road on the R. Paddlers wishing to avoid substantial rapids downstream are advised to take out here. Alternatively, whitewater paddlers may want to put in at this point to avoid flatwater upstream. By road this site is 1.3 m. W of Scotts Bridge and 0.8 m. E of the upstream bridge in the hamlet of Fine.

About a half mile below this point the East Branch begins to narrow and Class II rapids build to Class III by the time the first bridge in Fine becomes visible. Class III rapids continue below the bridge, accelerating briefly to Class III-IV as the river turns L and divides into three channels. The middle channel has the most water and requires skirting a hydraulic on the R before dropping into a larger hydraulic at the foot of an island. This drop is rated Class IV. The L and R channels are narrower and the R may be blocked by logjams; their difficulty is roughly comparable to that of the main channel. The entire rapid should be scouted in advance from the upper bridge and the nearby road on the R. Paddlers should note that a hydroelectric project is being considered for this area, known locally as the Antwine Bridge Gorge. These rapids would be destroyed and the impact on rapids downstream and upstream is unclear. Various groups, notably the Audubon Society and the American Whitewater Affiliation, are contesting the project.

Rapids dissipate below the second bridge at Fine; this bridge is on Route 58 connecting Fine and Edwards. In the 4.2 m. from the Route 58 bridge to the next dam above South Edwards the East Branch drops 80 feet, according to the topographic maps; it is the opinion of the second author that the total drop is closer to 110 or 120 feet. Rapids below this point range from Class III to Class VI. This section is similar to the lower Moose above Fowlersville and is best suited for expert paddlers. The scenery, however, is certainly sufficient to entice less skilled paddlers willing to make numerous carries which are quite arduous.

Flatwater extends about a mile and a half before the next rapid is encountered. Scouting is advised for this rapid, preferably from a

small island between the middle and R channels. The middle channel
is preferred; it drops 3 feet into a hydraulic, turns R and drops an
additional 10 feet. It is rated Class IV–V. The R channel may also
be run and is slightly more difficult. The L channel is unrunnable
and flows beneath a small footbridge connecting the L bank and a
small island. There is a camp on this bank, so paddlers should carry
on the R.

In about 0.2 m. the river veers R and enters a small gorge. Exit L
to scout. The L bank is steep and overgrown, making scouting difficult.
A short bushwhack leads to an unimproved jeep trail for those wishing
to carry. Those desiring to run this rapid should stay R of an exposed
boulder, then proceed straight down a 15 foot wide sluice dropping
15 feet over a distance of 10 yards. This drop is rated Class V.

A second camp appears shortly on the L bank. In 0.3 m. there is
a drop of 20 feet in two channels. The L channel is completely unrunnable; the R channel is Class VI. There are no major obstructions,
but a series of huge holes presents a significant danger. The next
drop occurs in 200 yards. This is a 10-foot near-vertical drop, rated
Class V, with a substantial hydraulic below. This is followed in 25
yards by a 25-foot vertical waterfall that is unrunnable. To the L of
this waterfall is a beautiful ledge of pink granite. Further to the L
there is an interesting and challenging "sneak" run, which consists
of a narrow channel angling to the L, then turning sharply (130
degrees) to the R before rejoining the main channel below the falls.
This channel is about 60 yards, with a total drop of 25 feet. Stay to
the outside of the R turn to avoid boulders and logjams. Drops in
this channel are frequent, with a rating of Class IV.

A quarter mile below the waterfall is a 200 yard long Class III
rapid consisting of large waves and no obstacles. Two hundred yards
below this is a Class III–IV rapid ending in a 5-foot pitch and a
tricky hydraulic. The river is flat from here to the next dam in 1.2
m. The East Branch squeezes through a narrow gorge before widening
into the impoundment. Paddlers can well imagine what kind of rapid
was formed at this point before the dam raised the water level and
destroyed it.

The river widens and presents a peaceful interlude until the next
dam. A narrow bay to the R is reached in 0.8 m. and allows access
to Route 58 if so desired. At the dam exit L and carry 0.25 m. over
a dirt road to the next power plant. This dam is an impressive 70-
foot structure. Enterprising paddlers can run the Class III–IV gorge
below the dam. Access to this gorge, which carries the overspill, is

very difficult and involves climbing down the steep L bank and crawling under the aqueduct. Eddies are very small and turbulent.

Below the power plant is 0.2 m. of flat water crossed by the Blue Line before yet another dam is reached. Carry L on a dirt road to a power plant in 50 yards and put in at a small side channel, which quickly merges with the main channel. Above this confluence, the main channel drops about 40 feet in a complex series of Class VI drops. Paddlers entering the East Branch from the side channel must contend with Class II–III rapids. These gradually subside to flatwater by the time the bridge at South Edwards is encountered in 0.5 m. Take out at this bridge on the R bank. Below the bridge a Class III rapid begins. It quickly escalates into a Class V–VI rapid, which may be run on the far R down a sloping ledge before turning sharply L to negotiate a series of ledges. Take out on the R bank and carry 0.1 m. back to the bridge.

From the bridge, proceed N on a light-duty road which forks in a quarter mile. Either fork takes you to Route 58. Turn R to return to Fine. Below South Edwards, the East Branch drops 40 feet in the next mile. Flatwater continues from this point to the village of Edwards, reached in 5.2 m.

LITTLE RIVER

Upper Segment, 4 m. (6.4 km.)
USGS: Newton Falls 7.5

The Little River describes a course roughly like a fishhook. From its sources E of Benson Mines it flows SW to loop around Star Lake, with which it has no connection, and then N and NE to join the Oswegatchie below Browns Falls. The lower segment of 7 m. is a steep slope for intermediate whitewater paddlers in late April and early May. An upper segment of 4 m. below Heath Pond (not shown on the accompanying map) is canoeable all summer. The owner of the land posts the two access roads against hunting and trapping but permits public fishing access. For put-in, carry 0.4 m. around a locked gate on a spur road on the N side of Route 3 2.1 m. E of the Wanakena turnoff (5 m. W of Cranberry Lake Dam). Heath Pond appears on the R. The outlet (Little River) winds through a broad marsh. There are several small beaver dams. In 1.5 m. the creek widens into a reservoir. Take-out is at the far SW end (beached boats mark the landing), where a spur road of 0.3 m. meets Route 3 across from the road to Inlet.

Bridge on Route 3 to Aldrich, 12 m. (19.3 km.)
USGS: Oswegatchie 7.5

The midsection of Little River between the bridge on Route 3 and
Aldrich is a pleasant cruising reach of 12 m. Water levels in the
upper level are usually adequate through June. A few beaver dams
and deadfalls are minor obstacles. A gorge and falls at the midpoint
require a carry. The lower reach between the falls and Aldrich is
canoeable all summer, although it may be necessary to line some
rapids. During periods of low water it may be advisable to put in at
Aldrich and paddle upstream with a downstream return.

The bridge on Route 3 is 1.5 m. E of the center of Star Lake
Village. Earlier editions of this guide described this area as a
facsimile of Milton's Hell, "a dismal situation waste and wild."
This was due to the huge mounds of tailings from iron-ore pits,
dust streamers on windy days, starved-looking flats downstream,
and water which was turbid brown with sediment. But the situation
has begun to improve with revegetation of the mounds. In addition,
several small booms across the river below the Route 3 bridge have
helped contain some of the pollution. These booms can be paddled
over. A slow transformation is in store as you wind down snaky
loops through the flats and slowly leave the mountain of tailings.
The sluggish stream gradually deposits its load and clears to
transparent amber. Vegetation gains on the banks — marsh grass,
cattails, and alders. The current quickens and the hills and evergreens close in a tight gap at 3.5 m., where the Youngs Road crosses.
A short carry is necessary here as the river flows through narrow
culverts. Below this all prospects please.

The volume of water markedly increases about a half mile below
the Youngs Road where Tamarack Creek enters. The stream winds
through an alder swamp for a mile, with views of a handsome
aspen-crowned hill ahead. At the base of this hill the current
quickens in a ravine. Soon a footbridge is reached as a private
inholding is approached. Below the footbridge are riffles where a
logging bridge formerly spanned the river. The waterfall is 0.3 m.
ahead. Exit L as a clifftop cottage comes into view on the R. The
easiest carry begins about 70 feet above the rim of the falls and
proceeds inland about 150 feet before swinging R to parallel the
stream. This route takes you through a fairly open lane and avoids
the rough, densely wooded ground near the gorge. Follow the lane
till you come to a line of yellow paint blazes marking the boundary
of state land. Follow the blazes NW down a draw to level ground in

a hardwood stand, where the going is easier. Leave the blazes on the state land side and aim at a point on the river just below its extreme northerly bend. Here the rapids end in a final barrier, a reef of boulders. Put in here. (The reef is a convenient turnaround point for those paddling upstream from Aldrich, a distance of 5.5 m.)

The remaining section of river is entirely in the Forest Preserve. In the next 2 m. there are several stretches of Class I rapids separated by flatwater. At low water it is generally easier to line these than to carry around them in the dense undergrowth. The river flows through a snug corridor lined with beautiful spires of balsam fir.

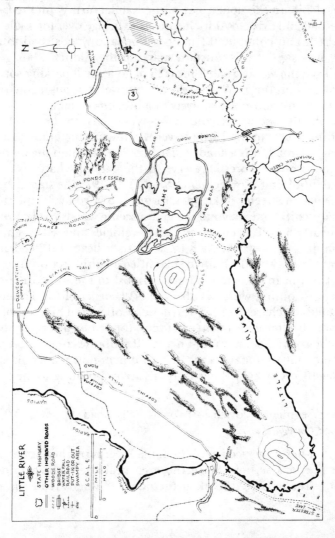

You then come to a small triangle of meadow on your R—an irresistible rest stop to judge by the trampled grass and joe-pye weed. From this perch it is spellbinding to watch the clear water roll around a bend and sparkle in shafts of sunlight filtering through the tall firs on the opposite bank. Below this the river winds through a marshy floodplain between hardwood hills. This used to be an elongated pond, named Aldrich Pond, before the dam at its foot broke out many years ago.

Aldrich is simply a cluster of hunting camps at the N edge of the Forest Preserve. From Route 3 take the turnoff for the hamlet of Oswegatchie. In the upper part of the hamlet turn W on the Coffins Mills Road and drive to Aldrich. Cross the bridge over the Little River in Aldrich and continue 0.1 m. to a one-lane woods road to the S. There is a sign at this junction marking the Aldrich Management Area. Take the woods road S for 0.25 m. to a small parking space for several cars on the L. Walk L on a faint trail to a put-in site on the Little River just above the spillway of a broken-out dam.

The woods road where your car is parked has another use besides providing access to the Little River. Following the grade of an old logging railroad, it is a shady drive of 4.7 m. through the maturing hardwoods of the Forest Preserve to the gate of what was a large private inholding (*Oswegatchie SE 7.5*). In 1975 the state acquired the 4,500-acre Streeter Lake tract, formerly owned by Schuler Farms of potato-chip fame. Beyond the gate a scenic woods road continues S for nearly 6 m. It is closed to motor vehicles and will eventually become just a footpath. At 3 m. it skirts a beautiful bend in the Oswegatchie's Middle Branch, classified in this section as a wild river. Continuing S, the road goes almost to the SW corner of St. Lawrence County, which is also the NW corner of the Totten and Crossfield Purchase. In 1878 Verplanck Colvin and his crew of state surveyors built a monument of stones, topped by a copper bolt, to mark the corner. Some vandal made off with the copper bolt many years ago, but an undated granite monument now marks the site. A boulder 10 feet away still has Colvin's arrow pointing to the corner.

Lower Segment, Aldrich to Browns Falls Road, 6.2 m. (10.0 km.)
USGS: Oswegatchie 7.5

The put-in for this section of the Little River is reached as described in the previous section. Since the area near the Aldrich bridge is posted, it is advisable to park at the one-lane woods road and carry to the fishing access on the R bank above the bridge. In the next 6.2 m. to the bridge on Browns Falls Road, the river drops 220 feet at a relatively uniform gradient of 35 feet per mile. Major rapids alternate between Class II and III, making this a suitable run for intermediate level paddlers. There is no formal gauge. Water levels are best assessed by examining rapids along Browns Falls Road. Adequate levels are usually found in early to mid spring.

Shortly after the put-in the river flows beneath a railroad bridge. The rapids begin in 1 m. as the river begins a number of sweeping turns. At normal levels there are two Class II rapids from 200 to 300 yards in length divided by a short section of flatwater. A quiet stretch is then followed by another rapid which begins as a Class II for 200 yards and then, below a small "picnic" area on the R bank, builds to Class III for 75 yards. The river is noticeably more narrow here, with standing waves two to three feet high. The best course is straight down the middle, with no notable obstructions. Rapids then alternate between Class I and II until just before the confluence with Sucker Lake Outlet at 2.5 m., where the difficulty level approaches Class III for 50–100 yards.

In the next 2.4 m. to the bridge on the Oswegatchie Trail Road longer cruising sections are punctuated by a number of Class I and II rapids with no noteworthy difficulties. In this section the Little River begins a long turn to the E as it approaches the hamlet of Lower Oswegatchie and houses become visible. One section of rapids approaching Class III difficulty comes as the first house is visible. Another is a fairly technical stretch for 0.25 m. before the Oswegatchie Trail Road bridge. Continue under the bridge another 0.25 m. past a small creek confluence on the R to Route 3, where one can take out on the L bank immediately under the bridge.

It is possible to continue an additional 1.4 m. to a bridge on Browns Falls Road. Here, the river strikes a meandering course to the N and joins the Oswegatchie River below the Browns Falls power plant at a point 0.3 m. below Browns Falls Road. There is a short Class II rapid below Route 3 as the river begins a sweeping turn to the L. As the Browns Falls Road is approached, a red house at a sharp turn to the R marks the beginning of a technical 50 yard long Class III rapid. Class II rapids then persist until the river turns sharply to the L, where there is another 50 yard long Class III rapid. Class II rapids continue to the bridge. Take-out is on either bank and involves a steep, difficult climb up to the road.

GRASS RIVER

We have an ongoing quarrel here in Canton-on-the-Grass/Grasse. Most people of this village, including the editor of our local weekly, the *Plaindealer*, insist on the spelling "Grasse" as having more cachet. The highway department humors them by its sign at the village bridge. But the county historical society favors "Grass" on grounds of antiquity. Siding with the latter, I tried to state the case in a letter to the editor, as follows:

"To the *Plaindealer:*

"Anyone who gets quoted as rarely as I do is especially sensitive to misquotation. In your Grasse Roots column, which last week was devoted wholly to the Grass(e) River, you quoted me as calling the South Branch an orphan because it has escaped the attention of engineers and developers. That doesn't make sense in my philosophy. A river is lucky to escape the notice of engineers and developers. Who wants to see those five beautiful waterfalls replaced by dams and aqueducts or surrounded by subdivisions? What I said was that the South Branch is orphaned by the state. It is almost entirely within the Adirondacks, where the state owns over two million acres of forest-preserve land but not one acre on the South Branch inside the park.

"To be an orphan is to suffer deprivation. The South Branch of the Grass(e) is deprived of the full measure of protection that owner-ship by the state or The Nature Conservancy would confer on it, while at the same time opening it to the public. Private ownership risks degradation of the river in the long run and deprives the public of access. How many North Countrymen have seen all five of those waterfalls? (Since this writing the state has acquired a small foothold on the South Branch.)

"In Canton everybody loves the Grass(e), just as in Potsdam everyone loves the Ra(c)quette, but we and they are fiercely divided on the spelling of the two names. As long as we are united on essentials, we can risk quarreling over trifles. True, 'Grasse Roots' makes a lovely pun and in that sense has, as you say, more 'panache.' But consider that we are a dairy county, often the leading one in the state. The river anciently named 'Grass,' wholly inside our county, is a fitting symbol of our major source of wealth....

"Antiquity is on the side of 'Grass.' The other day I ran across a copy of a document now little known and hard to find—the 1798 Patent of the Macomb Purchase, which clinched the sale of nearly four million acres at the top of the state. This document supports the view that the river we all love was named, more than 180 years ago, not by an unbalanced Frenchman with panache, but by a plain Anglo-Saxon who saw meadows, believed the evidence of his senses, and had the foresight to recognize a promising resource, our grass."

At the time I thought this a definitive reply to the Grasse faction. Not so. The quarrel goes on. People don't respect antiquity any more. It seems clear that the river got its name from the grassy meadows at its mouth, as Franklin B. Hough surmised in his county history of 1853 and as is strongly implied in the Macomb Patent, which reserved the mouth of the river for the St. Regis Indians: "The Indians of the Village of St. Regis have built a mill on Salmon River and another on Grass River, and . . . the meadows on Grass River are necessary to them for hay . . . ; it is therefore also agreed and concluded between the Deputies and said agents and the said William Constable and Daniel McCormick for themselves and their associates, purchasers under the said Alexander Macomb of the adjacent Lands, that there shall be reserved to be applied to the use of the Indians of the said Village of St. Regis . . . a tract of one Mile square at each of the said Mills and the Meadows on both sides of the said Grass River from the said mill thereon to its confluence with the River St. Lawrence."

Gazetteers of 1813 and 1842 knew only "Grass." But about the middle of the 19th century spellings began to diverge. French's *Gazetteer* of 1860 and an atlas of 1865 have *both* spellings. So has a county highway map of 1976. USGS maps have "Grass." The DEC Adirondack Map has "Grasse." So we are still in a muddle—a self-inflicted muddle, for the authoritative source in all such disputes is the federal government's *Official Standard Names Approved by the United States Board on Geographic Names.* There it is "Grass."

Greenleaf Chase compiled a list of forty of the more spectacular waterfalls in the Adirondack Park for the Spring 1974 issue of *Adirondack Life.* Eleven of them are on the Grass River and its three branches. More than half of the forty are in private land, including nine of those on the Grass. Early conservation commissioners were reluctant "to buy scenery," in the phrase used with disparaging intent in old annual reports. To the layman, buying scenery in a state park would seem a justifiable use of his taxes.

We line our highways with rights-of-way, protective zones, where the motorist can pull out of the traffic stream for a rest, a snack, or a choice view. Why do we not do the same for our most beautiful highways, the rivers? asks John Kauffmann in *Flow East*. "We should do for our waterways what we do for most of our other routes. . . . If we could treat our rivers like our roads, we could have beautiful, permanent river parks through every part of the country. . . . They are the best and in some places the only corridors along which we may pass from the contrived to the natural world in our search for self-renewal and understanding."

Public involvement is sometimes effective. Since 1972 preservationists in the Canton area have been urging state purchase of the Lampson Falls tract on the main stem of the Grass at the northwest corner of the park. When Commissioner Biggane was shown color photos of this scenic river corridor, he said, yes, the state ought to buy it. Since then, other commissioners passed through the revolving doors of the DEC, but Biggane's decision was not reversed. After lengthy and difficult negotiations, the 598-acre river corridor was acquired by the state in 1979, to preserve forever the wild beauty of Lampson Falls and the cascades in the gorge below it. A few years later the state purchased an adjoining tract that included Harper Falls on the North Branch, so that now at least two of Greenleaf Chase's eleven Grass River waterfalls are accessible to the public.

The Grass describes a great sickle course of 115 m. from the SE corner to the NE corner of the state's largest county, St. Lawrence. It empties into the St. Lawrence River 9 m. E of Massena. About 45 m. of the South Branch and main stem, 14 m. of the Middle Branch, and 25 m. of the North Branch are inside the Blue Line. Until recently, access to the entire system was severely limited by the absence of even the smallest parcel of state land.

The lower half of the river has long been a favorite canoeing stream. It was at Canton on the Grass that J. Henry Rushton designed, built, and tested his classic all-cedar canoes in the last quarter of the 19th century and, early in the 20th, his wood-and-canvas Indian Girls. From his shop on Water Street canoes went to all parts of the country and abroad. Some are still in use today, while others are preserved as museum pieces and heirlooms. This story is told in *Rushton and His Times in American Canoeing*, by Atwood Manley with my assistance.

In May each year Canton holds its Rushton Memorial Canoe Race on the Grass above the Main Street Bridge. Below the village too the Grass is a pleasant pastoral canoeing stream as far as Massena. But there is hardly a canoeist in these lowlands who does not dream of running the upper river someday, especially the South Branch, in country where the whitetail roams and no cows ruminate on the banks.

To do so has not been easy. It is one of the anomalies of the Adirondack Park that a river as attractive as the South Branch in remoteness and interest to both cruising and whitewater paddlers has been inaccessible to the public for one hundred years. This is not because the South Branch is too steep and obstructed; there are cruising reaches of considerable length. It is because the state has owned no land on this branch inside the Blue Line except a small rest area at the bridge on Route 3. In 1990, however, the state acquired a conservation and recreation easement from the Yorkshire Timber Company that opened a navigable reach of about 8 m. S of Route 3. And in 1991 the Nature Conservancy purchased outright a narrow, two-mile tract of 529 acres extending along the river from Grass River Flow to the bridge on Route 3 and 0.4 m. on the N side of the highway. Known as the Sykes tract, this will be transferred to the state and become the first parcel of Forest Preserve on the entire 40 m. of the South Branch inside the Blue Line. It is a key tract for paddlers because it makes possible egress from the eight navigable miles S of Route 3 and opens access to a route N of the highway. Even so, all land below Route 3 is posted by private owners and game clubs. Of the three bridge crossings on public roads, two are impractical points of access because they are soon followed by posted falls.

The South Branch below Route 3 does not deserve its fate as a neglected orphan of the state. Few Adirondack rivers surpass it in variety and beauty. Five of its waterfalls—Copper Rock, Rainbow, Flat Rock, Twin, and Sinclair—would be outstanding attractions in any region less richly endowed with scenic rivers. Yet three of them are completely hidden from public view, and two can be only partially glimpsed from a public road when the leaves are off the trees. River runners are prohibited from carrying around any of them.

The Middle and the North branches, the two chief tributaries of the South Branch and main stem, are almost entirely inside the Blue Line. Both are classified scenic in the state rivers system. They are shorter, smaller, and steeper than the South Branch and are for the most part inaccessible to the public.

The two streams are prized by members of the game clubs that have access to them. The public in St. Lawrence County also prizes them, though it sees little of them. When a nationwide real estate developer purchased 24,000 acres on the North Branch with the intention of impounding the waters and subdividing the land for a large community of second homes, a spontaneous movement sprang up in the county to stop the scheme. "Citizens to Save the Adirondack Park," they ambitiously called themselves. People from all over the state and out of state joined this informal group till it numbered several thousand contributors. It also found powerful allies among long-established conservation organizations. Meanwhile, the master plan for the zoning of private land in the Adirondacks was passed by the state legislature, and the development corporation eventually abandoned its plan of subdivision. It sold the entire tract to a lumber company, which now manages it as a timber reserve and continues the leases to game clubs. The latter post access sites and carries around waterfalls.

The county road through the town of Clare crosses the Middle Branch 1 m. above confluence with the South Branch. Local landowners do not seem aware that the right of way on a public road extends far enough outside bridge abutments to allow one to lower a canoe into the water, and that there is no title to running water. If you wish to gain access to the main stem of the Grass by putting in on the Middle Branch at the bridge on the Clare Road, you must be prepared for a possible confrontation with a local landowner just for carrying your canoe around the bridge. There is no practical public access to the main stem in the hamlet of DeGrasse; fortunately there is access to the main stem at an alternative site in state land.

In 1984 the state purchased the Harper Falls tract on the North Branch and thereby opened a short whitewater run on this stream to its confluence with the main stem.

NORTH BRANCH

Clare Road to Russell, 6.5 m. (10.5 km.)
USGS: West Pierrepont, Hermon 7.5

Access to the lower North Branch is possible on the Clare Road (see sketch map p. 58) at a bridge 4 m. N of the Middle Branch bridge and 3.8 m. S of the intersection with the Russell-Pierrepont

Turnpike. Minimum water levels are indicated by a 4-foot clearance between the water surface and the bottom of the bridge. Levels are likely to be too low during late spring and summer. This section consists mainly of Class II and III rapids with one Class III-IV drop and one carry around Harper Falls. The total drop from here to the confluence with the main stem is 170 feet, with approximately 50 feet of this drop occurring at Harper Falls.

Below the bridge the North Branch meanders through a flat, marshy area for 1.2 m., eventually completing a wide turn to the L around a ridge. The first rapids are met as the river completes this turn and are easy Class I building to Class II. The Class II rapids continue for 0.4 m. without a break as the current quickens and the river narrows. At this point there is a turn to the R in a Class III-IV rapid. Boulders clog the R channel and force the paddler to the middle of the river or, preferably, to the L where there is a moderate-sized double hydraulic. The river soon turns L, and in 150 yards there is an obvious horizon line. This signals Harper Falls, a completely unmanageable falls in several distinct pitches of 50 feet. Harper Falls can be carried on either side, though the R side is easier. If any of the eddies on the R are missed, there is a large eddy on the L just above the falls.

Below the falls are several hundred yards of Class II rapids ending in a 0.25 m. section of flatwater. The river again narrows in continuous Class II rapids for 0.3 m. A cable is stretched across the river at this point and is low enough that paddlers need to stay alert in order to avoid hitting it. Below the cable the river quickens to Class II-III rapids for 0.3 m. before fading to a Class I stretch, which continues to the confluence with the main stem. The next 2.7 m. of river consists of easy Class I and II rapids to the village of Russell.

SOUTH BRANCH

Massawepie Lake, Outlet, and Massawepie Mire, 4 m. (6.4 km.)
USGS: Childwold 7.5, Tupper Lake 15

The South Branch becomes canoeable just before entering a vast, almost treeless marsh below the mouth of Burntbridge Outlet known as the Massawepie Mire. To the N a feeder of the South Branch can be explored before June 1 and after September 1. The Massawepie Lake track is owned by the Otetiana Council of Boy Scouts, which has a cooperative arrangement with the DEC. The tract is kept open to the public except at the above time. Camping and swimming are not allowed and parking is restricted to designated areas. Paddlers must register near the Superintendent's office. This beautiful expanse of timberland and glacial lakes was once the site of the fashionable Childwold Park Hotel.

Access is by dirt road from Gale on Route 3. A prominent sign headed "Massawepie Scout Camps" marks the entrance. In 0.5 m. the road turns L onto an open field and then climbs a wooded esker. Ponds are strung like beads alongside this narrow ridge. On the W side are Massawepie Lake and Boottree and Town Line ponds; on the E are Catamount, Round, Long, Horseshoe, and Deer ponds. These waters are connected by carry trails. A glance at the map suggests several possible combinations for canoe cruising. Other trails encircle Massawepie Lake or visit outlying features of interest. The signs put up by the scouts seem inspired by Disney as well as Boone. A visit to the area awakens nostalgia in any overgrown Boy Scout. Other people will find interest in the beautiful timber and the glaciated landscape. The fingers of the retreating glacier left some fanciful carvings and deposits between and around pond basins and marshes—eskers, kames, kettle holes. "Kame-and-kettle topography," a geologist friend calls it. The lumber company that operated here in earlier days had the good taste to leave fringes of tall red and white pines on the shores.

The best launching site on Massawepie Lake is about 1.2 m. from Gale. The lake comes into sight on the R and a short spur road connects with the beach.

Massawepie Lake feeds the Grass through its outlet on the SW. At that end of the lake are pine-clad twin eskers, one of which bisects two long narrow bays. The other, on the W, separates the lake from landlocked Pine Pond. It is pleasant to walk along the crests of the two ridges on a carpet of pine needles and look down at water on both sides.

The entrance to the outlet is inside the mouth of the outer bay. But the most interesting way to reach the brook is by Pine Pond. Paddle N about 0.2 m. into the westernmost bay and look for a short trail, L, under a tall pine that has (1992) an active osprey nest in its top. Put in on the pond, bypassing a cove at the S tip, and cross to a hemlock grove on the SW shore. Carry S for 200 yards to a landing on the outlet of Massawepie Lake. Before putting in, climb the ridge top on the L for an overlook, through big pines, of the great Grass River Flow, void of trees except for a few islets of tamarack and aspen.

The meanderings of the outlet brook are, for the first mile, contained within a narrow tamarack and alder swamp edged by higher ground. The loops widen as hills and trees gradually draw back and one enters a funnel-shaped northerly projection of the marsh, where there are long views over low terraces. Below the Scout's property the outlet enters property of the Grasse River Club. There are numerous beaver dams on this portion of the brook. If you have patience enough to cope with them, you can continue to confluence with the South Branch (3.2 m.) and then proceed down the Grass River Flow to Route 3 or up to the Yorkshire Road bridge as described in the following section.

Yorkshire Road bridge to Route 3, 8.6 m. (13.9 km.)
USGS: Long Tom Mountain, Childwold, Brother Ponds, Cranberry Lake 7.5; Tupper Lake 15

Closed to the public for one hundred years, the upper reach of the South Branch has been opened to public boating by the state purchase of a conservation and recreation easement from the Yorkshire Timber Company. This access is closed to the public after mid-October, during the big game hunting season. Take the Massawepie Road S of Route 3 from Gale. Drive 4.9 m. to the first crossroad beyond the one posted by the Grasse River Club. Turn R here, then bear L at a fork; proceed 0.2 m. to a gate and park 30 yards back from it. Carry on the L of the gate for 100 yards to put-in at the bridge. A short upstream paddle is possible before the river becomes too constricted.

Downstream, the South Branch twists and turns through a narrow channel averaging 15 to 20 feet wide. Alders dominate the banks. The Grasse River Club is soon passed. Both foreshores from here to Grass River Flow are owned by this club. Use them only for carries, not for camping, hiking, or lingering. Below the club building, Burntbridge Outlet enters from the L. A low road bridge about 2 m. below the put-in obliges one to duck.

Below this bridge the shores begin to open. Sedge grass alternates with alders. Paddlers have the rewarding experience of cruising through the Massawepie Mire, a 900-acre peatland in this glacial outwash plain. The largest of its types in the Adirondacks, it has been proposed for registry as a national natural landmark. Wildlife sightings are frequent through the mire, especially near beaver colonies and wood duck boxes. Boreal species such as the spruce grouse and the brown-capped chickadee may be spotted. About 3.2 m. from put-in an incongruous outcrop looms up in this flat wetland, Burnt Rock, which rises a sheer 40 feet above the deep pool at its base.

Below Burnt Rock Massawepie Lake Outlet enters on the R, though its entrance may be difficult to spot. (This outlet provides another entrance to the South Branch.) Two short carries are necessary below here, one at a log jam and one at a low road crossing (not shown on the topo maps). About a mile below Burnt Rock the South Branch begins to widen upon approaching the Grass River Flow. The Flow is an artificial impoundment, as the presence of several large dead trees attests. At one time the Flow was somewhat wider than it presently is, reaching a maximum width of 0.5 m. A breaching of the dam about twenty years ago resulted in significant dewatering. A narrowing of the outlet gap of the Flow by the earthworks has again impounded the river, although not quite to its original extent. The Flow is 1.9 m. long, with its foot a distance of 6.6 m. from the Yorkshire Road bridge.

The outlet of the Flow, choked by a logjam, is spanned by a bridge on a road connecting with Route 3 in a quarter mile. A carry down the private road is not allowed, although the DEC is pursuing the possibility of a legal takeout here. In the meantime, the best available opportunities require continued downstream travel. The Nature Conservancy purchase of the Sykes tract and its subsequent transfer to the state open these lands to public use. At the foot of the Flow, take out on the R bank. Cross the road to a faint trail just behind a Forest Preserve sign and go about 20 yards to put-in below the rapids.

There is a major logjam about 0.6 m. below the dam. A road over the bed of the old Grasse River Railroad, adjacent to the L bank, affords an easy carry. Shortly below, yellow DEC canoe-carry discs on the R mark the beginning of a carry trail to Route 3, which allows you to avoid additional carries around several rapids downstream. Follow the discs up a faint foottrail, climbing a 40 foot ridge to the point where you intersect a logging trace. Bear R and then descend the ridge on the L, putting in on Balsam Pond. Paddle across the pond to a small clearing and proceed through open woods until again intersecting the logging trace. At this point Route 3 is visible. Each brief carry is about 0.1 m., and the short paddle across Balsam Pond is about 0.15 m. It is also possible to take the logging trace its entire distance around the E shore of Balsam Pond. The takeout point is about 0.35 m. W of the Shurtleff Road and 1.15 m. E of the state parking area next to the river. Look for a Canoe Launch sign.

Below this carry the river turns to the right, narrows, and drops 15 feet over 25 yards. This rapid is rated Class II-III and is likely to contain trapped deadfall. In the next 1.4 m. there are four distinct rapids, of Class I-II, which consist of shoals and rock gardens. The final rapid, a Class II, is located next to the parking area. Take out on the R either above or immediately below this rapid. Note that all rapids are scratchy, even at mid-to-late spring levels. Carries are short but congested along the banks. The bed of the old Grasse River Railroad follows the L bank for the most of this section, crossing over to the R bank about 0.5 m. before the takeout. This serves as an alternate carry route for those desiring it.

Below Route 3, 16.4 m., maximum round trip (26.5 km.)
USGS: Cranberry Lake, Brother Ponds, Tooley Pond 7.5

In its study report on the South Branch of the Grass, the APA recommended a 17.5-m. canoe route from the vicinity of the Route 3 bridge E of Cranberry Lake to the head of Rainbow Falls—a segment classified as scenic—if easements for carries could be obtained. This is a large *if.* Prior to 1982 the state had no program for opening restricted canoe route. It does have such a program now, but progress is painfully slow and undertain. A seeming opportunity to acquire a large tract on the South Branch E of Cranberry Lake fell through. The tract was offered for sale, the state made a bid, and then the owner either decided not to sell or considered the bid too low. After a long wait with no response, the state withdrew its bid. This tract would have opened several points of access to the South Branch.

The lower half of the route is in timberlands of Champion International, where two game clubs hold leases. Both clubs are adamantly opposed to use of the river by canoeists. They refuse to permit carries around the 100-foot drop of Copper Rock Falls and at other rapids. Following one or two unpleasant experiences with canoeists, the caretaker of one club patrols the Tooley Pond Road at the takeout sites of Newbridge and Rainbow Falls. To complete this run is to risk confrontation with this game club.

Owners and lessees in the upper half of the route have in the past been more accommodative. Previous printings of this guide cite an agreement with owners of Rustic Lodge for access below 1.2 m. of rapids over a private drive and a short carry trail. But soon after the 1981 edition was off the press, Rustic Lodge changed hands for the third time in less than a decade. The road into it is now gated and the present owner prohibits its use even as a carry. East of the bridge on Route 3 (Rustic Lodge is on the W) another private road used by the Cranberry Lake Fish and Game Club is also gated.

One alternative is a round trip from the Route 3 bridge not only descending the rapids but also poling and tracking up them on the return, taking full responsibility for your own safety. So there is a contradiction in this route. Intermediate to advanced skills are required in the 1.2 m. of rapids below the bridge, while the remaining 7 m. to the head of Deerlick Rapids is a cruising level with a drop of barely 10 feet. Scenically, however, it should be interesting to all paddlers.

The Route 3 bridge over the South Branch is 4.7 m. W of Sevey Corners and 3.9 m. E of Cranberry Lake. On the E bank is a highway rest area. It provides legal access. Put in either above or below a Class II-III rapid adjacent to the parking area. The water level of this rapid is a good indicator of how scratchy subsequent rapids will be. In the next 1.2 m. the river drops 60 feet in a series of rapids ranging from Class I to Class V. The first notable rapid occurs 0.3 m. below the bridge and is an easy Class I. In the next 0.5 m. rapids occur regularly and range from Class II to Class III-IV. At a constriction of the river where boulders line the banks, the river drops 10 feet over a distance of 40 feet in a dangerous Class V. The next major drop occurs in 0.2 m. and is a Class III-IV of about 6 feet. Flatwater begins shortly thereafter. Another alternative for the round-trip cruise was opened in 1992 with a gift to the Nature Conservancy of the roadbed of the old Grasse River Railroad from Conifer to Cranberry Lake. This grade parallels the South Branch on the R bank. Cleared of new growth, it affords an easy carry of one mile from Route 3 to the first faint logging trace on the L. Turn on this and descend about 150 yards to the river at a point below the last sharp drop in the rapids. From this point the difficulties are minor—a fallen tree or two, two short easy rapids between the mouths of Irish Brook and Twin Ponds Outlet, bridge pilings close enough to catch driftwood. This cruising level is canoeable all summer, but parties choosing to run the rapids should plan on a spring trip prior to mid-May. No trip should be taken during the big game hunting season.

An early morning start is desirable. Even so, it may not be possible to extend the downstream run as far as Deerlick Rapids, 8.2 m. Since camping is prohibited in these private timberlands, the round trip must be made in one day. The upstream paddle takes at least a third more time than the downstream one.

For the first 1.8 m. the banks are densely wooded. Then one emerges from the shadows into a flood of sunlight. Low terraces of marsh and meadow grass, dotted with islets of trees and shrubs, extend for several rods on each side, and beyond is a solid wall of forest. For the next 3 m. the stream meanders through this delightful natural park. Wildlife is frequently sighted in this corridor. Occasional deadfalls may impede travel.

The abutments of a bridge of the abandoned Grasse River Railroad soon appear on each side of the stream. The bridge is out. In a reversal of the usual order of change, the upper South Branch is wilder today than it was a half century ago. Then a bustling short line ran from home base in Conifer into the valley of the Grass, following the stream for most of its 16-m. course to Cranberry Lake. The Emporium Forestry Company built the railroad in 1913 to carry logs. In 1915 it began carrying passengers and mail too. A 1-m. spur connecting it with the Childwold station of the New York Central's Adirondack Division enabled summer residents and tourists to reach Cranberry Lake in a convenient and pleasant way before that village had good road connections with the outside. At its third and last crossing of the river, the railroad turned S to follow the shore of Silver Pond into Cranberry Lake Village.

At the peak of operations the Grasse River Railroad had a roster of 21 locomotives, both of the rod and Shay types. Summer people in the area grieved when the tracks of the short line were removed after World War II. Americans are ambivalent about wildness. They want to preserve it. Yet to some older people today the most meaningful thing about the upper Grass River is that a unique little railroad once rumbled, belched, and whistled along its banks.

Just beyond the railroad grade is the marshy delta of Dead Creek. In another mile is the iron bridge on the Windfall Road. The channel is often narrowed here by collected driftwood.

The Windall Road is now part of a private game preserve and is closed to public use. Originally it ran from Cook Corners to Sevey. Today its place is taken by the state highway 2 m. S, which joins the old road 5 m. farther E. The Windfall Road has a history. It once linked the farms of pioneer settlers in the area, who came shortly after the Civil War. They were attracted by a clearing in the forest a half mile or more wide and 25 m. long, from Cook Pond ENE across the Grass River to Sevey Corners and on into Franklin County. This was the path of the great windfall of September 20, 1845, the most severe tornado ever recorded in northern New York.

After the mass of uprooted timber had dried, some hunter, impatient with its impenetrability, set fire to it. Nearly 20 years later a traveler, Nathaniel Coffin, described the result of the fire and rot in his *Forest Arcadia of Northern New York:* "We at length saw through the gloom of the forest the opening of the great windfall, which, under the burning rays of a meridian sun, contrasted with the darkness of the woods upon its borders, shone like a band of gold.... The broad savannah of the windfall, bare of trees and covered with wild grasses, rose and fell, as far as the eye could reach, in graceful undulations." But the families that settled the western end of the windfall in the 1860s and 1870s did not find the land as fertile as it had looked to them and to Coffin. Except for a settlement of trailers and hunting camps at Cook Corners, no one lives on the Windfall Road today. Only cellar holes mark the locations of the old farmhouses.

Reforestation and natural growth have made the path of the windfall hard to trace. But along this section of the Grass, at least, the aspect is still somewhat as Coffin described it over a century ago: the wild grasses undulate in the breeze, and the savannah sines like a band of gold in contrast to the darkness of bordering woods.

At a low wooden bridge about 1.3 m. below the Windfall Road, the current quickens a little, and in the next mile to Twin Ponds Outlet there are two shore Class I rapids easy to descend but a stiff pull upstream unless poles are resorted to. Beyond them is a pleasant quiet stretch between low but mostly wooded banks. As the stream bends from W to N between rising banks, however, the current quickens again, and soon Deerlick Rapids are reached, the signal for turning back for those who have come thus far. The stretch from here to Newbridge on the Tooley Pond Road is wild and splendid. It is also strenuous, the river dropping 150 feet in several rapids and in a 0.6-m. long gorge and steep cataracts known as Copper Rock Falls. The run is impossible without a long carry at the falls and perhaps shorter ones at the Class II-III rapids.

The section from Newbridge to Degrasse equals or surpasses the upper river in scenic value. Its waterfalls have not yet been tampered with. Rainbow Falls in its constricted gorge and spacious Twin Falls are of outstanding beauty. The more modest Sinclair Falls, which can be reached on a spur road, is a favorite subject of local artists. This section too is private land. The Tooley Pond Road gives occasional glimpses of the river.

Degrasse State Forest to Russell, 11.5 m. (18.5 km.)
USGS: Degrasse, West Pierrepont, Hermon 7.5

State acquisition of the Lampson Falls tract in 1979 makes possible a run of 11.5 m. in a varied and uniquely scenic river corridor, ending in the village of Russell outside the Blue Line. In the first 4.5 m. the river meanders over a floodplain so flat, at least on the E side, that no grading was necessary on a private landing strip screened from the river by trees. These flats were probably the bed of a postglacial lake plugged by a slowly melting ice lobe on the N.

At Lampson Falls an abrupt change takes place. The river plunges into a gorge nearly 6 m. long, with steep heavily-wooded banks and outcroppings of bedrock. The 40-foot drop at the falls is followed by 0.8 m. of smooth water. In the next 1.1 m. comes a dramatic series of nine cascades—some in divided channels, some abrupt, others flume-like. Wildwater alternates with quiet pools. The rock is the hard, resistant Precambrian series that tapers from the northwest corner of the park to an isthmus at the Thousand Islands and connects the Adirondacks with the Canadian Shield. On a stage geological map the Lampson Falls corridor of the Grass is shaded as "thin discontinuous drift over Precambrian rock." It is a gallery of rock and greenery.

Below the last of the cascades, the descent is more gradual in 4.3 m. of almost continuous Class I-II rapids. The last 0.8 m. is flatwater in a broadening valley of cleared fields. The total drop in the 7 m. from Lampson Falls to Russell is 220 feet.

This run accommodates a wide range of paddling skills, but the novice should turn back at Lampson Falls. The practiced beginner making the whole run in an open canoe must be prepared to carry or line his craft in at least eight places and be experienced in Class II rapids. Advanced skills are required to run the 1.1 m. of cascades and flumes rated from Class II to Class V.

Late April and May provide the medium high water level most desirable for this run. In summer wading would be necessary in shallow parts of the rapids. Fall rains usually restore adequate water by late September.

A morning start is advisable. Numerous carries are time consuming. Time should also be allowed for rest and leisure. Cameras, however, should be reserved for a visit to the Lampson Falls tract on foot; there is risk of shipping water in the rapids even if you carry around all the cascades. The entire corridor is open for public fishing. The DEC stocks the river with brown trout at the Degrasse State Forest. Pike and small-mouthed bass are also caught.

Above the hamlet of Degrasse* the South Branch leaves the park

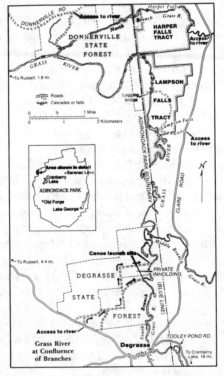

---

*Originally named Monterey. In the 1880s the name was changed to De Grasse (now Degrasse) in honor of the French admiral who served in the American Revolution. "Grass" was established as the name of the river long before the renaming of this hamlet.

boundary. After picking up the Middle Branch to become the main stem, the river flirts with the Blue Line, making three re-entries. The North Branch joins the main stem 2.5 m. outside the Blue Line.

The Degrasse State Forest provides legal access. Taking the Degrasse-Russell Road, County 38, turn off the blacktop 1.2 m. NW of Degrasse (6.4 m. SE of Russell), at the DEC sign "Degrasse State Forest." A pine plantation, the forest is a mostly level, sandy plain crisscrossed by single-lane logging roads in normally good condition. To avoid wrong turns, follow directions closely and check mileages on your odometer. Proceed N from the entrance 0.15 m.; E for 0.8 m. to a T; here turn L (N) and proceed 0.25 m. to the first R turn, where in 1980 a sign "Canoe Launching" was mounted (signs are volatile). Take this road in an easterly direction for nearly a half mile to its end. From the parking lot, carry about 40 yards to the river and then turn R for the most convenient put-in, a graded cut in the bank. (The accompanying map shows two put-in sites. The downstream one (N) should now be considered abandoned. The map was made before the DEC improved the upstream (S) access to the river. The latter shortens driving distance in the state forest, adds a half mile of cruising distance on the river, and offers a shorter and easier carry.)

From the improved put-in site it is 4.5 m. to the head of Lampson Falls on meandering smooth water complicated by sloughs and curlicues of abandoned channel. At 1.5 m. the Middle Branch of the Grass enters obscurely under a canopy of silver maple foliage, punctuated by the skeletons of dead elms, some standing, others fallen halfway across the river. Below the junction the South Branch becomes known as the main stem. A few widely spaced camps soon appear on the R bank. After crossing Burns Flat, the river makes an oxbow bend, and the sheer cliffs of a small mountain come into view on the L. The river now re-enters the park in the Lampson Falls tract (L bank to the head of the falls; both banks below) for its last 2.9 m. inside the Blue Line.

As the falls are heard, draw toward the L bank. (Here and at the cascades below, remember that the current next to shore is slowed by friction, while a few feet out it is faster. In crossing from one velocity to another the canoe may spin out of control and possibly flip if it hits an obstacle. A back ferry is often the best maneuver—back-paddling at an angle with the shore as you prepare to land.) Several openings in shrubbery make possible landings, one of them just a dozen feet above the brink. The carry around the falls is short and easy, down open rock alongside the sheet of sliding water.

A spit of bedrock jutting out from the R shore almost encloses a wide pool below the falls. Its terraces make an ideal picnic site and overlook. Here many years ago a Frenchwoman, then chairman of the modern language department of a North Country college, the daughter of a French army general, and herself an archpatriot, exclaimed in an unguarded moment: "There is nothing so beautiful in all France!"

Another Frenchwoman, celebrated in literary history and in politics for her opposition to Napoleon, once owned Lampson Falls as part of her 35,000-acre holdings in the northwestern Adirondacks. Madame de Staël, "mistress to an age" as a recent biographer calls her, dreamed of a possible refuge for herself and her children in the new nation across the Atlantic. A friend of Gouverneur Morris and of several French emigrants who settled in northern New York, especially James Donatien Le Ray de Chaumont, she was persuaded to buy large tracts in St. Lawrence County, convinced that these lands would be a good investment for her heirs. Though Madame de Staël and her son Auguste planned visits to America over a period of eight years, neither ever made the trip or saw Lampson Falls. It is just as well. A Paris salon, not wilderness, was necessary to her happiness. Unlike her 20th century compatriot, she had little taste for natural scenery. Nor did her Adirondack lands prove a good investment for her heirs. Forty-five years after her first purchase (which included the Lampson Falls tract), her son-in-law, the Duc de Broglie, tired of taxes and low valuations, sold all her land in St. Lawrence County. Today the town of Clare, of which she once owned more than half, has only 116 inhabitants (1980 census). But the value of its natural scenery has finally been recognized. In 1979 the state paid $325 an acre for the Lampson Falls tract, which in 1801 Jacques Necker, Madame de Staël's father, had bought for her at one dollar an acre. (For a fuller account of this story, see my article "Lampson Falls" in the March-April 1980 issue of *Adirondack Life*.)

A low narrow ledge extends across the channel at the foot of the pool below Lampson Falls. It should be examined from the spit. At low to medium water levels it can't be run without a scratch.

The next 0.8 m. is smooth water with one constricted passage in a basin of bedrock. There is a fine hemlock grove on the R bank.

The dynamics resume under a logging bridge built in the 1970s. Here the river funnels into the first of several pitches. The next 1.1-m. reach is a cornucopia of riverscapes: compressed channels alternating with wide pools, dome-shaped or elongated islands of tawny to orange-colored rock dividing wildwater flumes; sandy coves;

sentinel pines and hemlocks gripping the rock and penetrating its crevices with their roots; a long finger of bedrock deflecting the course of the river in two 130-degree bends.

In early June the L bank below the logging bridge is flowery with masses of pink lady's slipper, foamflower, wild lily-of-the-valley, and bunchberry; in August, with cardinal flower in rocky niches. Be careful where you step on the carries. Don't remain to camp. The thin layer of duff on the knolls is highly flammable, and the next visitors will not be pleased to find traces of a camp. What the guide Orson Phelps said of the mountain view from Upper Ausable Lake applies here: this "ain't the kinder scenery you want ter hog down."

There are nine falls or cascades in the 1.1 m. below the logging bridge with ratings from Class II to Class V. All but two are best carried on the L. The short Class II flume under the footbridge should be run on the far L and may require paddlers to duck at high water levels. Watch for the substantial hydraulic on the R. The second and third pitches are flumes dropping about 10 feet, each rated Class IV-V. At high water levels there are continuous rapids in the 100 feet between these two drops; a mishap in the first drop can be particularly dangerous. The first flume ends in a succession of large powerful hydraulics easily capable of flipping a boat. The second drops into a nasty hole surrounded by a powerful swirling eddy. The next pitch is an easy Class III drop of 5 feet, best run on the L. This drop can be lined in a narrow channel on the R at high water. The fifth pitch comes in a quarter mile and is a Class III drop. This drop can be carried over a rocky point on R shore. To run the rapid, negotiate a series of ledges while the river turns L. The river immediately turns sharply to the R and drops 6 feet. Run this down the center through a wide hydraulic. This drop should be scouted first as it is quite scratchy. The sixth drop is unrunnable on the L; the R channel is Class IV and can be scouted from the island or from the R bank. This channel veers to the R and then turns sharply L while dropping 5 feet; there is an additional 3-foot drop at the foot of the island.

Below the sixth drop at the N end of the Lampson Falls tract, the river swings from N to SW. Around this bend are three more falls in quick succession in a strip of state forest just outside the Blue Line. The last two can be bypassed in a single carry of 0.25 m. if one wishes to avoid some mild Class II rapids between the two pitches. The seventh pitch is a Class III-IV drop of 6 feet. It can be scratchy even at moderate water levels. Run on the far L and line up with a prominent roostertail wave. The eighth drop offers an interesting possibility for the enterprising paddler. The major R channel is too constricted to run, but at high water there is a very narrow (6 to 8 feet) quick flume down the L which drops 12 feet over a distance of 100 feet. Care must be taken to avoid being turned sideways while going down this Class IV flume. The ninth drop cannot be run on the L. The R channel requires a complex maneuver on the far R around boulders situated between two large pitches, the first of 6 feet, the second of 3 feet. Scouting from the R is advised before attempting this Class IV-V rapid.

Below the last cascade is a fast, exhilarating float of 4.3 m. No carries are required and only Class I-II rapids are encountered. There is little need for maneuvering. Keep the canoe pointed into the standing, scalloped waves which mark the deepest channel.

The Blue Line is crossed at the N-to-SW bend mentioned above, but the corridor remains scenic. In the next 2.5 m. to the confluence of the North Branch, Palmer Hill on the R is a state forest outside the park. Two cables cross the river, the lower one just above the North Branch junction. The North Branch is a brook trout stream. It has been overfished in recent years since a new logging road, connecting with the Donnerville Road out to Russell, made it possible to drive cars to a point on the bank 0.1 m. above the mouth.

From the North Branch junction it is 2.8 m. to the bridge in Russell. (The last 1.8-m. stretch is not shown on the accompanying sketch map; see the *Hermon* topo map.) A second car should be parked at the SE corner of the bridge for the shuttle back to the Degrasse State Forest.

The Lampson Falls tract can be reached more directly than from the put-in at the Degrasse State Forest. The entrance, "Grasse River State Forest", is a gated spur road off the Clare Road (County 115), 16 m. S of the post office in Canton. Visitors from the SE can take the slow but adventuresome Tooley Pond Road from Cranberry Lake to Degrasse; then continue N on the Clare Road 4.1 m. to the same spur. From the gate it is a half mile walk on a good gravel road to the head of Lampson Falls (the first 0.35 m. of the spur is between parcels of private, posted land). This is the only public access for visitors on foot.

A trail marked with red DEC discs circles around the pool below Lampson Falls to the terraced spit and overlook, continues down-stream on the E bank, crosses the river on a bridge, and resumes its downstream course on the W bank. For connoisseurs of wild river scenery, the mile below the bridge, alongside a series of cascades, is of outstanding interest.

RAQUETTE RIVER

The nice thing about many North Country names is that everyone can exercise his imagination in explaining them. The bad, that they lead to testy quarrels among the pundits. There are partisans for "Racquette." Others insist that "Racket" has the stamp of antiquity, an English equivalent of an original Indian name meaning "swift" or "noisy." And indeed, "River Racket" appears over and over again in the field notes of Benjamin Wright, Macomb Purchase surveyor in 1799. But majority opinion has settled on "Raquette," of French heritage. Why? Well, the configuration of the river's mouth is said to resemble a snowshoe, and "raquette" is the French word for that artifact. Another flight of imagination is that Raquette Lake was the first body of water to acquire the name, from a pile of rotting snowshoes found on its shore. They were abandoned there during a spring thaw, so the story goes, by Sir John Johnson and his party of Loyalists as they fled to Canada during the Revolution. No other surmise has surpassed this one for titillation, so we'll settle on "Raquette."

Like most rivers of the NW watershed, the Raquette rises in a chain of lakes in the central Adirondacks and flows for many miles over a flat or gently sloping plateau before tumbling over the rim into the St. Lawrence Valley. Morainal deposits and eroded cols have altered its course, and probably even the direction of flow of the upper stream, since preglacial times. It has the convex profile of a young river.

The Raquette is the longest river of the NW Adirondacks and the second longest in the state. The distance from its source in Blue Mountain Lake to its mouth in the St. Lawrence is about 170 m. In the upper two-thirds inside the park, the course is mostly zigzag or meandering.

Geologists think that the Raquette is considerably longer than in preglacial times; that it has captured the headwaters of two other drainage basins. The main axis of elevation in the Adirondacks runs

S through Clinton and Essex counties to the Marcy region, and then, with an offset to the W, SW through Hamilton County. The Raquette hugs the western slope of this divide in northern Hamilton and southern Franklin counties. A valley cuts across the axis SE of Blue Mountain Lake. Here a low glacial moraine less than a mile wide now separates Blue Mountain Lake from the Rock River, a feeder of the Hudson. Through this valley, it is believed, Blue Mountain and Eagle lakes once drained into the Hudson; Utowana, Raquette, and Forked lakes drained WSW into the Moose. Long Lake probably drained into the Hudson through another moraine-plugged cross-axis valley at Round Pond and Catlin Lake, where a canal was once proposed (and even begun) to link Long Lake with the Hudson. Preglacial feeders of Long Lake were a N flowing stream from a col at the rapids below Forked Lake and a S flowing one from a col at Raquette Falls. The damming effect of glacial deposits, linked with erosion of the cols, diverted the drainage of all these lakes—Blue Mountain, Eagle, Utowana, Raquette, Forked, and Long—into an expanded Raquette River system.

The sizable lakes of the headwaters, along with Tupper Lake and Simon Pond at midcourse, assure an adequate flow through summer months. The Raquette is the deepest and broadest river of the NW watershed. It also has the longest cruising mileage inside the Blue Line—112 scenic miles of forest, marsh, lake, and mountain.

The Raquette is the central part of a great valley that bisects the Adirondack Dome from Boonville to Plattsburgh. Linked with the Moose in the SW and the Saranac in the NE, it has been a main artery of travel since 1840. Do not expect the quiet and seclusion you can still find on several other streams. The Raquette is everybody's river. Motorboats churn its waters between the carries except for two sections classified scenic: the 6 m. from the foot of Long Lake to Raquette Falls and the 13 m. from Sols Island to Moosehead Rapids. But the attractions of the river far outweigh the noise and congestion. Thousands of canoeists float down to Axton or Tupper Lake each year.

The Raquette is a companionable stream. You meet interesting, relaxed people on it. This has been going on since two young New Yorkers met a party of Indians at Raquette Falls in 1843; since 1858 when two other New Yorkers met Louis Agassiz, James Russell Lowell, Ralph Waldo Emerson, and seven other celebrities of Philosophers' Camp. Today Boy Scouts outnumber celebrities. But a canoeist hardly ever leaves the river without some human contact, warm, intriguing, or comic. And if lucky, he may also enjoy some blessed long silences in the wilder parts of the river between Long Lake and Axton and between Piercefield and Carry Falls Reservoir.

Other rivers of the NW watershed, such as the Grass, the St. Regis, and the Deer, have little or no history. They lead into a timeless world. But a tour of the Raquette is a tour through Adirondack history. The people you meet may know something about that history. You should be prepared. The shortest way is to read a small book by Charles W. Bryan, Jr., *The Raquette: River of the Forest* (1964), and to visit the Adirondack Museum, which is conveniently located about 1.5 m. up the hill from the landing on Blue Mountain Lake where the Raquette cruise starts. Harold K. Hochschild tells the full story of Raquette headwaters in his *Township 34* and the seven revised extracts from that book.

Some of the highlights to brush up on are the escape to Canada of Sir John Johnson during the Revolution; the pioneer settlement at Long Lake; the advance of lumbermen up the river from Potsdam and the perils of log driving; the feud on Eagle Lake between the dime-novelist Ned Buntline and the angry woodsman Alvah Dunning; the Sabattis family of Indian hunters and guides; the first luxury camps; the tourist hotels; the world's shortest standard-gauge railroad, on the Marion River Carry; steamboat days; days when picnic points were littered with champagne bottles instead of beer cans; the evolution of the guideboat; Verplanck Colvin and the Adirondack survey; Mother Johnson's at Raquette Falls; honest John Plumley and his patron Adirondack Murray; Nessmuk's three summer cruises in light-weight Rushton's that made canoeing history; the rise of Tupper Lake; Noah Rondeau, hermit of Cold River.

The Raquette cruise can be made in sections at different times; or all at once, with or without side excursions, in a week or longer. Canoes can be rented and provisions obtained at hamlets along the route. Lodging is available too; a motel room on the waterfront can be welcome on a rainy night. But accommodations are not readily found in the 40-m. stretch between Long Lake Village and Tupper Lake (Corey's near Axton can be tried) or in the 44.5 m. between Tupper Lake and South Colton. A camping trip means heavier loads on the carries but freedom from schedules. There are state lean-tos (though never enough for peak traffic in July and August) at intervals from the headwaters to Tupper Lake. But it is wise to take a tent or tarpaulin in case the lean-tos are full.

Below Tupper Lake there are no lean-tos or state-built fireplaces. This part of the river is not described in the state circular "Adirondack

Canoe Routes," nor has the state improved carry trails or prepared camping sites. But there are attractive sites for improvised camps on state land at Moosehead Rapids, Moody Falls, and below Jamestown Falls. Also available are several sites developed for the public by Niagara Mohawk Power Corporation. This lower part of the river, especially from Piercefield to Carry Falls Reservoir, deserves to be better known than it is.

The average gradient is only 3 feet a mile above Piercefield. In the 16 m. below Piercefield Flow it steepens to nearly 10 feet. In the next 22 m. the average is 23 feet per mile, but the falls and rapids that many of us remember have been stilled in reservoirs and diverted through penstocks, around which the canoeist must carry unless he chooses to leave the river at the first of the reservoirs, Carry Falls.

The segments into which the cruise is divided below do not suggest day-by-day objectives. Much should be left to chance. Bad weather may indicate an early stop, or you may want to linger in one place and take a side excursion. You may also pass several lean-tos before finding an unoccupied one. The segments are determined by the location of access roads permitting the cruise to be made in one or two-day stints, with a car at each end or a pick-up arranged for.

Blue Mountain Lake to Forked Lake Carry, 18 m. (29 km.)
USGS: Blue Mountain Lake, Raquette Lake 15

The opinion that South Inlet and the lakes it drains (Sagamore, Mohigan, and Kora) are the true headwaters of the Raquette is based on the fact that these lakes are at higher elevations than Blue Mountain Lake. However, since the latter is fed by brooks off the highest peak in the region, there is support for the traditional view that the Eckford Chain (Blue Mountain, Eagle, and Utowana lakes) is the principal source, though the river first acquires its name as the outflow of Raquette Lake. The mound of glacial till in the valley SE of Blue Mountain Lake is the divide between the NW drainage of the Raquette and the SE drainage of the Hudson.

A fitting preface to the cruise is an overlook of Raquette headwaters from the summit of Blue Mountain, 2,000 feet above the lake. The 2-m. trail starts across the highway from and just below the entrance to the Adirondack Museum.

Canoes can be launched at the small public bathing beach (enclosed by a low railing) across from the Fire House in the hamlet. Canoes should be carried across the E end of the beach to a pier-like projection of sand and rock.

Blue Mountain Lake has a maximum depth of 102 feet. Its elevation of 1,789 feet is kept constant by a low dam at the outlet of Utowana Lake. Its waters are very clear and, set deep within a ring of mountains, reflect every mood of the changing sky.

It is 2 m. past several islands to the bridges over the outlet. Beyond stores and houses, vacation homes have taken the place of the big hotels that in the 1880s made Blue Mountain Lake one of the most fashionable resorts in the East. The W end of the lake is less developed. A glance back before entering the narrow channel into Eagle Lake shows how Blue Mountain got its name.

Two bridges cross the channel into Eagle Lake. The stone and wood one is a memorial bridge erected in 1891 by William West Durant in honor of his father, Dr. Thomas Durant, builder of the Union Pacific and the Adirondack Railway to North Creek.

Eagle and Utowana lakes are long and narrow. They too have privately owned shores but with fewer camps and longer reaches of unbroken woods. Proceeding down the chain and into the Marion River, one has a growing sense of remoteness. The present scene is very different from the bustle of early century, when, with its steamboats and Marion River Carry Railroad, this was a main line of travel stretching all the way to the mansions on Fifth Avenue.

Nearly a half mile above the dam at the foot of Utowana Lake is a lean-to in a narrow corridor of state land. Below the dam is a carry of 0.5 m. around shallow rapids and along the route of the former Carry Railroad, once the world's shortest standard gauge railway. (The locomotive and a passenger coach are on display at the Adirondack Museum.) From the carry a trail goes N to Sargent Pond. The Marion River becomes navigable near the remains of a steamboat landing.

The Marion River, classified scenic, winds through marsh and swamp. Rich aquatic growth makes it a feeding ground for waterfowl and deer. The valley contracts at the western end, and the flat top of a cliff on the R bank makes a good tent site on state land. The distance from the carry to the tip of Woods Point on Raquette Lake is 5.5 m. The direct route downstream swings N around the point. Osprey Island on the L was Adirondack Murray's favorite campground for many years; it is privately owned today.

Raquette Lake is the fourth largest body of water (excluding Lake Champlain) in the Adirondack Park. Its intricate pattern of bays,

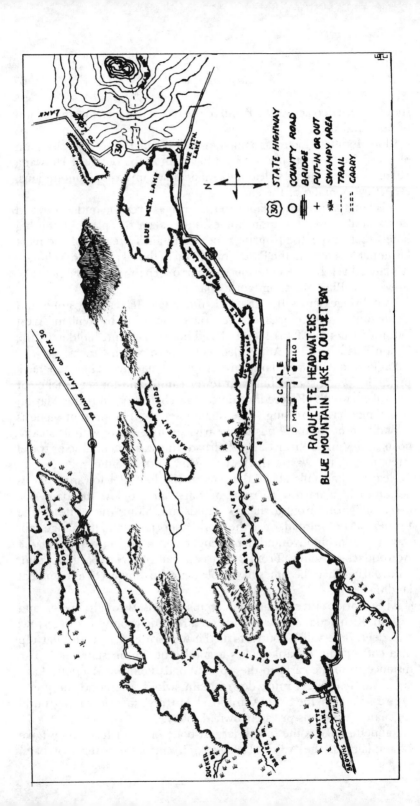

RAQUETTE HEADWATERS
BLUE MOUNTAIN LAKE TO OUTLET BAY

SCALE
0 MILES 1 KILO 1

STATE HIGHWAY
COUNTY ROAD
BRIDGE
PUT-IN OR OUT
SWAMPY AREA
TRAIL
CARRY

N

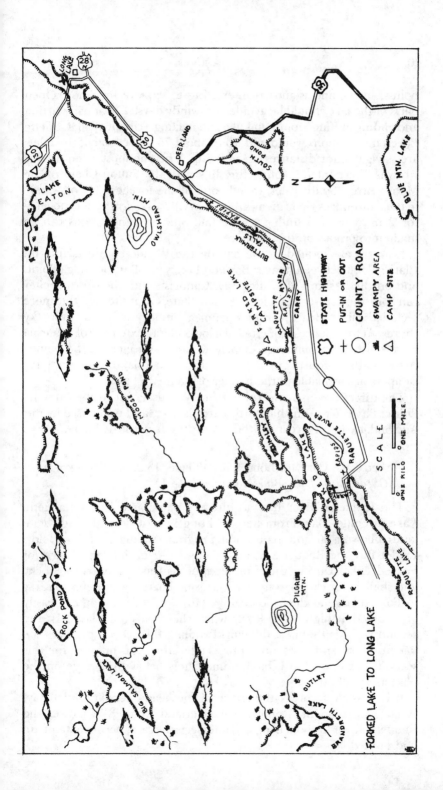

FORKED LAKE TO LONG LAKE

points, inlets, and islands is interesting to explore by canoe. Open parts of the lake should be avoided on windy days. A boat trip starting and ending at Blue Mountain Lake and making a circuit of all Raquette Lake's indentations would add up to about 75 m. Several of the inlets are navigable for distances up to 2.5 m. The one most often used is Browns Tract Inlet, a connecting link with the Fulton Chain of the Moose River. South Inlet, called "one of the loveliest bits of water" in the Adirondacks in Murray's *Adventures in the Wilderness,* is canoeable for 2 m. to a pool under a waterfall. Shorter penetrations can be made into brooks on the W shore.

Lean-tos are located in the bay on the W side of Big Island, on Clark's Point between Beaver Bay and Lonesome Bay, on Tioga Point, and on the N shore of Outlet Bay. Canoeists with their own shelter can join the crowd at Golden Beach State Campsite, try the more secluded Silver Beach, or pick from a number of green or rocky shores. At first glance Raquette Lake looks like an extension of suburbia because of the prominence of private camps on most of the points. Actually, three-fourths of the shoreline is state land. Provisions for campers are available at the hamlet of Raquette Lake.

The direct downstream route from Woods Point to the carry in Outlet Bay is 6 m. The half-mile carry is over land purchased by the Adirondack Land Trust in 1992. Camping is permitted here.

Forked Lake Carry to Long Lake Village, 13.25 m. (21.3 km.)
USGS: Raquette Lake, Blue Mountain Lake 15

The Raquette River first acquires its name as it leaves Raquette Lake in Outlet Bay. From here to Long Lake it flows through state land following a land acquisition program ending in 1986. Below Outlet Bay the Raquette winds its way for 2 m. into the E arm of Forked Lake. During the summer months this section is too rocky and shallow for easy passage, and cruising boaters will prefer to carry to Forked Lake as described below. However, this section can easily be paddled at high water levels when the rapids are Class I-II; the second rapid is the most difficult. Paddling this section bypasses the 0.5 m. carry and does not appreciably affect the mileage for this section. Put in on the L bank immediately below the bridge on the blacktop road off Route 30.

It is possible to break the cruise of the headwaters at Outlet Bay. A blacktop road off Route 30 at Deerland winds SW, crosses the Raquette River in about 8 m., and intersects the carry between Raquette and Forked lakes.

Canoeists continuing downstream cross the 0.5-m. carry on a dirt road to Forked Lake. The direct route lies through the E arm of Forked Lake to the outlet. There are primitive campsites and a lean-to on the S shore; and at the outlet (the Raquette), a public campground where tent sites are assigned by a caretaker.

Forked Lake, 7 m. long, has three arms resembling wide river channels. The shores are beautifully wooded. Sheltered from wind, the surface is often smooth, reflecting the gracefully arched branches of handsome pines. Most of the shores are a carefully guarded private park, but the southern end of the lake can be explored. The outer half of the W arm is state land and available for camping. Brandreth Lake Outlet enters here; it is canoeable for about 2 m. The outer 1.5 m. of the S shore of the E arm is also state land.

In the last century it was possible to make a round trip of 114 m., with carries, from Blue Mountain Lake, by way of a chain of ponds N of Forked Lake, to Tupper Lake, with a return by the Raquette River. As described in E. R. Wallace's *Descriptive Guide to the Adirondacks* (1875–1899), the route proceeded through Raquette headwaters, turned N in Forked Lake to Little Forked; continued N through Cary, Sutton, Bottle, and Rock ponds with their connecting streams or carry trails to Little Tupper Lake; thence into Round Lake and down Round Lake Outlet and Bog River into Tupper Lake. Paddling to the N end of Big Tupper, the canoeist then entered the Raquette and proceeded upstream to the head of Long Lake, where he carried to South Pond. Here the logic of the trip breaks down with a long, hilly carry of 3 m. back to Blue Mountain Lake; in the old days, horse and wagon were no doubt available here. It was also possible to begin at South Pond, go down the Raquette, and reverse the course through the lakes and ponds, with a terminus at Blue Mountain Lake. This round trip is not open to the public today because the ponds N of Forked Lake are in a patrolled private preserve.

The Raquette drops 116 feet in the 5 m. from Forked Lake to Long. Some cruising paddlers choose to bypass this rough section by arranging for truck transport from Forked Lake Campsite to Deerland. It can be potentially dangerous for inexperienced boaters or for skilled boaters carrying heavy camping gear. Those who stay with the river encounter Class II and III rapids and Buttermilk Falls. At the end of Forked Lake is a dam owned by the Whitney Company. If the dam's sluice gates are open, the R channel makes an exhilarating run; if they are closed, carry on the R and put in immediately below the dam. At high water there are continuous Class II-III rapids for the next 0.8 m. These are followed by Class I rapids for the next

0.7 m., ending at the first lean-to. A carry around these rapids begins at the Outlet and follows a paved road for 1.6 m. to a landing below the lean-to.

The river is now flat and easily canoeable for the next 1.5 m. to Buttermilk Falls. The falls appear just after the road becomes visible for the first time. There is a carry of 0.1 m. on the R bank, marked by a state trail sign. Buttermilk Falls drops a total of 40 feet and is completely unrunnable. It is celebrated in Adirondack Murray's tall tale, "Phantom Falls." The falls is a popular picnic ground today with an impressive array of rock terraces leading to the shoreline.

Below Buttermilk Falls are several short rapids rated Class I-II. At 0.5 m. there is another state marker on the R. This carry trail is 0.5 m. long and ends at two lean-tos almost invariably occupied to overflowing at the height of the season. Those wishing to paddle these sections are confronted with Class II rapids which build rapidly to Class III. There is a short carry trail from the lean-tos at the foot of the rapids to a small turnout off the blacktop road.

The river is now navigable to the head of Long Lake through watery meadows of pickerelweed and pond lilies. The next state land is on the W shore of the lake in the bay N of Moose Island. Cliffs here leave limited space for camping.

Long Lake is a widening of the river in a fault basin probably enlarged by glacial action. The average width is about a half mile and the length is 14 m. Sheltered by mountains, the surface is often calm. In any case, prevailing summer winds favor downstream travel. The canoeist can relax and enjoy panoramic views. Long Lake is at its best on a still day in late September when it reflects the rich colors of its wooded slopes.

As its S end the lake is narrow and shallow. The E shore and parts of the W are lined with boarding camps, cottages, and motels. A trail nearly opposite Deerland used to lead to the summit of Owls Head Mountain (2,780 feet), but was abandoned after the Big Blow of 1950. This mountain was a popular ascent as early as the 1850s while most of the High Peaks were as yet unclimbed. Lines of tourist travel then were mainly confined to the waterways.

A few pioneers settled on the S part of Long Lake in the 1830s and 1840s. In 1841 the Reverend John Todd, author of *Long Lake*, found a small settlement of eight or nine families. Among these settlers and their sons were craftsmen who contributed to the development of the Adirondack guideboat and who became skilled guides.

The present village of Long Lake is 4.5 m. from the head. For campers it is the last source of provisions on the cruise before Tupper Lake. Connecting the two parts of the village, Route 30 crosses a narrows on a bridge and causeway. The hotel, stores, restaurants, and motels are mostly on the E shore. The Lake Eaton State Campsite is 2 m. W off Route 30.

Long Lake Village to Axton, 23.3 m. (37.5 km.)
USGS: Blue Mountain Lake, Long Lake 15; Kempshall Mtn. 7.5 × 15

Canoeists can put in at two public beaches, one on the E side of the bridge and the other a state boat launching site on a blacktop road which starts from Route 30 about 20 yards SE of the post office. The distance from the village to the foot of Long Lake is 9.5 m. Widening to a maximum of 1 m., the northern half of the lake commands splendid mountain views. The first one to catch the eye, N of the bridge, is the massive notched skyline of the Seward Range in the distant NE. For the New York City surgeon Dr. Arpad Gerster, "the serrated skyline of Mount Seward" as seen from his camp on the W shore was "the finest view in the North Woods." Other peaks often in view are Blueberry and Kempshall on the E and Buck Mountain on the W. Kempshall (3,360 feet) can be climbed by a 2.5-m. trail which starts on shore 5 m. below the village.

About 2.5 m. down the lake from the village, the Big Marsh is on the L and Catlin Bay on the R. The next prominent feature is Round Island, midway between two promontories. Joel T. Headley was long ago struck by the beauty of this island. In his *The Adirondack* (1849) he wrote, "I wished I owned that island—it would be pleasant to be possessor of so much beauty."

The N end of the lake is much less developed than the S, particularly in the last 6 m. Over half of the E shore is Forest Preserve, the western edge of the High Peaks Wilderness Area. The Northville-Lake Placid Trail parallels this shore to Plumley's Landing, 1.5 m. from the foot of the lake, where it turns E to cross the Cold River at Shattuck Clearing. At many places on the E shore ribbons of sandy beach backed by dense forest provide good tent sites, and ten lean-tos are located between Catlin Bay and the foot of the lake.

Lean-tos on Long Lake would be more readily available to transient canoeists if it were not for violations of the rule prohibiting occupancy by the same party for more than three nights. Groups coming down the lake in motorboats with a cargo consisting of bottled-gas stoves, beach umbrellas, chairs, tables, and other paraphernalia have in the

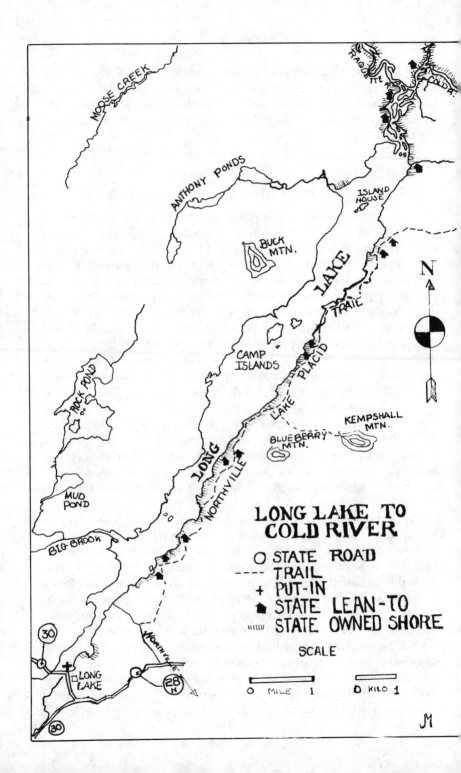

MOOSE CREEK

RAQUETTE R.

COLD R.

ANTHONY PONDS

ISLAND HOUSE

BUCK MTN.

LAKE

TRAIL

ROCK POND

CAMP ISLANDS

LAKE PLACID

KEMPSHALL MTN.

LONG

BLUEBERRY MTN.

MUD POND

NORTHVILLE

BIG BROOK

LONG LAKE TO COLD RIVER

O STATE ROAD
--- TRAIL
+ PUT-IN
STATE LEAN-TO
STATE OWNED SHORE

SCALE

O MILE 1   O KILO 1

N

30

NORTHVILLE

LONG LAKE

28 N

30

past settled in at a chosen lean-to for periods up to three weeks of free vacation. Having observed this pattern of behavior for several years, Frederick Hackett, owner of a camp on the W shore and friend of canoeists, complained about it to the DEC Commissioner. The reply promised measures to put an end to this illegal occupancy.

Recent acquisitions of land by the state, through intervention of the Nature Conservancy, greatly enhance the pleasures of camping near the foot of Long Lake. One is a tract on the E shore from the old Harper's stone dock, opposite the final island, to the outlet. The other, acquired in 1977 by the Adirondack Conservancy and turned over to the state, is 55 acres on the W shore formerly known as Camp Riverdale. This includes the outlet of the Anthony Ponds, a rest stop for migratory birds. There is also a fine sandy beach, the best bathing beach on the entire lake.

The outlet is a network of marshy islands, intersecting channels, sandbars, and sloughs. Avoid the narrow channel at the extreme R. The shallow, winding main channel is on the L side of a long narrow island. Avoiding sloughs to R and L, bear NNW past the Lost Channel Lean-to. Beyond it and a big boulder, the channel divides around an island. The boulder is a glacial erratic, sketched by the artist Homer Martin in the 1860s. To pass directly down the Raquette, keep L.

COLD RIVER

USGS: Long Lake, Santanoni 15, Kempshall Mtn. 7.5 × 15

To go up Cold River 1 m. to the lean-to at Calkins Creek, take the R channel and then turn R up Cold River proper. (A little S of Lost Channel Lean-to, on the R, is Lost Channel, which can sometimes be negotiated by canoe to Cold River. Several beaver dams have to be pulled over. This is a fascinating, swampy side excursion.)

The Calkins Creek Lean-to has an attractive site on an open knoll near the junction of Calkins Creek and Cold River. If lucky enough to find it unoccupied and clean, you may think it the pleasantest camp on the whole cruise. This is especially true during May when water levels are still high enough to permit boating a half mile farther up both streams. But don't count on getting much sleep. This is a gamy lean-to. If coons or bears don't make a racket in your cooking gear, you still will be kept awake half the night trying to sort out the raucous mating calls accompanying a chorus of passionate whip-poorwills.

Cold River is a hard-core "wild river." It was among the elite few so classified in the state's original Rivers System act of 1972: 14 m. from Duck Hole to the mouth and 3 m. of Ouluska Pass Brook. No one had any doubts about its qualifications as the wildest and most remote river in the state. Certainly not Noah John Rondeau if he had still been living. It was his deliberate choice of site as a maximum security hideout from civilization. And he lived there for twenty years, under the towering domes of the Santanonis and the Sewards, as hermit and "mayor of Cold River."

Now and then a quixotic canoeist pops up with the scheme of ascending the Cold to Rondeau's old digs, or what remains of them, some 10 m. upstream. Those who try abandon their canoes somewhere along the way and take to the trail, first on the L bank to Shattuck Clearing and then along the Northville-Lake Placid Trail on the R bank. The first edition of this guide discouraged this attempt. "Shallow, steep, and rocky," it said, "the Cold River is navigable for 1.5 m. above the mouth in the spring or after heavy rains." But it is wrong to set a limit to what canoeists will try, as I discovered a year later in reading "Huck and the Hermit's Homecountry—Cold River," in the August 1976 issue of *Canoe* magazine. James Davidson and John Rugge, co-authors of *The Complete Wilderness Paddler*, tell the amusing story of learning "the art of river browsing" on the Cold River in, of all seasons, the month of August, when the irrigation systems of rock gardens and sandbars are functioning at minimum efficiency. They admit that nobody in his right mind would think of canoeing this river, yet they did, and came to the conclusion that "dogged 25-mile-a-day paddling marathons are not the only way to travel" and that "the Cold River teaches us how to appreciate a river the way Huck Finn would appreciate it, slowly, and with supreme satisfaction at its utter lack of purpose." They never reached Rondeau's by the water route, but they probably broke previous records. "Who's crazy enough to go 25 miles when they've got this?" they ask.

So all the limits are off for any Huck Finns or hermits out there.

RAQUETTE RIVER *(Cont.)*

On returning to the Raquette from Cold River, keep in the R channel around the island at the mouth. For 6 m. below Long Lake the Raquette is a languid stream meandering over a wide, silent valley floor. Its R bank continues to border the High Peaks Wilderness Area to the mouth of Stony Creek. Moose Creek, which flows through a big swamp on the W, is navigable for about 2 m. above its mouth. Finally the hills close in as one approaches Raquette Falls. This is a landmark for canoeists, for it means a 1.3-m. carry on a hummocky old tote road on the NW slope of Lookout Mountain.

At Raquette Falls the river pitches 80 feet over a highly scenic, rocky bed. Cruising paddlers should carry over the tote road on the R. Those who are curious about the falls, which can't be seen from the carry trail, should scramble over the rough river trail skirting escarpments directly over the water. Actually, most of the falls can be paddled by those with advanced whitewater skills, although there are two dangerous 15-foot drops which should be avoided by all but the most skilled and caution-minded paddlers. The entrance rapid is a 100 yard long Class II ending abruptly in the first 15-foot drop, rated Class V. This drop is U-shaped and is best negotiated straight down the middle. In the next 0.7 m. rapids are continuous, building steadily to Class III-IV before the second falls (Lower Falls) plunges through a gorge. There is no clear marker indicating the approach to these falls and the horizon line is very difficult to see until it is too late. Prior scouting is therefore critical to determine a suitable exit eddy. Just above Lower Falls is a Class IV pitch which turns sharply to the L before dropping over the 15-foot, U-shaped ledge. This final drop is rated Class V–VI and is particularly dangerous due to the nature of the hydraulic below the ledge. Persons scouting this drop should note the many potholes on the adjacent ledges, a clear sign of extreme turbulence at high water levels. Below here is a short Class III–IV rapid, a pool, and then a final descent over a Class II–III boulder garden. The carry trail then enters on the R as the river exits the gorge and returns to calm water. Cruising and whitewater paddlers are forewarned that many canoes have been wrecked in an attempt to run the rapids and that a life was lost here in April of 1976. Currently, a wrecked canoe adorns the R bank at the foot of the falls. Perhaps this canoe would serve as a more effective warning to paddlers if it were located instead at the top of the falls.

Nearly every canoeist has a story to tell about Raquette Falls. The earliest I know concerns two young New Yorkers. Though unable to find any information about the Raquette, they determined to explore it in the summer of 1843. Starting from Long Lake in a heavy yawl, the only boat they could secure there, they wrecked it in the rapids above Raquette Falls. An improvised raft also proved a failure. There

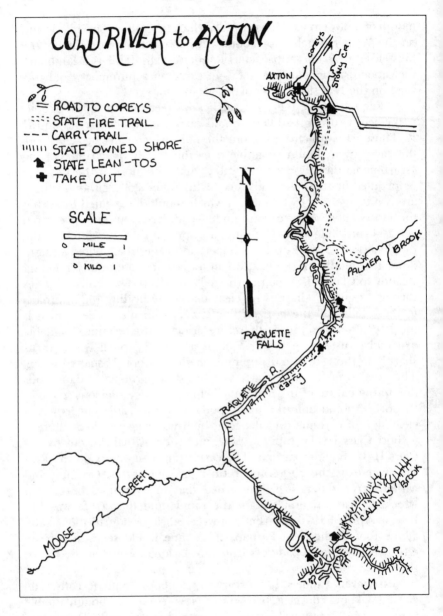

weren't many travelers on the Raquette in 1843, but as they were beginning to despair of either continuing their downstream trip or getting back to their starting point, a party of five Indians and a baby in a birchbark canoe came into sight. The city men hired this party as guides. One of the Indians was named "Mitchell" (Mitchell Sabattis?). He proceeded to make a second canoe of materials drawn "from the closets of the woods." The two canoes continued down river for 75 miles to Matildaville (now Colton). There a farmer told the New Yorkers that they were the first white men to come down the river "all the way from up south."

Those who complain today about the long carry at Raquette Falls should heed the story told by the Honorable Amelia Matilda Murray, maid of honor to Queen Victoria. Crossing the Adirondacks from E to W in 1855 with Governor Horatio Seymour, his niece, a Mr. H—, and three guides, this lady was equal to any hardship. "The signs of a trail were at times hardly visible," she wrote about Raquette Falls; "a gigantic timber felled by storms, or by time, crossed the obscure path, sometimes every twenty yards; deep bogs and slippery rocks impeded it, and we had often to retrace our steps or seek a blazed tree before we could find our way; each individual of the party straggled on as he or she could, with their load. . . . And so we all at last reached our intended camping place, a beautiful spot." After the evening meal around the campfire, the party settled down to a game of whist with a dirty pack of cards supplied by one of the guides. It rained during the night—"just enough," said the indomitable lady from Buckingham Palace, "to make us more sensible of the blessing of fine weather."

My own story about the carry shows the folly of believing everything you read in guidebooks. The year was 1939, the trip from Old Forge to Saranac Lake, and our only guide was the latest edition of the Conservation Department's "Adirondack Canoe Routes." It mentioned a two-wheeled, hand-drawn cart which would be at one end or the other of the carry. My companion and I, green at canoe touring, had a heavy, rented wood-and-canvas craft which had soaked up 15–20 extra pounds of paint and water. Not having a yoke, we had so far "doubled the carries," as old-time guides used to say—once over carrying the canoe in tandem and again carrying the two packs. Viewing Raquette Falls carry with distaste and not finding the cart at the head, we assumed it must be at the foot. Leaving everything behind, we set out confidently to fetch it. We found it at the other end all right, the axle broken, the wheels flattened, and ten years of rot on the crumbling spokes. So, back for the canoe. Then back again for the two packs. Tripling the carry, we logged 6.5 m. where 1.3 should have sufficed. This experience taught me two things: (1) apply two grains of skepticism to all guidebooks; (2) go light. Specifications for *singling* the carries are a lightweight canoe equipped with yoke for one man to carry, while the other shoulders all duffle in one backpack.

At the foot of the carry is a meadow of a dozen acres. Here a century ago travelers enjoyed the best flapjacks in the wilderness at Mother Johnson's boarding house. In more recent years a lodge here (destroyed in a fire) was the summer home of Charles W. Bryan, author of *The Raquette*. After his death, this historic site was acquired by the state and became a ranger headquarters.

There are two lean-tos in the clearing and two more a half mile downstream. The river resumes its languid meandering over bottomland in the next 6.5 m. to Axton. There is another lean-to below the junction of Palmer Brook and still another above the mouth of Stony Creek.

The 30 miles from Raquette Falls to Piercefield is the longest "level" on any northern Adirondack stream. The descent is about 12 feet, and nearly half of that is taken in one plunge over Setting Pole Dam.

At Axton the river makes a wide bend from N to W. Here it is possible to make connection with the first auto road below the village of Long Lake—the road from Coreys that swings E near Axton and crosses Stony Creek within 0.3 m. of the Raquette. Long before roads existed in the central Adirondacks, this area was an interchange for boat travelers switching from the Raquette to the Saranac or vice versa. A low divide of glacial drift separates the two drainage systems by one mile between the Stony Creek Ponds and the bay at the S end of Upper Saranac Lake. This fragile barrier possibly diverted the upper Saranac from original drainage into the Raquette at this point.

Indian Carry, the traditional name for this divide, has long been the Times Square of the woods. Jesse Corey, the first white settler, who ran Rustic Lodge at the N end of the carry, reputedly gathered a large collection of arrowheads and Indian pottery in this vicinity. For white trappers and later tourists, Indian Carry was still the hub of travel. Today the carry is as essential to canoe touring as it ever was. The standard long cruise begins at Old Forge on the Moose River, enters the Raquette chain through Browns Tract Inlet, shuttles to Saranac waters at Indian Carry, and ends at Saranac Lake Village or beyond.

The transfer can be made in two ways. Large parties often land at Axton and hire a truck at Coreys to transport canoes and duffle over 3 m. of road. Small parties usually take the scenic water route through the Stony Creek Ponds, which shortens the carry to an easy 1.1 m. The mouth of Stony Creek is obscure. It is 0.5 m. above Axton and lies between two landmarks on the R shore—a state lean-to in a birch grove and three prominent boulders. Paradoxically, the winding creek has a sandy bottom notable for absence of stones.

By the creek it is 1.7 m. to the first of the ponds. Here the outlet and the inlet (Ampersand Brook) lie side by side. (With patience in hauling over beaver dams and sandbars, one can paddle up Ampersand Brook some distance.) The summer colony known as Coreys is mostly confined to the W shores of the three ponds. To the SE are views of the Sewards and nearby Stony Creek Mountain. It is 1.2 m. through two ponds to a new trailhead. The former carry of 1.3 m. began from the small NW pond and proceeded along the Coreys Road and Route 3, an ambiance too closely resembling Times Square. In 1989 the purchase by ADK and the Land Trust of a private inholding on Route 3 made possible a more harmonious and shorter carry of 1.1 m. through the woods. An ADK crew constructed a model carry trail of 0.5 m. from the NW bay of the elongated middle pond to Route 3 directly across from the woods road of 0.6 m. to Upper Saranac Lake.

The half mile between the mouth of Stony Creek and Axton is a pretty stretch on the Raquette. In this section a private game club has stretched a cable across the river and operates a small ferry for its members. This section is likely to offer some adventure with wildlife. A mother duck lures intruders downstream while her young mysteriously disappear in eroded passages under banks. Once I watched a red squirrel, with urgent business on the opposite shore, shorten its crossing by running out to the end of an overhanging maple, take a belly flop, swim lustily ahead of the canoe, and, after a shakedown, scurry up the bank to check on the beechnut crop.

Axton is simply a small clearing with a ramp-like sandy beach separated from the main channel by a small marshy stream and backwater. Once the site of a lumber camp (Axe-town) and, at the turn of the century, of the Cornell School of Forestry, Axton today has no memorial of its past except plantations of red, white, and Scotch pine, Douglas fir, and Norway spruce. There is parking for several cars. Boaters should be forewarned that both this spot and the parking spot at upper Stony Creek Pond have been the sites of vandalism and theft. Lock your vehicles and leave no valuables in sight. A short spur connects the beach with the Coreys road, whence it is 3 m. to

Upper Saranac Lake. There is no lean-to at Axton, but it is a good site for a tent camp.

Axton to Tupper Lake, 16.5 m. (26.5 km.)
USGS: Long Lake, 15; Tupper Lake 7.5 × 15

In this reach the Raquette takes 16.5 m. to cover an air distance of 7. The channel describes a wonderful pattern of single and double oxbows with flanking lagoons and crescents of lost channel. It is easy to lose one's way in the maze. Local stories are told of boaters who start for Tupper Lake on a cloudy day, get lost in the Oxbow, and end toward evening back at Axton. Occasionally a wide loop washes the bedrock of a hill, but mostly the river meanders between banks held together by the roots of silver and red maples and just high enough in summer to keep it from sprawling wide over its floodplains. In spring it is in a glorious state of uncontainment. Those who complain of the monotony of this reach should try it in late April or the first week in May. Banks and tree trunks are under water. Wholly or half submerged posted signs on the L become the only reliable guide to the channel in some places. The canoeist can make cutoffs, shortening the trip measurably—or lengthening it if he has a poor sense of direction. Gliding through maple groves is such an effortless kind of bushwhacking that you feel like a disembodied spirit in a strange, ghostly realm.

The Axton-Tupper Lake reach has not always been thus. When ten notables from Concord and Boston and their guides came downstream from Stony Creek in August 1858, on their way to an encampment on Follensby Pond, the current was probably as slack as it is today. It was slack enough to deceive that nature poet and pillar of American literature, Ralph Waldo Emerson. He failed to notice the slight inclination of the water grasses and thought he was going "up Père Raquette stream" instead of down. Much else was different, though. The banks were higher then, and great white pines up to 200 feet tall made a canyon for the dark, silent stream to slip through.

The change came in 1870. Lumbermen who had had trouble in getting logs downstream built a dam at Setting Pole Rapids which raised the level ten feet, created a reservoir at Raquette Pond, and flooded thousands of acres of timberland 28 m. upstream to Raquette Falls. Timber that had not been cut was now drowned, and for many years skeletons lined the channel, which reeked of decay. The delta of the Raquette, which early visitors to Tupper Lake described as a

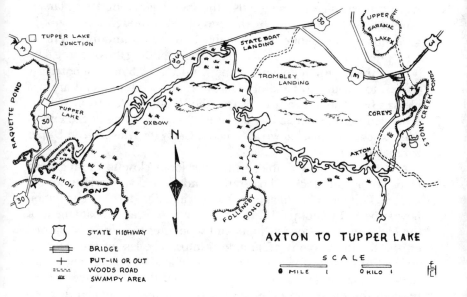

beautiful park-like meadow dotted with groves of trees and shrubs, was now mostly submerged. The protest was so strong that the dam was lowered in 1885 to its present level. The revegetation of a century has brought back on higher banks some spruce, balsam fir, and cedar and a few of the pines. And the silver and red maples make a fine display of color in September. The sprawling river with its rich aquatic vegetation is a feeding ground for ducks. Most trippers are satisfied with what they see today and are unaware of the devastation caused by the old dam.

On reaching the main channel from the recessed beach at Axton, one swings R to go downstream. After many a bend, the outlet of Follensby Pond is reached in about 3.6 m. If you are looking for it, you may be misled by several sloughs on the L. A broken-out dam and causeway are visible from the main channel. The USGS map of 1955 reflects conditions either of spring flood or prior to the breakout, for it shows a wide backwater here. Today the wide mouth soon narrows into a snaky ribbon. In his poem "The Adirondacs" Emerson describes the creek much as it is today:

> . . . . a small tortuous pass
> Winding through grassy shallows in and out,
> Two creeping miles of rushes, pads and sponge.

As of this writing (summer 1994), the state has announced plans to purchase Follensby Pond by the end of 1994, though it may not be accessible to the public for some time. Look for announcements in DEC press releases or *Adirondac* magazing regarding the opening date.

From the mouth of Follensby Pond Outlet it is 2.5 m., in a northerly course, to Trombley Landing. On the R at a westerly bend are two pleasantly situated lean-tos. Also on the R, but hidden from view by a wooded island encircled by backwater, is the landing at the end of a fire truck trail once known as Sweeney Carry (to Wawbeek on Upper Saranac Lake).

At 1.5 m. below Trombley's the river loops close to the highway. Here are a state dock, a boat ramp, and a spacious parking lot 3.5 m. E of Tupper Lake Village on Route 3 and 30. Marks of civilization now appear. In another 1.2 m. the river washes an embankment of the highway at a second N loop, and soon after a clearing is reached on the R with a colony of summer camps. The last of the camps is a signal to prepare for a test of navigational skill. A half mile below them is a tempting lagoon on the L. Avoid this. You have not yet reached the maze known as the Oxbow (an understatement). Keep in the main channel as it begins a slow turn to the L and follow it, S, around a semi-circle till you are heading NW. Here you come to a break in the L bank where the main channel bends back on itself at a 150-degree angle. If, instead of making this L turn, you continue around the circle, you will soon be headed back toward Axton.

The direction is now consistently SW. A mile below the Oxbow is LeBoeuf's Bridge on a private road to Follensby Pond Park. The channel straightens for the next 0.7 m., and a scenic vista of Mt. Morris appears over a grassy marsh. The river then bends sharply N to make a few more extravagant loops, but a convenient cutoff channel, L, takes one directly into Simon Pond. Mt. Morris is dead ahead. Paddle W across the lake 1 m. to the bridge on Route 30, where the Raquette empties into the foot of (Big) Tupper Lake.

There is parking space on the S side of the bridge but no state land for camping on the E shore except at the far S end. In Moody (L to a state boat launching site, 0.7 m.) there are motels; also on the outskirts of Tupper Lake Village, R.

Campers have some distance to go before reaching state land or developed campgrounds. The only lean-to on the direct downstream route is one built and maintained by the International Paper Company. It is open to the public free of charge and is now listed in state recreation circulars as the Sorting Gap Lean-to. It is located at a small sand beach on the W shore across from the river delta (NW of the bridge), on the S-facing shore of a bay; old booms are still visible. There is also the privately-owned Blue Jay Campground on the lakeshore S on Route 30. Much of the W shore of Tupper Lake S of Grindstone Bay is state land, and there is a lean-to in Black Bay about 5.5 m. from the bridge.

The next campground on the direct route is at Setting Pole Dam, 5.25 m. downstream. However, Tupper Lake maintains a large campground and beach on Little Wolf Pond (see *Saint Regis 15*). This can be reached from the N end of Raquette Pond either by carrying 2 m. or by paddling about 4 m. up Wolf Brook. The roadhead for the carry and the mouth of the brook are within a quarter mile of each other on the N shore of Raquette Pond. The carry goes through village streets. Navigation of the brook is slow. Though the current is slack, the stream is remarkably crooked in its upper reach. In the last century Wolf Brook was a link in a 29-m. chain of waters and carries from Saranac Inn, via Rollins, Big Wolf, and Little Wolf ponds, to the Raquette River; but this route is now closed because of private land and long-abandoned carries.

A 1.5 m. trail up Mt. Morris starts at the Big Tupper ski lodge, reached by a road turning E from Route 30 in Moody. One can also ride the chair lift and continue a short distance on foot to the summit. The fire tower on this peak was the first one built in the Adirondacks. It is no longer used, but open rock gives unobstructed views.

For canoeing on Tupper Lake, see the section on the Bog River. Lake Simond makes another attractive side excursion. It is surrounded by private land, but Adams Island, owned by the Nature Conservancy, is open to visitors who come by boat (no camping). It is off Pilot Point; what looks like a peninsula on the USGS map is in reality an island, pleasantly wooded and commanding fine views of the mountain-ringed S bay of the lake.

Tupper Lake (bridge on Route 30) to Piercefield, 7 m. (11.3 km.)
USGS: Long Lake, Tupper Lake 15 or 7.5 × 15

The foot of Tupper Lake where the Raquette enters is shallow and marshy. Islands of aquatic vegetation form a labyrinth across the direct NW route. The delta of the Raquette is listed in the APA's *State Land Master Plan* as a natural area of special interest. The best way to become acquainted with it is to weave through devious channels on a NW course wherever possible. It is probably time-saving, however, to stay in the roundabout main channel marked by buoys and bearing W toward the opposite shore before turning N.

Only the shoals of the delta divide Tupper Lake from Raquette Pond. The main part of Tupper Lake Village is on the E shore of the latter; on the N shore, in the flats, is the part of the village formerly known as Faust.

On the W side of Raquette Pond, a field of rushes and pickerelweed more extensive than the survey map indicates keeps one on a northerly course. Finally it is possible to turn W into the funnel-shaped outlet bay. Aim for the railroad bridge. If the way through Raquette Pond seems long, you are rewarded by a backward look from the vicinity of the railroad bridge. One of the most splendid mountain panoramas of the Adirondack Park opens across a broad expanse of water. Most prominent are Stony Creek and Ampersand mountains and the Seward, Sawtooth, and Santanoni ranges.

From the bridge to Setting Pole Rapids Dam the river is several hundred feet wide and shallow in places. Canoeists who do not follow the motorboat channel marked by buoys should look for submerged rocks and logs. The deciduous woods on both shores are transformed in early fall into a brilliant tapestry of color reflected on the still surface.

Just below the railroad bridge is a monolith in the river known as Captain Peter Sabattis Rock, after the father of the family of Indian hunters and guides that ranged up and down the Raquette for over a century and a half and left their names on a mountain, a railroad station, this rock, and an island. Captain Peter, who died in 1861 at Long Lake, kept a record of his reputed 111 years on a notched stick. He got his title by leading a party of surveyors about 1812 in mapping an "old military road" westward from Lake George through the wilderness. Adirondack rock is a fitting symbol for Captain Peter, who said that he had never slept in a white man's bed.

The river narrows near the concrete dam at Setting Pole Rapids (the name comes from the poles guides used to ascend the original rapid at this point). The landing is a sandy beach on the R at the edge of a clearing maintained by the town of Altamont for picnicking and camping. A gravel road connects with Route 3 about 4 m. W of the Tupper Lake Veneer factory and 1.4 m. E of the highway bridge in Piercefield.

Setting Pole Rapids, prior to the building of the dam in 1870, was the favorite camping place of a renowned fly fisherman, George

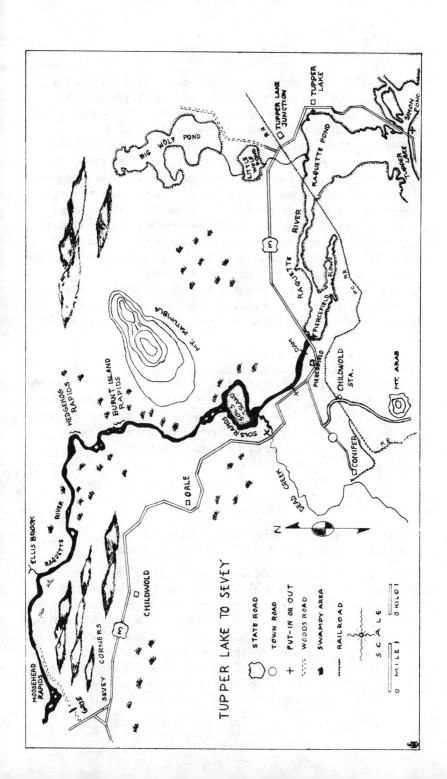

TUPPER LAKE TO SEVEY

STATE ROAD
TOWN ROAD
PUT-IN OR OUT
WOODS ROAD
SWAMPY AREA
RAILROAD

SCALE

0 MILE 1

0 KILO 1

MOOSEHEAD RAPIDS
GATE
SEVEY CORNERS
CHILDWOLD
ELLIS BROOK
RAQUETTE RIVER
HEDGEHOG RAPIDS
BURNT ISLAND RAPIDS
MT. MATUMBLA
SOLS RAPIDS
SOLS ISLAND
GALE
DEAD CREEK
CONIFER
MT. ARAB
CHILDWOLD STA.
PIERCEFIELD
PIERCEFIELD FLOW
RAQUETTE RIVER
RAQUETTE POND
BIG WOLF POND
LITTLE WOLF POND
TUPPER LAKE JUNCTION
TUPPER LAKE
SIMON POND
TUPPER LAKE

Dawson. Here, he said, was finer sport than any other point in the wilderness. But the dam spoiled the place for him, and not long after, the native brook trout of the Raquette were supplanted by the bass, northern pike, bullheads, and perch of today.

The carry to the foot of the rapid below the dam is about 150 yards. The current is strong for a short distance. As Piercefield Flow is approached, Mt. Arab comes into view and finally fills the horizon on the L. Keep well off the R shore of the flow to avoid stumps. The bottom land was not cleared before flooding. The easiest take-out is on the upstream L side of the Rt. 3 highway bridge at a gravel turnout. Niagara Mohawk maintains a fishing access site at the end of a gravel road off the NW side of the bridge. There is suitable parking here, but the steep banks make it difficult to launch a boat.

Plans exist for a carry on the R bank from the bridge to a point below Piercefield Dam, but they must await completion till the DEC has procured an easement on an existing road with an extension on a new trail.

A two-hour side excursion from Piercefield is the ascent of Mt. Arab (2,500 feet). The 1.5 m. trail is reached by taking the road toward Conifer off Route 3 in Piercefield. At 1.9 m. turn L at a fork, cross the railroad tracks, and, as the road climbs, look for a Mt. Arab trail sign on the L. The peak has an open summit with good views toward Raquette headwaters to the SE (Blue Mountain is prominent on a clear day) and partial views of the High Peaks to the E.

Piercefield to foot of Moody Falls, 14.2 m. (22.9 km.)
USGS: Tupper Lake 15; Mount Matumbla, Childwold 7.5

The Raquette is now a big stream 125 to 250 feet wide. The average discharge at the gauging station below Piercefield Dam is 1,249 cubic feet per second, and the range between maximum and minimum is over 8,000 cfs. Regulation of the dam causes wide daily fluctuations. Greater volume and velocity add an element of danger absent from the languid waters above Piercefield. This is a fascinating part of the river, varied in scenery, sporty and tranquil by turns, and accompanied by frequent sightings of wildlife. An osprey is sometimes seen, as well as many ducks and an occasional small shore animal. One hot day in

August I counted 16 deer cooling themselves and feeding in a quarter-mile stretch of Moosehead Stillwater.

This corridor was recently opened to public navigation through gifts by the International Paper Company to the state (a corridor 500 feet wide along the L bank in the town of Piercefield) and to the Conservation Fund on the E side of the river. At this writing (1993) the DEC has not yet marked and improved carry trails around rapids. Most carries are short, but the upper half of a long 1.6 m. one around Moosehead Rapids is choked by blowdown and very difficult. We recommend that, in 1995 and probably 1996 as well, this section of the river be attempted only by paddlers of intermediate to advanced skills, at ease in the Class II-III waters of Moosehead Rapids. Once current problems are solved, this section will become one of the most popular in the state for novice and skilled alike.

Put-in is reached by turning off Rt. 3 onto Main St. on the NW side of Piercefield. Proceed 0.15 m. to a dirt parking area on the L and carry 30 yards to a public beach. The Geological Survey gauging station is located on the L bank, just below the beach. Canoeists wishing to avoid Class II rapids in the next 1.6 m. can reenter the river by Dead Creek, 2.4 m. below the Piercefield bridge. The state maintains a rest area on the grassy banks with ample parking space. The creek is navigable downstream a winding 0.8 m. into the Raquette.

From the creek mouth one looks across a broad expanse of water at the head of a divided channel. What looks like mainland across the way is actually Sols Island, a large oval-shaped mass nearly a mile across at its widest. It is named for one of Peter Sabattis' two surviving sons. According to tradition, Sol, the elder, was born on this island. Mitchell, the uneducated son, was a signal success as guide, friend of many patrons, community leader at Long Lake, temperance reformer after his own reform, and preacher. Captain Peter admitted his mistake in trying to educate the elder son. Indians, he is quoted as saying, don't take to book learning: "You can't polish a brick. Heap rub; bime bye, brick all gone."

Avoid the R channel at Sols Island. It is choked by a massive logjam and boulder jungle. The best procedure is to make a sharp L turn at the mouth of Dead Creek and go into the L channel, which is itself divided by a long narrow island. Below the lower tip of the latter, the river swings NE, Mount Matumbla comes into view straight ahead, and Sols Rapids are heard. These rapids are divided into Upper Sols and Lower Sols, which are separated from each other by a smooth

pool of water about 200 yards long. Upper Sols is the longer and
trickier rapid and should be scouted from shore before it is attempted
by skilled canoeists. On the mainland (W) shore is a faint carry trail;
the beginning above the turbulence is usually marked by trodden
grass. It passes through a spruce-balsam grove and ends in a bay
below the rapid in 0.25 m. Most of Upper Sols can be run by canoeists
practiced in Class II–III waters. The dangerous pitch comes at the
end, where the L channel drops into a large souse hole, divides around
a large boulder, and plummets into an even larger souse hole. The
R channel around some small islands is only slightly easier. The lower
pitches of Upper Sols are a dangerous Class IV–V since the souse
holes can easily trap a boat. To avoid these, take out at a short resting
place marked by a boulder and a leaning cedar tree on the L bank.
Put in on the pool between the two sets of rapids. Lower Sols is a
pitch of about 8 feet. It is best run on the far R over a 4-foot ledge
and then quickly back to the center (rated Class III–IV). This route
avoids a large V-shaped ledge which would take the paddler into a
series of nasty hydraulics, rated Class IV-V. A trail crosses the tip of a
point on the L shore, allowing an easy carry. Avoid encroaching upon
the camp back from this point.

For the next 2.7 m. relax and enjoy the scenery. The river widens
in a floodplain as a braided channel weaves around and between
several green islands. Then both banks steepen again at a wide
bend to the W around the base of Mount Matumbla (2,688 feet),
the highest elevation in St. Lawrence County. By tradition it was an
Indian burying place. In the gorge at its base, where rapids and
cascades might be expected, there is instead a beautiful stillwater
interrupted by only one fast riffle. Hunting camps on the L shore
are hardly visible under a dense canopy of evergreen and hardwood
foliage.

The Mount Matumbla stillwater ends at Burnt Island. Before running the short rapids here, take a backward look at a lovely stretch
of the river below Mount Matumbla. The upper part of Pier Rapids
at Burnt Island can easily be run in the L channel at medium to
high water. At low level a poorly irrigated rock garden requires a
carry or towing the canoe in mid-channel. About 100 yards below
Burnt Island is the lower part of Pier Rapids, a natural rock dam
with a 2-foot pitch, rated Class II. A narrow breach is not easy to
locate in a downstream approach. There is a carry of 50 feet on
the R bank.

The river now widens, washing several islands and boulders. In midstream at a sharp L bend is a commodious circular boulder with a flat top. Catching the breeze, it makes an ideal lunch or rest stop in bug season.

About 0.6 m. below this archipelago are Hedgehog Rapids, Class II, approximately 200 yards long and with standing waves up to three feet at high water. Here guides of the last century used to reverse their guideboats in order to have clear vision ahead while using their oars to brake and steer. Obliged to crouch low so that the guide could see over his head, the anxious sportsman in the reversed stern seat saw little of what was going on as the small craft bounced over the waves. The best course is L of center. The carry of 200 yds. on the L shore is rough but drier and shorter than on the R bank.

Past Hedgehog, one can relax for the long reach of 5.7 m. named Moosehead Stillwater after the mountain that terminates it. On summer days this is the section where one is most likely to see deer wading in the shoals. At 1.7 m. below Hedgehog is a pretty wooded island. Here on the R is the mouth of one of several Windfall Brooks in the same ENE path of the great windfall of 1845. Below the island is the site of an old bridge. A logging road connects this site to Rt. 3 just E of Childwold. In 1993 and 1994, International Paper opened this road to the public from mid-spring to September 15. Future decisions to open this road will be made on an annual basis. When open, this road allows the trip to be divided into two sections and provides legal egress for those wishing to avoid the long carry at Moosehead Rapids. Quick current continues past the head of Smith Island, where there is a two-story cottage.

Below Smith Island the stillwater continues for 3 m. through marsh and swamp. Moosehead Mountain is often in sight on the L. Just as this quiet reach is becoming a little monotonous, the shore on the L begins to rise, then on the R. The tall pines of the Forest Preserve appear, and soon, as one rounds the N side of Moosehead Mountain and heads WSW, Moosehead Rapids are heard at the upper end of a gorge. The trip to this point takes about 4 to 4½ hours with a break for lunch.

Trippers who have two days at disposal and intend to continue downriver to Carry Falls Dam might consider camping here. The way ahead is long and rough whether by land or water. An evening's reconnoitering will aid in the decision. With compass and topo map, you might occupy the rest of the day by bushwhacking up Moosehead Mountain; the round trip takes about two hours. Views from the summit are limited since the removal of the old firetower. In any case, the strip of Forest Preserve on the L bank near the head of the rapids is worth exploring for its noble specimens of white pine, yellow birch, hemlock, and red spruce.

State land begins, on both banks, about 0.4 m. above the rapids. On the L bank two small brooks (not shown on the *Childwold* map of 1968) trickle down from the mountain. The one nearer the head of the gorge marks the location of a carry trail. If you choose not to run the rapids, follow this trail along the brook, away from the river, to a fork. Turn R here and proceed in a westerly direction. Beyond a short section of poorly drained ground, the trail leaves state land and enters International Paper timberlands, where it joins first a disused branch of a logging road, frequently covered by blowdown, and then a maintained one. Formerly the logging road could be followed all the way out to Route 56 at a point 0.7 m. N of its intersection with Sevey Road. But in 1984 International Paper erected a gate near the W end and posted it against trespass. (Pending the outcome of negotiations between the state and IP, this road should not be used for either egress or access. Under present conditions, the next legal exit from the river is a foot trail on state land at the foot of Moody Falls.) Continue the carry past two grassy roads to the R and then the culvert of a brook. Take the next fork on the R and go past a hunting camp to a put-in site on a point where there is smooth water. The whole carry is 1.6 m.

Moosehead Rapids lie in a scenic gorge at the base of Moosehead Mountain. They are best run at medium high water when they do not exceed Class III difficulty. But they are 1.25 m. long and require constant alertness and skilled maneuvering in a shifting channel. Intermediate level paddlers will find this stretch delightful and can take advantage of the many eddies to "play" this stretch. Cruising canoeists running this rapid for the first time should occasionally pull over to the shores to examine the narrower passages. The most difficult portion of these rapids is the final drop in a braided section just before the river makes its turn to the N. The main channel here flows between two islands. Although this drop does not exceed Class III difficulty, boaters should take standard precautions to avoid wrapping around the rocks below.

This final pitch can be avoided by an easy 0.15-m. carry on the R mainland shore. The irregular land mass on the topo map that looks like a sawtooth-shaped peninsula is really a low-lying island separated from the mainland by a narrow rocky channel. One should land near the head of this channel on the R and carry to smooth water at the W end. There is a confusing cluster of islands where the river makes its N bend.

Continuing downriver, make the northerly bend in the Raquette below Moosehead Rapids and proceed 0.2 m. to an island. Bear into the R channel here, though there is a low ledge at its head that may require a lift-over. Moody Falls is just below the island. It is a twisting chasm where the river drops about 22 feet. Highly precise maneuvering is required to avoid rocks and boulders where boats can easily be pinned. Careful scouting, advanced skills, and safety precautions are necessary for this dangerous Class V-VI falls. According to folklore, a French Canadian logger once shot the falls on a wager and escaped with his life. Not so lucky were the father and son whose names the falls bear; one dark night they were drawn over the rim and drowned.

The easier carry is on the R bank. The landing is a flat rock above rapids in the R channel. The carry is 0.2 m. A narrow sliver alongside the falls is state land. The L bank is also state land, but the carry on that side is hilly and rough. At the foot of fast water on that bank, however, is a good camping site. This site is the beginning of a carry trail to Route 56 as described in the next section.

Moody Falls to Carry Falls Dam, 9.3 m. (15.0 km.)
USGS: Childwold, Carry Falls Reservoir 7.5

The logging road off Route 56 (0.7 m. N of the Sevey Road intersection) cannot at present be used for access to the Raquette, pending negotiations. Meanwhile, canoeists can use a faint trail of 0.2 m. on state land that reaches the river at the foot of Moody Falls. Go 1.3 m. N of the intersection of Severy Road and Route 56 and park on the E side of the highway just before the northern end of a short loop road on the W side. Climb a graded bank and look for a trail beginning at a double-boled white pine. This carry, partially cleared in 1993, descends a ridge and ends at a point on the L bank next to a pool 100 feet from the base of Moody Falls.

Below Moody is a scenic reach of 0.8 m. between high banks. The current is moderately fast. The river narrows abruptly at a gateway of bedrock at the head of Jamestown Falls, a tumultuous winding staircase which widens out in a final sharp pitch over a ledge. Jamestown is a good place to unpack the camera. Like Moody, it is an extremely dangerous falls, rated Class V-VI. Though straighter and less technical than Moody, the hydraulics below the ledges are substantial. The national slalom team chose Jamestown Falls as a training site in 1988, after arranging special releases from the Piercefield Dam.

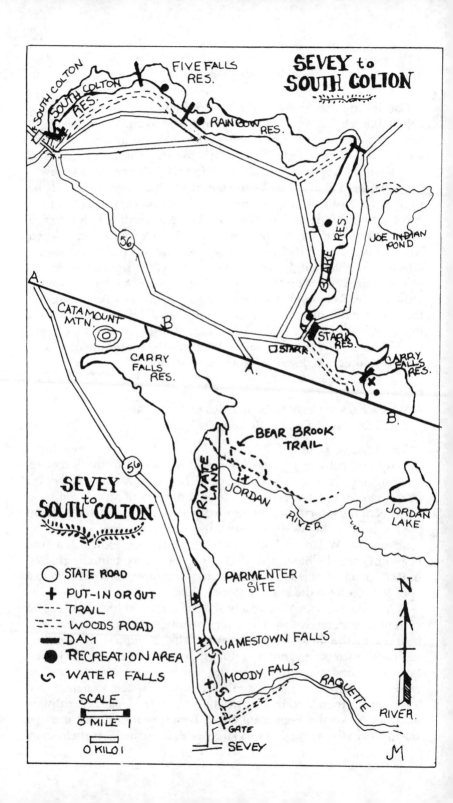

A lodge of the Jamestown Club stands on a knoll on the R bank. The club's lands include also a narrow strip along the L bank, west of which is Forest Preserve. Though most of the carry trail is in private land, it is not posted (except perhaps in hunting season), and I am told that the club does not object to its use as a carry so long as no litter is left. Take-out is in a bay on the L shore just above a big white pine where rough water abruptly begins. The trail passes over an outcrop near the water, goes into a small stream bed, and then, below the upper fall, draws away from the river on a side hill where there is less brush to contend with. It joins paint blazes marking the line between Jamestown Club property and state land and comes to the river's edge at the foot of rough water. The carry is about 0.3 m.

For the next mile both shores are state land. A brook enters the pool below the falls on the L. Just below its mouth is a small clearing and a spur road of 0.3 m. out to Route 56 (2.1 m. N of Sevey). This is a possible exit for those who wish to avoid the reservoirs and dams below. This road is passable by vehicles with high clearance, but passenger cars are advised to park at a turnaround by a designated campsite midway down the road. (No camping is allowed closer to the river.) The trip downstream from Piercefield to this point is nearly 16 m.

When Carry Falls Reservoir is full, the backwater extends almost to the pool below Jamestown Falls and all but eliminates two sets of rapids in the old riverbed—Long and Hall's. A quarter-mile bend of fast water is all that is left of the former, once nearly a mile long and ending in a boulder jungle. But at times of drawdown to low levels in the fall, Long Rapids are recreated.

Rounding a bend, the river widens into the reservoir, and the Parmenter Site comes into view on the L shore. This is a boat landing and campground maintained for the public by Niagara Mohawk Power Corporation. A blacktop road of 0.7 m. connects it with Route 56.

The Parmenter Site provides plots for tents or trailers, a parking circle near the water, fireplaces, picnic tables, drinking water, and toilet facilities. A caretaker assigns plots for overnight camping for a fee. There is no charge for parking or day use. The site is convenient for put-in and take-out.

Reservoir fans can have a field day in the next 22 m. of the Raquette, scene of the largest hydroelectric installation on New York State's inland waters. There are seven reservoirs which make quite respectable lakes when mud banks are not exposed. With the exception of Higley, the lowest and oldest, construction was begun in 1951 and completed in 1957. All the bottom land was cleared before flooding, as now required. The most picturesque phase of the operation was the burning of stumps that followed cutting. Viewed from the old Hollywood Road, now underwater, it was an eerie prospect at night. Over a vast floodplain formerly known as the Great Bog, not a tree was left standing, but myriads of stumps burned like the campfires of a large Iroquois war party on some stern mission against the Hurons of Canada.

While Niagara Mohawk negotiated for the land along the river and for water rights, the discovery was made that over 15,000 acres in the township of Hollywood were acquired by a wealthy merchant, one Jabez Bacon, of Woodbury, Connecticut, in 1804, either by purchase or as compensation for his financial aid to the Colonies during the Revolution. Jabez Bacon was a descendant of Sir Francis Bacon. The Canton attorney responsible for clearing title to this land got a thorough refresher course in British and American history as he studied the genealogy of a proud family and contacted the 135 living heirs of Jabez Bacon in various parts of the world.

The Hollywood Road is a nostalgic memory. Parallel to Route 56 but closer to the river bank, it cut across game trails where the deer came down to drink at night and morning and could almost invariably be seen in numbers. Also gone is the Hollywood Hotel on the L bank, where sportsmen for several decades had "their dailies with their deer," the newspapers coming by stage from Gale's or Potsdam. Across the reservoir at the mouth of the Jordan River, the cottages of a summer colony are still standing but have been moved back to escape flooding. The Jordan Club fought the power development for nearly thirty years to keep their Eden intact, but were too few to prevail. Mauled by bulldozers and tamed in reservoirs and aqueducts, the Raquette is no longer the unique wild river it was when, in its final plunge off the mountain plateau, it was free to orchestrate its theme with variations—rapid-fall-rapid-pool.

Niagara Mohawk has done what it could to make us forget the old river. It provides picnic areas, boat ramps, swimming beaches, and campgrounds. Canoe cruising is encouraged and is of course less strenuous than on the old river, though the variety and the excitement are gone. Power company officials ask only that, for safety, canoeists do not launch in the tailraces below power stations. Though the tailraces may not look dangerous at first glance, the surge as motors begin working (by remote control) can swamp a canoe.

It is 6 m. from the Parmenter Site to the boat ramp, L, at the foot of Carry Falls Reservoir. The mouth of the Jordan River is passed at 1.7 m. Below it the artificial lake widens to a maximum of 3 m. When full or near full, as it generally is through Labor Day, its shores and islands are attractive.

Rounding a rugged bluff named Bog Mountain, one follows the L shore to a boat ramp at the dam. There is ample parking space here. Below the dam, which is 70 feet tall and impounds a storage reservoir of 3,200 acres, is a small picnic area. To reach the dam by car, take the Stark and Carry Falls roads off Route 56.

Carry Falls Dam to South Colton, 14 m. (22.5 km.)
USGS: Carry Falls Reservoir, Stark, Sylvan Falls, Rainbow Falls, Colton 7.5

For those who tire of the reconstructed Raquette, there are convenient exits at each dam by way of the Power Project Road. Boat ramps and picnic areas are marked on the new 7.5-minute maps and on a chart of recreational facilities obtainable from the Niagara Mohawk caretaker at the McNeil Campsite on Blake Falls Reservoir.

Boats can be launched at the picnic area just below Carry Falls Dam. Stark Reservoir, 1.2 m. long, has two retaining dams, one on the L at the old channel (now mostly dry in summer) and one at the R at the head of a penstock and a new channel. Land at the R of the latter dam and descend over crushed rock along the penstock to the generating plant. Here take the blacktop road R and follow it about 0.4 m. to a L turnoff that goes to a point at the end of the tailrace. The whole carry of about 0.8 m. is the longest of the series but mostly on a good road.

Blake Falls Reservoir is 3.75 m. long. The old channel at Blake Falls is not canoeable. Paddle through the narrow channel of the intake on the L to a sand ramp. The carry follows a gravel road down to the parking lot at the powerhouse and continues on a trail on the L bank of the tailrace to a point where the channel begins to widen. The whole carry here is about 0.5 m.

Rainbow Falls Reservoir is 3.8 m. long. There are summer camps on the S shore. The carry is at the L of the dam over the blacktop road and a switchback spur, 0.3 m. Below Rainbow Falls is a small parcel of Forest Preserve on the L shore. The W boundary of this tract also marks the boundary of the Adirondack Park. Most of the 1.5-m. long Five Falls Reservoir lies outside the Blue Line. The carry, nearly 0.6 m., goes past the generating plant and out a long narrow spit to the end of the tailrace.

South Colton Reservoir, 1.7 m. long, is the last before the village. The Raquette cruise could well end here if one has a car waiting. The last dam is so close to the Route 56 bridge in the village that there is little point in putting in below it unless one wants to shoot the short rapid under the bridge at favorable water levels (inspection from the bridge is advised) and continue downstream another 2 m. to the Higley Flow State Campsite.

Infiltrated by history, motorboats, and power developments, the Raquette has limitations as a "river of the forest." The evasive canoe tripper is likely to echo Byron's comment on Lake Geneva: "There is too much of man here." But the Raquette is irreplaceable if you choose your season well. On the upper river you can escape the fleets of canoe campers and the powerboats in the weeks before Memorial Day and after Labor Day. The section from Piercefield to Carry Falls Reservoir, where traffic is always light, is best reserved for summer.

COLD RIVER (Cont.)

Duck Hole to Mouth, 14.0 m. (22.4 km.)
USGS: Long Lake, Santanoni 15; Kempshall Mountain 7.5 × 15

Cold River is best thought of as a side trip from the Raquette as described above. It has, however, been paddled downstream its entire length by Doug Hardy and myself (Don Morris) in the spring of 1979. This downriver trip presents major logistical and physical demands and is recommended only for those seeking a true wilderness adventure. This description is based on memory but has been confirmed and revised by Gary Koch (1989).

A certain degree of craziness is required to attempt the complete downriver trip. The Cold's headwaters are very remote and difficult of access, particularly when carrying paddling gear. A number of major issues must be addressed before attempting this section. For one, there are several steep stretches of technical rapids where carries are difficult, especially if the party has camping gear. Second, camping along the way may be difficult, not because of a lack of available sites but because most parties will want to travel as lightly as possible because of the difficulty in reaching the headwaters. Third, the shuttle of vehicles may be time consuming depending on the choice of exit route. And finally, this area must surely rate among the worst for black flies and mosquitoes during the brief season when the river is paddleable.

Proper planning is critical for this trip. The Cold is only paddleable at very high water levels after the ice has gone out or perhaps after extended periods of heavy rain. It would be very frustrating to carry to the headwaters and find the water level too low; so it is important to use good judgment or to check in advance with a Forest Ranger or other knowledgeable person. The party must also decide whether to do the entire trip in one day or to camp overnight. Doug Hardy and I chose to do the trip in one day and found ourselves hiking and paddling continuously from 5:30 A.M. to 11:30 P.M. Persons choosing this option should be prepared for a grueling trip and nighttime paddling. Camping is preferable, but it is difficult to carry the necessary gear to the headwaters and around steep sections of the river. Furthermore, it is not a good idea to paddle any of the steep technical sections with excess weight. The ideal option is to arrange to have friends bring camping gear for you and meet at a lean-to near the mouth. Though this option obviously requires additional planning and cooperation, the effort may very well pay off.

The best way to get to Duck Hole is to proceed E from the hamlet of Newcomb on Route 28N and bear L at the intersection with Route 2B. Take the first L onto Route 25 and proceed to the parking lot at the end of the road, traveling along the Hudson River past the mine site at Tahawus, the old MacIntyre furnace, and the Upper Works site. There is a trailhead near the outlet of Henderson Lake, where the Hudson River first acquires its name. Go N on this hiking trail with Henderson Lake on your L and the MacIntyre Range on your R. At the junction with Indian Pass Trail at 1.25 m. veer SW then NW to the Preston Ponds. Stay to the R of Upper Preston Pond while proceeding to Lower Preston Pond and eventually to the intersection with the Northville-Lake Placid Trail at 4.4 m. Turn SW and proceed 0.5 m. to the shelter at Duck Hole. From there go S on a hiking trail to the spillway at the W end of Duck Hole. Put-in is on the R bank below the spillway.

The total mileage for this access trip is 6.5 m. with an elevation gain of slightly over 350 feet as one crosses the divide between the Hudson and Raquette drainage areas. Though this trip is long and strenuous, any other access requires additional mileage. Note that water access to Henderson Lake, the Preston Ponds, and that portion of Duck Hole where Preston Ponds Outlet enters is prohibited. The previous owners, NL Industries, were occasionally willing to grant permission to paddle across these waters on an individual basis, but only during the month of May. NLI recently sold these tracts to a new company which has not indicated whether or not a similar policy will continue. The state is interested in purchasing an easement which would allow legal water access to Duck Hole throughout the paddling season, thus shortening the carry considerably.

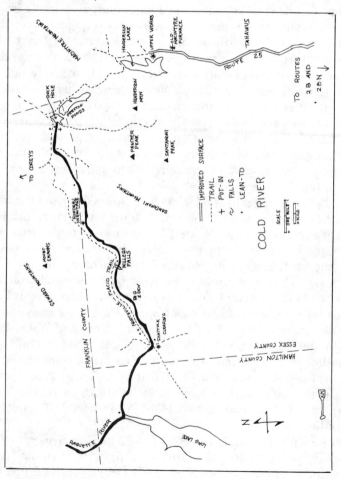

Once on the water, paddlers meet a definite but by no means relaxing change of pace. The Cold drops 120 feet in the first 1.4 m. to the confluence with Moose Creek, with roughly half this drop occurring in the last 300 yards. This section requires frequent and meticulous scouting as the drops are very steep and technical. The current moves swiftly in narrow channels, making it difficult to determine the safest course. The risk of being pinned on boulders or downed trees is substantial. This section is rated Class IV-V and is the most difficult of the entire run.

Below Moose Creek the river enters a steep gorge known as Cold River Canyon. The river drops 100 feet in the next 1.8 m. and rapids are predominately Class II and III. The ruins of an old cable-car crossing and an old cable car itself are visible here. Below the gorge the river enters an extended marsh known as Cold River Flow, about 1.7 m. long, fed by a number of small streams. Near the end of the marsh, on the R bank, is the former site of Noah John Rondeau's hermitage. For those with time on their hands this makes an interesting side trip on the Northville-Lake Placid Trail.

Exiting the marsh, the river drops another 200 feet in the next 5.8 m. to Big Eddy, passing the Ouluska and Seward lean-tos. Next to Seward Lean-to is Millers Falls, a formidable Class IV-V drop of 8 feet with powerful hydraulics easily capable of holding a boat. Below these falls a straight dike extends across the river bottom. Careful scouting is advised. The next rapid of significance is a 4-foot drop into the beginning of the pool known as Big Eddy, rated Class III-IV.

After Big Eddy the Cold becomes wider and does not exceed Class II as it flows past several shelters to the confluence with a second local stream known as Moose Creek at Shattuck Clearing, where there is a suspension bridge at the Northville-Placid trail crossing. Just above this bridge the river drops about 20 feet in 100 yards, with individual drops ranging between Class II and Class IV. Flatwater continues for an additional 3.5 m. to Calkins Brook, where there is a shelter, and then for a final 0.5 m. to the confluence with the Raquette River. Much of the last several miles can be paddled as part of an upstream float from Raquette River. At the confluence paddlers can turn L and proceed upstream through Long Lake to Long Lake Village or turn R and paddle downstream to Axton's Landing. The trip to Long Lake Village is preferable if the party wants to minimize the length of the shuttle run back to the Henderson Lake trailhead.

BIG BROOK

Route 30 Bridge to Long Lake Village, 7.3 m. (11.75 km.)
USGS: Long Lake, Blue Mountain Lake 15; Kempshall Mtn. 7.5 × 15

Four miles W of Long Lake Village Route 30 crosses Big Brook. Putting in here, one can cruise downstream to the mouth in Long Lake (4.7 m.) and continue 2.6 m. farther to the public boat landing in the village of Long Lake. This trip should be attempted only at high water level in spring (late April to early May) or in exceptionally wet fall seasons. At other times shallow riffles can make it, literally and figuratively, a drag.

Upstream travel is currently restricted. Below Route 30, the gradient averages 12 feet per mile. At high water rapids do not exceed Class II in difficulty.

Big Brook is stocked with brown and speckled trout by the state. It flows through a trough-like corridor of moderately steep slopes and rough, bouldery terrain. The floodplains are quite narrow. The midsection of state land is especially scenic. White pines tower over the evergreen canopy of red spruce and balsam fir. Elsewhere a mixed forest of northern hardwoods and conifers prevails.

A half mile from the lake one passes under a road bridge, and the brook widens into a marshy bay. Turn S in the lake toward the village unless you intend to continue down the Raquette to Axton or Tupper Lake.

BOG RIVER

The Raquette is a touch-and-go feeder of Big Tupper at the extreme foot of the lake. Its entrance and exit are sluggish and undramatic. The other principal feeder, the Bog River, enters the head of the lake with all the panache of a prima donna, in silvery cascades over shelving rock. Bog River Falls is spanned by a gracefully arched bridge and set between high wooded banks.

A tributary of the Raquette, the Bog is a maverick among the rivers of the St. Lawrence Basin in the direction of its flow. Rising in headwaters only a third of a mile from sources of the Oswegatchie, it hugs the southern boundary of St. Lawrence County on a persistent easterly course till its final swing NE into Tupper Lake.

Above Hitchins Pond the Bog is flat water favorable to canoe cruising. But this section of the river has been closed to the public in the

20th century till now. It is an example of the sequestration of many Adirondack waters in private preserves. What happened to most of the watershed of the Bog also happened, in the forty years around the turn of the century, on the Moose, the Beaver, tributaries of the Hudson, the chain ponds N of Forked Lake, and the three branches of the St. Regis. For a long time after the creation of the Forest Preserve in 1885, the state was reluctant to "buy scenery," so that many tracts suitable for public recreation passed into the hands of individuals and corporations.

A. Augustus Low, after acquiring wealth as a partner in his father's shipping and importing business in Manhattan and Brooklyn, fell in love with Adirondack wilds. He built a summer home near Robinwood on Bog Lake, one of the headwaters of the Bog. In the 1890s he proceeded to buy more and more contiguous land till, by 1896, he owned a forest empire of about 40,000 acres, or two-thirds of Bog River drainage. In 1900 Silver Lake, renamed Lake Marian after Low's wife and daughter, became his permanent home.

Low had inventiveness and energy. He commercialized his new empire. He built a handsome railroad station at Horseshoe to replace the shabby one of the Adirondack Division of the New York Central. His Horseshoe Forestry Company floated logs down the Bog to his sawmill at Hitchins Pond and later built 15 m. of trackage. He built a three-story boarding house at Hitchins for his employees. For several years, before the fad died, he bottled quantities of "Virgin Forest Springs" water for city markets. His maple syrup products also became a commercial success. He was said to have "the most sophisticated sugar bush" in the nation, an assembly line of tubs, pipes, and troughs which was the wonder of Adirondack natives. He exploited even the berry crop on cutover land, turning it into preserves for the market. He built a dam on the Bog to generate electricity, and when he needed more power, a second one.

Augustus Low loved the wilderness after his fashion. Ironically, when the forest fires of 1908 destroyed the greater part of his timberlands, he blamed the catastrophe on sparks from the railroad that another wilderness developer, Dr. Seward Webb, had built.

No one understood this phase of Adirondack history better than the late Kenneth Durant, whose family had a leading role in it. Commenting on the duality of men like Low, he said: "If this be paradox, make the most of it. They all had it—George Washington, Ethan Allen, John Todd, Joel Headley, all the Durants except me—sitting on the piazza at Saratoga Springs dreaming of wealth in wild lands.

. . . The parable of the talents teaches us that undeveloped land is a sin."

Augustus Low died four years after the great fire. His forest empire was subsequently split up among other private owners. Today access by road is only by permission and obliges the caretaker of a Boy Scouts camp to drive several miles to Sabattis to unlock the gate and escort the visitor. Access by water was, till recently, blocked at the Upper Dam at the head of Hitchins Pond. The carry here was closed to the public, thus shutting off access to 10 m. of flat water stretching to the head of Grass Pond on the N or to Bog Lake and Clear Pond on the S (*Wolf Mountain 7.5*). The dam backs up a long flow that gradually widens into what was once known as Mud Lake but is now an indistinguishable part of Lows Lake, as the flow is called today.

In celebration of the Forest Preserve centennial in 1985, the state purchased 9,248 acres of Bog River Flow. Now most of the headwaters are open to public canoeing.

Backcountry at the headwaters of the Bog was traditionally the last stand of the moose in New York State. The last moose was killed many times there in the middle decades of the 19th century. In 1859 Charles Marsh, a local hunter, killed "the last moose" near Bog Lake and became a hero in his native township of Fine. School was recessed so that the pupils could view the 1000-pound trophy exhibited in a sleigh. Sportsmen from the cities did not wish to be left out in the scramble to kill the last moose. Hence we have several vivid accounts of journeys up the Bog dating to the 1840s, 50s, and 60s.

All of them agree that going up the Bog, with its many tough carries, its crooks and turns, was a test of physical stamina. Alfred B. Street's guide, Harvey Moody, called it one of "the confoundest crookedest consarns in the woods." More, once at the headwaters, it became a test of spiritual fortitude. Street, Hammond, Headley, and Wallace could not find language strong enough to express their revulsion at the "dismal scenery" around Mud Lake. It was "the gloomiest sheet the wilderness contains," where "each member of the insect tribe holds high carnival." The vast bottomland was of "indescribable loneliness" and "weighed on the spirit." Once having been there, you never want to go back, says Hammond.

Today the Bog River Flow is very different from what it was in mid-19th century and after the fire of 1908. There are some barren acres and other patches where the preponderance of poplar grows monotonous, but on the whole, the forest has made a good recovery.

Some places were untouched by the fire. The Upper Dam has flooded a good portion of the "bog" and given once dying Mud Lake a new lease on life. A broad channel has taken the place of the once shallow, snaky outlet of Grass Pond. This remote, mountain-ringed pond, where until recently the golden eagle nested on the crags, is today the jewel of Bog River Flow.

A dam ordinarily sends a canoeist into a state of shock or righteous indignation. But just possibly the Upper Dam of the Bog has aesthetic as well as utilitarian justification. Shards of the desolation remain in fringes of drowned trees and in flats to the S, but much of the flow is very beautiful today with its wooded islands, piny headlands, and rocky mountain walls on the N. Yet there are grounds for rejecting the dam. A desolation so complete, like anything absolute, should have been preserved. Those sportsmen of the old days loved to boast of having got there in spite of physical obstacles and, once there, having sustained, like Browning's Childe Roland in another wasteland, great pressure on their sensibilities. We are denied that gesture of heroism today by the transformed scenery.

Bog River Falls and Tupper Lake, 7 m. + (11.3 km. +)
USGS: Long Lake, Tupper Lake 15 or 7.5 × 15

Tupper Lake has the shape of an arm slightly flexed at the elbow. It is 7 m. long and has a number of wooded, rocky islands. The E shore, along which Route 30 runs, is intermittently built up with private camps and motels. Keep your distance from it. It is best seen from the W side of the lake, whence its docks and camps are less prominent and the cliffs and mountains behind it more so. The W shore is likely to be wind sheltered. It is also interestingly irregular, with deep bays and headlands. About half of it is state land. There are numerous sites for camping and a lean-to in Black Bay.

Canoeists traveling the full length of the lake can put in at the bridge on Route 30 S of Tupper Lake Village, at the public boat landing in Moody, or at the village water intake station, a square brick building a little farther S. The essential part of the cruise is to skirt the W shore of Bluff Island or, better yet, to circumnavigate it. It is an elongated ridge of bedrock decorated with handsome red and white pines. At the SW is the Devil's Pulpit, a sheer cliff rising 100 feet above the lake. The name derives from an Indian legend that a god used this pulpit to proclaim the fate of any mortal who dared to listen. The only voice I have heard there came from three otters bobbing up and down in the water and saying "eek, eek"—an unfathomable message as oracles generally are.

County Line Island is bisected by the St. Lawrence-Franklin County boundary. State land extends S from Grindstone Bay on the W shore. From the outer part of this bay the N and S ends of the lake can be seen as well as distant Whiteface Mountain.

Ever since Alfred Street's *Woods and Waters* (1860), boaters and campers on Tupper Lake have praised its "liquid vistas" and its changing lights and colors. And there is certainly one day a year, perhaps two, when to launch a canoe on Tupper with a girl friend is to embark for Cytherea.

It must be still and sunny. The breeze, if any, must be light and from the south. A slight haze throws a purplish wash over sky, mountain, and glassy surface. Illusory horizontal lines of white light gleam where distant land meets water, and far shores seem to float in air like hovercraft. The season must be the first two weeks in October, and the leaves of white and gray birches and aspens must be near their peak of yellowness. When such a day comes, drop everything, put the canoe on the cartop, and drive to the causeway across Rock Island Bay near the S end of the lake.

At this time of year there are few or no motorboats. The summer residents have gone. But if it is a weekend, cars will be parked along the causeway. Cameras, pointed at islands as pretty as floral arrangements or at the double images of main shore, will be clicking off color film.

Push off from shore and head toward the three islands in the bay. Then turn S toward Bog River Falls. The slow approach from the lake is the best way to see the falls, which drop about 30 feet in three cascades. There is a picnic area here on state land. Carry about 80 yards up a steep bank on the R, cross a road, and put in in the outermost channel above the falls. Bog River is a stillwater to the Forks, 2 m. upstream. Beyond this, on both forks, rocks, rapids, and carries make the going too rugged for the mood of the day. Return to the lake and paddle slowly back to your car in the late afternoon sun, now at your back. The lake is even glassier, the purple tints deeper, and the birches more golden. Too bad that such a day must end.

The next few miles above the Forks are impracticable for upstream travel. The L fork, Round Lake Outlet (or Bog Stream), flows through a gorge in which long carries are necessary. It is closed to the public S of the St. Lawrence-Hamilton County line. The R fork, or the

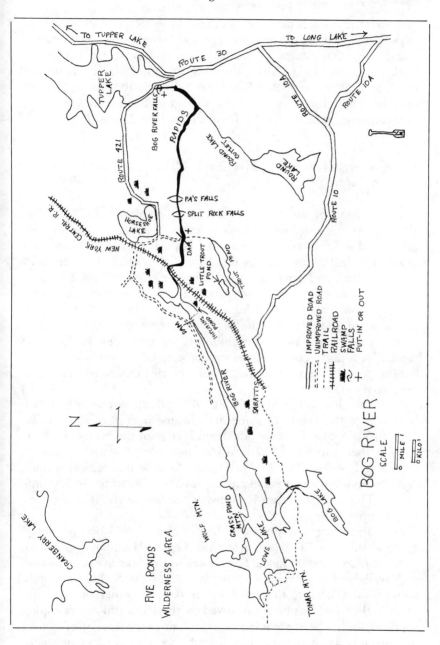

Bog River proper, is described in the next section as a downstream trip. In 1988 the Board of Geographical Names announced that it had changed the name of the last 2 m. of Bog River, below the Forks, to Round Lake Outlet, the name previously reserved only for the L fork. The name Bog River, according to the Board, applies only to the R fork. Nevertheless, this guidebook will keep with long-standing tradition and refer to the bottom 2 m. as Bog River.

Lows Lower Dam to Bog River Falls, 7.2 m. (11.6 km.)
USGS: Tupper Lake 15

This section of the Bog is classified as scenic by the APA. The DEC stocks the river with brook trout. It is about 40 feet wide at put-in and widens to 60 feet below the Fork. The drop in this section is about 90 feet (not including Bog River Falls), most of it coming in the first 5.2 m. and occurring at unrunnable drops or falls. For years the carries at these drops were posted by clubs thatleased from International Paper. But in January 1988 the DEC announced the purchase of Lot 11 from the paper company, consolidating state land on the lower Bog. The clubs will be permitted to use their camps for a period of years before the state takes possession of the buildings and razed them. Meanwhile, carries described below are open to paddlers.

Access to this section is via Route 421 off the S end of Tupper Lake. Cross the beautiful stone arch bridge over Bog River Falls. An informal gauge is on the upstream L edge of the bridge. If there is more than two feet of vertical blocking below the arch, consider the water level too low. The best time to canoe this section is mid-April to mid-May. Thereafter the rapids are liable to be shallow and scrapy. This is a great spot for viewing the falls as the Bog cascades into Tupper Lake.

From the bridge, continue to a L turn on the blacktop up a steep grade at what used to be the American Legion Mountain Camp and proceed to Horseshoe Lake. The shores of this lake are state owned and available for camping. At the W end of the S shore a woods road on the L leads to the lower dam in 0.7 m. Formerly impassable by cars, this road has been improved by the DEC and a parking lot for canoeists has been prepared near the dam. Carry across the restored dam and take a faint trail down the R bank. (A jeep road, now impassable even by jeeps but usable as a trail, continues through state land to beautiful, little visited Trout and Little Trout ponds, where lake trout fishing is good.)

Water drops over the 15-foot dam (which no longer generates power) and then over a double drop that is unrunnable except at very high water levels. The first drop is 2 feet; the second one of 4 feet ends in a river-wide hydraulic. In and below this are barely-covered rocks which could easily damage a boat. Very rocky shoals continue after this for 0.25 m. until an easy Class II rapids is encountered. The next 0.5 m. is beautiful flatwater paddling until Split Rock Falls, a 6-foot vertical drop, is encountered. As before, the rocks scattered across the bottom of this drop make a run unlikely except perhaps at very high water levels on the extreme R. The preferred bushwhack is on the L.

Below Split Rock Falls the river turns 90 degrees to the L with 50 yards of rocky, scratchy Class I rapids. Then the river makes a broad U-shaped turn to the L and in 0.3 m. flows under a bridge on a logging road. Under the bridge are two Class II drops and then a mandatory take-out on the L. Persons unsure of their ability to do proper eddy-turns are advised to take out before these two drops. Immediately below is Pa's Falls, a beautiful but formidable drop of 30 feet, twisting over three distinct pitches. Carry on either bank: the R bank is shorter and easier, while a carry on the L bank takes you past a tombstone for Pa.

Below Pa's Falls trees often block the river and make short carries necessary. In 300 yards a short Class I–II rapids is followed by 1.5 m. of flat meandering water. There are numerous signs of beaver, and spruce and alders abound. At one turn to the R the current quickens. In the next 0.75 m. the Bog drops 60 feet, beginning as Class II and quickening to Class III. In early spring ice walls tend to form on both banks and make the end of this run very fast and narrow with no eddies available. Under these conditions the difficulty level increases. Those wishing or needing to carry around these rapids should do so on the L bank, a difficult bushwhack.

A fisherman's camp appears on the R just before the confluence with Round Lake Outlet. It is possible to paddle up the Outlet a short distance till Class III–IV rapids on posted land are reached. The gorge above this point contains exciting rapids for the advanced paddler, but the land is heavily posted S of the St. Lawrence-Hamilton County line and access is not allowed.

Below the confluence are 2 m. of flatwater passing under a logging bridge at 1 m. Just above Bog River Falls proper is a set of slides 8 to 10 feet high. These are unrunnable because of the shallowness of the water and should be carried on the L to a picnic area by the bridge. The enterprising paddler may run Bog River Falls at optimal water levels when it is rated Class V. Just above the bridge start at the L bank and angle slightly toward the R. The river drops sharply just under the bridge and the paddler must stay to the R of a large pointed submerged rock, which spews a large roostertail wave. The paddler must thread a needle between the submerged rock (to the L) and a second, smaller rock six feet to the R. From here it is straight down a slide through waves into a hydraulic at the bottom. The falls are not very difficult technically but, because of their shallowness, should be considered very risky. A flip would be quite dangerous. The total drop of the falls proper is 20 vertical feet in 100 horizontal feet.

Lower Dam to Upper Dam, 3 m. (4.8 km.)
USGS: Tupper Lake 15

This section of backwater extends 3 m. to the head of Hitchins Pond, where Lows Upper Dam is located. Access to the lower dam is as described in the previous section on p. 108. Upstream from the lower dam the river alternately narrows between wooded banks and widens between low marshy shores. Just beyond cliffs on the S shore at the first narrows, lovely patches of twinflowers amid mossy rocks may be seen in bloom from late June into July. Beyond the railroad bridge lies the first of the large tracts acquired by the state in 1985. On entering Hitchins Pond, bear L. At the head of the pond, enter the tailrace of the inoperative power dam and look for a path up the R bank near the dam itself. Silver Lake Mountain looms nearby. A short bushwhack to the top of the prominent ridge provides a nice view of the surrounding area.

Bog River Flow and Lows Lake, 8.3 m. + (13.4 km. +)
USGS: Tupper Lake 15, Wolf Mountain 7.5

The upstream trip resumes at the head of the upper dam, accessible only by river, in a tract formerly owned by the Suffolk County Boy Scout Council. The next owner upstream is the Hiawatha Council, which also sold land to the state but retains some of its holdings. Two other tracts complete state purchases. The larger of these, 2,800 acres, surrounds Grass Pond and adjoins the Five Ponds Wilderness Area. It opens to the public an eastern approach to Oswegatchie waters.

In August of 1985 guests of the DEC gathered here at Hitchins Pond to celebrate the addition of nearly 10,000 acres to the Forest Preserve. Many of us felt that this purchase was the crowning event of the Forest Preserve's centennial. The Bog River Flow is a wonderfully scenic acquisition and a significant ecological one. In its loon population of over thirty birds it is second only to the Beaver Stillwater. Golden eagles once nested on the mountain ledges, and in 1985 a bald eagle was sighted. Eskers line the flow above Hitchins Pond. The craggy mountains of the northern shores contrast dramatically with swamp and marsh lands on the S. Most scenic of all, perhaps, is isolated, mountain-ringed Grass Pond. Consisting largely of waters, this new addition to the Forest Preserve is so admirably adapted to canoe cruising that it seems to demand classification as a canoe area.

The USGS maps in the heading are essential aids. All the headwaters are now open to canoeing with the exception of Clear Pond. The only obstruction is a floating bog, which was evidently detached from some upstream shore after the upper dam had raised the water level. It is now wedged in the channel about 0.8 m. above Hitchins Pond. It supports an undulatory carry at midstream, at the expense of wet feet and damage to vegetation. The easiest passage is a narrow channel along the N mainland shore which requires a short carry of 10 to 30 feet. During periods of low water it is generally possible to carry on the exposed bank rather than directly over the bog. The position of the bog—an interesting feature in itself, especially in the spring blooming season—probably shifts from year to year, but the extreme N or S end should remain the easiest and least damaging passage. The distance from the upper dam to the W end of Lows Lake (at a conspicuous point on the mouth of Tamarack Pond Outlet, where a trail into the Five Ponds area can be picked up) is 8.3 m. or more, depending on how you thread the islands.

In line with the prevailing SW winds and shallow, Lows Lake is choppy in a strong breeze. This factor needs to be considered, especially when cruising with camping gear. It is generally best to follow the N shore, taking advantage of the shelter provided by the islands. If the lake is too choppy, it is possible to bypass the main body of the lake by carrying the N shore between campsites 19 and

23 and proceeding over a crossway to the W of site 25; these sites are shown on the map provided by the DEC at the put-in. Camping is possible at numerous sites. The state has designated several camp-sites along the flow for the first mile above the dam, on the perimeter of Grass Pond, and at the W end of Lows Lake. Additional campsites may be found on some of the islands, although a few of them remain in private hands. The area forest ranger can provide additional information about those islands where camping is permitted as well as conditions requiring a permit. No camping is allowed around the buildings at the Upper Dam.

Side Excursions   *USGS: Tupper Lake 15*

Two excursions on foot at the S end of Tupper Lake offer notable views for little effort. Travelers on Route 30 can hardly fail to notice two conical shaped peaks with partially bald tops close to the high-way on the E. Each is in a block of state land surrounded by privately owned Litchfield Park. The one off the tip of South Bay, unnamed on the topo map but locally called Litchfield Hill or Goodman Hill, rises 600 feet above lake level. It can best be ascended from what remains of a narrow abandoned blacktop road running NE from the clearing and picnic ground at Lumberjack Spring, 0.6 m. S of the lake. The spring, protected by an enclosure, is surely up to the standard of Low's best Virgin Forest Springs Water.

To climb the 2,160-foot peak, walk up the blacktop road about 0.5 m. and then turn L into the woods (no trail), following the height of land to the peak. Trees block the view toward Tupper Lake, but open rock and a grassy meadow afford views in other directions. Toward the E on a clear day is a bit of Bavaria. About 3 m. away the towers of Litchfield Castle rise from deep woods, and beyond is the noble skyline of the High Peaks. The castle, which the grandson of the builder affectionately calls "an anachronism of the first order" and "a magnificent Edwardian dream," was finished in 1913. It has two towers, walls from three to six feet thick, and nearly 100 rooms.

The other peak, named Coney Mountain, has an elevation of about 2,270 feet. It gives much the same view of the High Peaks, but an intervening ridge blocks a view of the castle. It is most easily ascended by a hunters' trail along the Franklin-Hamilton County line, marked by blazes. (Land on the S side of the line is private.) The county boundary is about 1.25 m. S of Lumberjack Spring. The faint trail leads to the height of land (a steel boundary marker) in a saddle. Turn L here and ascend a rocky spine to the bald summit. The grassy top is a pleasant place to pass the noon hour.

Here on Coney Mountain in 1772 one Archibald Campbell and a group of Indians ended their survey of the northern boundary of the Totten and Crossfield Purchase. They had bushwhacked E from the NW corner some 30 m., chopping blazes to establish the boundary of the first major land purchase in the central and western Adirondacks. By the time they reached Coney, they were tired. But they had another, more sufficient reason for ending the ground survey here, content with a line of sight eastward. "The rum gave out" was the clinching explanation in Campbell's field notes.

In the fall of 1972, two centuries later, staff members of the Adirondack Museum climbed Coney Mountain to commemorate the anniversary of Campbell's aborted survey. After lolling about under the September sun, they descended and drove a few miles to the nearest bar to share a celebratory shot of rum. Things are too easy today.

JORDAN RIVER

USGS: Carry Falls Reservoir, Childwold, Mount Matumbla 7.5

The Jordan is a little river, hardly more than 40 feet wide at its mouth and only 18 or 21 m. long, depending on whether you take its source to be Sunset Pond or a mountain brook. Because of its remoteness in an area N of Tupper Lake and E of Carry Falls Reservoir where there are no public roads, it is comparatively little known. Its fans are a fortunate few: the owners of a large private park and their guests, members of a few game clubs, and a small number of woodsmen who have discovered the parcels of state land back there where gray jays (the whiskey jacks of Canadian forests) parachute down from the trees and shadow intruders with ghostly, ill-intentioned whisper among themselves; where spruce-fir swamps are as hauntingly primitive and boreal as anything to be found in the Adirondacks today; and where white pines tower above all else from the hummocks and knolls of the swamp. Back in 1799 the Macomb Purchase surveyor Benjamin Wright was impressed by the pines of the Jordan valley. His field notes mention "a fine body of Pine Timber of good (quality) quantity near the large creek which falls into the Racket River on the East side." The pines are still there in the 44% of state land in the watershed (some of it the original Forest Preserve of 1885) and in the Kildare Club, a private park. The state acquired an additional mile-square lot on the river in 1989.

The remoteness and unspoiled beauty of the Jordan watershed prompted the novelist Philip Wylie, a guest at the Kildare Club, to make that private park with its virgin forests a setting for *The End of the Dream.* "Faraway" on the "Mystery River" is the site for the final vestiges of civilization in the 21st century. Wylie is remembered at the Kildare Club for his ability to call loons on Jordan Lake to the edge of the dock.

The APA rivers survey team estimated that 88% of the 18 m. from Marsh Pond (Sunset Pond on the topo map) to the mouth of the Jordan is canoeable stillwater. The problem is getting to it. Access to the upper stream is blocked 5 m. N of Tupper Lake at a gate with a full-time gatekeeper. At the mouth, the first 0.7 m. is canoeable when Carry Falls Reservoir is full, but above that is a steep 1.3 m. of rapids and cascades. A carry around these rapids is possible but extremely difficult. It is best to stay 20-30 yards inland to minimize encounters with deadfalls. Even so, several parties have attempted this carry and given up.

There is legal access to the stillwater above the rapids. This is over a state trail from the edge of Carry Falls Reservoir. Instead of going directly up from the mouth, this trail starts 1 m. N of it in a cove at the mouth of Little Cold Brook. It passes through blocks of state land that touch only at one corner. It approaches the river (R across a strip of overgrown meadow) a little way above the foot of the stillwater. The distance by this trail, up and down grade, is 2.7 m. A long way to carry a canoe. The Bear Brook Trail, as it is called after a feeder of the Jordan, is traced on the sketch map "Sevey to South Colton" on p. 94, but the USGS map *Carry Falls Reservoir* is essential for locating the trail's beginning.

State purchase of Lot 31 in 1989 made possible a shorter carry to surmount the rapids. Take the Bear Brook Trail for about 0.7 m. till it emerges in a broad meadow, shown in white on the topo map. Near the W end of the meadow leave the trail and head S on a compass bearing for 0.2 m. till you intersect a jeep road. Follow this road E till it branches. Take the R branch for several hundred yards to the camps of the Stag Club, where flatwater on the Jordan begins. You are now in the block of state land purchased in 1989. The club is permitted to retain its camps for ten years, but meanwhile this site and an additional 1.5 m. of river corridor are open to the public. By this route the total carry distance is 1.4 m., considerably shorter than the state trail alone which reaches the river well above the foot of the flatwater.

The first edition of this guide suggested, for the hardy, a two-night camping trip beginning on Carry Falls Reservoir. Several parties have made this trip, according to report. One detailed report from Peter Brown describes difficulty in negotiating the muddy Bear Brook trail and dealing with the punkies while camping in the meadow.

Those wishing to paddle the rapids on the downstream return should have intermediate whitewater skills and should do so only during periods of high water. In this stretch the Jordan drops 80 feet. Rapids begin as Class II-III and, within 50 yards, there is a drop of 15 feet in two pitches over a distance of 20 yards. The first pitch is potentially dangerous, a 5-foot drop onto a turbulent pillow followed immediately by a sharp S-turn and a sloping ledge dropping 6-8 feet. This is Tebo Falls, rated Class IV-V, where a French Canadian log driver, Thibault, lost his life, according to the fine old ballad: "And we found his drownded body on Racket flood below."

In the next 0.4 m. there are constant, technical rapids ranging from Class I to Class III. A large boulder then divides the current in half. Stay R and negotiate a tricky drop of 5 feet, rated Class II-III. Rapids between here and the backwater above the mouth are constant and technical but do not exceed Class II in difficulty. A nineteenth-century map of this area refers to this stretch of rapids as "Rickey's Rapids."

Remote little rivers like the Oswegatchie above High Falls, the Cold, the upper Chubb, the Deer, and the Jordan bring one in closer touch with wilderness left in the Adirondacks than the larger streams. Ever since spending a couple of days as a guest in a Jordan Club camp at the mouth of the Jordan in 1931, this river has figured in my conception of a wilderness paradise. The impression was reinforced by an opportunity to canoe on a midsection of the stream as guest at the Kildare Club. But some parts of the river are not so beautiful. The spruce, fir, tamarack, and cedar swamps are often screened from view by long files of alders on the banks. Maybe Bill Frenette has a better idea. When he wants to get away from everything on a solitary weekend of camping, he uses his canoe only to cross the Raquette below Jamestown Falls and then bushwhacks through the woods to the midsection of the Jordan via Deer Pond. After one such fall trip, he wrote to me: "I really feel I'm in the wilderness in this country."

ST. REGIS RIVER

The 15-minute *Saint Regis* map shows over 150 lakes and ponds ranging in size from a stone's throw to 8-m. long Upper Saranac Lake. To canoeists, this generous display of blue nudity is the centerfold of Adirondack topographic maps.

These lakes and ponds in the southern half of Franklin County are the headwaters of three rivers, the West and Middle branches of the St. Regis and the Saranac, with a little of Raquette River drainage thrown in. In Township 20, St. Regis and Saranac headwaters are so closely intermingled that it is a Chinese puzzle to separate them on the map. But soon the systems part, the Saranac flowing S through Upper Saranac Lake before veering on its long NE course to Lake Champlain; the two branches of the St. Regis flowing NW to their junction at Winthrop and then swinging NE. The Grass, the Raquette, and the St. Regis run roughly parallel courses in drainage basins that narrow toward their mouths. They empty into the St. Lawrence in separate channels within a span of 7 m.

When wilderness was unwanted, Township 20 was valued at eight pence an acre. New York State sold it at that figure in 1792 to a land speculator, Alexander Macomb, as part of a deal involving nearly four million acres. A century later, armed now with a conservation law protecting the Forest Preserve, the state bought most of Township 20 back. Here the Adirondack beaver made its last stand after becoming extinct elsewhere in the park. A colony of five to ten carried on in these waters through the turn of the century until Harry Radford and others successfully reestablished beaver in the Adirondacks.

Much of Township 20 was devastated by forest fires in 1903. The fires skipped over some areas, especially low-lying stands of hemlock, spruce, and balsam and also pines on the fringes of ponds. Today there is an intermixture of young hardwoods and softwoods on the slopes and of mature softwoods in swampy places. Many shores are accented by tall pines that escaped the fire.

During the last thirty years, overuse and inappropriate use have degraded some of the lovely headwater ponds of the Saranac. This is especially true in the Fish Creek area S of the railroad tracks. Two popular state campsites draw thousands of visitors every summer, along with their campers, trailers, tents, and powerboats. Ponds that can be crossed in three to fifteen minutes by canoe or rowboat swarm with high-speed motorboats. In the 1960s and early 70s this plague was rapidly extending to the more remote ponds N of the railroad tracks, most of which are in St. Regis drainage. Outboard motors were taken in by float planes in summer and by snowmobiles to tent-platform sites in winter. Snowmobile trails were opened. Then came the *State Land Master Plan* of 1972. As approved by the Governor, this established a new category of zoning—a canoe area. Only one was designated as a start—the St. Regis Canoe Area. It is bounded on the S by the railroad tracks and on the N by the William Rockefeller preserve. It contains 58 bodies of water. Motorboats and snowmobiles are now prohibited; tent-platform permits have been canceled. The area is reserved for hand-propelled boats and for fishing, temporary camping, snowshoeing, and ski touring. The wilderness character of the St. Regis Canoe Area has been largely restored and its attractiveness to canoeists enhanced. The new silence in this pocket-sized wilderness is wonderful.

The headwaters of the West and Middle branches are divided by a low quarter-mile ridge between Green and Little Long ponds at the SE base of St. Regis Mountain. Together, the two branches encircle the mountain range except on the W side, where they run parallel courses. Below the Fish Pond chain, the West Branch soon passes into a private park and is inaccessible to the public. The Middle and East branches, however, have several reaches ideal for canoe cruising with public access.

WEST BRANCH

St. Regis Canoe Area: The Nine Carries, 11.5 m. (18.5 km.)
USGS: Saint Regis 15; Upper Saranac Lake, Saint Regis Mtn. 7.5 × 15

The *Saint Regis* map is to the canoe tripper what the *Marcy* and *Santanoni* quads are to the mountaineer. There are mountains here too, but they are modest ones rising at most to the 2,873-foot elevation of St. Regis Mountain. Some are worth climbing for their views. But the main attraction is the numerous ponds. Each one has a distinctive character; even the color of its waters is distinctive. None is so large that you tire of it. Several reclaimed trout ponds are stocked by the state and afford good fishing: Little Green, St. Regis, Ochre, Fish, Little Fish, Lydia, Nellie, Bessie, and Clamshell.

The principal source of the West Branch is St. Regis Pond. The infant stream then flows through Ochre, Fish, and Little Fish. Feeders join it from outlying ponds. It is too narrow and obstructed for canoeing till it leaves Little Fish. The headwater ponds, however, are a world in themselves.

A state fire truck trail of 5 m. traverses the St. Regis Canoe Area and ends at Fish Pond. This trail is open to the public for foot travel. The truck trail can be reached from the Adirondack Fish Hatchery off Route 30. On the loop road into the hatchery grounds, there is a dirt road 0.35 m. W of the bridge. Drive N on this and cross the RR tracks. The continuation straight ahead and then R goes to a public launching site at Little Clear Pond, which is the start of the Nine Carries route. To reach the gate on the truck trail, turn sharp L across the tracks and drive a rough 0.6 m. W to a last R turn, passing several driveways to abandoned tent-platform sites. Take this for 150 yards to a parking circle on a high bank above Little Green Pond at the gate of the truck trail. From here it is a pleasant hike through varied woods to Fish Pond for those substituting foot for canoe travel.

The route of the Nine Carries is a circuit of West Branch headwaters that begins at Little Clear Pond and ends either at Hoel or Long Pond. Two cars are essential if take-out is at Long Pond. If the Hoel Pond take-out is chosen, two cars are desirable, although it is possible for a pair of canoeists with one car to split up at the N end of Hoel, one walking E along the RR tracks to the starting place while the other paddles across Hoel Pond to take-out (afternoon winds might hamper a single paddler). In any case, the public landing on Hoel should be visited before the trip begins in order to note its location on the SE shore.

Drive W on Route 30 from the hatchery and take the blacktop road turning R across from the W entrance to Saranac Inn. At 0.3 m. the road forks. Take the R fork and cross the golf course to the edge of the woods. Turn L here and continue to the NW corner of the clearing, where the road, now dirt, swings R onto state land on Hoel Pond. There is parking space for several cars.

If Long Pond is chosen as the objective, drive a second car over the Floodwood Road (the L fork on the golf course), cross the RR

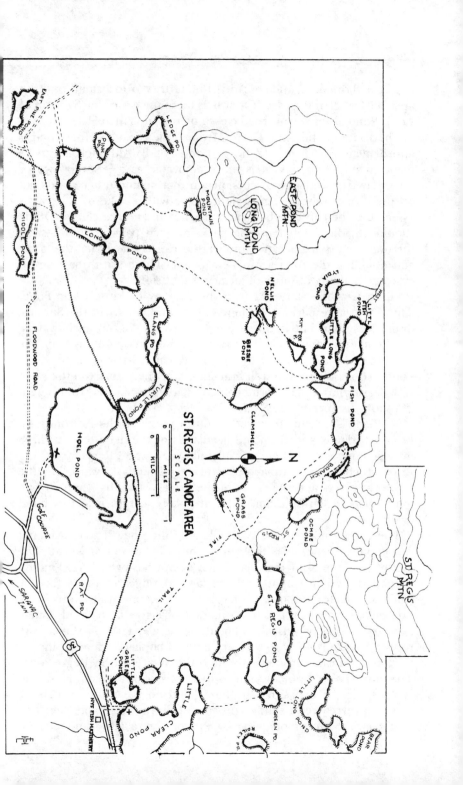

tracks at about 4 m., and continue 1 m. farther W to a small parking area 100 feet N of the road. Carry 0.25 m. to the bay of the SW arm of Long Pond along a spur road closed by the DEC in 1990.

The route of the Nine Carries from Little Clear to Hoel Pond is approximately 11.5 m. (12 m. to Long Pond). Although it can be made in one long day, it is more enjoyable as a leisurely two or three-day trip, with side excursions on foot or into other ponds not on the direct route. A lightweight canoe with a yoke or a kayak is essential if the trip is to be a pleasure, not an endurance test. Duffle should be consolidated in one pack for each pair of canoeists. In this way, one person can shoulder the canoe, the other the pack, and doubling the carries can be avoided. There are three lean-tos en route and any number of attractive tent sites.

Put-in is at the state beach in the SW bay of Little Clear Pond. There is a large parking lot here. This pond is part of the Saranac drainage system but is the readiest access to West Branch waters. Paddle its full length. The first carry on the direct route is from the NW corner of Little Clear to a dock on a marshy inlet of St. Regis Pond, 0.6 m. Where the trail branches, take the R fork (on the same NW bearing) to a plank bridge over a marsh to put-in. From here it is a short distance to the S bay of St. Regis Pond.

St. Regis is one of the most beautiful ponds in the Adirondacks. From its islands and from the headlands of the deep bay on the S by which one enters, there are splendid views of St. Regis Mountain. Rows of white pines, their tops bent permanently leeward, line the shores in places and the crests of the ridges. Now that there are no motorboats to harass them, loons are likely to return to this pond every season.

There is a lean-to on the W headland of the S bay. The E headland is a good tent site, as is the sandy bluff of the central island. The mountain slope N of this island may tempt bushwhackers. Finding a good route over or around the layered ridges of the S face by compass and topo map is a challenge. (The only trail is on the N side of the mountain.) A more modest objective is the wild, lonely tarn in a fold between ridges about 0.8 m. above the N shore. Any route you take is likely to lead to stands of big hemlock and pine.

The direct canoe route is through the W arm of St. Regis Pond. The outlet (West Branch) tumbles over a fish-control dam. Here one has a choice of bypassing the next pond on the route by making one long carry over a spur to the main fire truck trail and thence to Fish Pond, 2 mi; or of going by way of Ochre Pond and making two carries which add up to about the same length. The carry trail from Ochre is known as the Ridge Trail. It begins in the NW corner of St. Regis Pond, about a quarter mile N of the outlet bay. An alternative, at favorable water levels, is to paddle down the outlet into Ochre Pond.

The Ridge Trail, so called because part of it follows the crest of the St. Regis Esker, was first constructed as a snowmobile trail. But now that motorized vehicles of all kinds are banned in the St. Regis Canoe Area, it is maintained exclusively as a canoe carry. Too bad to degrade it with the toil, sweat, and partial sightlessness of carrying a canoe. It is a beautiful trail through varying stands of mature hardwoods and conifers and aisles of tall white pines on the esker near Fish Pond.

Ochre Pond is a small gem encircled by apparently virgin stands of spruce, yellow birch, and white pine. A piny knoll on the NE (part of the St. Regis Esker) is a good tent site. The old carry trail out to the fire truck trail is on the L side of the outlet. The new Ridge Trail runs a parallel course on the N side of the West Branch and also comes out at Fish Pond. A sign in the NW bay of Ochre locates it. It is more interesting than the truck trail.

After crossing a fair-sized brook, the Ridge Trail gradually ascends the esker. In a saddle on the crest there is a fork. Taking the R fork, one can descend to a sliver of water known locally as Mud Pond, canoeable for a quarter mile. But in doing this, one misses the majestic aisle of white pines on the fork that goes straight ahead on the crest. Remaining on this, one can go out to a point on Fish Pond. Just before the point a short trail descends the L side of the esker to the SE bay of Fish. Paddle directly across the bay, past the mouth of the inlet, to a launching site at the end of the fire truck trail. This route replaces the trail from the esker to the S bank of the inlet, no longer in use since deadfalls destroyed the footbridge over the inlet.

Fish Pond is sufficient reward for the labor of getting there. Smaller than St. Regis Pond, it is just as beautiful in its setting at the base of massive St. Regis Mountain. An overnight camp (there is a lean-to on the S shore and another on the N) gives a chance to enjoy changing lights and colors on the pond; to explore other ponds in the cluster by canoe; to climb the cliffs of the N shore from Blagden Lean-to; or to tramp along the crest of a winding esker from the carry trail between Fish and Little Long ponds, first N, then W to the foot of Lydia Pond, much of the time looking down to waters of different hue on both sides of the hogback ridge. At its widest part, where the esker divides into a northern and western extension, there is a pretty round pool in a deep depression. This dimple is one of many kettle holes in the morainal sands of the area, where remnant blocks of ice formed natural refrigerators after the retreat of the main body of the glacier.

G. H. Chadwick, who made a study of Adirondack eskers, named this one the Lydia Pond Esker. It is a nesting area alive with birdsong in May and June. White-throated sparrow, wood thrush, and ovenbird carry on through summer. Here a blackburnian warbler once lit on the bill of my companion's cap, a rare incident that stamps a lasting image of the scene on the memory.

The route continues from Fish Pond into Little Fish by the outlet and a carry of a few yards. Crossing Little Fish to its SW end, one carries over the steep esker to Little Long Pond. From nearby mountaintops this pond stands out because of its striking shade of green. Little Long is the outermost pond in the main route, but a side trip to the W end of Lydia Pond leads to a large concentration of pitcher plants and sundew. Little Long Pond marks the parting of the ways for parties headed for either Hoel or Long Pond.

(1) *For take-out at Hoel Pond.* Paddle to the E end of Little Long and take the steep carry over the esker to the SW bay of Fish Pond, which commands a striking mountain view. You can put in for a short paddle to the S tip of the bay or continue to that point on foot to reach the carry trail to Clamshell Pond.

Clamshell is the highest pond on the route. The carry is hardly more than a half mile but seems longer because of the ascent. Clamshell is notable for bugs and swallows. The latter are forever skimming over the surface in pursuit of the former. This helps to distract the insects, but not enough to make the big flattish rock on the W shore the ideal place it should be for a lunch break.

The height of land between St. Regis and Saranac drainage is reached on the next 1-m. carry between Clamshell and Turtle ponds. The descent from a 1,900-foot elevation into a swampy stream bed is steep and rough. The last carry and the shortest of all is over the RR tracks from Turtle to Hoel. Here one sets a course SE to the public landing near the golf course.

(2) *For take-out at Long Pond.* This alternative route, about a half mile longer, should be avoided before the middle of June because of a poorly drained carry trail. Long Pond, however, is well worth a visit. It is the largest body of water on the route and is interesting to explore because of its irregular shape and beautifully wooded shores.

Now that the tent-platform camps and the motorboats are gone, it is more appealing than ever.

From the SE end of Little Long, take the carry trail to Kit Fox Pond. Cross this (¼ m.) to the SW end for the carry to Nellie Pond, at the base of Long Pond Mountain. Bessie Pond can be skipped by taking the carry trail marked by a sign on the S shore of Nellie. For a full quota of ponds Bessie can be sampled with just a short detour. Look for a spur trail, marked with blue trail discs, which leads L off the main trail, marked with yellow canoe-carry ones. Proceed toward the E shore, where you will pass a picnic table on the knoll, a nice amenity on the Nine Carries. Earlier editions of this guide stated it was possible to probe the outlet of Nellie. A decrease in the outlet's volume has made this impractical except perhaps during unusually wet seasons.

The 1.5 m. carry, once in the low spots an exasperating mire, has been greatly improved by ADK trail workers, who substituted flat stones for the treacherous corduroying. The last third of the trail, on dry rolling ground, is pleasant. It passes through a plantation of Scotch pine and Norway spruce on a carpet of needles and through masses of bunchberry, blooming in mid-June. The trail ends at the northernmost bay of Long Pond, whence one paddles S and then W 2.5 m. to take-out at the W end of the SW arm.

The 40.5 m. of the West Branch from its outlet at Little Fish Pond to the Blue Line is the most tightly locked-up river of the northern Adirondacks. State land extends for only 1.3 m. below Little Fish, and then for the next 14 m. the river flows through a private park. Access roads are all private, requiring paddlers to begin at Little Fish. Here the West Branch is fairly wide, though shallow and obstructed by deadfalls. There is a fish barrier dam at the head of a small ravine followed by mild rapids. In 1.3 m. the river passes into a private park. Below this is a series of game clubs, all of which post the banks, and carries around waterfalls and shallow rapids are presently restricted. Because of this, paddlers are limited to a short round-trip from Little Fish, feasible only for those camping nearby. Even if carries were permitted, a complete downstream trip to Parishville would not be practical, as it would require a unique combination of long sunshine, favorable water levels, and endurance-style paddling. This is regrettable because the West Branch would make an exciting run for whitewater paddlers and, with its five named falls and extended stretches of marshland, a beautiful trip for cruising paddlers as well. This trip must await state purchase of property or an easement near a mid-point.

MIDDLE BRANCH

Headwater lakes and ponds: The Seven Carries, 9 m. (14.5 km.)
USGS: Saint Regis 15; Upper Saranac Lake, Saint Regis Mtn. 7.5 × 15

The route of the Seven Carries is an old favorite. Many a guide
and party of hotel guests traversed it in days of glory of Paul Smith's
Hotel and the Saranac Inn. Those fashionable resorts lay at opposite
ends of the route. Lunch baskets were prepared at one or the other
hotel, and parties of several boats each made an all-day outing of it.
The carries were then, and still are, in excellent condition, fit for
the "most delicate ladies," to use pastor Murray's Victorian way of
describing the easier paths over uneven Adirondack ground. The
longest foot trail on the route is but 0.6 m. Ten lakes and ponds for
seven short carries seems a bargain, even without a guide to carry
the boat. And you can cheat a little by omitting the first pond and
carry.

The highest of Middle Branch ponds accessible to canoeists is Little
Long Pond at the SE base of St. Regis Mountain. It is a central link
in the Seven Carries. The first two ponds of the route drain into
the Saranac, and the next two into the West Branch of the St. Regis.

The easiest access at the S end of the route is the loop road off
Route 30 that passes through grounds of the Adirondack Fish Hatchery. Turn N off the loop 0.35 m. W of the fish ponds onto a dirt
road, which forks just across the RR tracks. The continuation straight
ahead and then R goes to the public landing on Little Clear Pond,
where there is a large parking lot. A sharp L turn on the N side of
the tracks and then, at 0.6 m., a R turn lead to the landing on Little
Green Pond, the traditional start of the route for those who once
portaged by wagon from the Saranac Inn. Except during the middle
hours of the day, this is a pond of long shadows, cast by tall pines
on the high banks. The carry on the E shore is 220 yards.

Since Little Green is quite small, some prefer to begin the trip on
Little Clear Pond and thus reduce the carries to six. Little Clear is
attractively wild. On the E shore across from the launching site is a
good sand beach. (Neither camping nor fishing is permitted on this
pond.) Carry trails at the NE end lead to Grass Pond and Green Pond.
The main route, however, lies over a carry trail at the NW end, near a
marshy inlet. Keep a NW direction on this trail for 0.6 m. to a plank
bridge across a marsh and a dock on a canoeable inlet of St. Regis
Pond. Pitcher plants bloom here in June. As one enters the large

pond and then paddles E around the tip of a peninsula, the pine ridges of St. Regis Mountain fill the northern horizon. In fact, the mountain is in view from various perspectives on most of the route.

Prevailing winds assist in reaching the E end of St. Regis Pond, but sometimes make the landing tricky through wave-tossed driftwood. The carry is about 200 yards. Green Pond is even littler than Little Green, but is otherwise well named for the color of its water. It is quickly crossed to the carry at the NE corner. This 0.25-m. trail ascends about 40 feet to the height of land on the route and leads to Little Long Pond, at an elevation of 1,654 feet. Here the drainage of the Middle Branch is reached. The pond, bisected by a narrows, is lined with white pine.

At the NE end of Little Long is a short carry to Bear Pond. Paddle N on Bear and then E around a point. Still on a due E course, a short carry over a bluff dips into the lovely basin of a bog and tiny pond. Bog Pond, a highlight of the trip for the botanist, is surrounded by a floating garden of moss, leather-leaf, wild cranberry, pale laurel, Labrador tea, sundew, bog rosemary, and pitcher plant. Several of these plants bloom in June.

The carry from Bog Pond to Upper St. Regis Lake is the last of the seven carries. The three remaining lakes are connected by navigable channels (see map on p. 130). The shores are privately owned, but the lakes are open to canoeists passing through. The trip can be terminated on Upper St. Regis Lake by paddling 0.6 m. ESE across the bay, past two islands, to a public dock on the L side of a private one. There is space for visitor parking here. A spur road connects the landing with Route 30, 4 m. from Paul Smiths and 2.8 m. from Lake Clear Junction.

Upper St. Regis, Spitfire, and Lower St. Regis lakes were once the domain of the enterprising hotelier Paul Smith. He bought thousands of acres of cheap cutover timberlands, including the shores of the three lakes, and sold lots to the wealthy patrons of his hotel for vacation homes. By 1890, Paul, wealthy now himself after an early life spent in trapping and guiding, surveyed his domain with pride: "I never saw anything like it! There's not a foot of land on that lake [Upper St. Regis] for sale this minute, and there's not a man in it but what's a millionaire, and some of them ten times over. . . . I tell you if there's a spot on the face of the earth where millionaires go to play at house keeping in log cabins and tents as they do here, I have it yet to hear about."

Many of the camps on the two upper lakes have passed to other hands since 1890, but some are still owned by the original families, down to the fifth generation. There are no tents now, but a few of the original log cabins remain. One still walks from the sitting room to the dining room on a carpet of pine needles. As families grew in size and guest lists lengthened, so did the number of cabins until many camps resembled hamlets. Camp Topridge, built by the late Marjorie Merriweather Post, has sixty units atop the esker at the W end of Upper St. Regis.

The life of the private camps at the turn of the century was the envy of foreign visitors. Its essence is well caught in *Camp Chronicles* (1952, 1964), the recollections of eighty summers of camping on Upper St. Regis and Spitfire lakes. Summing up her feelings, Mildred Phelps Stokes Hooker writes: "As a child, when anything went wrong, I would say to myself, 'Never mind, we're going to the Adirondacks,' and just the thought of this place would make me happy again."

Today the boathouses of Upper St. Regis Lake are virtual museums of water craft—Rushton and Peterborough canoes lovingly cared for, guideboats handmade by Adirondack artisans, several classes of sailboats, and of course motorboats for utility. The Idem class of sailboat was designed especially for these lakes, and one of them is on display at the Adirondack Museum. The St. Regis Yacht Club has held sailboat races since the 1890s.

The canoe route continues through the narrow channel connecting Upper St. Regis and Spitfire lakes and then bends to the NE toward the outlet, a broad winding stream through marshy flats known as the Slew. This was the route taken every Sunday by a flotilla as the summer people set out for church services at St. John's in the Wilderness, often making a race of it.

On Lower St. Regis Lake a broadside wind may make tacking advisable. In recent years the waters of this lake have been murky, but Paul Smith's College has taken measures to clear up the pollution. The route of the Seven Carries ends at a public landing on the W end of the open campus beach. The total distance is about 9 m. The trip can be extended NE through Osgood Pond, Jones Pond (Lucretia Lake), Rainbow Lake, and the North Branch of the Saranac (see Osgood River and Saranac River, North Branch).

An enjoyable half-day circular tour of the three St. Regis lakes can be made from Paul Smith's College. The direction is SW across the Lower Lake to the outlet bay and then down the Middle Branch to Keese Mill Dam. Here starts the only carry, 0.6 m. It goes L from the dam over the road to Camp Topridge. At 0.4 m. it turns L on a trail into the woods, marked by a red arrow on a stone beside the road. The red blazes soon turn to yellow. The trail climbs the St. Regis Esker and then descends, past a little pond (kettle hole) on the L, to the long narrow bay at the W end of Upper St. Regis. (If you have taken the reverse course and are looking for this trail from the lake side, don't go quite to the head of the bay. There is a big white pine about 100 or 150 feet from the end of the bay on the E shore that may have a poster on it. There is a fair landing here. No-trespassing signs are intended for hunters only as a security measure for college students on field trips. College officials have given assurance that canoeists and hikers are welcome on this trail at any time.)

Black Pond, a feeder of the Middle Branch N of Keese Mill, is worth a visit because of its pretty navigable outlet and its views of Jenkins and St. Regis mountains. Canoeists coming down the Middle Branch from Paul Smith's College should take out on the grassy R bank just above Keese Mill Dam and carry across the Brandon Road (also known as Keese Mills Road) 40 yards through a fishermen's parking lot to put-in on the tributary brook. Beyond the shoals of a floodplain the brook enters a ravine of rock and greenery at the base of the St. Regis Esker. It is a lovely passage of a quarter mile which one could wish longer. Surrounding Black Pond are three attractive leantos built by students of the college. The pond is 0.7 m. long. At its N end a carry trail of 0.3 m. leads to Long Pond, the head of this chain of feeders. It is less attractive than Black Pond. There are two lean-tos on Long Pond.

Side excursions in the Paul Smiths Area. The landforms of this area sooner or later lure the canoeist out of his craft. Aside from two attractive mountain climbs, a labyrinth of kames, kettles, troughs, valley trains, and eskers call out to be explored at lower elevations. The last deglaciation left a strong imprint here. An excellent discussion of the geology of the area, with graphic charts that can serve as trail guides, is found in two chapters of Michael Kudish's *Paul Smith's Flora,* obtainable from its publisher, Paul Smith's College.

Perhaps the most interesting glacial feature is a 10-m. long sinuous esker, easily traceable (with interruptions) on the *Saint Regis 15* topo map, from Mountain Pond through a gap enclosed by dramatic cliffs below Jenkins Mountain to Keese Mill, where the Middle Branch cuts through it at right angles; continuing S to bisect the waters of Upper St. Regis Lake and the Spectacle Ponds; then winding around the SE base of St. Regis Mountain and the piny N shore of Ochre Pond to end at a point in the E shore of Fish Pond in the St. Regis

Canoe Area. Kudish calls this the Jenkins Esker; Chadwick, the St. Regis Esker. Eskers are links with a geological past in a time frame that the layman can easily grasp, as little as 10,000 years ago. They have a powerful appeal to canoeists because they are rivers turned bottoms up (concave to convex) and converted into solids. They were formed by the outwash of glacial streams and, like rivers, are seldom straight for long but winding or meandering. Often they have tributaries. They also have braided sections where two or three parallel ridges are separated by islands. There is such a braiding below Jenkins Mountain, where the esker breaks into three parallel ridges. And a tributary esker from the E joins the main one on the S side of the Brandon Road at Keese Mill. On the N side of this road at the same location, one can observe the drift material composing an esker (sand, gravel, cobbles, small rounded boulders) in parabolic cross section at a gravel pit behind a fringe of trees.

All parts of the St. Regis Esker are open to foot travel in land owned either by the state or by Paul Smith's College. Some parts are made easy by informal or maintained trails on the crest of the ridge: an unmarked trail SSW from Route 30 at Mountain Pond into the gap under Jenkins Mountain; a trail at ridgetop between Upper St. Regis Lake and the Spectacle Ponds; and the Ridge Trail in the St. Regis Canoe Area described above. A trail N from Keese Mill Dam follows the E base of the esker alongside the drainage basin of Black and Long ponds. From this, the esker can be climbed at several points to follow game trails on the crest.

The trail up Jenkins Mountain can be reached three ways: (1) by walking a jeep road of 2 m., shown on the topo map, from Route 30; (2) by canoe to the head of Long Pond, where a foot trail leads NE from the lean-to and intersects the jeep road; (3) by a trail along the base of the esker and shores of the two ponds from Keese Mill, continuing to the intersection with the jeep road. The jeep road ends opposite the central ravine of Jenkins Mountain near a site once occupied by a ski lodge. Where the trail forks, bear R and descend a short slope. The trail then crosses a drainage basin through brush and begins to climb through the ravine, gradually bending L away from it toward the highest point on the range (2,514 feet). Several acres of flattish open space rock and meadow provide views and sleep-out space. The return trip can be made more interesting by bearing R (SW) at the fork and taking a loop trail marked with yellow blazes. This trail takes you over several parallel ridges of the esker past a number of kettle holes before meeting the foot trail connecting the head of Long Pond with the jeep road.

The trail up St. Regis Mountain is reached over a half-mile spur road S from Keese Mill Dam. It starts at a public parking lot outside the gate of Camp Topridge. Walking distance to the summit (2,873 feet) is 2.7 m. The trail is interesting for its variety of wildflowers in spring and summer; in early fall, for its brilliant color. The flat rock of the summit commands splendid views of a billowy expanse of forest green studded with countless lakes and ponds and backed on the E and SE by the High Peaks. On a clear day it is one of the grandest views in the Adirondacks.

There are several foot trails nearby. The most interesting are nature trails in timberland once owned by the college but now leased by the Visitors Interpretive Center. Considerable care has been taken in planning and constructing these trails. Accessible from the Center, they may also be reached from a point starting on the N side of the Brandon Road 0.4 m. W of Route 30. The Blue Trail, about 3.5 m. long, encircles a large, irregularly shaped marsh, through which the outlet of Barnum Pond flows. The trail leads through a variety of ecological systems and is continuously interesting. The E side of the trail affords views of St. Regis and Jenkins Mountains. Several shorter trips are possible for those not wanting to make the entire circuit. Lean-tos and observation areas are scattered about. All trails are also excellent for skiing and snowshoeing.

Keese Mill to St. Regis Falls, 28.1 m., discontinuous (45.0 km.)
USGS: Saint Regis 15; Meno, Santa Clara, Saint Regis Falls 7.5; Saint Regis Mtn. 7.5 × 15

From its outlet at Lower St. Regis Lake, the Middle Branch winds 42 m. to its first exit from the park below St. Regis Falls. Stillwater and moderate flow account for about 85% of the mileage, though not all of it is accessible to the public.

A sharp descent off the plateau begins in St. Regis Falls. After crossing the Blue Line 0.5 m. below the village, the river re-enters the park for 4 more miles in a northerly projection of the boundary which takes in the villages of Nicholville and Hopkinton. This section is part of a wildwater course known as the Silver Staircase.

For paddlers wishing flatwater cruises, the four sections described below require no carries once one is on the river. In two instances, a downstream float is possible; in the others, there is only one point of access, and canoeists must paddle upstream as well as down. There

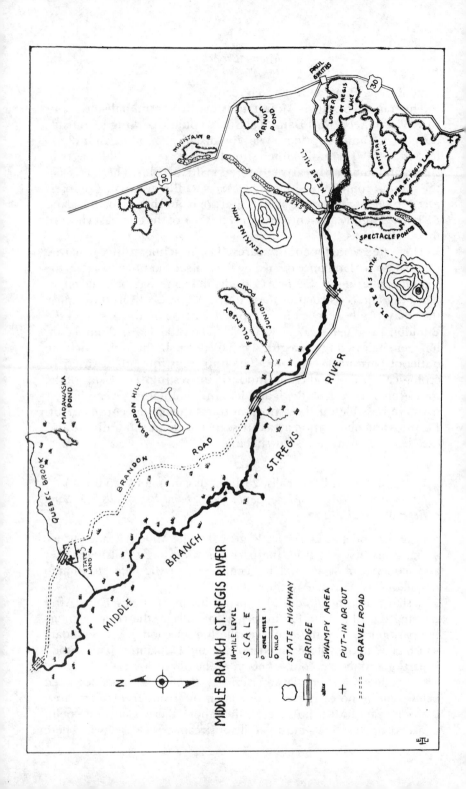

MIDDLE BRANCH ST. REGIS RIVER

16-MILE LEVEL

SCALE

0 ONE MILE 1

0 KILO 1

━━━ STATE HIGHWAY

╪ BRIDGE

🟡 SWAMPY AREA

+ PUT-IN OR OUT

::::: GRAVEL ROAD

N

is, however, a short whitewater run beginning below the bridge at Santa Clara. This section requires at least two carries and is described in Section IV of this chapter. There are public fishing rights in the first, third, and fourth levels, where the state stocks speckled, rainbow, and brown trout; the Sixteen-Mile level is private fishing waters.

I. *Two-Mile Level.* Although the Middle Branch widens to about 100 feet at the park boundary, below Keese Mill it is only about 30 feet at medium water level. Below Lower St. Regis Lake the river is very narrow and obstructed by overhanging branches. A canoeable level of 2 m. begins 0.6 m. below the St. Regis Church on the Brandon Road. Where the road makes a close approach to a loop in the river at a curve with several white guard posts, carry on the L down a short embankment to the river. In this section the stream is somewhat murky from treated sewage of Paul Smith's College. It clears in the Sixteen-Mile Level.

In the first mile the stream is shallow over bars of silt. Other obstacles are snags, deadfalls, and the remains of an old footbridge. Eelgrass waves in the moderate current. The R bank is a low marsh; the L is mostly wooded and rims the lower slopes of St. Regis Mountain. The last mile, where the stream meanders from one side to another of a marsh, has open views of the long ridge of St. Regis Mountain. In fall the hardwoods of the N slope make a brilliant display. Equally colorful at this season are the masses of winterberry on the R bank.

Class I rapids are heard around a R bend as the first bridge on the Brandon Road is approached. The take-out is in brush at the upper side of a cliff on the R bank, in state land. At the top of the cliff is a carry trail of about 100 yards out to the road. This short level is recommended only in spring and fall at medium to high water.

Below the first bridge on the Brandon Road, the Middle Branch enters the Ross private park. Through most of the summer the rapid visible from the bridge is too shallow for navigation. Experienced canoeists who are confident of their ability to run this rapid at medium to high water in spring should ask permission of the manager of the private park before continuing downstream about 3.6 m. to the second public bridge.

II. *Sixteen-Mile Level.* The smooth water at the second bridge on the Brandon Road is inviting, but about a mile downstream, in a private park, is Brandon Dam followed by a rapid. The owner, with whom I have corresponded, refuses permission for canoeists to carry around the dam and rapids, citing a fishery research program with Cornell University.

In the last century the marshy, meandering reach beginning above the second bridge was known as the Sixteen-Mile Level, a "grand secluded reach of boatable stillwater," as Wallace's *Guide* called it. In the ocean of marsh grass, landmarks familiar to the sportsmen of those days were Burnt Knoll, Indian Rock, and Buck Mountain. This level was noted for its fine specimens of brook trout. Today, closed to public access at its upstream end, the Sixteen-Mile Level is an example, all too common in the Adirondacks, of a small-boat route once well established but now restricted by private owners under the authority of the state's posting law. New York State could once make this and other rivers public highways for log driving, but it is apparently not yet ready to legislate right of passage (use of riverbed and foreshore to the extent necessary for navigation) for recreational boating. Perhaps in time it will carry out the APA's recommendation to purchase easements or fee title on the Middle Branch for canoe access and carries.

In his Adirondack survey of 1883, Verplanck Colvin made observations from Azure Mountain (*Meno* quad) and then ascended the Sixteen-Mile Level of the Middle Branch by boat. In his report to the legislature he mentions the "vast marshes which from Mt. Azure are seen to extend over an area of thousands of acres . . . of valuable timber." He continues: "The sixteen-mile level [is] a picturesque still-water which winds for miles through rich alluvial lands, now among alders and bushy swamps, and now through natural meadows. . . . Ascending the river, by boat, a journey of half a day, we landed where the water became swift and the banks of the stream precipitous, and climbing a gravelly, sandy ridge, marched eastward over wild, desolate, burnt lands, once covered with valuable pine timber. Aspens and birch brush were replacing the ancient evergreens, but we soon entered a dense dark forest of most majestic white pine, which extended eastward nearly to Follensbee pond." The burnt area is even larger today as a result of fires early in the present century; but it has a beauty of its own, dotted as it is now with islands of revegetation. One can only echo Colvin's remark in 1883: "It is to be regretted that the State is not the owner of this beautiful valley."

There is legal, backdoor access to a lower part of the Sixteen-Mile Level, with a return over the same route, at Quebec Brook. This brook is 14 m. W of Paul Smiths on the Brandon Road. Approach from the W is 11.2 m. over the Blue Mountain Road from its junction with Route 458 (Route 72 on old road maps). The Blue Mountain and Brandon roads connect as one at a town line. A small 140-acre tract of state land touches the Brandon Road 0.15 m. E of the bridge over Quebec Brook. Two truck trails, both gated and about 70 yards apart, lead S into this parcel. There is room to park two cars at a small turnaround halfway between these two trails.

For 0.5 m. below the bridge Quebec Brook is obstructed by fallen trees and boulders, and its banks are posted by the game club whose land borders on the tract of Forest Preserve. But the brook becomes navigable where the W line of the state land crosses it. From here it meanders through a marsh for about 1.3 m. to empty into the Middle Branch. The only obstruction is some overhanging alders. Depths are ample throughout the summer unless the season is abnormally dry. In the last century Wallace's *Guide* described Quebec Brook as an established canoe route, with carries.

The easternmost of the two truck trails is a longer and more difficult route. The westernmost trail continues S for 0.15 m. before fading. From this point it is a tough bushwhack of 0.25 m. around heavy deadfall and through a lush carpet of ferns. The carry, no longer flagged, is best reserved for those comfortable with topo maps and compass. The carry first veers W and dips before angling back toward the SW as it ascends a wooded plateau. Proceed on the plateau till reaching a steep bank overlooking the brook. Put in at a bend in the brook, shortly upstream from a notable braiding of the channel just discernible on the topo map. Some obstructions are likely up to the line of posters crossing the brook, but no further carries should be necessary from there to the mouth. Carry time is about 20-30 minutes. The passage down the brook takes about 25 minutes downstream; 35, upstream.

Emerging from the mouth of the brook brings a sense of liberation. The river here is exceedingly beautiful. Straight ahead, across a terrace of tall waving marsh grass, is a grove of tamarack and balsam fir. To the L is the long ridge of Buck Mountain. Downstream there is a fine view of two haystack-shaped peaks, Azure and Brushy Top. In remoteness, solitude, and wild beauty, this stretch of stillwater is probably unsurpassed among Adirondack rivers.

Before proceeding up or down the river, note the mouth of Quebec Brook well for identification on the return trip. Sloughs and curlicues of lost channels are easy to mistake for brook mouths. There are distinctive features about the mouth of the brook, however.

Remember that these are private hunting grounds and fishing waters, and that camping or any other use of the shores is prohibited.

One must return the same day and over the same route. The Sixteen-Mile Level ends 2 m. downstream at a rocky chasm of fast water. The drop is about 60 feet in the next 1.5 m. to a bridge on the Blue Mountain Road where Class I rapids may be seen. Upstream the stillwater extends for about 10 m. to rapids below Brandon Dam. Effective cruising range is thus about 12 m., doubled by the return trip. An overnight camp on the parcel of state land would enable one to get an early start for a full day's cruise on the river.

This access to the Sixteen-Mile Level is legal under New York State law. Put-in and take-out are on state land. No carries are necessary if the cruise is limited to the waters described above. One caution: do not attempt this trip during the big-game hunting season.

III. *Santa Clara Level.* Put-in is a lovely pool above the bridge on Route 458 in the hamlet of Santa Clara. Nearby is a campground developed for public use by Champion International in cooperation with the DEC, an elaborate installation with rain shelters over picnic tables and fireplaces. The site is at the downstream end of the Santa Clara Level. There is no upland access (the road to Spring Cove and Madawaska Pond is private). The round trip is 11.2 m. and, with no allowance for errors in navigation, takes about four hours of unhurried paddling time. The objective is the foot of a rapid in a gorge at the upper end of a straight.

For the next 3.5 m., the river is a broad backwater above a dam in Santa Clara. The shores are heavily wooded, with evergreens prevalent. At Trout Brook Flow the river bends W between banks of bedrock. Goose Pond Brook comes in on the W as the river turns S again. Near Reeves Hill, where a private road crosses the river, the stream narrows and snakes from side to side of a marshy valley, with occasional views of Azure Mountain. Sloughs and lost channels complicate navigation, and one must watch the current to stay in the right channel.

Near Spring Cove the main channel makes some improbable maneuvers. In spring, when the river sprawls wide over its floodplains, the channel is hard to follow. Do not be misled by ribbons tied to alder branches; these mark the location of hunters' traps, old or new, and may lead you into a cul de sac of a slough. The best clue (short of the 7.5-minute *Meno* topo map) is little balls of foam floating down from the rapids above.

Not far above these erratic twistings the river straightens between rising slopes, and a staircase of fast water comes into view at the end of the corridor. This is the signal for a return over the same route.

IV. *St. Regis Falls Level.* The fourth and last level within the park is a reach above St. Regis Falls, with access at both the upstream and downstream ends. This reach ends above the dam in St. Regis Falls at a picnic ground on the L bank. This is reached by the South River Road, which turns off Route 458 in the center of the village and, on a gravel surface, continues S along the river to Santa Clara. Upstream access is at one of two places, depending on whether one wants only a flatwater cruise with no carries or would like to include a whitewater run with at least two carries. The flatwater cruise begins 5.2 m. above the picnic ground (or 1.2 m. below the church in Santa Clara for those coming from the E). Here the road makes a close approach to a loop in the river at an 8-foot drop in the river. Look for a carry trail that descends to the river, and follow the shore onto bedrock at the head of the cascade. There is a narrow strip of state land here between the center of the river and the road. A cruise beginning at this point and proceeding to St. Regis Falls is 6.4 m. long.

The other place to begin this section is at the campsite described in Section III or at the Route 458 bridge in Santa Clara. This whitewater float is 2.1 m. long. There is flatwater for 0.3 m. below the bridge to a log boom extending across the river. The next 0.4 m. contains difficult rapids and a treacherous cascade. All or part of this section may be carried on the L on a very faint and seldom used trail which parallels the bank about 30 feet above the river. This carry amounts to a difficult bushwhack through brush and fallen trees.

Immediately below the boom is a 10-foot drop. This is runnable only on the far R and is rated Class IV. In the next 250 yards there are Class III rapids until the river enters a narrow chasm with vertical cliffs on each side, making an exit from the river virtually impossible. At this point the river drops precipitously for 20 feet in the next 40 yards. A large knife-edged boulder divides the current into two frothy channels, each a dangerous Class VI. Below this cascade is a Class III rapid which extends for several hundred yards until South River Road is faintly visible high on the L.

Flatwater begins at a notable bend to the R and continues for 0.4 m. until meeting a Class III ledge. This is best run on the L to avoid a large hydraulic. Shortly below this rapid large boulders line both banks. Take out on the L bank as soon as the boulders are visible and carry around a 12-foot tumble onto scattered boulders, rated Class V-VI.

From here the Middle Branch meanders until it merges with the

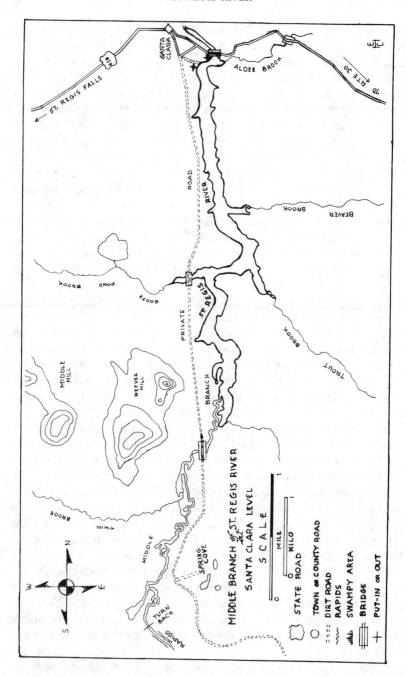

MIDDLE BRANCH of ST. REGIS RIVER
Santa Clara Level

SCALE

MILE

KILO

STATE ROAD
TOWN or COUNTY ROAD
DIRT ROAD
RAPIDS
SWAMPY AREA
BRIDGE
PUT-IN or OUT

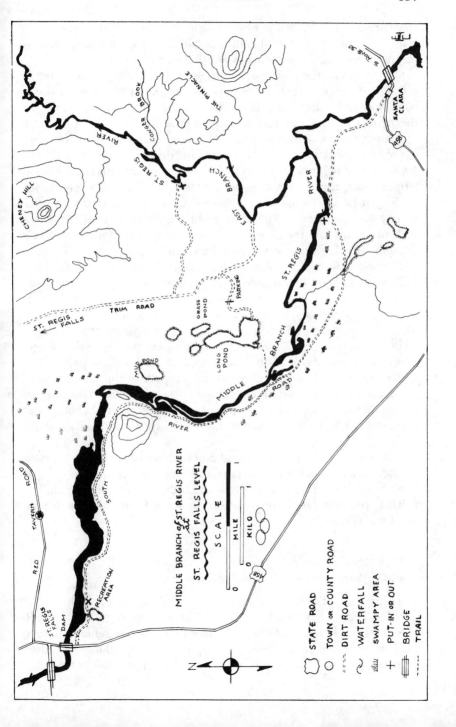

MIDDLE BRANCH *of* ST. REGIS RIVER
at
ST. REGIS FALLS LEVEL

SCALE

MILE

KILO

STATE ROAD
TOWN OR COUNTY ROAD
DIRT ROAD
WATERFALL
SWAMPY AREA
PUT-IN OR OUT
BRIDGE
TRAIL

East Branch 1.6 m. below Santa Clara. Beyond the confluence the Middle Branch is flat until camps become visible on the L bank as the river once again approaches South River Road.

Shortly below these camps, the river makes a 100-degree bend to the R and drops 8 feet, as mentioned above. Take-out is on the L bank, either immediately above this bend or below the cascade. At the bend the river narrows considerably to 20 feet. The current is very swift and those running this drop must take care to avoid being swept to the outside (L) of the turn. This drop is rated Class III-IV. Immediately below it is a series of standing waves and then a small ledge before the river widens to 100 feet. The L bank here serves as the put-in for the flatwater cruise to St. Regis Falls. In dry weather it may be necessary to continue down the faint trail on the L for 0.25 m. or track through shoals, but in spring and fall water levels are generally high enough to run these mild rapids.

The remainder of the run is all deep stillwater with no obstacles. Hilly shores alternate with swamp and marsh. In 3 m. the river widens into the backwater above the dam in St. Regis Falls. The R bank is wild throughout, but a number of weather-beaten shacks on the L bank are eyesores. The trip is more scenic going upstream. It can be done as a round trip, starting from the picnic ground in the village, or even 1.5 m. above if one wants to avoid the widest part of the backwater. In spite of the presence of trappers in the camps strung along South River Road, otters survive to raise families. One August day my companion and I watched three young otters bobbing and diving playfully in the middle of the river just 2 m. above St. Regis Falls.

In addition to the picnic ground and bathing beach above the dam in the village, there is a campground along scenic falls on the R bank below the village. The DEC maintains a nature center on the L bank, reached over a dirt road on the R off Route 458 a half mile W of the village.

St. Regis Falls to Nicholville (Silver Staircase), 7.1 m. (11.4 km.)
USGS: Saint Regis Falls, Nicholville 7.5

This section of the St. Regis is a nearly continuous run of whitewater ranging from fairly easy Class II to Class V. The overall drop is 450 feet for an average gradient of 63 feet per mile. In general, a good deal of technical maneuvering is required through long and often complex rapids. This section has acquired the name Silver Staircase, which can be best appreciated by an observer standing on the rim of the gorge above Nicholville. The best time to make the run is early spring or during periods of heavy rainfall in autumn. Because of the length and complexity of the rapids, advanced skills are required. The paddler must feel comfortable running extended Class II-IV rapids where scouting is not always feasible.

Part of the route lies outside the park. A half mile below St. Regis Falls the Middle Branch winds outside the Blue Line for 3 m. and then re-enters for the next 4 m. in a projection of the park boundary which juts N on the Franklin-St. Lawrence County line to take in the villages of Nicholville and Hopkinton.

The put-in is at the campground off Route 458 in the village of St. Regis Falls. A good site is about 100 feet upstream from a footbridge which is often washed out by spring ice. An advantage of putting in here is that the distance from the surface of the water to the bottom of the footbridge serves as a crude gauge. There should be no more than 3.5 feet of clearance between the water and the bottom of the bridge on the R side. At this level the river's waves and hydraulics become smaller, but there are many exposed rocks. Precise manuevering is required in order to make this run cleanly at lower water levels. Anyone unsure about the water level or his skills is advised to walk the campground trail on the R bank and scout the first several hundred yards. If this section is considered too rocky or too difficult, the trip should be canceled, for the river becomes more difficult downstream.

Below the footbridge a section of Class II rapids extends approximately 0.3 m. You will then see a horizon line with a large rock mass about one-third of the way over from the R bank. Pull over, preferably to the R bank, to scout this dangerous drop. There is a short carry here to a small pool below. At this point the river drops 8 feet in two distinct channels. The L channel drops over the ledge into a churning hydraulic with large, exposed boulders immediately downstream; it is rated Class V. The R channel also drops over the same ledge and is rated Class IV. The hydraulic below it is not as dramatic as the one on the L but is nonetheless capable of holding a boat or logs. The approach to this drop is tricky, and there are submerged rocks in the hydraulic below. Immediately below the drop is a diagonal run to the L through a series of curling waves and roostertails. Here the river drops another 6 feet in about 30 yards and is rated Class III. Class II rapids follow to the first island, where Class III rapids are then encountered for several hundred yards before tapering off. As the river turns L, a pool of flatwater extends for approximately 150 yards. Up to this point the river has dropped about 80 feet in 1.0 m.

Paddling through the pool, you can see a horizon line formed by a washed-out dam at the site of what was originally referred to as Ploof Falls. The state has refused an easement or land sale to Adirondack Hydro Development, a private company considering development of the site for hydroelectric power. Thus, rapids and access above and below the dam will not change. This dam must not be run. Take out on the L bank at a DEC demonstration center. (The center can be reached by turning R off Route 458, 0.3 m. W of the lower bridge in St. Regis Falls. This gravel road forks at about 0.8 m. The R fork takes you to a parking lot at the demonstration center, while the L takes you to the piers of an abandoned bridge. Either of these points may be used as alternate put-in sites or take-out for a shorter trip, although the access road is often muddy during the spring when water levels are most favorable.)

After carrying around the dam on the L bank, you can either put in below it or carry further down the L bank till milder rapids are found. The several hundred yards immediately below the dam are among the toughest on this run. The preferred route is a quick ferry to the R side of the river in order to avoid a large hydraulic in the middle. Continue R until passing a large boulder about 50 feet from the R bank; then bear L or straight ahead. This section is Class III-IV and a flip here would result in a long swim where access to shore would be difficult. For this reason paddlers may prefer to put in downstream on the L bank.

In the next 2.4 m. between the dam and Lake Ozonia Outlet the river drops 200 feet for an average gradient of 83 feet per mile. Most of this section is lined with beautiful cedar banks. The river is full of Precambrian rocks and ledges resistant to erosion. There are no definite courses through these rapids; constant maneuvering is required.

Below the Class III-IV section described above the river gradually fades to Class II by the time it reaches the piers of the above-mentioned bridge at 0.5 m. below the dam. About 0.25 m. below the bridge the gradient steepens as the main current veers L of the first island. The next several hundred yards are Class III-IV. These gradually subside to Class I-II rapids until Lake Ozonia Outlet joins the river from the L.

It is 0.5 m. from Lake Ozonia Outlet to the bridge on the Days Mill Road, which connects Route 458 and the Port Kent Road. Below the bridge the rapids turn to easy Class I for about 1.1 m. Here there is a transition from the Precambrian rock of the Canadian Shield characteristic of the upstream stretches to a softer conglomerate, basically Potsdam sandstone. The character of the rapids changes from complex rock gardens requiring technical maneuvering to gently sliding ledges with standing and diagonally curling waves.

As the river takes a sharp turn to the R, the gradient again steepens as the banks close in. The last 2.2 m. are known locally as The Gorge and have an average gradient of about 50 feet per mile. Vertical or near vertical cliffs are separated by less steep slopes on which vegetation manages to cling. The white cedars, hemlocks, and white pines of the R bank are deeply gouged by the ice floes of spring breakups.

All the rapids in the upper part of The Gorge are relatively straightforward Class II-III and remind one of the Salmon River near Pulaski. About 2.0 m. below the Days Mills Road bridge are the remains of a concrete foundation for an old mill. It is advisable to pull out here to scout the rapid immediately below the ruins. There is a good eddy by the L bank to secure a boat, but scouting is made difficult by the steep banks. It may be easier to wade if water depth is not too great or temperature too cold. A Class IV rapid drops approximately 15 feet in 30 yards. A "sneak" route on the far L entails paddling down a shallow tongue of water and then punching through a moderate-sized hydraulic at the bottom. The preferred route requires you to begin on the R in order to avoid several wide, offset hydraulics near the top of the rapid. Approximately halfway down you can either go straight or angle to the L to end in the center of the rapid. Diagonally shaped waves tend to push the boat to the L anyway.

Below this rapid are several Class II-III rapids. At one, Miller Brook cascades dramatically into the river from the L. Take-out is on the R bank under the bridge on Route 11B. One may continue an additional 3.3 m., with an average gradient of 40 feet per mile, to Fort Jackson. This section consists of frequent Class II rapids which may be very rocky at low water. Take-out at Fort Jackson is at the bridge in the hamlet and is somewhat difficult because of the steepness of the banks.

On approaching Hopkinton from the W on Route 11B, motorists wonder about the sign announcing entrance to the Adirondack Park. All around are open pastures and fields of hay, corn, and potatoes. Could this be the Adirondacks? But kayakers on the Silver Staircase know the justification for this aberration of the Blue Line. And others can verify it by taking the all-purpose trail which begins across from the Nicholville cemetery on the Port Kent Road and runs about 3 m. upstream on a high terrace with glimpses through the pines of the vivid silvery dynamics of the river below.

EAST BRANCH

My first discovery of the East Branch as cruising water was in map reading. The old 15-minute *Santa Clara* map showed a reach of 15 m. with a drop of only 50 feet. Wonderful. Why hadn't I heard of it? A trial run increased the surprise and pleasure.

I soon found out why I hadn't heard of it. Posters throughout the stretch were intended to keep canoeists off the river as well as fishermen and hunters. This part of the East Branch was one of the river cruises of the northwest watershed entirely closed to the public or open only in part, not as continuous downstream floats. However, the situation on the East Branch is now improved over what it was prior to 1974.

The East Branch drains Meacham Lake. This large lake of 1.9 square miles at the headwaters helps to give the river a fairly equable flow all summer, as do the heavily wooded or marshy shores with their slow release of water. The average summer width is about 60 feet, though in marshy places the river sprawls out in sloughs and crescents of abandoned channel. Twenty-two miles long from Meacham Lake to confluence with the Middle Branch, the East Branch lies entirely within the Blue Line. The only dam is a state one at the outlet of Meacham Lake. The rest of the stream is in its natural state. The 15-m. reach lies in a U-shaped valley. The ridges on both sides rise from several hundred to a thousand feet above river level. During the retreat of the ice cap this valley was almost certainly a glacial lake, plugged at its N end by an ice lobe in the narrow gap where Everton Falls breaks over a sill of bedrock.

The East Branch is essentially a cruising river. The first 1.0 m. below Meacham Lake, however, represents an exhilarating but potentially dangerous run for expert whitewater paddlers. Immediately below the dam the East Branch drops 20 feet in 40 yards. This drop is extremely difficult (Class VI) and the prominent boulders at the bottom are particularly hazardous. Put in below this drop on the R, shortly before the foot trail enters posted land; the L bank is posted also. Scratchy Class II rapids predominate for the next quarter mile until a jeep trail and abandoned house appear on the R. Below here the river begins a series of turns as the gradient increases and rapids increase to Class III difficulty; stay L. In 100 yards the river becomes increasingly congested as rapids become Class IV for a short stretch before returning to Class III. In 150 yards the East Branch turns sharply R. Stay R for the next 60 yards as the river plummets through a highly technical Class V drop. The total drop is about 20 feet, with a notable 6-foot drop in the middle of the rapid. Below this point rapids return to Class III and briefly to Class III-IV before exiting the ravine. Rapids fade from here to the confluence with Rice Brook in 0.2 m. Paddlers may exit here or continue downstream as described below. Those considering the first mile below Meacham Lake are cautioned that all rapids are technical and scratchy, even during the spring. In addition, all rapids must be scouted from the river as both banks are privately owned.

The ideal float trip on the East Branch starts 1.0 m. below Meacham Lake and extends downstream to Everton Falls. Most of the 50-foot drop is concentrated in a 2.5 m. stretch where the hills close in. There are four rapids in this ravine, with the most difficult rated Class II. All can be run at medium high water with the precautions noted below, allowing a continuous run of 15.0 m. to Everton Falls. However, these rapids and a series of deadfalls which span the river pose a number of potential obstacles to a successful downstream trip. Carries around these obstacles are restricted and one risks prosecution for trespassing. The APA has recommended that an easement be negotiated for a canoe carry around the last rapids. Until such an easement is secured by the state, paddlers are advised not to attempt the full 15-m. downstream cruise. Therefore, this section of the East Branch will continue to be described in two discrete parts, below Rice Brook and above Everton Falls.

Take-out above Everton Falls was also restricted prior to 1974. Consequently, less than 3 of the 15 m. (the head of the run to the first rapid) were legally open to the public.

In 1974, however, The Nature Conservancy, through its Adirondack Committee, bought 530 acres around Everton Falls. This land runs for about 1.7 m. along both shores of the stream. Canoeists now have access at the Everton Falls Preserve.

Rice Brook to first rapid, 5.6 m. (9 km.) round trip, or 6.0 m. (9.7 km.) total to Nine-Mile Level
USGS: Meacham Lake 7.5

Access to this upper stretch is Rice Brook, which enters the East Branch 1.6 m. below Meacham Lake. Approaching from the E, one turns L off Route 30 onto Route 458. The embankment over Rice Brook is 0.9 m. from this junction. The banks on both sides of Route 458 are heavily posted. A legal put-in appears possible if canoeists stay strictly within the allowed right-of-way. The downstream end of the culvert is easier but is more likely to involve trespass and paddlers may find themselves confronting the landowner. In view of this difficulty and those described below it is advisable at this time to forego this section and put in at Everton Falls as described in the next section. (The new highway, relocated since the 1964 survey map, crosses the brook only 0.1 m. above the mouth.)

Rice Brook enters the river below fast water. About 1 m. downstream is a collapsed footbridge over which one can float. This part of the river is constricted between rising banks heavily wooded with conifers. Ranks of parallel and intersecting ridges make an interesting skyline, notched by spiry balsam firs. During the nesting season the shores are alive with warblers.

Continuing downstream, a second collapsed footbridge is encountered. Immediately below this footbridge is a collection of deadfalls which span the entire width of the river for a depth of 10 to 15 feet. Carries on the banks are conspicuously posted; carries over the deadfalls would be extremely difficult and are of questionable legality since the deadfalls are in contact with the shores and possibly the river bed. These deadfalls were observed at high water levels in the spring of 1986. It is possible that they may flush out over time, in which case no special obstacles are encountered above the first rapid. Otherwise, it will be necessary to turn around at this point, with the round-trip distance less than the 5.6 m. mentioned in the heading. Below the deadfalls are two minor rapids. The East Branch then approaches a high ridge on the R with a bench placed to overlook the river. Below this ridge is a Class I-II rapid and then the Class II rapid referred to in the introduction to the East Branch. This rapid is in front of Cedar Bridge Camp and drops two feet while passing under a low footbridge. Negotiation of this rapid requires simultaneous ducking and maneuvering and is much easier in a decked boat than in an open boat. Immediately below this footbridge is a second, even lower footbridge. The water is still here and at medium high water there is just enough clearance for a boat to pass if the paddler lies down in the boat. (At high water the clearance is less than 1 foot.) Since the owners of the camp prohibit carrying on shore or wading, downstream access is functionally barred unless paddlers are lucky enough to cruise during optimal water levels.

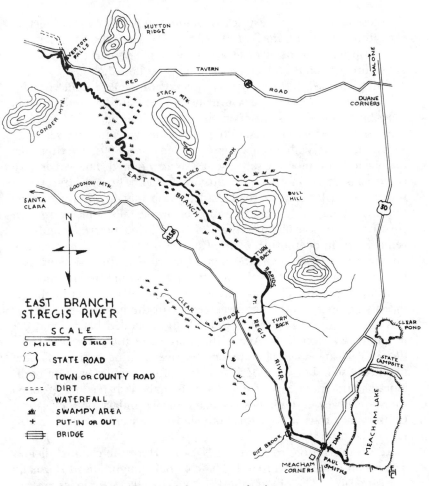

Nine-Mile Level, 18 m. (29 km.) round trip
USGS: Santa Clara, Lake Titus, Meacham Lake 7.5

The Nature Conservancy's purchase of the Everton Falls Preserve opens the Nine-Mile Level as a two-way cruise. This is a stillwater meandering through a marsh which varies in width from 100 yards to over a mile. Beyond the marsh grasses, spirea, leatherleaf, willow, and holly, long files of spruce and balsam fir mark the bases of the hills. Scattered groves of white cedar and white pine appear along the banks. The higher slopes are covered with aspen and the northern hardwoods. The APA recommended originally a classification of "wild river" for this segment but later changed it to "scenic," probably at the insistence of a paper company and its lessees.

Access is the Red Tavern Road (Route 99) 8 m. W of its junction with Route 30 or 7.2 m. E of St. Regis Falls. Here the road makes a close approach to the river in a narrow pass between hills. Everton Falls plunges about 18 feet over smooth granite ledges.

This place has a history. After completion of the Port Kent-Hopkinton Turnpike about 1830, a tavern and inn for teamsters and a sawmill were built at the falls. Later in the century the hamlet of Everton grew up as the conifer forest of the river valley was intensively logged. When the marketable timber gave out in the 1890s, Everton, like many another lumbering settlement, was abandoned. The woods have come back to cover this once thriving scene. The only traces that remain are a logging railroad grade, a crib pier in the river above the falls, a pillar of stone and masonry below the falls, some overgrown clearings, and possibly an artifact of plain living not yet found and removed from deep brush by the Conservancy's cleanup crews; also, on the *Santa Clara* map, the name "Everton," which designates a loop road, a segment of the old turnpike, parallel to the modern blacktop highway. The eastern quarter mile of the Everton Road, directly across from the falls, was the site of the hamlet.

A carry trail of 125 feet is located on a wooded bank about 0.2 m. above Everton Falls. Above this put-in site the Nine-Mile Level (9.3 m.) is canoeable all summer, the river cutting a deep channel in alluvial soil. The meandering stream often doubles back on itself. Sloughs and fragments of old channels make rich feeding grounds for waterfowl. At 1 m. posters mark the boundary of the Nature Conservancy tract. Above this both shores are leased to game clubs; do not land on them.

At 1.3 m. is a big rock on the N bank. Here the channel divides around an oval-shaped island. The channel straight ahead is usually not canoeable. The one on the R should be taken. It circles around the island in quickening current. Two short rifts challenge passage, but they can be surmounted if the course is well chosen. This is the only bedrock exposure and the only fast water on the Nine-Mile Level.

About a mile above this mild rapid is the boat landing of the Red Tavern Club. At 4 m. is a pine grove on a low eminence known as Burnt Knoll. Above this, Little Cold Brook makes its obscure way into the river. The next landmark is an unusually long straight-of-way lined with tall balsam fir. Another 1.5 m. of windings run to the edge of the *Santa Clara* topo map. The next mile is shown on the lower L corner of *Lake Titus*. Here Big Cold Brook comes in from the E.

The meanders continue for another 1.5 m. in the section shown on the *Meacham Lake* map. Then the marsh ends as wooded banks close in, the stream straightens out somewhat, and the current quickens. Whether one can surmount the first mild rapid that now appears depends on determination and the water level. Ahead, at the second upstream rapid, the Jennings Road (now abandoned) once crossed the river. United States troops used it on a march through the wilderness from Lake Champlain to Lake Ontario in the War of 1812. Where it once crossed there is now a private footbridge.

The return trip to Everton Falls (the only legal put-in or take-out) can usually be made in three-fifths of the time of the upstream one. The skyline looks quite different in the perspective of the downstream float.

Two nature trails of less than a mile each are maintained in the Everton Falls Preserve. Both start on the highway, one on the N side 0.3 m. above the falls and the other on the S side 0.5 m. below the falls. They are marked with silver discs.

Camping is not permitted on Nature Conservancy preserves. However, there is a 350-acre tract of state Forest Preserve, where camping is permitted, on the L bank 0.9 m. below the falls. To reach it, put in at Bristol Brook (the first culvert on the highway below Everton Falls) and paddle downstream 0.6 m., in a canyon of balsam fir, to the head of a Class I rapid. Scout it from the L bank to check on water level and ledges to avoid. In summer it is usually necessary to carry on the L bank. The W property line of the Conservancy tract crosses the pool below the rapid. The L shore for the next 0.1 m. is privately owned, but at the head of another rapid and cascade the E boundary of the Forest Preserve tract is reached. There is a good landing in a cove at the head of fast water. (Note that, on breaking camp, you must paddle upstream to the property line of the Conservancy tract and follow it 100 yards out to the highway.)

Lower East Branch and the St. Regis Falls Level, 9 m. (14.5 km.)
USGS: Santa Clara, Saint Regis Falls 7.5

Below the W boundary of Everton Falls Preserve, the next 3 m. of the East Branch cannot be run without carries on posted lands, especially at Jewell Falls. The last 2.3-m. stretch above the mouth, however, is bordered by state land and, in combination with the level above St. Regis Falls on the Middle Branch, makes a pleasant downstream run interrupted by two or three carries. This trip should be made in spring or fall or a day or two after heavy rains in summer. The rapids of the lower East Branch are too shallow to be run at water levels below medium high. The cascade midway down the first and longest of these rapids is difficult to negotiate safely, but the two other rapids are easily runnable with sufficient water. The drop is about 35 feet. This section of the East Branch is shown on the sketch map of the St. Regis Falls Level of the Middle Branch, p. 137.

To reach put-in, drive W from Everton Falls nearly 5 m., or E from St. Regis Falls 2.5 m., on the Red Tavern Road. Turn E then S on the Trim Road (avoid the Trim Hill Road). At 2 m., just beyond a ruined log cabin on the L, turn L through a field reforested with young pines. This spur soon enters the woods, again emerges into a meadow, and ends on a high bank above a loop in the East Branch. This is state land suitable for camping. From here one can paddle upstream 0.5 m. before encountering rapids.

Downstream from the landing, the river describes three horseshoe bends and then straightens out at the base of the Pinnacle of Conger Mountain, 550 feet above the river. The rest of the course to the mouth is a winding gorge with steep banks beautifully wooded with balsam fir and white cedar. In about 1 m., around a R bend, the first and heaviest stretch of whitewater is encountered. Rapids quickly escalate to Class III until a series of ledges is encountered approximately 150 yards from the beginning of the rapids. The first ledge drops about 4 feet, followed shortly by a second drop of about 8 feet, and then by a final drop of 4 feet over a ring of boulders just submerged at medium high water. These three ledges occur over a distance of only 50 yards and are rated Class IV-V. The first two drops are relatively straightforward, although the current is swift and the hydraulics large. The last drop is scratchy with only a few narrow channels possible; the swiftness of the current makes it difficult to identify the channels and align properly for them. Scouting is highly recommended. Note that the eddies above the ledges are small and difficult to enter, so scouting is best begun from the beginning of the rapids. At the head of the rapids there is a carry trail on the L bank so faint that one soon loses it in the brush. Close to the river the going is rough and often wet. An alternative is to angle up a slope to the top of the ridge, where an old logging road parallel to the river makes the footing secure but adds distance. The whole carry of about 0.3 m. should be reconnoitered without a load to find the best route. If the water level is adequate, the mild rapid below the cascade can be run to shorten the carry.

The next stretch of fast water is about 0.4 m. below the first. With enough water, it is sheer fun. Keep the canoe pointed into the strongest current.

The last rapid above the mouth rounds a sharp bend. The ribbon of strong current is even narrower here. Below this, the East Branch empties into the Middle, which is noticeably wider and deeper.

For 0.35 m. below the junction, the Middle Branch is smooth. Easy rapids start at a L bend. Those wishing to avoid these rapids should take out on the L bank and follow a trail 0.1 m. to the South River Road. Carry 0.2 m. down the road to another trail which leads to the base of a cascade. The cascade and the rest of the route to the picnic ground in St. Regis Falls are described above (Middle Branch IV, p. 135). The whole distance is 9 m. The trip takes four to five hours with ample allowance for lunch and carries.

OSGOOD RIVER

The Osgood is a miniature river; hardly more than a creek, in fact. But it is one of the most delightful cruising streams in the Adirondacks. Inconspicuous on the map and only 14.5 m. long, it is usually overlooked by canoeists. As the principal feeder of Meacham Lake, it is in reality an upland extension of the drainage of the East Branch of the St. Regis. All but 3 m. of its course is canoeable.

Except for a few camps on the lower third of the stream, the Osgood is untouched by development. Most of its course is in, or borders, state land. Its shores are varied in vegetation and contour, rising steeply in piny eskers and flattening in spruce and tamarack swamps, sphagnum bogs, or swales of grass, alders, and backwater. Pendent to the stream are several ponds in deep pockets of the hills, their short outlets cutting through the narrow esker that separates them from the river.

The Osgood is a specimen garden of the North Woods. It is rich in interest to the amateur botanist, geologist, and ornithologist or to any lover of uneven ground and moving water.

In the days of Paul Smith the stream was better known than it is now. It is part of a water route from Meacham Lake to Paul Smiths via McColloms, Chain Lake, Follensby Jr. Pond, and the Middle

Branch of the St. Regis. From McColloms on, this route is now closed to the public.

The Osgood is deep enough for navigation throughout the summer. In a few swampy places it spreads out to 100 feet or more, but the characteristic width of 25–40 feet keeps one in intimate touch with the shores. Along with its pond headwaters and Meacham Lake at its mouth, it can agreeably fill two days of cruising, with time to spare for side excursions. State-land boundaries (two thirds of the river corridor) are shown on the 7.5-minute *Meacham Lake* map, so that one can tell where to land and stretch amidst the pine needles and blueberries of the Osgood River Esker or where to camp overnight. In camping, a stove is advisable. There is risk of starting a ground fire in the dry duff of the esker, where there is no bedrock to build fires on.

At this writing the APA has released its recommendations (not yet approved by the Legislature) for classifying the Osgood under the Rivers System. Its measurement of the length of the stream, 12.6 m., is I believe an underestimate not taking meanders sufficiently into account. But the study team was impressed, calling the Osgood "an excellent canoeing" stream and "a worthy addition" to the Rivers System. The most interesting feature of the report is the recommendation that this short stream receive all three classifications: recreational (Osgood Pond area), wild (state land below Osgood Pond to the fire truck trail), and scenic (fire trail to Meacham Lake).

Headwaters of the Osgood, 10 m. (16.1 km.)
USGS: Saranac Lake, Saint Regis 15; Bloomingdale 7.5 × 15

The shores of Osgood Pond are private, but the pond can be reached by canoe from Jones Pond (Lucretia Lake) on the E or from Church Pond on the W. A cruise of 10 m., including 3 m. of retracement, can begin at one of these places and end at the other. Put-in at Church Pond takes advantage of prevailing winds.

There is a small landing on Church Pond 0.15 m. E of Paul Smiths corners on Route 86 at a dirt road on the N side. Paddle ENE through the hourglass-shaped pond (St. John's in the Wilderness is on the R at the narrows); through a navigable brook into Little Osgood Pond; and thence by a narrow, umbrageous canal into Osgood Pond. It is a varied passage with no carries.

The eastern approach is at the N shore of Jones Pond. From Paul Smiths, drive E about 1 m. to a fork in the road at the Brighton

Town Hall. Take the L fork here, a blacktop which soon skirts Jones Pond after crossing the bridge over the outlet. There are two or three put-in sites close to the road, in the vicinity of a carry trail to Rainbow Lake. The state-owned shores around the SW half of Jones Pond are mostly swampy, but a point of dry land on the N shore near the outlet is state owned and suitable for camping. Jones Pond is at its best in late October, when the tamarack thickets on the SW shore are a mass of glowing antique gold against a background of dark evergreens.

The outlet is a quiet stream dropping only one foot in its 1.5-m. course to Osgood Pond. Except for one short stretch of shoals, where wading is usually necessary, the stream is deep enough to float a canoe through summers of normal rainfall. Birds are attracted by the varied, lush vegetation rooted in the deep glacial soil of what Chadwick calls Paul Smith's Esker, a long sinuous ridge from Onchiota SW past Jones Pond to Osgood Pond. (Michael Kudish believes that the W end of this ridge is not an esker but an outwash valley train.) The brook is at its best in late May, when warblers are active and the pastel colors of emerging foliage contrast with dark evergreens. A half mile from the mouth one passes under a bridge on a blacktop road which services camps on Osgood Pond and allows river access.

On entering the pond, paddle NW into the deep bay of the overflow, or Osgood River. From headlands on the pond, a stillwater extends downstream 3 m. The river is wide for about 2 m., narrows for 0.5 m. to a W bend, widens again, and finally funnels into a ravine of shallow rapids with a low log dam at the head. This marks the end of navigation. Only the fanatic will stick with the next 3 m. Bill Frenette, who did, reports having an interesting walk under his kayak. An expecially troublesome area is known among trappers as the Thousand Islands, a wetlands jungle where, in one place, the river pours through a hole in the ground and vanishes. Bill calls his trip "good for character building, patience, perseverance, etc. The river does disappear. I had laughed at that prospect in your description until I found myself in a cul de sac and no sign of where in hell the river was! It goes down a hole like the last water from the tub. A miniature whirlpool." This on a postcard report of his trip.

Turn back and make the best of your disappointment by studying the shores on the retracement. Greenleaf Chase describes the upper Osgood as follows: "To see and feel the spruce swamp and bog in true dimensions, take a canoe trip . . . [across] Osgood Pond to about a mile below on its outlet. Here the spruce-tamarack swamp close on both sides suddenly gives way to a large sphagnum bog on the

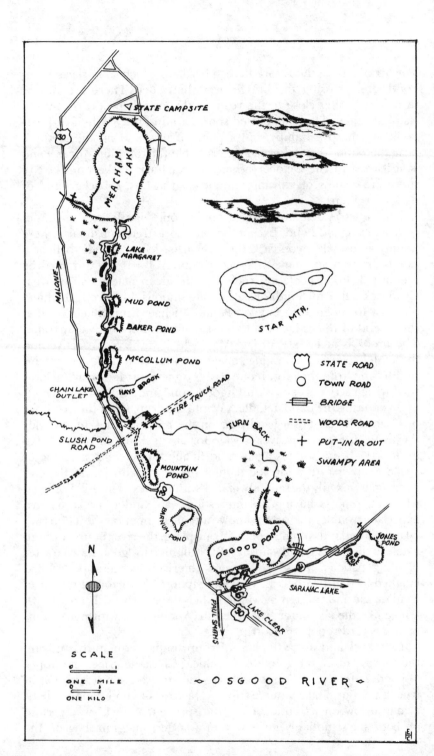

STATE CAMPSITE

MEACHAM LAKE

30

MALONE →

LAKE MARGARET

MUD POND

BAKER POND

McCOLLUM POND

CHAIN LAKE OUTLET

HAYS BROOK

FIRE TRUCK ROAD

SLUSH POND ROAD

TURN BACK

STAR MTN.

STATE ROAD
TOWN ROAD
BRIDGE
WOODS ROAD
PUT-IN OR OUT
SWAMPY AREA

MOUNTAIN POND

30

BARNUM POND

OSGOOD POND

JONES POND

SARANAC LAKE

PAUL SMITHS

30

LAKE CLEAR

N

SCALE

0   1
ONE MILE
0   1
ONE KILO

← OSGOOD RIVER →

west side. At the confluence of Blind Brook one can venture out on an almost pristine muskeg wildness. Brown-capped chickadees flitting along the edge and the spotting of a clump of white-fringed orchis make this a memorable trip." After an APA study of the upper half of the stream in May 1977 by Gary Randorf and George Nagle, Gary remarked in a letter: "It is a rich area botanically and wildlife-wise. We saw black duck, hooded merganser, mallard, osprey, sharp-shinned hawk, red-tailed hawk, great blue heron, ruffed grouse, beaver, king-fisher, spotted sandpiper, gray jay, and migrating warblers."

Turn WSW upon reentering Osgood Pond and pass the low green lawn of a point midway on the S shore. Head S between the point and an island into the deepest end of a sickle-shaped bay. Here is a launch site, accessible from a road a quarter mile N of Route 86. Just to the W, a little probing will disclose the entrance of the narrow canal, dug by hand about 1900 so that summer cottagers could float to services at St. John's or to dinner at Paul Smith's Hotel. A nature trail parallels the canal, passing several lean-tos owned by Paul Smith's College but accessible to the public on a first-come, first-served basis. The cruise ends at the SW corner of Church Pond. Gravestones in the cemetery on the knoll bear such names as Apollos (Paul) Smith, Clifford Pettis, and Edward Livingston Trudeau.

Lower Osgood and Meacham Lake, 8.5 m. (13.7 km.)
USGS: Saint Regis 15, Meacham Lake 7.5; Saint Regis Mtn. 7.5 × 15

Among flatwater cruises the lower Osgood is unsurpassed in variety of riverine scenery. The last advance and retreat of the glacier modified its course, hollowed wetlands and kettle ponds tributary to the main stream, and deposited eskers on which pines flourish in the deep mineral soil.

The Osgood flows into Meacham Lake. The cruise ends with a crossing of the S bay of the lake into the outlet (East Branch of the St. Regis). The take-out is a state parking lot at a dam over the outlet and a highway bridge on Route 30, 0.15 m. N of the junction of Route 458.

The put-in designated in previous editions of this guide, the Route 30 bridge at Spring Lake Outlet, has been abandoned for several reasons: possible encroachment on private land, congestion on the highway as canoes are unloaded, limited parking, and the fact that this site is below a beautiful upstream corridor.

Three put-in sites, all on state land, are now recommended. The two uppermost are N of Mountain Pond and are reached by the eastward extension of the Slush Pond Road off Route 30, marked by a sign "Hayes Brook Horse Trail." This is 3.8 m. N of Paul Smiths or 5.6 m. S of the take-out site. Drive 0.4 m. on this woods road to the second of two parking areas and look for the gate of a fire truck road on the N side. This road, with branches, makes a fine hiking trail through both pine reforestation and natural growth. The glossy leaves of trailing arbutus carpet the forest floor for over a mile N of the gate in what may be the largest concentration in the Northeast of this now rare flower. Called "Plymouth Mayflower" on the Massachusetts coast, it was, according to Whittier, the first flower to greet the Pilgrims after their winter of hardship. Here it usually blooms about the middle of May. Look for the waxy pink and white blooms hidden under the leaves and enjoy the scent but do not otherwise disturb the plants.

Carry 0.4 m. over the fire road and put in just upstream of the bridge. The river is very narrow here and may be too obstructed for passage. If so, carry back up the fire road 50 yards to a point halfway around the first bend to the L. A faint foot trail to the R leads to a good landing. The first 0.5 m. is a sporty run in strong current and a narrow channel. Windfalls may be a hazard. Clumps of royal fern are prominent in the lush vegetation of the banks. Where the stream divides, keep L. Alders and willows now close over the channel and oblige you to duck or clutch at branches to slow the craft, disengage it from a tangle, and guide it. There are three reasons for choosing this access during May: cool weather for the carry; medium high water to ease passage in the narrow channel; and, down on your knees, surprising shy, fragrant arbutus bloom. From this access, the float to take-out is 8.5 m.

Don't suppose that you are less privileged if the month is June or any other. The Osgood is an all-season charmer among cruising rivers, even if the state legislature has blindly refused for several years to elevate it from a "study" river to an officially classified one. The next two put-ins have the advantage of shorter, though rougher, carries. To reach the first of these, drive 0.3 m. E on the same Slush Pond Road to the first large parking area on the L, an inverted V in shape. At the point of the V continue N 0.3 m. to the end of a section of the old Route 30 before it was relocated to the W. A circular clearing is large enough for two cars to park and turn around. Parties of several cars and canoes should drive over this spur by twos, unload, and return to the large parking area or to the take-out site. As a courtesy to other possible users, no car should be left at this dead-end.

The carry to the river is about 450 feet long over a course flagged with both yellow and orange plastic ribbons. The Ray Brook office of the DEC recognizes that a cleared carry trail is desirable here but is barred from making it till a unit management plan for this area, the Debar Mountain Wild Forest, authorizes such a trail. The flagged course starts at the R of a large white pine on the east (R) side of the clearing; avoid what appears to be a trail at the north end of the clearing. The flagged course is a moderately rough bushwhack over a faint trail blocked by deadfall and reaching the river at a lone cedar tree. Users of this access should paddle upstream a quarter mile for a view of the deep gorge between parallel eskers topped by tall white pines.

The third access is a new one, replacing the narrow, obstructed access via Chain Lake Outlet as described in earlier editions. Like the previous access it misses some upstream scenery but allows a relatively easy point of entry. It is off Route 30, 1.1 m. N of Slush Pond Road (4.2 m. S of Route 458). Park on the N side of a short section of guard rail along the E side of the highway. Parking is limited here to several cars. The 100 yard-long carry begins about 20 feet to the L of a State Forest Preserve sign and is marked with orange ribbons. It is through a fairly open stand of conifers, down and then back up a small depression. Near its end it is necessary to carry (or slide) down a steep embankment about 20 feet high. Put-in is a small, shallow slough. Paddle or line about 75 feet to the river. Additional orange ribbons mark this point for those making a return trip.

Above the mouth of Chain Lake Outlet the Osgood River Esker is often double, lining each shore. Below the mouth it is a single ridge on the R bank. With interruptions, it parallels the stream for the next several miles and is the distinctive scenic feature of the lower Osgood. It provides the sunny location and deep glacial soil favorable for pine, and groves of both white and red pine are well established on it. In some places the steep bank, carpeted with pine needles and berry bushes, drops directly to water's edge. The crest of the ridge is a pleasant solitary place to walk on.

Hays Brooks comes in on the R, its mouth choked with an impassable alder thicket; upstream, where a branch of the fire road crosses Hays, the brook is navigable, but a long carry is necessary to reach it. In another 0.3 m. Spring Lake Outlet comes in on the L.

Below this point, the Osgood swings away from the traffic noise of the highway. The channel is meandering and the current slow. The valley alternately narrows between high, pine-clad banks and sprawls out in marshes, where sloughs and fragments of old channels complicate the course. Ceaseless change is the order of this entrancing stream. In two places high banks and tall trees on both sides form miniature canyons. There are numerous deadfalls and beaver dams.

Early August is a colorful season on this part of the stream. Wildflowers then in bloom include yellow loosestrife, monkey-flower, fireweed, pickerelweed, wild calla, closed gentian, turtlehead, joe-pye weed, purple-fringed orchis, and the incomparable cardinal flower. About 0.7 m. below Spring Lake Outlet, where the river washes the base of the esker, a climb to the ridge top discloses McColloms Pond on the other side.

McColloms is the first of four ponds on the R, mostly hidden from view by the esker. Three of them drain into the Osgood through breaks in the ridge. All three are worth a visit either by climbing the esker or, in the case of Baker and Mud ponds, paddling up the short outlets. Baker, the prettiest, is at its best on a still, sunny day in October. Lake Margaret, the fourth pond, is landlocked.

By beaching your canoe on the SE shore of Mud Pond and climbing the ridge to the E, you can intersect a hunters' trail that skirts the S slope of Cherry Hill. A more interesting excursion is bushwhacking up Star Mountain, which from an open ledge on top gives a view S and SE over the Hays Brook valley. To climb the mountain, beach the canoe on state land about 200 yards downstream from the outlet of Mud Pond and circle N and then E into a draw. Ascend the draw eastward, and near its head set your course ENE at 55 degrees, corrected from true north. This should take you to the top of the W peak of the Star range. The round trip takes about two hours. On your return to the river, you should not have to spend more than five minutes looking for your canoe. Topo map and compass are essential.

In its last mile the Osgood winds through a wide marsh accented by a few gray skeletons. Berry shrubs cover these wetlands, which are a nesting ground for redwings in spring and a feeding ground for cedar waxwings in late summer and fall.

As you emerge from the mouth into Meacham Lake, beside several white cedars, Debar Mountain is prominent to the N. Paddle across the shallow S end of the lake. In 0.5 m. the outlet (East Branch of the St. Regis) is reached. Follow this 0.6 m. to a landing and parking lot near the state dam and the highway bridge on Route 30. If your party has two cars, one will have been left here. If not, and if you have no bike for the shuttle, a favorable spot for picking up a ride back to the Mountain Pond Road is a filling station, tavern, and a motel 0.2 m. S on the highway. A one-car party can of course begin and end a cruise on the lower Osgood at the Meacham Lake outlet. The Osgood bears doubling.

Instead of ending the trip on the outlet, one can paddle N 2 m. on Meacham Lake to the large state campsite. Meacham is entirely surrounded by Forest Preserve. The state campsite, however, opens the lake to a summer influx of powerboats.

A trail from the state campsite leads to the summit of Debar Mountain in 3.7 m. The first two miles are a pleasant walk through woods over rolling ground; most of the ascent is concentrated in the last 1.7 m., with a final very steep pitch. Debar is the dominant peak of the Osgood River-Meacham Lake valley, rising to 3,305 feet. Views from the summit are somewhat obstructed now that the fire tower has been removed.

DEER RIVER

The Deer River has its source in the brooks of Debar Mountain not far from the northern boundary of the park. From its principal headwater pond, Lake Florence, it flows NW across Franklin and St. Lawrence counties to merge with the main stem of the St. Regis at Helena before emptying into the St. Lawrence a few miles below.

The Deer is nearly everything a river can be except big. It is surprisingly narrow for its length of nearly 70 m. Those who see it at the few access points in the upper half of its course might conclude that it is uncanoeable for any worthwhile distance. This is not so. Its still waters run deep. And in rough water sections some of the rapids can be run at medium to high water in spring and fall. Elsewhere short carries suffice.

The Deer is miniature, secretive with its closely compressed banks, small shady pools, underground rivulets honeycombing spruce thickets, funnelings in bedrock, islets in braided channels, and ribbony meanderings in a remote silent meadow. The canopy over one divided fall and round pool is so dense you have the feeling of entering a cavern. It is a stream for trout fishermen and connoisseurs of little rivers.

For the cruising canoeist, the greatest attraction is a winding 8-m. level known as Deer River Meadows. This is a narrow, secluded, tidily wild valley flanked by ranges rising 600 feet above the valley floor. It is probably the bed of a postglacial lake once plugged at the N

end by a moraine delta and sill of bedrock, now the site of High
Falls. Alders obscure the view in the lower half of the meadow. But
in most of the upper half there are open views over parklike flats to
enclosing hills. It is an other-worldly place. No river corridor in the
northwest sector of the park gives so complete a sense of isolation
and remoteness. "A memorable experience," said a paddling companion of mine as we completed the cruise at Newbridge.

In the past, few intruders have visited the Meadows because of
the posted carries above them and the turbulent waters at the downstream access. In 1984 and 1985, however, a 14-m. downstream cruise
from the Red Tavern Road to Deer River State Forest, outside the
Blue Line, was opened to public canoeing for a limited spring season.
The St. Regis Paper Company (now merged with Champion International) agreed to enter into annual agreements with the Adirondack
Mountain Club to open the river in May and most of June. Several
members of the Laurentian Chapter of ADK were permitted to clear
six short carry trails in miles 2.4 to 4.2. Prospects for the future are
uncertain in view of the steep rise in liability insurance rates that
took place in 1986.

Deer River Flow, 2.7 m. (4.3 km.)
USGS: Lake Titus 7.5

Deer River Flow is an artificial widening in the town of Duane.
Above this backwater the Deer can be penetrated only a little way
before numerous deadfalls block the channel.

The Y-shaped flow can be legally entered at two ends. Fifteen miles
N of Paul Smiths, bridges on Route 30 and the Cold Brook Road
give access at the head. State land on Horseshoe Pond Outlet (S of
a bridge on the Red Tavern Road 0.5 m. W of Route 30) gives access
to the E prong of the Y.

The chief attraction of the flow is its mountain views. Its NW-SE
orientation provides a frame for the twin peaks Debar and Baldface.
Closer by, on the W, are two others whose names derive from an
enterprise of early settlers—Furnace and Orebed mountains. In 1838
the Duane brothers erected a forge for manufacturing iron. One of
the brothers, James, a son-in-law of the Adirondack landowner William
Constable, was the first settler in the town of Duane in 1825. The
best mountain view is obtained from the vicinity of the dam on the
W prong of the Y.

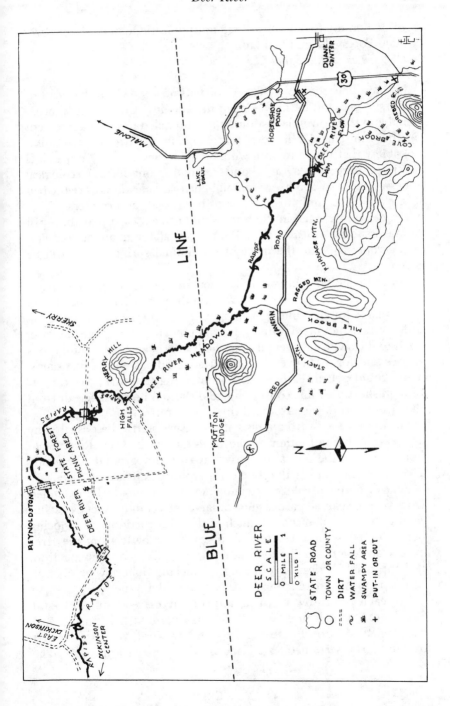

Bridge on the Red Tavern Road to upper bridge in the Deer River
State Forest, 14 m. (22.6 km.)
USGS: Lake Titus, Santa Clara, 7.5

In 1986 only the upper 2.4 m. of flatwater (down to the head of
the first rapid and back) was open to canoeing. Champion International and the Adirondack Mountain Club failed to reach agreement
on the 6-m. corridor in corporate ownership. Since there is still a
possibility that the route as a whole may be open in the future, it is
described here. It is a varied and fascinating one in four ecological
zones—marsh, spruce-fir swamp, hill-encircled meadows once the bed
of a glacial lake, and mixed forest of hardwoods and conifers.

Canoeists interested in the route should watch each year the April
or May issue of *Adirondac,* the ADK periodical, for an announcement.
If the route is open, the dates of the limited spring season will be
given.

Several conditions are necessary for an optimum trip. The party
should be a small one of not more than three craft. Two cars should
be available for the shuttle. You should be experienced in paddling
little rivers in mountain country. If work is not to overbalance pleasure,
you should have a lightweight canoe with yoke or a kayak for numerous
carries and for maneuvers at uncharted deadfalls and beaver dams.
You should get an early start, not later than 10 A.M.; the carries,
though short, are time consuming, and there is no possible exit from
the river short of the take-out bridge at 14 m.

For those coming from a distance, an early start is best assured by
an overnight camp either at the take-out site in Deer River State
Forest or near the put-in at a privately-run campground a half mile
E on the same road or the state campground at Meacham Lake.

Finally, if the privilege of canoeing this river is to be extended
from year to year, all parties must observe the conditions set by Champion International, owner of much of the river corridor; no canoeing
before or after the set dates; no access to or away from the river
except at designated sites; no littering; no hiking or straying from
the approved carries; no camping, picnicking, loitering or fires on
company property, which extends N to the Blue Line.

To reach put-in by the eastern approach, drive 18 m. N of Paul
Smiths on State Route 30 to Duane Corners, turn L on the Red
Tavern Road (County Route 14), and proceed W past the first
bridge to the second one, 2.3 m. By the western approach, take

the Red Tavern Road opposite the central school in St. Regis Falls for 12.5 m. to the Deer River bridge.

The Deer River State Forest at the take-out is worth visiting for itself. It contains over 10,000 acres along a scenic corridor of the Deer as it descends off the plateau. The area is tastefully planned and well maintained by a resident DEC unit. Small picnic areas are scattered for several miles along the water's course at cataracts, falls, gorges, or winding stillwater. The fact that all roads are sand or gravel helps to check overuse. Overnight camping is allowed free of charge. For longer stays a permit is required. The headquarters building is on a gravel road S of Route 11B from the hamlet of East Dickinson, a DEC sign marking the intersection.

The shuttle route on the E via Malone and Bangor is 31 m. The shorter western one is recommended. Drive W on the Red Tavern Road from the put-in site to St. Regis Falls, N to Dickinson Center, and E on the Cemetery Road, the extension of which enters the state forest. Continue E on the main gravel road past widely separated picnic sites to the first bridge. Just beyond it, take the L fork for about 2 m. to a traffic triangle at the Reynoldston Road. Take the R fork, cross the intersection, and continue E 1.5 m. to the uppermost bridge over the Deer, the take-out site. The total distance is 24 m.

The first segment below put-in is meandering flatwater in a marsh. The carries are concentrated in two comparatively short sections. The first of these, miles 2.4–4.2, is in Champion International property where members of the Laurentian Chapter of ADK have been permitted to clear and mark carry trails. The first two, at a rapid and a waterfall, are on the L bank; at the next rapid, on the R. The channel then divides around an island. Bear R and, if necessary, line your craft over a ledge. Soon you hear the second waterfall, a twin cascade. Carry on the R bank, launch again in the small pool below the falls, and paddle across it to an iron bridge on an abandoned road. The braided channel below the bridge is obstructed. ADK has cleared a carry on the R bank a little way back from the river. The last carry in this section is on the L bank at a small rapid.

At 4.5 m. the woods give way to the long marsh known as Deer River Meadows, and the stream is now a meandering stillwater of 7.5 m. in a bed of sand and silt. There are no obstructions now except a possible beaver dam not flushed out in the spring breakup. Relax and enjoy your situation. It could hardly be improved if the date is May 20 to 27, the skies clear, the temperature 60 degrees with a light breeze, and the blackflies trailing behind as you keep moving with gentle strokes. The alders that at first line the banks soon end, and now the eye roves over an expanse of meadow grass tossed in the breeze. The low banks are as even and neat as if a giant plow had gouged out the sinuous channel. Seated, you ride just high enough to see over the banks to scattered hummocks of shrubbery in the marsh and to the slopes of Mutton Ridge on your L and Sugar Hill on your R. Narrow files of dark evergreens line the bases of the hills, and above them the hardwood slopes are in the year's subtlest color harmony, the pastel shades—buff, pale green, pink, rose—of catkins, flowers, and leaf buds beginning to open. Linger in these open spaces shut off from the world by the florescent hills, for alders will close in again in the lower half of the Meadows.

The Blue Line is crossed unnoticed at 7.5 m. At 10 m. a hunting camp looms up on the R, the only sign of man in the Meadows— the only building in the entire run. At 12 m. the hills that have enclosed the marsh converge to a narrow still of bedrock. As the glacier wasted, this gap was once plugged by a lingering ice lobe to form a backwater lake in the Meadows.

In the last two miles the Deer puts off its languor in a burst of renewed energy. The first half mile is particularly trying. Shortly after a camp on the R the sound of High Falls becomes audible. High Falls begins as a narrow, twisting Class VI drop settling down to Class IV ledges. It is a very dangerous rapid, prone to logjams, and only the bottom portion can be considered runnable. The carry on the R bank is actually an unimproved bushwhack, best attempted a little way back from the river where the woods-wise may faintly discern an overgrown logging trace. Below the falls and its downstream ledges is a short level of 0.25 m. before a series of two Class II drops followed by a Class III-IV drop. Here the L bank is only slightly less impossible than the honeycombed R one, and wading through the shoals may be preferable. Nearly a mile of flat water ensues before two short rifts signal the beginning of another display of gymnastics, this time an unrunnable falls followed by a short Class III drop just before the bridge. Here the state owns both banks, and you will find two short carries on the R bank around the rifts and a final carry on the L around the falls.

As the terminal cataract becomes audible, draw into the pointed end of a cove of rock on the L. The last carry of nearly 0.2 m. extends to the take-out bridge, where a car should be waiting for you. You might have arranged with a friend to drive you to put-in and then to go to the take-out. Your friend should not be bored in passing the day exploring and trout fishing in this delightful park.

Deer River State Forest, Newbridge to Church Road Bridge, 8.6 m. (12.2 km.)
USGS: Santa Clara, Saint Regis Falls 7.5

This section of the Deer River is a study of remarkable contrasts. The section below the upper bridge (Newbridge) contains intermediate-size rapids alternating with quiet stretches. The drop is 80 feet in 2.6 m. with most of it occurring in the first half. The next section from Reynoldston Road bridge to the lower bridge in the State Forest is flat and meandering. Below the lower bridge is one of the steepest and most challenging sections of whitewater in the Adirondacks, much of which is runnable by advanced decked boaters during periods of very high water. The total drop is 200 feet in 3.1 m. Most of the gradient occurs in a concentration of rapids in the middle of the run. Paddlers may run this entire section of the Deer or choose a shorter section more suited to their tastes. A number of take-out sites make the latter choice possible.

Put-in for this section is the upper bridge in the Deer River State Forest on a gravel road connecting the Reynoldston Road with the Walkerville Road. Directions to this bridge are given in the previous section. From the put-in the Reynoldston Road bridge is reached by going back W for 1.5 m. to the first intersection, turning R, and proceeding N for 1.0 m. The lower bridge is reached by proceeding straight through the above intersection and going SW for an additional 1.7 m. The Church Road Bridge (not shown on sketch map) is reached from Dickinson Center by proceeding 1.9 m. NE on the Cemetery Road and turning R onto Church Road. It can be reached from the lower bridge in the State Forest by proceeding 2.5 m. NW to the intersection with Cemetery Road, turning L for 0.8 m., and then L again on Church Road.

At Newbridge there is a carry trail on the R below the bridge. This enables the paddler to bypass a complex and dangerous Class VI drop. Put in 200 feet downstream from the bridge at the first pool or run the last Class III-IV drop before the pool. Flatwater continues for 0.25 m. above two Class III drops. Each of these is scratchy but can be run down the middle into moderate-sized hydraulics at the bottom. Scouting is advised because of the scatchiness. A Class II rapid follows and then, at the first island, a Class III rapid.

Another Class II rapid and then a Class I are encountered before a tapering to flatwater for 0.5 m. After a sharp turn to the L the river constricts noticeably at a washed-out dam. There is a short carry trail on the R at a break in the dam wall. The wall continues 100 feet to the end of a short dirt road connecting with the Reynoldston Road. Put in across from the first house on this road. It is possible to run the short, narrow Class III drop over the dam, but an immediate turn to the L is required in order to avoid a large boulder. This area tends to be heavily constricted with deadfalls, however; careful scouting is advised. The Reynoldston Road bridge is reached in another 0.2 m. and can serve as an alternative put-in or take-out.

The Deer now assumes a major change in character as it becomes flat and meandering, eventually flowing past the lower bridge at 5.5 m. This section is a dense marsh with alders bordering the river. Many dead elms appear as sentinels standing watch. At 5.2 m. evergreens begin to crowd the banks as the current quickens and forms a Class I rapid. The lower bridge appears shortly thereafter.

This bridge serves as a convenient take-out. The next section drops 200 feet in only 3.1 m., resulting in an average gradient of 64 feet per mile. The gradient is quite deceiving, though, as much of the drop is concentrated in a particularly steep, narrow stretch. This is a section for expert paddlers willing to scout frequently. Either bank suffices for short carries; longer carries are generally easier on the R bank. Below the picnic area is an easy Class I rapid. Then the Deer pulls out all stops. At the next drop the river plummets over 20 feet in three channels. The left and middle channels are Class VI drops; the right channel drops 3 feet into a hydraulic before screaming into a 160-degree turn to the L through an 8 foot wide chasm. This highly unusual drop is rated Class IV-V and sets the stage for what is to follow. All rapids from here to the next picnic area are highly technical, require careful scouting, and can only be negotiated by precise maneuvering. At least 12 distinct drops rated between Class III and V follow the first major drop. For all practical purposes most of these run together to form far more complicated drops. Notable among these are a 100 yard long Class IV beginning at the top of a boulder garden, a series of Class V drops around an island across from a small cabin, and a Class IV-V zigzag around a boulder. The first campsite by the road is visible after this last drop at 7.1 m. Below the campsite is a 300 yard long Class III followed by a tumultuous 150 yard long Class V as the river turns R and drops very quickly. Immediately below this rapid is a 16-foot falls, which continues under a footbridge to a Class VI drop. The Forest Road is adjacent to the river at this point (7.5 m.) and can serve as another take-out. Paddlers choosing to continue may put in 30 yards below the footbridge at the top of a 100 yard long Class III-IV rapid. This rapid gradually tapers to quick-moving water which continues to the Church Road Bridge 1.1 m. below the falls. Class III rapids are visible below this bridge and may look enticing. However, there is no permissible take-out before the bridge in Dickinson Center, where the river begins yet another Class IV-V descent over a series of dangerous ledges.

The upper Oswegatchie, East Branch, and *below,* virgin pines above High Falls

Garrie Stevens

S. S. Slaughter

Pink granite troughs and flanks of the Oswegatchie's Middle Branch

Perry Yaw

Above, Massawepie Lake, between twin eskers.
Below, Lampson Falls, Grass River

Duncan Cutt

Two flumes of the Grass River below Lampson Falls—Don Morris
in the kayak

S. S. Slaughter

Raquette River
Above, The beach in Long Lake Village
Below, Moody Falls

Thomas Finch

On the Jordan River

Herbert McAneny

St. Regis Canoe Area
Left, The carry
Below, Green Pond

Clyde Smith

James Schaller

Duncan Cutter

Middle Branch St. Regis
Above, Outlet of Lower St. Regis Lake
Left, The Silver Staircase near Nicholville

Duncan Cutter

East Branch of the St. Regis
Above, The stillwater above Everton Falls
Below, Everton Falls

Duncan Cutter

Deer River
Above, A hidden-away waterfall
Below, Bill Frenette running the rapids

Duncan Cutter

Saranac River
Above, A campsite on Middle Saranac Lake
Below, Aquatic garden on the river between Middle and Lower Saranac lakes

Duncan Cutter

Rainbow Lake Esker, dividing waters that feed the North Branch of the Saranac

Bradford Van Diver

Mountain-ringed marshes of the upper Chubb River

Duncan Cutter

Whiteface Mountain from the Ausable's West Branch, near
the Conservation Monument

Betsy McCa

Above, Oxbow on the Boquet River above Wadhams
Below, Paul Jamieson, Middle Branch Oswegatchie

Duncan Cutter

SALMON RIVER

In general, rivers of the Adirondacks have fared better than mountains and ponds in attracting unique and stirring names. Names like "Oswegatchie," "Raquette," "Saranac," "Boquet," "Schroon," and "Sacandaga" are bait to canoeists. But folk imagination failed in scattering "Cat" or "Catamount" mountains and "Long" ponds all over the map and in naming four rivers of northern New York "Salmon," with a couple of "Little Salmons" thrown in. One of the Salmons rises on Tug Hill and flows into Lake Ontario below Pulaski. A second is N of Blue Mountain Lake. Another, in Clinton County, drains the NE slope of the Adirondacks, feeding Lake Champlain; it is not navigable within the Blue Line for any worthwhile distance. The fourth and northernmost, in Franklin County, rises in the brooks of the Elbow Range N of Loon Lake and takes a NNW course to empty into the St. Lawrence on the Canadian side of the border. It deserves a more distinctive name. People in Malone believe that there is no finer river in the Adirondacks.

A good way to make acquaintance with the Salmon is to do as the Maloners do on a Sunday afternoon: drive along the 12-m. stretch S of that county seat either on Andrus Street and the River Road or on Duane Street and the Duane Road. The river is often in sight. And for once, in settled country, Americans have not made a mess of a river corridor. The landscaping takes advantage of natural contours. The valley of trim suburban homes and farms gradually becomes wilder above Whippleville, a pleasant village where the two roads join as one. After winding upward through the gorge of Chasm Falls, the road breaks over the rim of the plateau and continues to border the river for nearly 2 m. more to The Bend.

Although most of this valley S of Malone was proposed for inclusion in park boundaries by the Temporary Study Commission of 1970, it was excluded in the extension enacted two years later. The reason is not clear. Below Chasm Falls is as pretty a reach of fast water as one could hope to find. The rapids are almost continuous and the gradient fairly steady. In spring it is a thrilling run for intermediate whitewater canoeists. The Malone Extension of North Country Community College used to sponsor canoe races here in late April or early May in Class II and III waters.

On the plateau above Chasm Falls are two cruising reaches of several miles each, one inside and one partly outside the Blue Line. The lower reach can be extended to a 9-m. downstream trip by starting on a tributary, Hatch Brook, and continuing down the Salmon, with no carries, to Chasm Falls. A third section, not recommended for cruising, lies mostly outside the Blue Line but is best reserved for enterprising paddlers with intermediate to advanced whitewater abilities.

Above Mountain View, 8 m. (12.9 km.)
USGS: Ragged Lake, Owls Head 7.5

In the 1850s the state built a dam on the upper Salmon to regulate the downstream flow for floating logs to mill. Mountain View Lake was thus created, and the outlet of Indian Lake was widened to the present broad channel connecting the two bodies of water. A small settlement grew up at the site of the dam. Mountain View, as it was called, became a popular summer resort after the Adirondack and St. Lawrence Railroad reached it in 1892. Hotels, inns, and summer cottages sprang up around the two lakes. But as tourist traffic shifted from railroad to auto, the hamlet went into decline. Passenger trains finally stopped running in 1957, and in 1960 the tracks were torn up. Today the hamlet of Mountain View has a shabby look. But summer residents have never ceased coming back to their camps on lakeshores.

Today the summer colony is growing again as people try to get away from main traffic lanes. Mountain View is favored by an isolated location on a mountain-ringed, split-level plateau. The name is appropriate. In all directions there is a bold skyline. Long flat-topped, craggy ridges alternate with conical peaks rising to 2,000 feet above Huckleberry Marsh, the lower level of the basin.

The river used to be navigable for small boats for 10 m. upstream from the dam at the foot of Mountain View Lake. But now a blowndown area cuts that distance in half. About 5 m. above the dam (2 by lake and 3 by river) is an abatis of fallen cedars across the narrow stream. Dense growth and blowdown make the shores nearly impenetrable for carrying. It would take hundreds of manhours of labor to clear the choked stream.

Under present conditions, the longest possible cruise above Mountain View starts at the public beach on Indian Lake. This is reached by driving 1.4 m. NW of Mountain View on the road to Owls Head and then turning R on a dirt road to the beach, where cars can be parked. The distance from here through Indian Lake, its outlet, and Mountain View Lake to the bridge over the Salmon on the Bryants Mill Road is 2.8 m. The Salmon gradually narrows as one paddles upstream. At 2.2 m. S of the bridge is a shallow sandbar. To go beyond this in the dry season, some wading is necessary. But in spring and fall one can keep afloat a mile farther before encountering the blowdown. Occasional mountain views open up. Kingfishers patrol the stream. Trout jump. Ducks and herons are commonly sighted.

If there are two cars in the party, the return downstream can be shortened by leaving one car at Bryants Mill bridge and ending the trip there instead of returning by the two lakes. In this case, the distance would be about 8 m. including the retracement on the river.

A pleasant side excursion in this area is the ascent of the prominent pyramidal peak, Sugarloaf. Though owned by a corporation, the land is unposted. From Bryants Mill bridge drive to the second jeep road on the R—the one just N of Deerfly Pond. Park here and hike NE on the jeep road to the edge of a high meadow, where Sugarloaf Mountain is in full view. Continue to follow the jeep tracks L across the meadow past clumps of quaking aspen. At about 0.4 m. the trail swings R away from the jeep tracks and into a depression. There is no sign, but the trail from here on has been marked with a combination of plastic lids and paint blazes—a red dot in a white field. It bears NE and E at a moderate grade. The hiking distance is about 1.4 m. to an outcropping just below the wooded summit on the W side. There are fine views of the valley of the Salmon, the two lakes, and the encircling peaks.

Mountain View Lake to confluence with Hatch Brook, 3.9 m. (6.2 km.)
USGS: Owls Head 7.5

The Salmon River plateau has two levels above The Bend. In the vicinity of Mountain View and Owls Head the elevation averages a little over 1,500 feet. The elevation of the flats known as Huckleberry Marsh is slightly under 1,300. Between these two levels the river slashes through bedrock on a steep staircase. High Falls, in a state forest just outside the Blue Line, is the most scenic part of the gorge. Hikers can reach it by driving 1.4 m. NW of Mountain View toward Owls Head and then turning L on the Barnesville Road. The trail to the falls is not marked. It starts as an obscure tote road about 0.2 m. S on the R side of Barnesville Road in a scrubby clearing. As the tote road enters the woods trending SW, it narrows to a trail. The walk to the head of the falls takes 10 to 15 minutes. Here is a small shady flat above the river, a stone fireplace, and space enough to pitch a tent, on state land.

Put-in for this section is immediately below the dam on the NW end of Mountain View Lake. Carry over a short foot trail beginning at Pond Road and proceeding on the R over an old railroad grade.

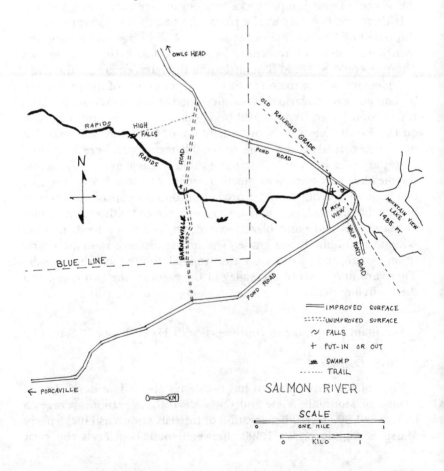

Boats may be launched below the dam or 15 yards further downstream below some riffles. In 0.2 m. the river flows beneath a spur road connecting two different portions of Pond Road. This bridge serves as an alternative put-in. Carry down the upstream R bank until you intersect a grassy jeep trail. Proceed an additional 20 yards and put in at a small clearing. It is 1.4 m. from here to the next bridge (now closed to traffic) on the Barnesville Road. To this point the river is flat with fair current and offers a short but appealing cruise. Cruising paddlers are advised to stop at Barnesville Road unless they are willing to make an arduous carry around High Falls and the rapids above and below it. The distance for this carry is slightly over a mile through dense undergrowth punctuated only occasionally by faint game trails. Cruising paddlers who wish to see this are advised to use the hiking trail as described above.

The next portion of the Salmon offers a short but interesting white-water run for those with intermediate to advanced skills. Two brief Class I rapids are encountered in the first 0.3 m. In the next 150 yards rapids quickly escalate, ending in a series of closely grouped and technical Class IV ledges and a 4-foot drop. Class I and II rapids continue below here for 0.3 m. to the foot of a small island. Stay L of the island and negotiate a straight 3-foot drop. Immediately exit on the R to carry around High Falls. High Falls is an unrunnable drop in two parts, the first of 35 feet and the second of 20 feet. The first drop is especially impressive as it twists and winds down a channel sometimes as narrow as 12 feet.

The gradient is very even in the next 0.9 m. below the falls. Rapids are continuous Class I and II, with brief spurts of Class III. Paddlers should note that this entire stretch of rapids is very rocky and is best suited to short boats. The rapids are best run at high water levels, even though eddies will be small and difficult to reach. Because of this, the overall difficulty rating for this section may be considered slightly higher than the above ratings for the rapids. The final half-mile to the confluence with Hatch Brook is smooth water.

Hatch Brook and Salmon River to Chasm Falls, 9 m. (14.5 km.)
USGS: Owls Head 7.5

Once the Salmon drops to the level of Huckleberry Marsh at the confluence of Hatch Brook, the next 4.4 m. to Chasm Falls is a delight-ful, scenic float. This lower level is best reached by putting in on Hatch Brook. The two streams together make a cruise of 9 m. A strong current moves one along at a fast pace. A non-stop float takes a little over two hours.

Put-in is at the bridge over Hatch Brook on the Pond Road 3 m. W of Mountain View on the way to Duane. Take-out is the bridge over the Salmon at Chasm Falls or the state picnic area and boat landing 0.8 m. above the bridge. Two cars are necessary for the trip unless one is ready to walk back to the starting point over the Duane Road and the California Road. Hitching a ride over these little traveled roads cannot be counted on. The walk of about 5 m. is an easy one over a sandy plain, covered with second-growth woods and almost as level as a landing strip. The road surface is firm enough for a shuttle by bicycle. Hops were once grown on these flats. The old farms are now abandoned, and the state has acquired the land.

Hatch Brook runs a corkscrew course of about 4.6 m. between the bridge on the Pond Road and the junction with the Salmon. If one uses the path at the SW corner of the bridge for launching, he should first inspect the rift under the bridge. At low water it is better to take a few strokes upstream and then, turning, draw close to the piling on the R. One can also make a short carry downstream on state land 50 yards W of the bridge; the stream loops W parallel to the road.

One encounters very few rocks in lower Hatch Brook. The channel cuts through deep alluvium (the bed of a postglacial lake), and the bottom is almost entirely of firm sand. There are no obstructions except a beaver dam or a windfall not yet removed by local fishermen. But sharp bends and strong current make the run a test of skill for the stern paddler. A craft not over 15 or 16 feet is advisable. The brook is canoeable throughout summer.

In the first mile there are a few hunting camps on the R. Beyond the last of these, the stream enters state land, and the woods recede as one winds through a broad marsh. Groves of tamarack break the monotony of the flats. In places the banks are so deeply eroded that the terraces are above eye level. The Blue Line is crossed well above the mouth of the brook, but state land continues.

The mouth is undramatic. The Salmon is only slightly wider as one first enters it. If you turn upstream on the Salmon, however, you encounter the resistance of a strong current in the half mile of smooth water to the base of the rapids below High Falls.

Downstream on the Salmon, the current is moderate to strong. There are no obstacles except a few slightly submerged boulders in the lower part of the run. The corridor is varied and beautiful with

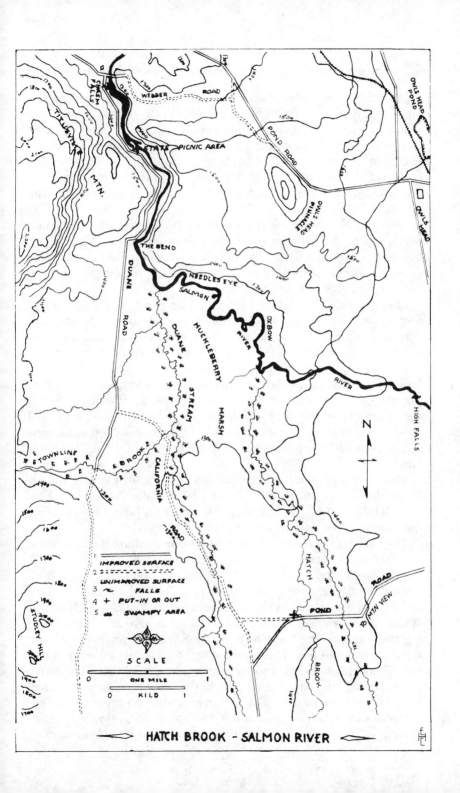

HATCH BROOK - SALMON RIVER

rapidly changing vistas. On the L, across Huckleberry Marsh, is the long craggy ridge of Titusville Mountain. On the R the stream draws steadily closer to a range of hills, seeking a way to break through the wall at the N rim of the plateau. One such attempt at Needles Eye fails, and the river swings abruptly away from a steep poplar-covered hill back into the marsh. Sandbars pushed up by the current are covered with animal and waterfowl tracks in the rich feeding ground of the marsh.

Swinging NW below the confluence of Duane Stream, the Salmon heads straight for another seemingly impenetrable wall. Colliding, it bends sharply R and finally succeeds in piercing the barrier ramparts, gliding smoothly through a narrow cleft which, until now, has been hidden from downstream paddlers.

This abrupt right angle is known as The Bend. The Duane Road now appears on the L and, on the other side of it, an attractive private camp in an inholding. The camp has had a succession of owners since the late 1870s, when it was operated as an inn known as the Myrtle Bower House. From high ground behind the inn, a New York artist of the last century made a panoramic painting of the Salmon River Valley valued at several thousand dollars when it was exhibited at the National Academy of Design. Today the hill above the house at The Bend is private, but much the same view can be enjoyed from a higher elevation, the crags of Titusville Mountain.

The river now flows quietly through the cleft in the hills for 1.6 m. to the bridge above the dam at Chasm Falls. At 0.8 m. below The Bend, on the L, is a small picnic area maintained by the DEC. One can take out here or continue to the bridge.

The pleasant brook-river route may become nothing but a memory. For fifty years various proposals have been made for a dam much larger than the present one at Chasm Falls. It would be a huge earth embankment presumably at The Bend. This old proposal is now being revived in studies by the St. Lawrence-Franklin County Regional Water Resources Planning Board. Consultants have advocated flooding the whole of the lower level of the Salmon River plateau to an elevation of 1,340 feet. This would wipe out all of Huckleberry Marsh and all of Hatch Brook and the Salmon as described in the above route. Brook trout would disappear in the warmed waters of a reservoir. The folklore of the brook and river would become meaningless. Advocates of a dam argue that the 4,500 acres to be flooded (ninety percent of it state land) are of "little economic value." They happen to be, however, a rich feeding ground for wildlife. The planners are not quite sure what the benefits would be: additional power perhaps. But the area is sparsely settled and doesn't need additional power. There would not be enough to make long transmission lines feasible. Downstream floods are hardly a problem. Only local and minor damage has been caused by spring floods on the Salmon, mostly as a result of ice jams. So the planners are forced back on "recreation" as the great potential benefit. Canoeists of America, speak out.

Chasm Falls to Whippleville, 4.9 m. (7.9 km.)
USGS: Chasm Falls, Malone 7.5

At Chasm Falls is a dam operated by Niagara Mohawk and situated just below Webber Road. A penstock carries much of the river's flow to a reservoir and generating station about a mile downstream. The drop in this section is a dramatic 280 feet, most of it in a narrow, twisting chasm that extends for 0.6 m. below the dam. This section is completely unrunnable. The top and bottom of the gorge are posted, but there are several dirt turn-outs on the road connecting Webber Road and Duane Road. Park here and scramble down the steep hillside for the best views.

Access to the lower Salmon is at a recently built picnic and day use area developed by Niagara Mohawk. This area is just N of the intersection of the above-mentioned spur road with Duane Road. (Note that Duane Road is referred to as Route 25 as it proceeds N from this intersection and Route 27 as it proceeds SE.) There is a short path leading 100 feet upstream from the parking area to a gauging station. The absolute minimum for this section is 1.5 feet. In the next 4.9 m. the Salmon drops 230 feet for an average gradient of 47 feet per mile, making this a suitable run for intermediate level whitewater paddlers.

Class II rapids predominate immediately below the put-in, increasing slightly in difficulty the first two times the river veers towards Duane Road. Class I rapids then continue as the Salmon flows under the bridge on the Titus Mountain Ski Road and build slightly as a second bridge, now closed to traffic, is approached. Below this second bridge the Salmon enters a wide plain. Be on the lookout for large boulders appearing on the L bank slightly less than a mile below the ski road. Pull out at these boulders to carry around a falls of about 35 feet in a series of four pitches. The carry is a difficult one of about 60 yards and involves sliding one's boat over and around the large boulders. The L bank becomes posted at this point so that re-entry is necessary just below the falls. The entire R bank of the falls is heavily posted.

Immediately below the falls is one of the two most difficult stretches on this part of the Salmon. Just after the put-in is a series of tricky Class II–III ledges, which are then followed in 100 yards by a Class III boulder garden. Easy Class II rapids then predominate to the Duane Road bridge at 2.9 m. A town park here provides a pleasant break or an alternate point of egress. Flatwater and mild rapids alternate between this bridge and the next, located on a dead-end gravel road. Below here, the rier begins a long sweeping turn to the L beneath some power lines, signaling the return of Class II rapids just outside the hamlet of Whippleville. At the site of the bridge on the River Road in Whippleville is the second stretch of fairly difficult rapids. Here there is a complex Class III rapid requiring the paddler to first negotiate a double hydraulic and then maneuver through a short boulder garden. Take-out on the R. There is a small dirt turn-out along the upstream side of River Rd. that offers limited parking. Rapids do not exceed Class II between here and the outskirts of Malone, where several dams prevent an uninterrupted trip further downstream.

Side Excursions in the Salmon River Area

There are enough attractions for the amphibious tripper in this split-level valley at the northern rim of the Adirondack plateau to justify a camping trip of two or three days. Ample tracts of state land, shown on the 7.5-minute maps, provide a variety of choices for tent sites. Scenic, lightly-traveled roads of sand, gravel, or blacktop crisscross the two levels of the valley and climb draws in the hills. Four excursions on foot are described below.

I. The crags of Titusville Mountain provide a good lookout over the valley. The round-trip hike takes about 2½ hours. The USGS map *Owls Head* and a compass are essential.

On the Duane Road S of The Bend, there are two houses on the L at 0.75 m. Near the first one, on the R, an old tote road bears W toward a saddle in the long ridge line of the mountain. Follow this to a brook that drains, not the saddle, but a fold between the main ridge and a parallel one. The direction swings toward the N as one climbs steadily up the ravine (no trail). Where the grade lessens near the top, climb out of the ravine to the long flattish summit ridge.

Second-growth hardwoods interfere with views from the top. But by keeping a little below the crest and walking SSW, seeking the near-vertical pitches on the L, one comes sooner or later to small grassy plots at the top of the crags and to open views over the valley.

II. The pinnacle called Owls Head rises 700 feet above the upper level of the valley. The mountain range of which it is a part is privately owned, but a trail to the stone face has in the past been open to hikers who do not fish, hunt, or camp on posted land. Inquire at the filling station in Owls Head. From the hamlet, you can drive 0.5 m. NW on the railroad grade and power line. The rails were removed in the 1960s. If the grade is closed by a cable, take a parallel road to a farmhouse, then turn L onto the railroad grade and proceed 0.2 m. farther. Park on the R and walk through a breach in a fence. Turn L on a jeep road which, on entering denser woods, becomes a well-worn foot trail in the same northerly direction. Ascending at a moderate grade, the trail swings NE and then E on a high bank above Bell Brook. After crossing and recrossing the brook, it swings S under a steep slope. The main trail now leads directly into the mouth of a cave, where one can walk upright. For the branching trail to the summit, climb the rocks at the L of the cave and continue up a steep pitch to the wooded crest. A hundred feet below, on the far side, is the open rock of the owl's forehead. A leisurely ascent to this point takes a little less than an hour.

Splendid views open up. The flat upper terrace of the valley is directly below. Across it, in the SW, are the prominent summits of Debar and Baldface. To the S are the Goldsmith and Plumadore ranges, with the Sable and Loon Lake mountains beyond them. To the SE is a long line of peaks, past the bold hump of the Elbow Range to distant Whiteface. To the E is a broadside view of Lyon Mountain—the *lion couchant.*

III. One of the most striking features of the view from Owls Head is a rectangular bog about one mile S of the hamlet of Owls Head. The bog is worth closer inspection, especially in early June. The southerly extension of the railroad grade bounds it on the E and can be used for access. One can drive on the single-lane road of the grade (passing might be difficult) if the cable is down, or walk. Since the Mountain View end of the grade is usually closed, those who drive should turn R at the crossroad 1.6 m. S of Owls Head in order to intersect the Pond Road between the two hamlets.

A half-mile square and treeless, the bog provides the best lowland view of the peaks and ridges encircling the valley. It is also interesting for its great variety of bog vegetation. It is at its best in early June when the cotton grass, spread over the whole area, unfurls its terminal tufts. The bog is then carpeted in white, with accents of pink in the clusters of bog laurel. You can imagine yourself in a California meadow.

IV. If you are adept at orienteering, a bushwhack up a trailless peak on state land is recommended (*Owls Head and Debar Mountain 7.5*). It is the ascent of Baldface, the eastern twin of Debar, from which it is separated by a deep mountain pass. The climb can be made on the N ridge from a ravine that crosses Route 99 2.3 m. E of the intersection of the Pond Road. But state acquisition of the Debar Pond tract, a private park before 1981, has opened a more interesting route. It gives access to the base of the mountain by a short paddle across a surpassingly beautiful pond in the notch between the twin peaks.

Enter the tract by turning S on a one-lane road off Route 99 0.3 m. E of the intersection of the Pond Road. Then drive one mile to a parking lot. A gate is visible farther S on the same road at a 25-acre inholding retained by the former owner. Walk a few yards S on the same road to the head of a canoe-carry trail on the R. The first part of the 0.3-m. trail is a boardwalk over wetlands of the pond's outlet.

From the put-in site, the way to bushwhack up Baldface is clear by its NW ridge, which rises midway along the E shore of the pond. Take care to keep on the crest of the ridge on both the ascent and the descent, to avoid near vertical cliffs just S of it. The ascent of 1,300 feet from pond level to the 2,867-foot peak takes about one hour. The top is open rock with full-circuit views over a wilder landscape than that seen from Titusville and Owls Head mountains. Below on the E is the Hatch Brook valley. On the W, and close by, the sparkle of Debar Pond enlivens the somber circumambience of conifer forests.

Although most Adirondack summits under 4,000 feet are wooded over the top and have only limited views if any, there are enough exceptions (a burn; a summit cleared by Colvin's survey team) to repay a lifetime's exploration in the nearly six million acres of the park *outside* the High Peaks Wilderness Area. Bushwhacking is a small price to pay for an escape from overcrowded trails, a summit free from litter, and, in the case of Baldface, an abundance of tangy mountain blueberries in August and a grand view.

CHATEAUGAY RIVER

Two small rivers, the Trout and the Little Trout, head between the Salmon and the Chateaugay. They are too steep, narrow, and rocky for canoeing inside the Blue Line. Posted land limits access to a few bridges where the two streams look more inviting to fishermen than to canoeists.

The Chateaugay (*Chateauguay* in Canada) is the easternmost of the rivers draining directly into the St. Lawrence. According to Beauchamp, there is no historic reason for a French name. He believes that the name is of Indian origin and is *Chateuaga*.

In the last two-thirds of its course across the plains of southwestern Quebec, the Chateauguay is a placid river winding through farmlands and woodlots. Upland, in its 16 m. from the Chateaugay Lakes to the Canadian border, it drops a torrential 1,000 feet. Most of the other rivers of the St. Lawrence Basin show small to moderate amounts of erosion. The Chateaugay, on the other hand, cuts a deep box chasm in slabby sandstone with near-vertical walls of 100 feet and more. Much of the drop below the Chateaugay Lakes is concentrated in short sections of the river located just upstream from the bridge on Pulpmill Road, between High Falls and Route 11, and in Chateaugay Chasm, located N of Route 11 (*Chateaugay, Burke 7.5*). At high water levels these sections would provide exciting whitewater runs for expert paddlers; but access is sometimes restricted and a number of carries are necessary, some of which are on posted land and therefore illegal. In the spring of 1989 a party did paddle portions of this stretch. Several falls are encountered, among them the majestic 120-foot drop at High Falls, as well as numerous rapids which range up to Class V and VI in difficulty. Members of this party encountered numerous problems with deadfalls spanning the rapids and had to scale very steep cliffs during their carries. Among the most interesting of their experiences was running a section of the river which flows through a large, man-made tunnel before exiting over a 10-foot drop.

In the last century, before the river canyons of the West were opened to tourists, Chateaugay Chasm rivaled Ausable Chasm and Watkins Glen as popular attractions in the East. Today, in the series of gorges below the village of Chateaugay, places once admiringly called Catherdral Rocks, the Bastille, the Niches of Jupiter, Giant Gorge, Vulcan's Cave, Rainbow Basin, and the Grotto of Juno, Venus, or Minerva are neglected and forgotten. In addition, the river has been tamed somewhat by two privately owned hydro-development projects. If old travel guides propel you to visit these scenes of "wild and rugged grandeur," you must do so by car on dead-end dirt roads and on foot, taking care to avoid trespassing on posted lands. Leave your canoe behind.

The headwaters are quite different. They consist of two large lakes, Upper and Lower Chateaugay; the connecting channel between them, called Chateaugay Narrows; and feeder brooks. The canoeist shares these waters with powerboats, for the lakes and the Narrows have been a summer resort since the mid-19th century.

Pioneers from Vermont, moving westward across the plains N of the Adirondacks after the Revolutionary War, crossed the Chateaugay Chasm at a lofty bridge known as Pioneers' Crossing. Some of them were lured up the valley itself, into the funnel-shaped opening in the hills where the two lakes form a natural pathway into the heart of the Adirondacks. Clearing land first in the valley N of the lakes, families like the Bellowses and the Merrills tried to make a living by farming. As farms proved unproductive in the harsh climate and thin soil, they moved up the valley, drawn into that inviting gap in the hills. As they moved, their occupations shifted from farming to sugaring, seining fish, lumber jobbing, hotel-keeping, and guiding. The Bellows family started the Bannerhouse on Lower Chateaugay, where in the 1850s A. F. Tait had a studio and produced several paintings of local scenes and activities. These were reproduced as popular Currier and Ives lithographs. The Merrills moved to the Lower Lake and finally to the Upper, where they ran the Merrill House.

Ease of access as well as beauty of setting, made the Chateaugay Lakes one of the earliest developed summer resorts in the Adirondacks. The Ogdensburg and Lake Champlain Railroad across the top of the state came within 8 m. of the Lower Lake. And in 1879 the Chateaugay Railroad was extended to the mines on Lyon Mountain, only 2.5 m. from the Upper Lake. By the 1880s families from New York and Boston were buying shore land for summer camps. This process has continued to the present. The Lower Lake and the Narrows are heavily developed. The Upper Lake also has a sizable summer colony, but steep slopes and swampy areas have preserved more open space. Camps are also better concealed. Upper Chateaugay is one of the most enjoyable lakes for canoeists.

Chateaugay Headwaters, up to 12.5 m. (20.1 km.)
USGS: Lyon Mountain, Ellenburg Center, Brainardsville 7.5

The fact that the Chateaugay headwaters are surrounded by private land creates problems of access. The ideal cruise would start on South Inlet (Middle Kiln Brook), which is canoeable for 3 m. above the Upper Lake. But the access road W of Standish, which crosses the brook 2 m. above its mouth, is gated and closed to cars. Local people walk over it, and conceivably the ambitious canoeist could park his car outside the gate and carry 1.5 m. to the brook. The distance from here through the two lakes to a bridge on the Cromp Road over the outlet is 12.5 m.

There are easier alternatives. On Route 374 boats can be rented and private landings can be used for a fee. Canoes can also be put in on the Narrows at a public auto bridge and at the single state-owned launching site. The latter is 7 m. S of Brainardsville on Route 374. A DEC sign marks the entrance to the large parking lot. There is a ramp for motorboats and a sandy cove for canoe launching. To the S, a shady trail of 80 yards near the water leads to a small clearing on a point usable as a tent site. The firm shelving sand on this point and at the launching site makes a good bathing beach. No fee is charged for parking and use of the beach.

From this midpoint one can paddle up or down the headwaters. The Upper Lake is 3.5 m. long; the Narrows, 4 m.; the Lower Lake, 2 m.; and the outlet as far as the first highway bridge on the Cromp Road, 1 m. North of this bridge the river is mostly too steep and obstructed for canoeing. The Blue Line as extended N in 1972 crosses the river near Brainardsville.

A story told in a family chronicle that appeared in a Malone newspaper and in book form in 1973 (*The Old Guide's Story*, by Charles E. Merrill) is worth repeating. The author's grandfather,

Paul Merrill, moved from New Hampshire to the Chateaugay Valley in 1823 and raised a family there in Spartan simplicity. The material rewards of farming in upland country were meager, but the Merrills were nature lovers and derived intangible rewards from their surroundings. There was one thing, however, that Paul Merrill missed in the new country. That was the white water lilies of New Hampshire ponds. He determined to make up for this deficiency. He made three arduous trips back to New Hampshire over a period of several years just to collect *nymphaea odorata* roots. The first two attempts at transplanting the fleshy tubers in shallow waters of the Narrows were unsuccessful. The sandy bottoms that make Chateaugay headwaters ideal for bathing were doubtless too infertile for mud-loving aquatic plants to get an easy start. The third trip in 1855 resulted in a modest success. A few white pond lilies began to grace the Narrows. Grandfather Paul did not live to see them, however. And it was some time after his death before the Merrills discovered that white pond lilies are native to Adirondack waters too. Grandpa could have spared himself those three long journeys.

If you look closely, you can still find at least one small colony of white lilies, mixed with yellow ones, in Chateaugay Narrows today. Perhaps they are descendants of Grandpa Merrill's New Hampshire roots. That love and that effort deserve a lasting memorial.

Adirondackers of the forever-wild school may find these waters too congested. Nevertheless, there is one place so unique, so startling, so grand that the eye selectively strips away docks, camps, speedboats, and bikinied sunbathers and sees it almost as Grandfather Merrill saw it, secretive and remote, over a century and half ago.

Only by water do you get the full effect. Paddle S through the widening Narrows from the state launching site. At 0.6 m., pass a rocky point on the L. Before you is a wide bay with islands. It is bounded, on the SE, by a low narrow spit of sand 500 feet long and, straight ahead, by a bulbous promontory called Bluff Point, which blocks a lengthwise view of Upper Chateaugay. A slight realignment would turn this configuration into an exclamation mark, the bluff an oversized period. Now look at the surface ahead. Extending out from the spit to a shrubby islet is a white line through the water. This is the reef that marks the division between the Narrows and the Upper Lake. Motorboat traffic is buoyed to the R of the islet, close to Bluff Point, in deeper water. Ignore the buoys. As a privileged canoeist, you can rub sensuously over the reef between spit and isle.

Now it is hard to ignore the bathers. In ankle-deep water some of them are wading the 200-yard-long reef. You would probably join them if it were not for the view that opens up on the SE. Across the watery foreground is the grand uplift of Lyon Mountain, highest and most massive of the peaks near the northern boundary of the park. This place where spit, reef, bluff, lake, and mountain meet fulfills the promise of that gap in the northern foothills which has lured pioneer, sportsman, artist, tourist, and summer resident up the Chateaugay for many generations.

Eastward from the Chateaugay Lakes lies another major watershed. The streams on the far side of Lyon Mountain drain into Lake Champlain.

If your direction is westward, however, the Wolf Pond Road from Standish to Mountain View is venturesome. It is a winding, one-lane dirt road used by lumber trucks and an occasional quixotic motorist. Avoid it if you are addicted to claustrophobia. The forest shuts you in as tight as a clam in its shell. Avoid it too in wash-out season or when pressed for time. Chances are that you will meet no more than one truck and one car in the 12.5 m. It is a road you will never forget. Until the town highway department begins to "improve" it.

NORTHEAST WATERSHED

The Lake Champlain drainage basin is the third largest in the Adirondacks, after the St. Lawrence and the Upper Hudson. Its area of 2,614 square miles exceeds that of the Mohawk or Black River basins. Its principal rivers are the Great Chazy, the Saranac, the Ausable with its East and West branches, and the Boquet. Two other rivers, the Salmon and the Little Ausable, also drain the Northeast basin. Neither of these rivers is paddleable for any significant distance as either a cruising trip or a whitewater trip.

With the exception of the Saranac, the rivers of the northeast are comparatively short and steep. They are offsprings of the High Peaks. Rising as mountain brooks on the main N-S axis of elevation, they tumble precipitously over cliff and through ravine, slacken somewhat on the ramp-like floors of intervales, and regain speed in their terraced descent into the Champlain Valley, with alternate smooth and turbulent sections.

The Ausable is characteristic of these mountain rivers. Its East Branch originates in runnels off the cone of Mount Marcy, highest of New York State peaks, and drops nearly a vertical mile in a 60-mile dash to Lake Champlain, which is only a mean 95 feet above sea level. It and the West Branch are the steepest rivers in the state.

Again excepting the Saranac, cruising reaches are shorter and fewer in the northeast than in the northwest. Trips of half to a full day are likely to include whitewater stretches of some length, which require a higher degree of skill and experience. For the steep, swift segments a kayak or a decked canoe is a better choice than the open tandem canoe. The latter can be reserved for cruising reaches of ample length on the Saranac and shorter ones on the other streams.

Bedrock lies close to the surface. The rivers tend to be shallower and, except in the chasms, wider than those of the northwest plateau. Most of the latter are canoeable all summer. But in the Champlain Basin, except for the Saranac, the rivers are best run in April and

May and again in the fall rainy season. The first two weeks of May usually provide good conditions. Water and air are not so chillingly cold by then. Snows are still melting in the mountains to keep the rivers fairly high. And the blackfly season hasn't begun. Opportunities also arise in the summer months after heavy rains. But one must be quick about it. These rivers respond fast to downpours and recede fast too, usually within 24 to 48 hours. Partial deforestation in the intervales and the Champlain Valley make the runoff cycle shorter than in the more heavily forested northwest sector.

It is a good precaution to examine water levels at several points from roads and bridges before committing yourself to an extended run. What may look like an adequate depth at put-in may turn into a thinly irrigated boulder jungle elsewhere.

Most of the streams in the Champlain Basin are crystal clear. The sharp tilt of the land eastward makes for good drainage. Swamps, bogs, and marshes are small and few in number as compared with other areas of the Adirondacks. The extensive spruce-fir-sphagnum swamps of the central and northwest plateau release into streams the tannic stain of decaying vegetation; the color ranges from that of weak tea to coffee. In the northeast the Chubb and the Saranac have this coloration. But most of the rivers, except where polluted in their lower courses, are transparently clear. They carry little sediment except during flood or after heavy rainfall. Stones on the bottom sparkle with polished brilliance.

For mountain vistas these streams have no match elsewhere in the Adirondacks. Although the best views are often behind one in downstream travel, oxbow bends give a fair sampling. Steep slopes, wooded except where broken by outcrops of gray-blue anorthosite, rise abruptly from the river's edge or across an open meadow.

The Saranac is unique in that it rises on the central plateau and cuts across the main axis of elevation to reach Lake Champlain. It is the longest river of the Champlain Basin. Its headwaters lie in the same broad upland valley where the St. Regis rises. But unlike the St. Regis, its course is northeasterly. The chain lakes and ponds at its head and its long journey through upland valleys make it an excellent, summer-long cruising stream as far as the dam at Union Falls. Between that place and the Blue Line, the Saranac is comparable to the other streams feeding Lake Champlain. Its whitewater sections are a challenge to the skilled canoeist.

Access is less of a problem in the northeast than in the northwest sector. There are fewer large individual and corporate landowners that control long river segments. There are more road bridges where the public right-of-way affords put-in space. There are fewer posted carries. Although restrictions in the northeast are generally less severe than in the northwest, readers are referred to the front of this book ("Northwest Watershed") for a discussion of a hoped-for lifting of the few remaining ones.

The state has acquired fishing rights on many of the trout streams. These easements provide permanent access to fishermen. They are limited to the enclosed parking lot if any, entrance trail, foreshore, and stream. Canoeists like to assume that these easements are intended for them as well as for fishermen. Actually, the state has acquired only the right to fish. Landowners retain control over all other uses. In practice few owners object to canoe launchings even though the party is not equipped with fishing gear and licenses. But if the party is a large one (say, more than three canoes) and access is dependent on fishing easements, permission should be asked of the landowner. He might well object to heavy use of an entrance trail or bank in wet weather, just as he certainly would to camping and littering. Esprit de corps among canoeists is essential. We must not endanger shaky privileges by presuming on them too far; not until right of access and passage is more firmly established in state law than it is at present.

There are fewer descriptions of side excursions on foot in following pages than in the foregoing ones. The reason for this is the availability of the Adirondack Mountain Club's *Guide to Adirondack Trails* with its extensive coverage of foot trails in the High Peaks Region. Amphibious travelers should consult it. The foot trails described here will not duplicate that guide but supplement it so far as attractions near the waterways are concerned.

GREAT CHAZY RIVER

"Chazy" is an adaptation of the French *Chézy*, name of a French lieutenant killed by Iroquois Indians in 1666 near the river mouth. The Great Chazy is 46 m. long. It is great only by comparison with the Little Chazy. The latter has its source outside the Blue Line. It does not join its namesake but empties into Lake Champlain 2 m. to the S, opposite the N end of Isle La Motte.

The principal tributary of the Great Chazy is the North Branch. The confluence is at Mooers Forks in northern Clinton County. Below Mooers the river is canoeable in spring for 20 m. to its mouth in Kings Bay. Both forks rise within the Blue Line. But inside the park boundary as extended in 1972, they are hardly more than mountain brooks, steep, shallow, and rocky. The main branch is included here because of the spacious, beautiful mountain lake that it drains and because of a tantalizing transformation that takes place perhaps a half dozen days out of the year.

If you happen to strike one of those days, you might be led to a wrong assumption. Natives say that the upper river is downright uncanoeable. But one day in August when my companion and I saw it from the spillway and two bridges below the lake, it was in flood. The clear, swirling blue-green water made a plushy cushion over the rocks and promised a fast, bouncy ride. The stream in fact looked glamorously canoeable as far as the next bend—a speeding conveyor belt into the unknown.

But we noted that the width is only 10–15 feet. Fallen trees, more treacherous than rocks, would be a problem as well as the steep gradient. We resisted the temptation. The way is open for explorers of less age and discretion. But they must choose their day with pinpoint accuracy.

The phenomenon we saw is rare. It is due, like many other things in Chazy country, to the enterprise of one William Henry Miner. An orphan who grew up in his uncle's home in Chazy, he became a wealthy builder of refrigerator cars and president of his own company in Chicago. But his heart remained in Chazy. He expanded the original 150-acre homestead of his paternal grandfather into the 13,000-acre Heart's Delight Farm. Here he bred stock, built a trout hatchery, and set aside a wild animal preserve. He built the two-million dollar Chazy Central Rural School, a forerunner in 1916 of the luxurious central schools of today. Another of his benefactions was a four-mil-lion-dollar hospital in Plattsburgh. After his death in 1930 his widow, Alice, carried on his philanthropies. The Lake Alice Game Manage-ment Area near the village of Chazy is now owned by the state, and in 1963 the Miner Foundation gave to the state the 700-acre tract near Altona which includes Miner Lake, an impoundment on the Great Chazy just outside the Blue Line.

William Miner's enterprise extended upstream as far as Chazy Lake. In order to provide an even supply of water on his property down-stream, he built the concrete wing wall and spillway, with controls, at the outlet. The wall raised the level of the lake and turned the outlet into an underground waterfall of great potential force. Another effect was not anticipated. Turbulent wave action on the raised, unnat-ural shoreline eats away at the banks, leaving dead trees, stumps, exposed rocks. In order to clean the beaches and repair damage, the shore owners' association requests, at intervals, that the town of Dannemora lower the lake level. The gates of the dam may also be opened to clear away debris that has accumulated against the grates. But the openings are infrequent. When they do occur, the upper Great Chazy is briefly transformed from its customary state of a purling rock garden into a just-possible canoeing stream.

Chazy Lake, 4 m. (6.4 km.)
USGS: Moffitsville, Ellenburg Mountain 7.5

Chazy Lake is nearly 4 m. long and has a maximum width of 1.5 m. Its mountain setting is as splendid as that of Upper Chateaugay Lake. Its southern end lies deep in the shadow of Johnson Mountain in the morning and of Lyon Mountain in the afternoon. Topknot and Ellenburg mountains frame it on the NW.

The lake is very choppy in a strong breeze. Parents in the neighbor-hood try to instill a sense of its dangers by telling of various drownings over the years. Marion and Clarence Bissonnette, who were lessoned in this way in childhood, recall a tragedy that occurred on a Memorial Day picnic of the Dannemora High School. Five members of the senior class, returning by water from an outing on Lyon Mountain, were drowned when their rowboat overturned in a violent storm. Winds sweeping down from the mountains caused unpatterned turbulence. Though not frequent, they can come with little or no warning.

Put-in near the head of the lake takes advantage of the prevailing SW winds of summer. The last navigable quarter mile of South Inlet is not easy to reach through brush and swamp. A more convenient site is 0.6 m. below the inlet where the Chazy Lake Road comes closest to the W shore, at the mouth of a small brook. Here there is an unposted parking space for two or three cars beside a sandy cove. A course down the W shore is suggested for shelter and emergency landings.

The distance from this put-in to the outlet bay at the N end is 3.3 m. All the way you have Lyon Mountain at your back, but on landing near the outlet, you are rewarded with the finest of all views of that important landmark. The lake is now foreground for the massive ridge, 6 m. long, spread out across the SW horizon and rising 2,300 feet above the surface.

Three centuries ago this shape suggested to French travelers on Lake Champlain a *lion couchant*. Quite appropriately, the first settler on the mountain was a sheep farmer named Nathaniel Lyon. In 1876 his granddaughter Hattie became the first woman to climb to the top. The logic of these facts led to a slight alteration in spelling.

The beach near the outlet is one of the developments that W. H. Miner conferred on Chazy country. His wall raises the lake to a level above that of the original floodplain at the N end. From Route 374, which encircles the bay, one ascends a gentle slope to reach the beach. The strip between beach and road is a pleasant place to linger. It is a small park landscaped with cedars, single or in clusters. A concrete pier, once the foundation of Miner's boathouse, borders a small public bathing beach. Bathers are in evidence only on the warmest summer days. The beach is exposed to prevailing winds, and the water is colder than that of most Adirondack lakes. Chazy is fed not only by numerous mountain brooks but by submerged springs.

Walking NW along the concrete wall from the beach, one comes to a gaily painted footbridge over a secondary channel of the outlet. A little way beyond is a concrete enclosure over the spillway of the main channel. If the gate under the spillway happens to be open, the Great Chazy pours out of a conduit ten feet below in a jet of wildwater exciting to watch. If it is closed, the Great Chazy belies its name.

There is nothing transitory and uncertain about Lyon Mountain. The 3.5 m. trail to the fire tower starts on the Chazy Lake Road 1.8 m. S of the junction with Route 374. You can now cut off nearly a mile of the hike by driving up the lower slopes to a parking lot. A tractor trail continues at a steep, steady grade to a point not far below the fire observer's cabin. It narrows to a foot trail over the last mile to the summit. The mountain's hardwood forest is mostly of pole size. A fire raged over the slopes in 1903, and the second growth has been logged since then.

The summit is more interesting than the trail. Broad and flat, it is strewn with fragments of Potsdam sandstone looking quite foreign amidst outcrops of Lyon Mountain granite. The sandstone comes from lower elevations several miles to the N and E. The glacier that once overrode the mountain hoisted the erratics some 2,000 vertical feet to their present resting place. Other features of note are a mountaintop spring and a cleft rock imaginatively called a "cave."

Verplanck Colvin built an observation station on the summit in the Adirondack survey of the year 1878. His guides labored for three days to carry the heavy theodolite up the steep slopes. On his first ascent Colvin was troubled by the plateau-like summit. He realized that much cutting would be necessary. The surrounding peaks selected as signal stations were all lower. His men worked for several days to cut lanes radiating out from the highest spot of ground in the direction of each of those peaks. Two weeks of hazy August days caused a further delay. But September brought clearing skies and successful observations. Colvin's reckoning of the elevation of Lyon Mountain was 3,809 feet, quite close to the 3,820-odd feet shown on the latest topo map made from aerial photographs.

Since the view is the main reward for climbing, you should choose a day of good visibility. Then you can see the St. Lawrence River and Mount Royal in Montreal, Lake Champlain and the Green Mountains, the High Peaks of the Adirondacks, and to the W the peaks of lesser size but great character on the northern fringe of the park.

There is also some satisfaction in standing on the crest between two drainage basins. The brooks on the NW slope flow to the St. Lawrence through the Chateaugay; those on the SW to Lake Champlain through the Great Chazy and the Saranac.

SARANAC RIVER

The Saranac has a will of its own. The ponds at its source are neighbors of St. Regis headwaters and Raquette drainage. Propinquity would seem to destine it for a course over the NW plateau. In fact, geologists think that the W part of the Saranac once had such a course. It may have flowed into the St. Regis through Upper St. Regis Lake or into the Raquette over Indian Carry. Only the flimsiest of glacial deposits separate it from those systems today. But the Saranac disdains this easy way out. Instead of penetrating the soft low mound of glacial till, less than a mile wide, at the S end of Upper Saranac Lake and joining the Raquette, it veers E to break through a sill of anorthosite at Bartlett Carry. After a circuitous course across the E part of the Lake Belt, it swings determinedly NE into a gap in the northern ramparts of the High Peaks. The Saranac and its North Branch are unique in cutting through the main axis of elevation between the St. Lawrence and the Champlain basins.

This willful course has consequences for canoeists. The Saranac has great diversity. It is a stream both of upland marsh and lake and of rugged mountain pass. It is for novice and expert and gradations in between. Its upper sections are suited for placid touring and exploration; its lower ones, for whitewater thrills and flips. Two-thirds of its fall comes in the last one-third of its course.

In the old days when streams and lakes were the only highways of the Adirondack interior, the Saranac Chain was Route 1. For travelers from the Eastern seaboard the commonest way into the wilderness was by train to Whitehall or Burlington and then by steamer on Lake Champlain to Port Kent or Plattsburgh. After a short lap by stage, and later by rail, to Keeseville or Au Sable Forks, tourists of the 1850s hired a team and wagon for the day's journey over the Western Plank Road through Black Brook and up Little Black Brook between Catamount Mountain and the Wilmington Range to Franklin Falls on the Saranac. Here the Franklin House served the noonday meal. The journey then continued through Bloomingdale to Martin's or Bartlett's on the Saranac Lakes. These hotels were induction centers reasonably skilled in easing the transition from Fifth Avenue or Beacon Hill to the wilderness. They supplied boats, guides, and provisions for camping trips of a few days or a few weeks in the wilds.

Martin's was on Ampersand Bay at the NE end of Lower Saranac Lake. Operated by its popular host, William Martin, from 1850 till the early 1880s, this hotel was the gateway to an intricate network of waterways where one could travel for weeks by boat and short carries. Thaddeus Norris, a visitor of the early 1860s, described Martin's and its patrons as follows:

> Martin's is a kind of jumping-off place from the civilized world into the wilds beyond: I have seen men embark at his landing with their wives, children, and other baggage; their cooking utensils, their India-rubber bags stuffed with luxuries, their bass-rods, which the owners essayed in vain to cast-fly with, and their highly finished guns that were innocent of the death of deer, all crammed into boats, when starting for the upper Saranac or some of the lakelets and ponds beyond the Raquette, to camp out for weeks. Many of these are people who live in luxury at home, who have become weary of Newport, Saratoga, and Nahant, and come out "to rough it." Some . . . repeat the excursion year after year, until the men become passable woodsmen, and the women right good squaws.

To those people, all the waterways were open, for the posting of private lands was not common before the 1890s. The Adirondacks were then a kind of Venice spread out over Switzerland. The three large lakes of the Saranac Chain were of course the Grand Canal. On August days two streams of guideboats, one leaving Martin's and the other returning, plied the blue sparkling waters. On Upper Saranac the traffic began to thin as routes diverged. Some turned W to Wawbeek and took the Sweeney Carry to continue their journey on the Raquette, through Tupper Lake, and perhaps on westward to the headwaters of the Bog or over the divide to the Beaver River and its chain of lakes. Others continued N to the Prospect House (later known as the Saranac Inn) at the head of Upper Saranac, to Paul Smiths, or on to Rainbow Lake. Many turned S at Indian Carry to go upstream on the Raquette, to explore its many tributary waters including the Whitney ponds, and perhaps to cross the divide into waters of the Upper Hudson or another divide into the Fulton Chain of the Moose River. Among the earliest to make the latter transit was Amelia Murray, maid of honor to Queen Victoria, who in 1855 crossed the Adirondacks from NE to SW.

Bearing the heaviest traffic, the Saranac Lakes of those days became a little hackneyed to wilderness buffs. Adirondack Murray advised people to hasten over them and do their camping elsewhere, away from the crowd. But all that is changed today. Paved roads are now the highways. The sweating guides who pulled their parties into the sunset on the Saranacs, against prevailing winds, have been replaced by do-it-yourself trippers with canoe carriers atop their cars. These fellows are sensitive to excess labor. They prefer to have wind and current with them whenever possible. So they drive to a put-in on Upper Saranac. This changes the perspective. The three magnificent lakes are no longer a hard pull to get to some remote destination in the "wilderness" but an end in themselves, as they deserve to be. The people one meets on them today are content to be there and not elsewhere. Too many of them are motorized. But the Saranacs offer enough to the canoe tripper to outweigh that disadvantage.

All permits for permanent camping at tent-platform sites have been terminated, and since 1975, 300 tent platforms on Lower and Middle Saranac Lakes have been removed. This has lessened motorboat traffic on the two lakes somewhat. There is a chance that the trend toward overuse of the beautiful Lower Lake may be reversed for a few years.

Even today, when the Saranac country is crisscrossed with roads, private shores are lined with cottages and mansions, and motorboats and water skiers swarm over the lakes, it is easy to understand the enthusiasm of those first tourists of the 1840s and 1850s. The upper river lies in a spacious basin enclosed by two belts of mountains running NE-SW across the central Adirondacks. The oval-shaped basin is over 30 m. long and up to 15 m. wide. It is rimmed by a rugged skyline consisting of the following peaks: Panther, Stony Creek, Ampersand, Scarface, McKenzie, Moose, Whiteface, Esther, Wilmington, Catamount, Silver Lake, Lyon, Norton, Elbow, Loon Lake, Sable, Jenkins, St. Regis, Long Pond, and Floodwood. A few interior peaks, such as Boot Bay and Alder Brook, are obstacles around which the Saranac and its North Branch circle. One of the principal sources, Lake Clear, is only 6 m. from the village of Saranac Lake by the railroad tracks, but the river scorns this pedestrian route for a scenic extravaganza of 28 m.

This interior valley was once filled with water. Only the mountain crests rose above the flood as islands. The successive levels of vast lakes as the retreating glacier uncovered lower outlets between the hills can be traced in the terraces and sand plains of Saranac country today. The lakes and ponds with which the basin now seems generously endowed are only remnants. Some lie in rock basins. Others owe their separate identity to deposits of glacial drift or sills of anorthosite. And still others, especially the smaller ones, occupy kettle holes left by slow-melting blocks of ice. The variety of shape, size, color, depth, and shoreline vista of bedrock or forest cover is great enough to occupy the exploring canoeist for many days. He will find some places he will wish to return to time after time.

Headwaters of the Saranac
USGS: Saint Regis 15; Upper Saranac Lake 7.5 × 15

The Saranac is Hydra headed. "We rise here," one of the alleged meanings of the corruption "Saranac," is a good joke. Where is here? (It is probable that "Saranac" is a corruption not of an Indian but of a French name.)

Weller Pond is the least acceptable of the sources that have been mentioned. It cuts out Upper Saranac Lake, sixth largest body of water in the Adirondacks. But to regard Upper Saranac as head is to overlook a maze of 37 ponds larger than pool size clustered around the N end of that large lake and draining into it. The largest of these, but not the highest, is Lake Clear. Three other waters clearly have a claim. Grass Pond is the most remote. But the highest of the pond sources are Mountain and Ledge ponds, each with an elevation of 1,670 feet. Mountain Pond has perhaps the better title to being the primary source since the brook that feeds it drains 2,533-foot Long Pond Mountain.

Pond-hopping among the 37 is a pleasant pastime from ice-out to ice-in. In winter the fun continues on skis or snowshoes. Only four of the ponds are entirely in private land. Another five are partly so but freely used by the public. The rest are surrounded by Forest Preserve, land which the state bought from the Upper Saranac Association in 1898. Some of the ponds are connected by navigable streams. Where there are carries, they are shorter than those in nearby St. Regis headwaters: rarely over a quarter mile.

The state maintains two large campsites, Fish Creek and Rollins Pond, in the headwaters, off Route 30. Provisions can be bought and canoes rented here. There are no lean-tos in this area but an abundance of attractive tent sites on the ponds. In general, the farther such sites are from the hubbub around the developed campgrounds, the more they are appreciated.

Some of the possible combination tours of headwater ponds are described below. Others can be arranged to fit time and inclination.

I. *Lake Clear to Upper Saranac Lake,* 5.5 m.   Lake Clear, easternmost of the headwaters, was once a link in a water route between two famous hotels, Paul Smith's and Saranac Inn. From Upper St. Regis Lake boats were transported by team and wagon 1.5 m. on the St. Germain ("Sangemo") Carry. After crossing Lake Clear, boating parties proceeded down the winding outlet for 3.5 m. to Upper Saranac and thence across the N end to Saranac Inn. But the St. Germain Carry is now abandoned. Though the state now owns the bed of Lake Clear, most of the shoreline is private. The upper half of Lake Clear Outlet is still navigable, however. Access is at the bridge on Route 30, whence one can paddle out into the lake or downstream 1.8 m. in a wide backwater to a dam. At the L of the dam is a short carry to the Forest Home Road.

Below the dam the outlet is choked with obstructions. A narrow dirt road passes through state land parallel to the stream on the W side. The road has been improved to allow auto access to private camps on Markham Pt., Upper Saranac. It is gated during muddy seasons. The road crosses Hatchery Brook, a tributary, in 0.25 m. and the outlet in 1.0 m. Parking near each bridge is very limited. Continuing beyond the second bridge, the dirt road crosses a vast swamp that has interest for botanists.

Little Clear Pond, W of Lake Clear, also drains into Upper Saranac. Its outlet, Hatchery Brook, is now utilized as a water supply for the Adirondack Fish Hatchery. A marked carry of 0.7 m. leads from Little Clear across Rt. 30 to Hatchery Brook. In the summer of 1994 DEC workers cleared a narrow channel through the numerous deadfalls spanning the brook. Even so, the going is obstructed in the 1.4 m. between Rt. 30 and the second bridge on the dirt road. The final 0.2 m. leading to Upper Saranac is fairly open.

A century ago Little Clear was a link in a second and more popular route between Paul Smith's and Saranac Inn. The Seven Carries, as it has always been called, is very much used today, and the carry trails are in excellent condition. Since most of the ponds it traverses are headwaters of the Middle Branch of the St. Regis, it is described under that heading.

II. *Follensby Clear Pond circuit,* 5 m. This circuit starts at either of two parking lots and launching sites at the SE end of Follensby Clear Pond off Route 30. One is 0.8 m. N of the entrance to Fish Creek Pond Public Campsite, and the other a mile farther N. Follensby Clear Pond is 2 m. long. Its irregular shape, with rocky points, deep bays, and pine-clad islands makes it a favorite with campers. Paddle to the N end. There, if desired, you can take a side excursion to Green Pond over a carry. (Green is also acessible from Route 30, over a marked carry 0.1 m. long to a public landing. Look for a sign on the W side of Route 30, 0.4 m. S of the turnoff to Saranac Inn Golf Course. The carry from Green to Polliwog is not recommended. It is a rough bushwhack over a steep esker to a campsite on Polliwog.) The main route is over a marked carry to Polliwog, located just to the SW of the carry to Green. It then proceeds through Little Polliwog and Horseshoe, where there is a carry back to Follensby Clear.

III. *Fish Creek circuit*, 10.5 m. from First Fish Creek Pond; 10 m. from the mouth of Fish Creek in the public campsite. Fish Creek and Rollins Pond public campsites are good bases for this and other tours in Saranac headwaters. Campers seeking isolation, however, prefer tent sites on the outlying ponds.

Paddle up Fish Creek in a slack current between marshy shores into Little Square Pond. Cross the E end of this pond and head into the pretty brook that drains Floodwood Pond. Unfortunately, the brook is navigable for small outboards as well as canoes. Follow the S shore of Floodwood around to an inlet at the SW end. A lightly loaded canoe can sometimes be coaxed up this brook with a little wading. There is a carry trail of 0.2 m. Pass through the full length of Rollins Pond and carry 0.1 m. to Whey. Carry 0.3 m. to Copperas Pond, and return to the starting point by way of Fish Creek. This is a varied, scenic tour. In summer it is much used, and motorboat traffic is often heavy in the vicinity of the public campsites.

IV. *Middle Pond circuit*, 12.5 m. This is like the preceding tour except that it widens the perimeter on the E and N. Start at the public landing and parking lot at the S end of Follensby Clear and paddle to the N end. After a short carry to Polliwog, head W through a narrows into a pond unnamed on the map. Carry 0.4 m. to Middle Pond (it seems farther); then 0.3 m. to Floodwood. Return by Rollins, Whey, and Copperas as described in III. Take Fish Creek for 0.8 m. downstream to a carry of 0.2 m. on the L to Follensby Clear and thus back to the start.

Floodwood Road. Across from the W entrance to Saranac Inn on Route 30 is a road that gives access to launching sites on Saranac ponds of the northern tier. Blacktopped at the start, then with firmly packed gravel, this road forks in 0.3 m. The R fork crosses the golf course, turns L to skirt the edge of the woods, and R to a public boat landing on Hoel Pond, where there is parking space for several cars. The L and longer fork goes W along the S edge of the golf course and enters deep woods on state land. In 4 m. it reaches Floodwood at the railroad tracks. Skirting Polliwog, Middle, and Floodwood ponds on the N, it affords alternate starting points for the circular tours in II, III, and IV above. The road continues over 2 m. beyond Floodwood to the W boundary of state land, extended on the S in 1991 by a purchase from the Floodwood Mountain Reserve, which allows access to two new ponds and a bushwhack up Floodwood Mountain. Rock Pond can be reached by a carry trail of 0.75 m., beginning 0.2 m. past the RR crossing. Bear R at the first Y. Just before Rock Pond comes into view take a faint spur to the L leading to a sandy beach at the E end of the pond. (The main trail continues to the outlet of West Pine Pond, where launching is more difficult.) Since trails connecting Rock and Floodwood Ponds cross private land, a return carry to Floodwood Road is necessary. Shortly to the W on Floodwood Road is a landing on East Pine Pond. Canoeists can now enter West Pine Pond via a short, steep carry over the esker dividing the two ponds. At 1 m. beyond the RR crossing, there is a small parking lot 100 feet N of the road. From here it is a carry of 0.25 m. to the bay of the SW arm of Long Pond, with much of the carry along a spur road closed by the DEC in 1990.

V. *Hoel Pond to Long Pond,* 4.8 m. This is a leisurely two-hour trip between the Hoel and Long Pond landings described above. Two cars are necessary for the shuttle. There is a short carry over the RR tracks at the NW end of Hoel Pond. The route continues through Turtle and Slang ponds to a 0.2 m. carry to Long Pond. On Long a twisting course of 2.2 m. leads to the end of the SW arm. Long Pond has many attractive tent sites. It is in the St. Regis Canoe Area where powerboats are banned. (See the sketch map on p. 119.)

VI. *Wide circuit,* 15 m. A party with one car can tour the perimeter of Saranac headwater ponds by closing the circle with an unencumbered walk of 1.0 m. Although this trip can be made in one long day, an overnight camp on some piny headland is recommended. The best put-in site is the public landing on Hoel Pond. From here to Long Pond the route is the same as in V. It diverges in the SW arm of Long Pond. Go only 0.25 m. into that arm and look for a carry trail to Floodwood Pond on the W side of the outlet. This is the longest carry of the route—0.8 m. The tour continues through Floodwood, Rollins, and Whey. The recent state purchase of lands from the Floodwood Mountain Reserve also includes Deer and Heavens Ponds. Deer may be reached by paddling to the SW corner of a long, narrow bay on the

W side of Rollins. A short trail leads to the RR tracks. Go N 50 yards to three green "FMR" markings on the rail ties. Follow the markings along a faint foot trail 0.2 m. long. Put-in on Deer is difficult because of the wide, marshy shore. Heavens Pond is reached by returning to the RR tracks, proceeding N for 0.25 m., and taking a trail signalled by three yellow "FMR" markings on the rail ties. Proceed W for 1.5 m. to the SE corner of Heavens. In the last century Deer and Heavens were part of a route from the Saranac Inn to Tupper Lake via the Wolf Ponds. This route is not open to the public.

Continuing through Rollins into Whey, one can proceed as in III or keep to the outer perimeter by taking a carry on the S shore 0.2 m. from the E end. This carry of 0.7 m. goes S, skirts Black Pond, and then follows the Rollins campsite road SE to Square Pond. Continue through the Fish Creek Ponds to First, the outer one of the group, and then paddle up shady Spider Creek. This outlet of Follensby Clear Pond is wide and shallow but canoeable. The shores are a North Woods garden. One wishes the creek were several times its length of 0.3 m. Paddle now to the Polliwog Pond carry at the NW end of Follensby Clear. At the head of the NE bay of Polliwog look for a sign marking a new 0.7-m. carry trail through the woods to the parking lot at Hoel Pond. This cuts the old roundabout carry nearly in half.

Two side excursions in the northern tier of Saranac headwaters are rewarding for those with compass and topo map and a familiarity with their use. The goal of one is Long Pond Mountain, a trailless peak that commands one of the best views in the Adirondacks. The other is perhaps the prettiest of all headwater ponds, Ledge.

VII. *Ledge Pond,* 2.5 m. (round trip) of paddling and carrying. Put in at Long Pond landing and paddle along the N shore of the SW arm to the Pink Pond Outlet. This brook surprises one by being canoeable all the way. Paddle along the S shore of Pink (it is pink with emerging spring foliage) to the W end. Bypass the first inlet and head for the second—the one that comes from the NW. Small beaver dams and silty shallows challenge passage up the brook. Persevere for about 15 minutes till the banks hem in your prow and you can go no further. The carry of about 0.3 m. begins at this point on an informal path that follows the course of the brook to its source in Ledge Pond.

Ledge Pond is interesting to circumnavigate. It has a point on the W shore ideal for camping, islets off the E shore, and a fine escarpment on the N shore which explains the pond's name. Ledge is usually deserted.

VIII. *Long Pond Mountain,* 11 m. from Hoel Pond and return, with 8 m. afloat and 3 afoot; 9.5 m. from Hoel Pond to a take-out at the

Long Pond landing; 8 m. from Long Pond landing and return. For trippers accustomed to bushwhacking and to using a compass, this is probably the most delightful and varied tour in Saranac headwaters. A full day should be devoted to it. Visibility should be good, skies clear, and temperature cool. The ascent of 900 vertical feet is made on the S face of the mountain, where openings in woods often expose the climber to the sun.

The logic of this amphibious trip is that Long Pond Mountain can't readily be reached overland. It is a canoeist's mountain. Most visitors to the Saranac country never see it at all. Yet it is strategically located so as to command the best possible view of the great oval basin in which upper Saranac waters lie, of the ring of mountains around it, and of the High Peaks beyond.

Although modest in height at 2,533 feet, Long Pond Mountain has character. It should have, considering the trials it has withstood. It lay in the path of the most severe tornado ever recorded in northern New York, the windfall of September 20, 1845. The storm's ENE course can still be traced by local names: the Windfall Club at Cook Corners, the Windfall Road, the Windfall House at Sevey, several Windfall brooks, and two Windfall ponds. One of the latter is less than 2 m. WSW of Long Pond Mountain. Much of the mountain's timber must have been laid flat by that tornado. The year 1903 brought another disaster when the fires of a dry season swept eastward from Tupper Lake almost to Saranac Inn. Ground fire then, or at some other time, must have destroyed the duff on the southern half of the mountain, exposing bedrock. Revegetation was slow. In July of 1966 a lightning fire broke out on the summit, burning several acres of grass and a fringe of trees before fire-fighters brought it under control.

Today a forest cover is coming back. Conifers, maple, and beech are beginning to appear among the still prevalent aspen, white birch, and cherry that commonly follow a fire. But much of the bone structure of the mountain still shows on the S face, and a handsome bone structure it is as seen on the water approach. The mountain is a propped-up natural park, meadows alternating with thickets, terraces and bare nubbles topping cliffs, and shady hollows with the imprint of deer beds in the ferns.

The Upper Saranac Association, which owned Township 20 before the state acquired it, had a trail up Long Pond Mountain in the last century. There was even a hut and fireplace next to a spring. Nearly all trace of that old trail from the N end of Long Pond is gone today.

Hopefully, no new trail will be built. It is more fun to find your own way, each choice nook then seeming like a private discovery. The entire S face from E to W has interesting irregularities. The shortest route, however, is from the E end of Mountain Pond.

Of the two water approaches, the one starting at the Long Pond landing off the Floodwood Road is the shorter. (The Hoel Pond one is more scenic, giving repeated views of the mountain from various angles as the water trail twists through Hoel, Turtle, Slang, and Long ponds.) Paddle through Long into its NW arm, round a point at the narrows, and continue NW to the carry trail to Mountain Pond.

At the landing, beach or hide your canoe. There is no point in carrying it over the 0.6 m. trail to Mountain Pond. Some rather surprising medium-sized Norway spruce, with drooping foliage, appear on the trail. Not a native tree, the Norway spruce was among other conifers planted in the Upper Saranac area at the turn of the century under the direction of Bernhard Fernow, an immigrant and the first professional forester in the United States. (Larger specimens of Fernow's Norway spruce can be seen on a short marked trail off Route 30 just W of the Wawbeek turnoff and 0.7 m. E of the junction of Route 30 and 3; also a mile farther NE on the fire truck trail to Deer Pond.)

At Mountain Pond, follow a fishermen's trail around the E end and then leave it as it swings W. Head due N through the woods. The uplift begins immediately. The grade is gentle at first but gradually steepens. There are cliffs, but they can be skirted. There are nubbles, and don't prematurely mistake several of them for the summit. You may have to descend short pitches into hollows. The ascent from the pond takes about one hour. The summit is an elongated open flat of grass and bedrock. The two ends and the middle unfold different views through an arc of about 300 degrees. The ponds of St. Regis, Saranac, and Raquette drainage radiate outward in sparkling lanes through the forest. One lane leads to the big glitter of Upper Saranac Lake. The whole of the great oval basin is spread out below in startling detail as on a relief map. Beyond the basin lies the blue serrated ridge of the High Peaks. The view is most colorful on a sunny day in late October when the tamaracks are turning gold and the crowns of aspen and birch retain a few yellow leaves to contrast with the dark conifer forest. For the moment at least you are convinced that you are looking at just about all of the best part of the good earth.

This part of Saranac headwaters N of the railroad tracks is in the St. Regis Canoe Area and is fully protected as wilderness. All motor vehicles are prohibited. It is quite otherwise with the ponds S of the tracks. They have been degraded by inappropriate use and overuse. For this, the two large public campsites on Fish Creek and Rollins ponds are largely to blame. The whole constellation of Saranac headwaters, south of the tracks as well as north, could have been the most delightful wilderness-in-miniature in the East. The extent of the degradation is tellingly put by John Kauffmann in *Flow East:*

> What a place to take a little boy on a canoe trip! Carries of a few hundred feet lead you from pond to tiny pond, each one Hiawatha's own. Not Fish Creek and Rollins ponds, anymore, however. There the constitution has been circumvented in the name of fire protection and concentration of use to preserve other areas. More than 600 campsites along some 2½ miles of waterfront now banish the wild forever. And there I confess, I lost my ambivalence and my cool toward what New York has done over the years in this tiny jewel box of wilderness waterways. The could-have-been wilderness was being lounged upon with beach chairs, for the Empire State was saying welcome, city man, to the wild Adirondacks on *your* terms. And the little boys who camped there in the elaborate tents and trailers would never, in old age, dream back to a first adventure in the wilds. Above the portable radios, they would not hear the Red Gods' call.

Saranac Lakes, 17.5 m (28.2 km.)
USGS: Saint Regis, Long Lake, Saranac Lake 15; Upper Saranac Lake, Saranac Lake 7.5 × 15

The longest tour of the Saranac Lakes, between state launching sites at the N end of the Upper Lake and NE end of the Lower, is 17.5 m. Put-in is adjacent to the point formerly occupied by that white colossus, the Saranac Inn. After surviving several years of disuse, the inn finally burned to the ground on June 17, 1978. The tour of the lakes can be shortened in a variety of ways as time, inclination, and weather suggest. The direction of travel should normally be from W to E to take advantage of prevailing winds. Winds shift, however, and a reverse course may be indicated. The following public launching sites allow a good deal of flexibility in planning a route:

Upper Saranac Lake: (1) State site at N end of lake on Back Bay off Route 30 at Saranac Inn turnoff; hard-surfaced ramp and lot for 40 cars and trailers. (2) Fish Creek Bay area, off Route 30; several put-in sites on headwater ponds. (3) Indian Carry at S end of lake, on gravel road off Route 3; sand ramp.

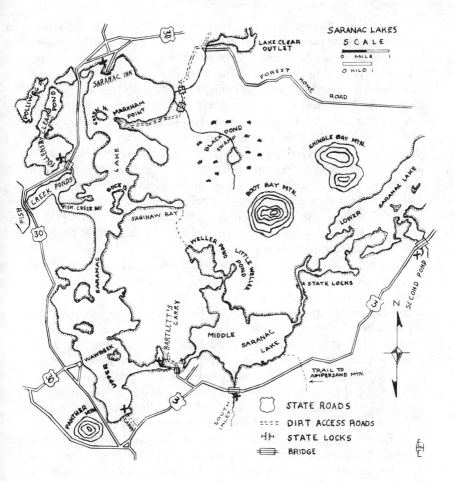

STATE ROADS

===== DIRT ACCESS ROADS

ᛁᛞᛁ STATE LOCKS

▭ BRIDGE

Middle Saranac Lake: (1) South Creek, a state site for canoes and other car-top boats on Route 3 about 9.5 m. W of Saranac Lake Village and 5.5 m. E of the junction of 3 and 30; stream navigable for 0.5 m. to lake. (2) Carry trail of 0.5 m. from Route 3 (about 8 m. W of Saranac Lake Village and 7 m. E of the junction of 3 and 30) down to a nice sand beach at the SE end of the lake.

Lower Saranac Lake: (1) Second Pond, 5 m. W of Saranac Lake Village on Route 3; hard-surfaced ramp and docks, with parking for 40 cars and trailers; caretaker assigns campsites on Lower Saranac Lake. (2) Ampersand Bay, reached from village by Ampersand Avenue or Edgewood Road; for canoes and car-top boats only.

The starting place I prefer is the foot of Follensby Clear Pond at the state parking lot and dock 0.7 m. N of the entrance to Fish Creek Campsite on Route 30. This shortens the tour by only 1 m. but spares 3 m. of exposure on the lake to the frequent SW winds of summer. The route proceeds down short but lovely Spider Creek into First Fish Creek Pond and thence into Fish Creek Bay.

Upper Saranac is 8 m. long. It is shaped somewhat like a dumbbell. From a width of 0.2 m. at the Narrows, it widens at the ends to about 2 m. Bold headlands, deep bays, and wooded or rocky islands make it interesting to explore. Most of the W shore is private, with numerous summer camps; over half of the E shore is state owned. There are tent sites on the state-owned E shore of Buck Island and on the bluff between Indian Point and Indian Carry at the S end of the Lake. Lean-tos are located about half way along the N shore of Saginaw Bay and on Indian Point.

Canoeists wishing to escape the powerboats and water skiers of Upper Saranac's summer colony can take an alternate route. Directly W of Fish Creek Bay is Saginaw Bay. Long and narrow, it is likely to be the quietest part of the lake. At the SE end is a carry trail of 1 m. to Weller Pond, from which a navigable outlet leads into Middle Saranac. The trail climbs about 150 feet before making a gradual descent. There are fine hemlocks and cedars at the far end. However, the first half mile is rough, and most canoeists prefer to take the more peopled route by lake and the shorter carry at Bartlett's. Weller Pond can be visited without a carry from Middle Saranac.

The S end of the Upper Lake has an earlier history than the N end. Rustic Lodge and Bartlett's date to the early 1850s, whereas Prospect House (later Saranac Inn) was not built till 1864. Jesse Corey was the pioneer settler on the lake. He built a cabin at Sweeney Carry, near Wawbeek, about 1830. In 1850 he moved still farther down the lake and built a popular inn, Rustic Lodge, on Indian Carry. In the present century this property became a private camp, and the carry trail was shifted to state land a quarter mile E. Jesse Corey is said to have found in the vicinity a large number of Indian artifacts which he dribbled out among his patrons. This and other evidence have led to speculation that a hunting camp or summer village of Algonquins was once located on Indian Carry. A few arrowheads have been found near here in the present century.

Of the old inns on the lake dating back to the last century, only the Wawbeek, after being closed for many years, torn down and rebuilt, served the public through the Lake Placid Winter Olympics of 1980; shortly thereafter it burned. The Saranac Inn survived for nearly a century, from 1864 till it closed its doors in 1962. For the next sixteen years it stood on its point as an empty monument to the past till it finally burned to the ground on June 17, 1978.

Some of the early patrons of the hotels hankered for family camps of their own. This stage of development has proved more durable, though it, too, has undergone changes. As families grew in size and guest lists along with them, so did the number of cottages or cabins until many camps resembled hamlets. Much care went into improving, enlarging, and decorating. Odd specimens found in the woods and along beaches served as symbols of main lodges or separate units. Mounted animal heads lined interior walls whether the owner was a hunter or not. Stones for great fireplaces were selected with deliberate care. One owner of Upper Saranac imported clay from England for his tennis courts.

A shortage of help after World War I put a strain on maintenance of these large camps. Family fortunes were reduced by climbing tax rates, division among heirs, and depression. An Upper Saranac camp that had cost $200,000 sold in 1938 for $75,000. The smaller camps have proved more viable, and demand for them is as great as ever. Some of the large ones have been split up among several individual owners. Others are passing into the ownership of charitable institutions, universities, or other organizations.

The little church on Chapel Island, east of Wawbeek, has survived all these changes. On summer Sundays canoes, sailboats, and power-boats still tie up for interdenominational services as they have since 1889. The original chapel burned in 1956 but was rebuilt two years later.

The outlet of Upper Saranac is opposite Wawbeek in a long narrow bay. Here, at the site of Bartlett's Hotel (now a colony of private camps known as the Bartlett Carry Club), the Saranac breaks through a ledge of anorthosite in a narrow gorge. The carry is an easement over private land. The present route of 0.45 m. is nearly twice the length of the original carry. The rerouting has led to confusion and wasted effort. Instead of paddling to the E end of the outlet bay, one now goes about 0.5 m. E and then swings NE to a marked landing (white sign) in Huckleberry Bay. Here one carries upgrade to the R, on a good gravel road, to a ridgetop. As the descent begins, look for a marked trail leaving the road on the L and going down to a landing on the Saranac River. (A lone kayaker I met on an October day had missed the turn off the gravel road and had carried his craft out to Route 3 before discovering his mistake.)

It is less than a half mile by the broad stream to Middle Saranac. The W shore of this lake is private and the remaining two-thirds is state owned. As a remedy for overuse of main shores and islands for camping, the DEC has designated 25 tent or lean-to sites on Middle Saranac Lake and Weller Pond. A camping fee ($9.00 in 1992) is charged by the night. Arrangements are made with the caretaker at the Second Pond launching site at the Route 3 bridge. No fee is charged prior to Memorial Day in May and after Labor Day in September.

Presenting a broad surface to the westerlies, Middle Saranac is easily whipped into whitecaps. Though shallower than the other two lakes, it is often rough when they are not.

If time allows, a side trip to Weller Pond through the marshy inlet is recommended. Before Boy Scouts discovered Weller's attractions as a campground, Martha Reben spent several seasons on it and wrote two books about her experiences, *The Healing Woods* (1952) and *The Way of the Wilderness* (1955). The islands and the main shore are state owned. Weller is so well known now that it is no longer the isolated gem it was till the 1950s. To recapture the isolation and silence, one must visit it on snowshoes or skis in winter. Then Middle Saranac and Weller make an ideal tour.

Little Weller Pond can be reached by a fork in the Weller Pond Outlet. The marshy banks of the stream are colorful in June with the blossoms of pitcher plants. Little Weller itself is bleak compared to its opulently wooded namesake.

An ascent of Boot Bay Mountain from Weller Pond is a challenge to bushwhackers. The trick is to return through trackless woods to your canoe on the E shore without straying into wetlands on the S or an expanse of shoreless, uneven ground on the N. A compass bearing should be taken on the mountain from Tick Island, and again from the W summit of the mountain for the return trip to the pond. To keep an accurate course, one person walks 70 feet or so ahead and takes directions from the compass holder behind him. At the start there are low ridges to get over before the steady climb begins. The going is fairly easy in tall timber with little undergrowth and little blowdown. You pass through a climax forest. But suddenly, about two-thirds of the way to the summit, the tall trees stop as if at a wall. The rest of the ascent is made over outcroppings under a canopy of birch and aspen. A fire swept over the upper part of the W face early in the century. Open spots afford views to the W over

Weller Pond and Upper Saranac to Tupper Lake. The ascent to the W summit takes a little less than two hours; the return, about an hour and a half—if direction finding is accurate.

On the return trip from Weller Pond toward the outlet of Middle Saranac, one enjoys impressive mountain views all the way. Ampersand and Stony Creek mountains fill the southern horizon and beyond them massive Seward. As you round Umbrella Point, the view expands to include several of the High Peaks in the SE. But it is noble Ampersand that dominates by its nearness. The first recorded ascent was made from Middle Saranac in 1872 by W. W. Ely, M. D., of Rochester, New York, maker of the first good detailed map of the Adirondacks. In 1873 Dr. Ely ascended Ampersand again with a work crew, cleared a small area of the summit for a view, and opened a trail by following a compass reading NW to the sand beach on the SE shore of Middle Saranac. Cutting trail from the top down, he ignored the human limitations of those going the opposite way and stuck to an uncompromising beeline. For the next 70 years people panted up the steep pitches of Dr. Ely's Spartan trail.

A few months after the trail was cut, Colvin and his team of surveyors and guides camped on the mountaintop for three days. Dr. Ely's small clearing was not enough for their job of mountain measuring. They felled timber on the whole crest. That is why Ampersand today has a bald top. Once the trees were gone, storms washed the duff off bedrock.

In the 1880s Henry van Dyke, patron of Bartlett's, Princeton professor, writer, and ordained minister, who used to preach on summer Sundays at the little church on Chapel Island, Upper Saranac, climbed Ampersand with his guide and wrote a glowing description for *Harper's Monthly*, July 1885. Since then, Ampersand has been everybody's mountain, like Monadnock in New Hampshire. About 1916 two brothers in their early teens, Bob and George Marshall, with their guide Herbert Clark, climbed the peak from their family camp on Lower Saranac. The experience so excited the boys that they went on, in the next few years, to climb all 46 Adirondack peaks of 4,000 feet or higher, several of them the first recorded ascents. Today a national wilderness area in Montana is named for the older of the brothers, Bob, whose career as explorer, forester, writer, conservationist, and founder of the Wilderness Society started on Ampersand.

Walter Rice, fire observer on Ampersand from 1915–1923, devoted years of labor to lessening the rigors of Dr. Ely's old trail. He built an elaborate system of log ladders and staircases, complete with railings and seats on lookout landings. His successors were not so careful to keep the stairs in repair, and finally the old Ely-Rice trail above the site of the former observer's cabin was abandoned. A new route, longer, less steep, and less spectacular, was opened from a point halfway up the mountain. Too bad. Serial outlooks over the lakes were reward enough for the rigors and vertigo of the old trail. The present one is already badly eroded. But it has compensations, especially toward the upper part where it winds through a narrow col and around cliffs and boulders.

The Ampersand Trail is 3.2 m. long from the lakeshore. In 0.5 m. it crosses the highway into a climax forest of hardwoods and conifers, including shadowy groves of tall hemlock. Higher up, spruce, balsam fir, and white birch prevail until one reaches the bare rock of the summit. The old fire tower was dismantled in 1977 by Moses Smoke, a Mohawk Indian, and the parts were carried off by helicopter. Ampersand is in the High Peaks Wilderness Area, and an artificial structure such as a fire tower is incompatible with wilderness under APA guidelines.

The view from the top is a celebrated one. To the E are the High Peaks; to the N and W, more lakes and ponds than you can count. But turn to the S for simple grandeur. At the base of the mountain is a single body of water, the glimmering crescent of Ampersand Lake, and beyond it an unspoiled wilderness of mountain slope and forest as far as the eye can see.

To return to the canoe route. Buoys mark the shallow channel on the approach to the outlet of Middle Saranac, which is hidden amidst the reeds and rushes of Bull Rush Bay. The first half of the next 2-m. stretch of river is a broad marshy flood-plain rich in water vegetation. The best season is mid-August, while masses of white pond lilies are still blooming and the blue spikes of large pickerelweed beds are at their best. If the foliage of scattered swamp maples has already begun to turn scarlet, you will conclude, perhaps too hastily, that there is no prettier natural garden in the Adirondacks than this.

About a quarter mile above the locks, at a bend, a large rock presents a symmetrical pentagonal face upstream. Wooded banks now close in as a lip of bedrock is approached at a short rapid. Here is the first of two sets of manually operated locks. A state lock tender is on duty through most of the boating season. In his absence canoeists can operate the locks by following posted instructions or can carry around them. The difference in level between Middle Saranac and Lower is only three feet; virtually all of the drop comes here.

Just below the locks on the R is a good tent site. Another, about 0.4 m. downstream, is the flat top of a 12-foot ledge facing SW toward the summer breeze. The entrance to Lower Saranac is a beautiful passage with cliffs on one side and a marsh on the other.

Once on the lake, avoid the large bay on the R and head NE into the Narrows. Keep nearly the same bearing through clusters of islands if your objective is the state landing in Ampersand Bay at the NE end of the lake. (The parking lot at this landing is locked from 8 p.m. to 8 a.m. If you headed for the landing on the outlet at Second Pond (which shortens the tour of the lakes by 2 m.), keep to the R of the bold cliffs of Bluff Island; and round Picnic Point into First Pond, where the river, wide and narrow by turns, twists between bluffs. The landing, R, is just beyond the highway bridge.

The removal of all 300 tent platforms on Lower and Middle Saranac, completed in 1977, has eliminated exclusive use of camp sites and lessened the intensity of use. The DEC has adopted a new program of a more primitive kind of camping involving a fee for overnight occupancy at approximately 60 tenting sites on Lower Saranac at widely spaced intervals on islands and shoreline. Most contain a fireplace, a table, and a pit privy. Powerboats, though not excluded, are not encouraged; docks at former tent-platform sites have been removed. The fee ($9.00 in 1992 and subject to increase) helps prevent overuse. A caretaker at the landing on Second Pond collects fees and gives each camper a map with an assigned location on it. Another caretaker patrols the lake by boat to check on campers who use other points of access, such as the Saranac River at the head of the lake.

Second Pond to Moose Pond Road, 16 m. (25.7 km.)
USGS: Saranac Lake 15; Saranac Lake, Bloomingdale 7.5 × 15

This stretch of the Saranac is a study in contrasts. The marks of time can be reckoned in aeons or decades. The river itself is not very old. The channel it follows here is thought to be postglacial. But the rock it washes is 1,100,000,000 years old. A geologist has called Route 3, the highway where the trip begins, "the road of anorthosite"; every exposure on it between the villages of Saranac Lake and Tupper Lake is the ancient gray-blue stone familiar to hikers in the High Peaks. The Saranac is the river of anorthosite. The basins of Lower Saranac, Kiwassa, and Oseetah lakes are eroded in it. It towers over the river above and below the mouth of Cold Brook.

This reach also winds through the heart of Saranac Lake Village, where the first settler did not arrive till 1819. Only in the perspective of Adirondack history is the village old. Through decades of rising and declining prosperity it has had a cosmopolitan air. Some of the tubercular patients who came here for the cure in the late 19th and early 20th centuries liked the village and its setting well enough to stay on into the third or fourth generation. The prosperous days of the sanatoria are long past. Saranac looks a little shabby in spite of the new high rises. But it is not garish like some resort towns. An Old World atmosphere lingers in some of the balconied store fronts of Broadway (which isn't) and Main, and in the cracked masonry walls along the river and the feeding ducks.

The river from Second Pond to the dam at the foot of Lake Flower in the village is infested with the powerboats of summer residents and tourists. But a little way up Cold Brook one can escape into the silence of a primeval forest. Below the village there are few powerboats, but the contrasts between developed and wild continue for several miles as heavily traveled Route 3 borders the river on the L and the 35,000-acre McKenzie Mountain Wilderness Area on the R.

Most of the 16-m. stretch is in back or slack water. The drop is only about 25 feet. The current quickens below the dam in the village, slackens again in a marshy area, and in the last 3 m. is alternately quick and slow. There is one short carry around the dam in the village.

Put-in is the state launching site 5 m. W of the village at the bridge on Route 3. The backwater here is known as Second Pond. Toward its E end, cedars bordering the N shore have been pruned by those landscape gardeners, the deer. The remarkably even understory is the browse line, or highest reach of the whitetailed deer from the snow-covered pond in winter feeding. This is a familiar sight wherever cedars line the shore of river or lake.

The river below Second Pond is marked by buoys and spindles. Going downstream, the black and white markers are to be passed on the R side of the boat and the red and white ones on the L. Canoeists can usually ignore them.

From Second Pond to Cold Brook the stream winds through dense woods. Its attractiveness is well known, and boat traffic is fairly heavy. There is a lean-to on the L bank on the approach to Cold Brook. Opposite the mouth of the brook is another desirable campsite for those carrying their own shelter, a shady flat where fishermen have cooked their catch for generations. Cold Brook was once famous for its two-pound trout. Today only little ones are caught. It is usually

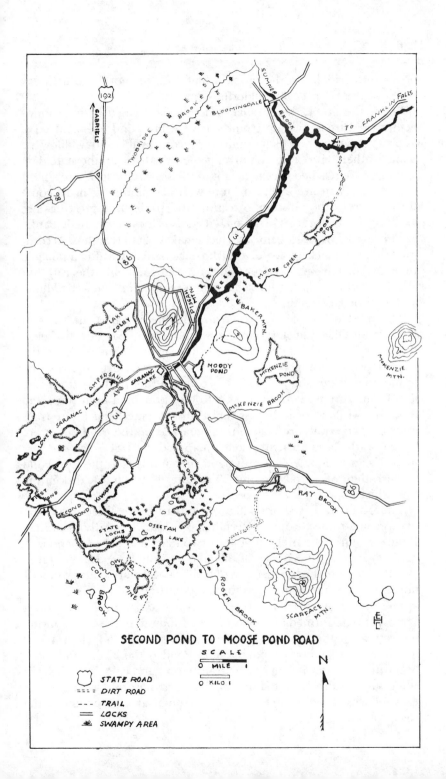

SECOND POND TO MOOSE POND ROAD

SCALE

0 MILE 1

0 KILO 1

N

State Road
Dirt Road
Trail
Locks
Swampy Area

possible to paddle up the brook a half mile or more into a climax forest of the High Peaks Wilderness Area.

Below the brook the Saranac widens in a flooded basin. Stumps of drowned trees stick up from beds of white pond lilies and serve as bird nests or pots of rich humus for ferns, shrubs, and wildflowers. Some of them rival a florist's arrangements. At 2.4 m. the state dam and locks are reached. At the height of the season the locks are almost continuously in use. A five-minute wait is common as boats come through from the opposite direction and smiles and greetings are exchanged. A short carry trail of 100 yards is located on the R bank.

The novelty of passing through locks makes people careless. According to a former lock tender, divers who once went down after a valuable ring dropped from a cruiser came up with not only the ring but also two wristwatches, a pocket watch, a manual on canoe paddling, and a set of false teeth.

The most enjoyable side excursion on this reach is the trails to Pine Pond. One trail starts on the S shore of the bay directly below the locks. The lock tender can point the way to it. One passes to the R of a private camp near the water's edge onto a jeep road that soon enters state land and finally becomes a foot trail. By this route it is 1.1 m. to Pine Pond. It is easy to go astray on a branching jeep road to Owl Pond or to bypass the R turn to Pine Pond where trails intersect. The trails are inadequately marked on the ground but are traced on the accompanying sketch map and the USGS *Saranac Lake* map. Use a compass. The prevalent direction is S to the Owl Pond turnoff, then SE. It takes about 20 minutes to reach a R fork in the trail which soon leads to the pond.

The other trail is shorter (0.5 m.) but involves a detour off the main canoe route through Oseetah Lake (known locally as Millers Pond). It starts obscurely (a boat or two may be beached there) in a marshy cove in the SW bay of the lake on state land. Here too it is essential to note the intersection of trails on the map so that you will not stray off to the S and miss the pond entirely.

The basins of Owl Pond (partly private) and Pine Pond (Forest Preserve) were formed by blocks of ice left buried in the sands during the retreat of the ice cap. The slow-melting blocks left depressions for these two landlocked ponds. Pine Pond is the larger and more beautiful. Its water is remarkably transparent and cold. The shelving white sand at the N end is one of the finest natural beaches in the Adirondacks. It commands a view of Ampersand Mountain in the background.

In the early 1930s, when I first visited Pine Pond, relatively few people knew of it. There was a good chance of having the white beach all to yourself. Now, however, people from the private camps on Oseetah and Kiwassa lakes and Owl Pond come there to swim, and Boy Scouts and other groups often encamp on the knoll of red pines above the beach. To avoid transistor radios and boisterous Scouts, it is best to pick a warm weekday in June or after Labor Day. Pine Pond is an object lesson in how the loveliest of natural areas becomes degraded by overuse and abuse. The white sand is often disfigured by articles which people have had the energy to carry in but not the decency to carry out. The rest of the shore (sand continues all the way around) is cleaner and in September is graced by blooming closed gentians, pearly everlasting, and ladies' tresses as well as by patches of ripe cranberries.

A trail continues to the S off the E side of Pine Pond. It passes through a climax forest in one of the oldest parts of the Forest Preserve and in 1.3 m. enters the ravine of Cold Brook amidst a stand of giant hemlocks. At East Brook (*Santanoni* quad) a branching trail (converted into a logging road when salvage crews took out fallen timber after the Big Blow of 1950) goes E to Averyville. South of this junction the continuation up Cold Brook is little more than a rough fishermen's trail.

Kiwassa Lake is a side trip that can be made by canoe through the channel E of Oseetah Lake. Its N and E shores are lined with camps.

The main route bears NE and N from the state locks to the dam in the village, a distance of 4.6 m. through the broad backwaters of Oseetah Lake and Lake Flower. From the former there are views of Scarface, McKenzie, and Whiteface mountains.

As one approaches the village of Saranac Lake, traffic becomes heavier, with craft of all kinds on the water. Early in July, annually since 1963, boat races are held beginning on the E shore of Lake Flower and ending at the Fish and Game Club beach 2 m. below the village. The races are in memory of Willard Hanmer, a guideboat builder. There are races for several kinds of craft, including family, racing and war canoes, kayaks, and guideboats. A carnival spirit prevails among participants and spectators.

Coming down Lake Flower, land on either bank above the bridge in the village. Carry across Main Street and down an alley between a white building and a red one to a good landing below the dam. High retaining walls line much of the river in the commercial section of the village. There are two Class I rapids. At medium to low water levels look out for submerged rocks in the vicinity of bridges.

Saranac Lakers have made an earnest effort to locate and eliminate sources of pollution on the river's course through the village. Sewage is treated at a modern disposal plant. Yet, in addition to the customary tannic stain of streams flowing through spruce-fir-sphagnum swamps, the Saranac is slightly clouded through most of the stretch from the village to the Moose Pond Road. This suggests that some sources of pollution have not been eliminated.

From the Lake Flower dam to the Moose Pond Road E of Blooming-dale, a distance of 9 m., the river is mostly smooth. The current is a little faster than in the upper river, and a tail wind often helps as the stream swings 'NE. The natural beauty of this valley between the McKenzie Wilderness Area on the E and the Saranac Esker on the W is marred by the highway cut, often close to the L bank, and by the gravel pits on the esker. The rumble of traffic is a discordant note. After noticing the purple loosestrife and steeplebush on the L bank, canoeists learn to fix attention on the R bank and mountain slopes above it.

Moose Creek is navigable for a half mile or so if you can find the true mouth in the maze of the delta. Sumner Brook offers a way of entering the river from Bloomingdale at medium high water when rapids just below the Route 3 bridge in the village can be run.

Below Sumner Brook, road traffic is less evident. The River Road to Franklin Falls (also known as Franklin Falls Road), which now parallels the river, is lightly traveled and often out of sight and hearing. The bridge on the Moose Pond Road is 1.7 m. below Sumner Brook. A little way below the bridge, on the L bank, there is state land on which one can camp. A more desirable camping site, if a car is available here, is on Moose Pond, 1.2 m. S of the bridge by a good gravel road. Moose Pond is now entirely state owned. There are fireplaces and picnic tables at the N end. A trail on the R leads to a snug clearing and large flat rock. Many other sites for tenting can be found by canoeing around this beautiful mountain pond.

Moose Pond Road to Union Falls, 12.5 m. (20.1 km.)
USGS: Saranac Lake, Lake Placid 15; Alder Brook 7.5; Bloomingdale, Wilmington 7.5 × 15

This too is a section of strong contrasts between the wild and the developed. Because of its summer colonies and power developments, the entire reach of the Saranac within park boundaries has been classified "recreational" by the APA. Yet there are scenic passages where man is little in evidence. Below the Moose Pond Road the river escapes from the large intramountain basin of the Lake Belt through a narrow valley that slopes toward Lake Champlain. In the 12.5-m. stretch to Union Falls it drops 150 feet, considerably more than in the whole upper course of 40 m. from Lake Clear. But the drop is not a steady one. Most of it comes in three sharp pitches of about 35 feet in Permanent Rapids, 54 feet at Franklin Falls, and 56 feet at Union Falls. Between these pitches are two placid backwaters, Franklin Falls Pond, 3 m. long, and Union Falls Pond, 6 m. They are broad enough to unfold superb mountain views as one crosses this main axis of elevation.

The water continues smooth for 1.5 m. below the Moose Pond Road. Near the end of this stretch a loop comes close to the road on the L bank; this is a good place to put in or take out according to your intention to run or not to run the rapids.

At the 1,500-foot contour the banks steepen and constrict the river in a gorge with walls 100 to 200 feet high. One glides swiftly into the ravine. Canoeists have given the next mile the name Permanent Rapids because, in seasons of normal rainfall, it is canoeable all summer. However, at low water levels the last 0.25 m. is typically very scratchy. Permanent Rapids closely parallels River Road and is a popular whitewater play spot for local paddlers. There are several put-in sites where the river approaches to within 20 feet of the road. Take-out is at the beginning of the slackwater of Franklin Falls reservoir, where the L bank juts out noticeably. There is room for several cars to park off the road at this spot. A short uphill carry of 50 yards is necessary. Both banks along the rapids are state land.

Starting with Class I riffles, this reach soon divides around a small island with the more sporting route around a ledge on the R. Class II rapids then begin as the river narrows and the banks steepen. The most difficult section, rated Class II-III at high water levels, begins where the river funnels between a low rocky point on the L and a high bank on the R. After 100 yards the river again widens and settles down. Numerous channels exist and most are scratchy. The take-out described above is found below 75 yards of flatwater. For those continuing past this point, the ravine widens into the reservoir. A small island directly ahead makes a good tent site.

The two most interesting features of Franklin Falls Pond are the

mouth of Still Brook in a deep bay on the R and views of Whiteface,
Esther, and Moose mountains framed between smaller peaks in the
foreground. A visit to the delta of Still Brook lengthens the route
through the reservoir by 1 m. The brook mouth is a rich feeding
ground for shore birds. On one visit we saw several ducks and kingfishers. A score of spotted sandpipers teetered on the sand and mud
flats. And as we poled a little way up the brook, five great blue herons
lumbered into flight.

At the foot of Franklin Falls Pond, a carry of 0.4 m. begins on the
upstream L side of the bridge and descends a hill on blacktop.
Nothing is left of the hotel or other buildings, strung out in a row on
each side of the road in the narrow ravine, of the hamlet of Franklin
Falls that grew up around a lumbermill. The settlement was destroyed
by fire in 1852. The mill and the hotel were rebuilt. Paul Smith was
married at the Franklin Falls House in 1859. After he had made his
fortune, he bought the land around the falls (known originally as
McLenathan Falls), closed the hotel, and by 1912 completed the
building of a hydroelectric plant on the site.

During the construction of the dam, the state secured an injunction
against Paul Smith's power company, charging it with flooding 270
acres of state land. Smith ignored the injunction. It was already too
late to save the trees. The Association for the Protection of the Adirondacks fought the case in court, and the suit dragged on till 1912.
Finally a decision was rendered in favor of the power company.

The carry of 0.4 m. around the power plant brings one to a put-
in site on the narrow ravine at the head of Union Falls Pond. Gradually
the shores of the reservoir widen to a maximum of over 1 m. In
some places the heads of submerged stumps are a hazard.

Woodruff Bay opens on the R at 1.5 m. Two cold mountain brooks
enter it, both draining the N face of Whiteface Mountain. The easternmost, Frenchs Brook, is worth a visit. It splashes into the bay over a
curving staircase of bedrock 20 feet high.

In the pool below the cascade, there used to be a large bed of
smartweed, its spiky clusters of pink blossoms carpeting the dark
water in August. On a return visit in August 1973, the cascade at
the mouth was as pretty a sight as ever, but the smartweed was gone.
Its disappearance is a mystery that strikes at the conscience of a guidebook writer. How many other changes will take place after he has
fixed conditions, hopefully for permanence, in print? Nature is a
magician skilled in acts of disappearance and transformation. To say
nothing of man.

Mountains at least are relatively permanent. The two long narrow reservoirs lie in a gap athwart the main axis of elevation in the Adirondacks, and the mountain views that each commands are quite different. On Union Falls Pond one must look back for a grand view of Whiteface, Esther, and Moose. Ahead or to the side are Duncan, Alder Brook, Catamount, and Silver Lake mountains, all with a generous display of gray cliffs amidst their forest cover.

At the foot of the pond a boom encircles the dam. The landing on the L is a private one in the hamlet of Union Falls. You should take out on the R bank in the angle formed by the boom and the shore. This is state land where a camp can be set up. Cars can be driven to this beach over a short spur from the E side of Union Falls bridge.

A car at each end or a prearranged pickup is recommended for this stretch and the next one. Hitching a ride is a poor prospect on little-traveled Rock Street and Alder Brook Road W of Union Falls and on the Casey Road NE to the Silver Lake Road.

East of Union Falls Pond is an interesting rock climb that can be made by any mountain hiker. Catamount Mountain is about 5 m. E of Franklin Falls on the Forestdale Road. Viewing it from this western approach arouses an itch to climb this unique peak rising abruptly from the flats of old pastures and potato fields. Directions for finding the obscure beginnings of the trail and following its twists can be found in the Adirondack Mountain Club's *Guide to Adirondack Trails* or in my article "Catamount Mountain" in the September-October 1959 issue of the *Ad-i-ron-dac.*

Union Falls to the Silver Lake Road, 4 m. (6.4 km.)
USGS: Alder Brook, Redford 7.5

From Union Falls to the Blue Line, the Saranac is stocked with rainbow and brown trout. Fishermen are often seen wading the rapids.

The 4-m. reach from the falls to the Silver Lake Road is wild and scenic. Its Class I-II rapids are best run at medium high water. You can check on the water level at the bridge at the end of the run. A gauge has been painted on the downstream L side of the Silver Lake Road bridge. Water levels above 1 foot indicate good to satisfactory conditions; levels between 0 and 1 feet would be scratchy but still negotiable. Paddlers should not confuse this gauge with an older, faded gauge on the upstream L side which reads almost a foot higher than the new gauge. Scanning the rapids above and below the same bridge is also a good indication of what to expect in the upper part of the run.

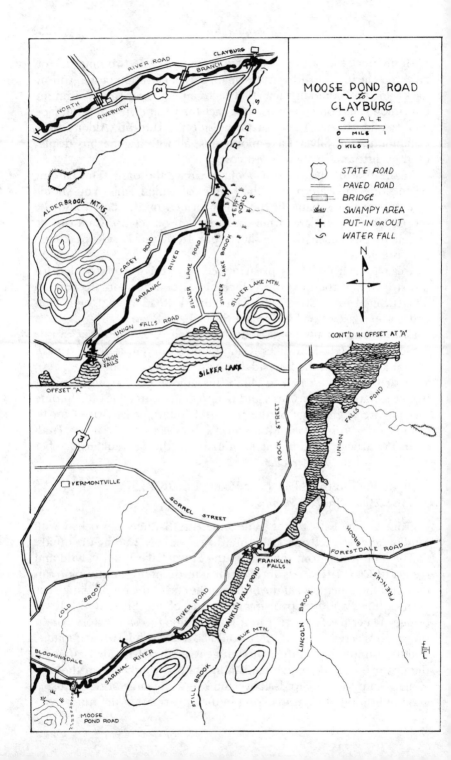

In general, the Saranac has a longer canoeing season than any other river of Champlain drainage. The upper part, with several large lakes to feed it, remains canoeable all summer. Most of the lower river does also when rainfall is normal or above. At the Union Falls Dam the power company does not shut off the flow. When the level is below the dam, what was formerly a turbine is opened to sustain some flow. Shortly after the third edition went to print a new hydroelectric project was developed at Union Falls. This resulted in significant dewatering of the stretch of rapids immediately below the falls. Minimum flow requirements for this project are too low to allow paddling below the dam; however, excess flows above the turbine capacity will be released from the dam during periods of high water. The increased flow may make it possible to paddle this stretch during very high water levels. Minimum flows downstream of the powerhouse should still be sufficient to allow cruising during the regular paddling season.

The drop in this section is about 35 feet. There are three sets of rapids. This stretch should be skipped by those who do not have Class II abilities. Exit is difficult on swampy, densely wooded terrain some distance from the road.

Canoeists who are continuing the trip from Union Falls and do not have a car there should carry across the bridge below the dam and turn R on the Casey Road. About 0.1 m. below the turn a gated gravel road on the R goes down to a power house. Although the road is marked "Danger," "Private," local people obviously use it on foot. At the bottom of the hill fishermen's trails lead to put-in sites in mild rapids. This makes the shortest (0.4 m.) and easiest carry. It is not necessary to go near danger points to launch a canoe. Niagara Mohawk Power Corporation has "an open land policy." It does not keep people off but asks them to leave the area in as good shape as they found it. The APA study report on the Saranac River recommends that a state launching site be developed on state land below the power company enclosure. Canoeists who hesitate to use the latter should inquire locally whether the recommendation has been carried out.

Though most boaters will prefer to put in at the site described above, an interesting alternative exists for skilled boaters during periods of very high water. On the L bank immediately below the bridge is a small boiling eddy. Access to this eddy is difficult because of the steepness of the bank and the fact that the eddy is not much longer than most boats. Once in the eddy a single stroke and a brace draw the boat into very swift current at the top of a 200-yd. Class III-IV rapid. The best course is to start slightly to the R of center in order to avoid a sharp pointed rock which is barely submerged at high water. Gradually move to the L, just skirting a ledge protruding from the R about halfway down. This entire rapid is full of large waves and holes which can easily knock a boat from its intended course. Because of its speed, narrowness, and tendency to contain items washed over the dam, careful scouting is advised.

Take-out at the Silver Lake Road may present some problems as all four corners of the bridge are heavily posted. It is possible, however, to take out here and still stay within the allowed right-of-way. The upstream R and downstream L banks both contain very faint trails from the edge of the bridge abutment to the road, with the downstream L bank being somewhat easier to negotiate and less likely to provoke disputes over the right-of-way. Canoeists continuing downstream should seek deeper water in the main current near the R bank and then, 100 feet below the bridge, work toward the center along a diagonal line of boulders. Those who wish to avoid a dispute at Silver Lake Road bridge have two options. The easier one, the first fishing access site below Tefft Pond Falls (see next section), has been used in the past but is presently in dispute. The other, a previously flagged bushwhack of 200 yards, begins at the head of the Class I rapid 0.8 m. upstream from the bridge. Start at a yellow property post and follow yellow blazes marking the Forest Preserve boundary. Follow this through dense blowdown to Casey Road at a point 1 m. from its intersection with Silver Lake Road (3.5 m. from the Union Falls Road intersection). The Forest Preserve boundary is shown incorrectly on the *Redford* map; it is actually located about a half mile further to the W, on the *Alder Brook* map.

A pleasant side excursion in the vicinity is the mile-long trail up Silver Lake Mountain amidst tall pines. The trail, 2.9 m. S of the Saranac River bridge, is on the E side of the Silver Lake Road at five mailboxes.

Silver Lake Road to Clayburg, 5 m. (8 km.)
USGS: Redford 7.5

This portion of the Saranac possesses the best and most challenging rapids on the entire Saranac River and is comparable to the Silver Staircase of the St. Regis in its sustained, dazzling display of whitewater. Though there are pastoral flatwater stretches, this section is dominated by long, complex series of ledges and by boulder gardens requiring much maneuvering. In the last 3.5 m. the drop is 200 feet, an average gradient of 57 feet per mile. Rapids range from Class II to Class V, making this a suitable run for advanced paddlers. Intermediate level paddlers can usually negotiate much of this run during early summer. There are fishing-rights easements on the trails along the L bank and out to parking lots on the highway. These facilitate scouting and carrying as the need arises.

Paddlers who stay with the river from Union Falls can avoid the disputed access at the bridge on the Silver Lake Road, 2 m. N of the intersection with Union Falls Road and 3.9 m. S of the intersection with Route 3 at Clayburg. Access is as described in the previous section and the same statements apply with respect to gauge readings.

Immediately under the bridge and continuing for about 150 yards is a fairly simple Class II rapid. The river then widens into a 1.4 m. stretch of flatwater known as Tefft Pond. This stretch bears the above name because the river channel and the marshy area surrounding it used to be flooded by a dam downstream. Since the breaching of the dam the backwater has drained out. Below this stretch the current quickens and the sound of falling water is heard. Here the river falls abruptly in a dangerous Class V drop known as Tefft Pond Falls (or locally as Garlic Falls). Paddlers should proceed carefully and immediately pull over. On the R bank a sign indicates a carry trail, which winds for approximately 50 yards through a boggy area littered with numerous deadfalls. There is an easier carry on the L, a fishermen's trail. The L channel of this drop takes a near vertical plunge of about 10 feet over exposed rocks and then cascades over and through a complex series of boulders where no discernable course exists. The R channel requires relatively little maneuvering, but the likelihood of flipping and possibly getting pinned is quite high. This route involves two drops, back to back, the first of 4 feet and the second of 8 feet. Both drops have substantial aerated hydraulics, particularly the lower one. The bottom drop veers sharply to the R, hiding partially submerged rocks which serve as a warning about a possible pin.

The carries end in a pool below the falls. In several dozen yards is one of the most difficult sections of the Saranac, approximately 0.3 m. long. It consists of a complex series of ledges and drops. Though most of the individual drops are only Class II-III in difficulty, the combination of length and complexity may be sufficent to warrant a Class III-IV rating. Paddlers with advanced skills who wish to avoid the Tefft Pond flatwater may want to put in at the first fishing access site 1.0 m. N of the Silver Lake Road bridge. A 400-yard carry upstream brings you to the L bank below Tefft Pond Falls. The public's right to use this access is under dispute.

The first drop in this series is the most difficult. The drop is about 4 feet into a diagonally shaped, turbulent hydraulic. After this, proceed to the L bank and negotiate a series of ledges. Most of these are wide and regularly shaped and hence have powerful hydraulics below them. The best way to run these is to ferry across the backwash, taking care not to be swept upstream into them, until a suitable channel can be found. Because of all this hydraulic action the downstream current is not as fast as one might expect from the steep (100 feet per mile) gradient. It is, however, full of cross-currents and is fairly difficult to read.

Toward the end of this section the rapids become easier, settling down to continuous Class II-III. The remnants of an old footbridge appear about 0.5 m. below Tefft Pond Falls. (Watch out for cables near the surface of the water next to both banks.) From here the river presents fairly continuous Class II rapids for approximately 0.4 m. before beginning to pick up speed. For the next 0.8 m. there are solid Class III rapids alternating with some Class II ones. These consist mainly of broken ledges with boulders and rocks scattered about. Several fishing camps appear along the L bank.

At approximately 1.2 m. below the footbridge the river completes a 160-degree turn to the L at the head of a small ravine. At this point a large boulder divides the river into two distinct channels. The rapid below this boulder is rated Class III-IV and should be scouted, preferably from the L bank. The L channel is the better course, although the R channel may also be run. Both channels drop about 3-4 feet into substantial hydraulics. There is a small eddy behind the boulder dividing the two channels. In 10 yards there is a second drop of 4-6 feet, also with a large hydraulic at the bottom. Large rooster-tail waves mark the best course down these drops. For the next 1.3 m. the Saranac gradually fades to Class II, then Class I, rapids until the confluence with the North Branch of the Saranac at Clayburg. Take-out is at the SE corner of the bridge over the North Branch.

Clayburg to High Falls Dam, 5.5 m. (8.9 km.)
USGS: Redford, Moffitsville 7.5

At Clayburg the river swings E into a broad valley. The North Branch enters at this bend, and the Saranac now becomes a major river, averaging over 100 feet wide and canoeable throughout a summer of normal rainfall. Aside from a short stretch above and below the upper bridge in Redford, rapids do not exceed Class II in difficulty.

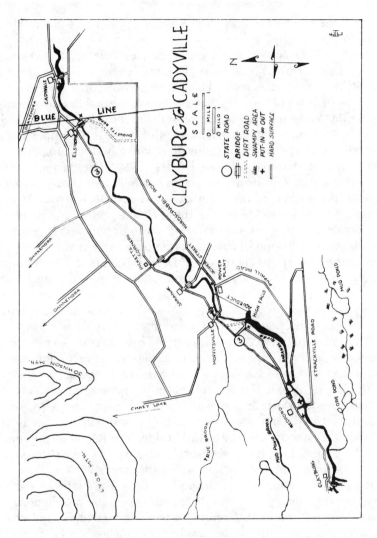

The most convenient put-in is the SE corner of the bridge over the mouth of the North Branch. Below the bridge one is soon swept into Class I rapids in the main stem. The current is moderately fast over a series of rifts. This is a pretty stretch with high wooded banks.

At 1.8 m. several rock islets are arranged in such regular rows that they do not seem natural. They aren't. They are man-made stays for booms which were used in river-driving days to sort logs according to the owners' symbols branded on them. Locally this segment of the river is known as "the Separator," though some residents have forgotten why.

Below the Separator and about a quarter mile above the upper bridge in Redford is a Class II-III rapid where the river turns to the R away from the road. This rapid consists of a series of five ledges with drops of 1 to 2 feet. These require the paddler to maneuver from side to side in tricky crosscurrents in order to avoid the hydraulics below each ledge. Immediately below this rapid is the upper bridge at Redford, where the river narrows considerably. This rapid, though fairly short and straight, is rated Class III-IV. The current is very powerful and may push an unsuspecting paddler into a large, powerful hole in the middle of the main current near the R bank. At high water levels it is possible to take the L channel. Here the current is less powerful, but some maneuvering through boulders is required. The bottom of this rapid contains large standing waves for 100–150 feet as the river drops about 8 feet. Decked boaters should take note of the "ender-hole" formed by water pouring over the final ledge on the R. There is a steep trail to the bridge from the slackwaters of a shallow bay on the L. This can serve as an alternate take-out and as a re-entry point for those choosing to carry these rapids.

On the L bank there is an unexpectedly easy carry of 0.3 m. around the whole series of rapids. To locate it, bypass the first faint trail up the steep bank and look for a second one just 10 feet above the first of the ledges. About 100 feet up the slope this trail forks. Take the R fork, headed downstream, which soon connects with a section of abandoned macadam road. Follow this smooth surface out to the road that crosses the upper Redford bridge, turn R, and on approaching the bridge, look for a well-worn path on the L, which descends to a good put-in site on flat rock below the rapids.

Redford is a quiet village strung out along the highway and the river between the two bridges. It has shrunk in size and importance since the middle of the 19th century, when it thrived on two industries, an iron mine S of the upper bridge and a glass works. Both are gone, and Redford glass is now a collector's item.

Continuing downstream in Class I waters, one passes under the lower Redford bridge in 0.7 m. In another half mile a rock juts hugely out of the stream—probably a glacial deposit. Banks now steepen to enclose a wide scenic trough of quiet backwater above the dam at High Falls.

There are in fact two dams, one intercepting the flow in the canyon known as High Falls, the other (R) at the head of a penstock through which the flow is now diverted. The original High Falls gorge, with a drop of 200 feet in 0.8 m., made an impressive wildwater scene before the building of the dam after World War II. Now the old channel is nearly dry except at flood.

Take-out is on the flats above the dam on the L. A half-wooded, half-open picnic and camping ground here is pleasant when not disfigured by litter. A loop road (the two ends are a half mile apart on the highway) connects this spot with Route 3. It is desirable to have a car here.

High Falls Dam to Cadyville, 10.8 m. (17.4 km.)
USGS: Moffitsville, Dannemora 7.5

For those continuing downstream from High Falls, the best arrangement is to transport canoes by car. The carry, though mostly downhill, is a long one of 1.7 m. Go N on a dirt road from the dam to Route 3, follow the highway into Moffitsville, and turn R across the bridge over the old river channel, now dry. At a fork in the blacktop, take the L, known as Soper Street. A good launching site is 0.7 m. beyond the bridge, at the E end of a private road into the power plant.

Between this put-in and the bridge in Picketts Corners, a distance of 2.3 m., the river makes two wide horseshoe bends. Class I rapids are almost continuous to within a half mile of the iron bridge at the Corners. They are easy to read and negotiate, and you skim over lapping waves at a good clip. At bankfull level in spring, care should be taken not to be swept into fallen trees or snags at bends; at other times you can relax and enjoy the fast float. During the dry season some wading may be necessary at one or two shallow rifts.

Beyond Picketts Corners the Saranac slackens to a serene roll amidst farmlands and woodlots. The valley widens and hills recede. You have the sense of leaving mountain country some miles before the Blue Line is crossed. The trip can be ended at a bridge on the Duquette Road, 0.1 m. S of Route 3 and near the hamlet of Elsinore. The distance to this point from the Moffitsville put-in is 7.2 m. The Blue Line, coinciding with the Schuyler Falls town line, is 0.1 m. downstream from this bridge. The SE corner of the bridge makes a convenient landing, with a trail up the bank.

Cadyville is 1.8 m. farther. A little way above the concrete bridge in the village is a public beach and picnic ground on the L where one can land.

A statement in the first edition of this guide requires updating. It remarked that I didn't know whether any canoeist had ever made the trip "on a long diagonal through the Adirondacks" from Old

Forge via the Moose, Raquette, and Saranac to the St. Lawrence
River and Montreal. I added that it was probably too late for such a
trip today because of the industrialization of the waterways outside
the park boundary. Well, in October 1976 I received a letter from
Tom Warrington, of Blue Mountain Lake, describing a 265-m. canoe
trip that he and Ernie LaPrairie had made the preceding month
from Old Forge to Sorel on the St. Lawrence. For Ernie, the motive
was to repeat a trip of 80 years earlier which his grandfather, Ernest
Blanchard, had made in an Adirondack guideboat from Old Forge
to Canada. Averaging over 35 m. a day including carries, Ernie and
Tom reached Sorel in seven and a half days. Their enthusiasm dimin-
ished on the long carries between Cadyville and Plattsburgh, on Lake
Champlain heading into a stiff northwester, and on encountering
the numerous dams and locks and the swarming motorboat traffic
of the Richelieu River. At Sorel, they found themselves in the midst
of a busy shipyard with huge tankers bearing down on their little
16-foot fiberglass canoe. The shores were lined with refineries and
storage tanks. They made a unanimous quick decision to cancel the
remaining 45 m. up the St. Lawrence to Montreal, against a powerful
current and alongside ocean-going monsters.

Tom and Ernie proved that the long diagonal is still possible. But
before attempting to follow them, others should read the day-by-
day account of their trip which Alice Gilborn wrote for the March-
April 1977 issue of *Adirondack Life*. The real theme of this article is
not so much the explicit one that the trip is still feasible as the implied
one: that we in the Adirondacks can be grateful for the creation of
the Forest Preserve in 1885, the "forever-wild" amendment of 1894,
and more recently for APA regulations designed to preserve Adirondack rivers in their near-natural state. As for the long diagonal, it
had best be terminated at the Blue Line.

Inside the park, the Saranac merits two cheers for its combination
of long scenic cruising reaches and exciting whitewater. The third
cheer should be reserved till such time as powerboats are banned
on the headwater ponds.

NORTH BRANCH

The North Branch of the Saranac rises in the Sable Mountains 11
m. N of the headwaters of the main stem. It follows an ENE course
for 28 m. to the junction in Clayburg. It is a small river and, in

most of its course, steep, shallow, and rocky. The midsection contains portions of whitewater which range from highly technical to suitable for intermediate paddlers. The last 6 m. above the junction, however, make an amusing float trip at medium high to high water in spring. Another attraction is the beaded lakes and ponds near Onchiota. From these waters an easy carry over a divide extends one's range into the Osgood drainage basin and thence to the St. Regis, Saranac, and Raquette.

A mile E of the crossroads hamlet of Onchiota is the Six Nations Indian Museum in as remote a part of the forest as could be found short of inaccessibility. No concessions are made to the national addiction to ballyhoo and maximum visibility. The museum was there before the road was paved, and the road is still lightly traveled. If you are not looking for the museum, you can drive by without becoming aware of its shy appeal for recognition of a heritage most Americans have forgotten.

Southern approach to the North Branch, 19 m.+ (30.6 km.+)
USGS: Saint Regis, Saranac Lake 15; Debar Mountain 7.5; Upper Saranac Lake, Bloomingdale 7.5 × 15

A scenic and varied two-day trip combines two previously described routes—the Seven Carries and Osgood Headwaters—to reach the chain lakes of the North Branch from the vicinity of Saranac Inn. An overnight camp on Jones Pond (Lucretia Lake) is suggested. A second car should be available for the shuttle back to the landing on Little Clear Pond from the bridge at Rainbow Narrows on the Mud Pond Road 0.6 m. N of Onchiota. Road connections, S to N, are Route 30 to Paul Smiths, 86 to the Brighton Town Hall, the Jones Pond Road to Onchiota, and the Mud Pond Road.

This canoe trail comprises a chain of 14 lakes and ponds (more with side excursions), some private and developed, others state owned and wild. The route of the Seven Carries is 9 m. long. The connection between it and Osgood headwaters is made by a 0.3 m. carry through the campus of Paul Smith's College. From the public landing on the Lower St. Regis Lake, carry N to the junction of Routes 30 and 86. Walk NE on 86 about 0.1 m. to a dirt road on the L, where there is a launching site on Church Pond. Paddle NE through a narrows to a short stream connecting Church with another small pond. Cross the latter and enter a narrow, shady canal which leads to a bay in Osgood Pond. Cross Osgood to the inlet at the E end. Proceed up this navigable stream to Jones Pond. Here the S and W shores are state owned and available for camping. The distance from Paul Smith's College to Jones Pond is 4.5 m., or a total of 13.5 m. for the first day.

The carry between Jones Pond and Rainbow Lake is the longest on the route, 0.75 m. (see the USGS map *Saranac Lake*). The trail is in part an easement over private land. The closest good take-out for the trail is about 80 yards W of a small inlet in the bay at the N end of the pond. Turn R on the blacktop for 70 yards to a trail (L) marked by red DEC discs and yellow canoe-carry ones. The trail climbs an esker and follows the ridge top to a gravel road. Here it jogs R on the road; then leaves the road on the L. The trail now leads down to a narrow cove at the SW tip of Rainbow Lake. (For canoeists starting their trip on Rainbow Lake, this carry can be shortened to 0.1 m. by driving a car to the last lap of the trail. Traveling NE on the Jones Pond Road, turn L on a gravel road at a small triangle 0.3 m. beyond Jones Pond. The trail (R) is 0.35 m. from the junction of the two roads. Orange ribbons on both sides of the road alert you to the location. There is room to park several cars at a small turnaround just past the trailhead.) Rainbow Lake was named for its shape, a long narrow arc.

Rainbow Lake Esker is the most interesting topographic feature in this area. In 1928 George H. Chadwick called attention to the remarkable development of eskers in the northern half of the Adirondacks, "perhaps unrivaled elsewhere." Among the best developed are those in the great oval, intramountain basin drained by the St. Regis and the Saranac rivers. In *Geology of the Saranac Lake Quadrangle* (1953), Arthur F. Buddington describes eskers as "irregular winding ridges of gravel and sand commonly broken and discontinuous with a form which often leads them to be called 'embankments,' 'hogbacks,' or 'horsebacks.' They are interpreted as river deposits . . . formed primarily in tunnels within and at the base of the ice sheet . . . parallel to the general direction of motion of the ice."

Eskers often bisect lakes or string them like beads. The Rainbow Lake Esker is a classic example, as a glance at the topo map shows. It is double, embracing Rainbow Lake. The western ridge, which splits the lake down the middle through its entire length, is, according to Buddington, "as fine an example of an esker as is commonly found." The parallel eastern ridge is discontinuous and less well defined. It follows the SE shore of the lake from Onchiota to converge with its twin between Rainbow Lake and Jones Pond.

Buddington suggests that the Rainbow Lake Esker might just as well be called the Adirondack Esker because of its extensions NE along the valley of the North Branch and SW across the northern half of the Adirondacks for a distance of 85 m. It crosses a low divide between tributaries of the St. Regis River near their heads, crosses the St. Regis at 1,620 feet and the Raquette at 1,500, and reaches an altitude of 1,800 on the divide between the Bog and the headwaters of the Oswegatchie. Continuing SW, it crosses the divide between the Oswegatchie and the Beaver at about 1,860 feet. Unlike a river, it rises and falls in altitude according to the underlying relief. Sophisticated map reading is required to visualize as one what Chadwick had considered separate eskers: i.e., Goldsmith, Paul Smith's, St. Regis, Floodwood, etc. For a descriptive study of Adirondack eskers and their flora and an aerial photo of Rainbow Lake Esker, see my article in *Adirondack Life*, November-December 1978.

Canoeists become intimately acquainted with the Rainbow Lake Esker in one way or another. The carry trail from Jones Pond climbs to, and for some distance follows, the top of the esker, which is dimpled with small kettle holes. The last part of the trail is in the narrow draw between the twin ridges just N of their convergence. For 4 m. through Rainbow Lake and Rainbow Narrows, the W ridge is on the L, running a serpentine course through the waters and separating Inlet, Clear, and Square ponds from Rainbow Lake. Navigable channels cross this esker in two places, one leading to Inlet, the other to Clear Pond. About a half mile of the esker N of the cottages between Rainbow Lake and Inlet Pond is state land, which can be explored. At the first bridge over Rainbow Narrows (opposite Square Pond), a gravel road climbs the esker, runs along the top through a stand of red pine, and descends at the E end of Clear Pond.

Powerboat traffic on Rainbow Lake is fairly heavy in summer. A resort has been established for over a century. James M. Wardner was the pioneer settler. He came to Rainbow Lake from Essex County in 1856 and a few years later opened the Rainbow Inn, where for the rest of his life he was a popular host to sportsmen and vacationers. Some of the guests at his inn acquired shore property of their own and built camps.

Motorboat traffic, as well as summer camps, thins out in Rainbow Narrows, the mile-long NE extension of the lake into which the North Branch flows. This is an increasingly wild and beautiful passage, with occasional views of symmetrical Loon Lake Mountain as one approaches the second bridge (the one on the Mud Pond Road).

West of the bridge is a narrow gap through which the North Branch enters Rainbow Narrows. Passing through this channel in a NW direction into a small pond, one comes in 0.25 m. to a pretty headland on the E shore. The outer part of the promontory is state land and makes an attractive site for overnight camping.

The North Branch can be explored upstream from this headland for at least 1 m. in spring, early summer, and fall. Influenced by a dam at the foot of Lake Kushaqua, the stream is wide at first and the flow is hardly perceptible. In October pine needles make a carpet of gold on these still, black waters. At 1 m. the stream narrows at a small rift. After wading this, one can proceed upstream through a marsh as the North Branch gradually narrows to a ribbon and beaver dams become numerous. How far one can go above the rift depends not only on the season but also on adverse effects of extensive timber cutting on adjacent paper company lands. Without a forest cover to retain surface water and release it slowly, the upper stream will probably not float a canoe much after spring runoff in future years. This is a pity. From the marsh there are good views of the Sable and Loon Lake mountains which the North Branch drains.

Rainbow Narrows to Mud Pond Outlet, 3.4 m. (5.5 km.)
USGS: Debar Mountain, Loon Lake 7.5

The last mile of this route is impracticable except at medium high to high water in spring and perhaps during the fall if rain is fairly heavy. At other times the trip should end at the dam at the foot of Lake Kushaqua, where the Kushaqua Road crosses the outlet to a junction with the Mud Pond Road. There is a faint carry trail on the L side of the dam. A two-car shuttle is desirable on these little-traveled roads. The Mud Pond Road is especially scenic in May, before the leaves are out, and from mid-October to November, after they have fallen. Then there are unobstructed views across Mud Pond to the dramatic skyline of the Loon Lake Mountains.

Put-in is below the bridge over Rainbow Narrows on the Mud Pond Road 0.6 m. N of Onchiota. The direction is NE into a tunnel under a railroad grade. Beyond this, the North Branch enters Kushaqua Narrows. The outlet of Buck Pond, where a large state campsite is located, comes in on the R. If the outlet is followed into Buck Pond, a carry over a road grade is necessary. A better way to reach the pond is to continue 0.25 m. farther in Kushaqua Narrows to a bay on the R and follow the S shore of the bay to a boat ramp and carry of 130 yards. Buck Pond has a diameter of about a half mile.

The main route continues N past islands into Lake Kushaqua. The large building on the W shore, once a sanatorium, was later owned and used by the White Fathers. Now they too are gone.

Below the lake and the dam, the North Branch and Mud Pond are quite shallow. The pond's name ignores the beauty of its mountain setting but accurately describes the condition of its bed. There is risk of stranding in the soft mud; wading is not an agreeable alternative.

Nevertheless, I found this passage enjoyable on a sunny, mild November first. I was alone; a heavier load would have meant some tracking in stream and pond. Under this go-light condition, the North Branch link made a pleasant float in the main current, with an occasional scratch. For the first 0.5 m. the stream ripples over pebbles and cobbles between high banks and under overhanging trees. In the last 0.25 m. the current slackens between low, marshy banks. A well-constructed beaver dam spanned the stream here. Vegetation had taken hold in the mud calkings, and the top of the dam was gay with forget-me-nots in lusty bloom. In home gardens this flower survives several frosts, but to find it in bloom in November on the Adirondack plateau was enough to make the trip memorable.

The entrance to Mud Pond is a narrow, sinuous channel amidst cattails. The delta is badly silted, and paddle must double as pole, sinking deep into the mud and resisting withdrawal. Water deep enough to float even a one-man canoe is not easy to find in the bay of the inlet. But the pond becomes deeper as one aims for the outlet.

A 19th-century guidebook describes an extension of this route to Loon Lake via the Loon Lake Outlet, which enters Mud Pond at the NE. All but a fifth part of this 1.7 m. stream was said to be navigable then. But now the proportion of float to carry is nearly reversed. Beavers made a mess of this stream once they were reestablished in the Adirondacks. And the carry is now closed to the public. There is no public access to the waters of Loon Lake; the shores of both lake and outlet are posted by an association of camp owners.

So one heads for take-out at the bridge over the North Branch as it leaves Mud Pond. Below this bridge (closed to vehicular traffic) is a cruising reach of only 0.4 m. before the stream narrows in a steep, rocky gorge. In the next 5 m. the North Branch drops 360 feet.

Irregularly shaped Loon Lake can be viewed at several places from Blue Spruce Drive on the E and Route 99 on the N. A popular hike in this area used to be the trail up Loon Lake Mountain from Route 99, 4.5 m. W of the Loon Lake post office. The start of the trail was an easement over a private woods road. Now that the state has abandoned use of the fire tower on the summit, the trail is no longer marked on the highway. Permission to use it should be obtained from the private owner.

Mud Pond Outlet to Clinton County Line, 9.3 m. (15 km.)
USGS: Loon Lake, Alder Brook 7.5

As the North Branch leaves Mud Pond, the topographic map suggests a prime whitewater run. In the next 2.8 m. the river drops 240 feet with virtually all this drop occurring in the last 2.2 m. for an average gradient of over 100 feet per mile. The gradient is very nearly uniform, however, resulting in continuous rapids of Class II and III difficulty. This rating is somewhat surprising given the average gradient and would appear to be an enticement to whitewater paddlers. It is important to note, however, that this section of the North Branch is quite narrow (10–12 yards), has virtually no eddies, and is frequently spanned by deadfalls. The result is an extremely dangerous river since the paddler would have no opportunity to avoid potentially treacherous strainers. This section is otherwise runnable, but should be attempted only by highly skilled paddlers willing to scout the river meticulously. Scouting is relatively easy because the Thatcherville Road closely parallels this section. The road is not maintained during the winter, however, and is generally inaccessible during early spring when high water levels are present.

A preferable put-in is downstream of Route 99, 0.9 m. SE of the hamlet of Loon Lake. The first several hundred yards consist of Class II-III rapids very similar to those above Route 99. Though the rapids are not very large, the same concerns regarding strainers and lack of eddies generally apply. The next 0.5 m. contains Class I rapids, again with the risk of strainers, before calming down to flatwater with current. The river flows close to several trailers at one point. About 100 yards below these there is an overhead cable across the river. This marks the approximate beginning of an extremely winding, narrow section of the river, which continues to Slab Bridge on the Goldsmith Road at 1.75 m.

Below Slab Bridge the river flows under first one, then a second, footbridge before opening to a view dominated by white birches. At 1.4 m. below Slab Bridge is a bridge, closed to traffic, which connects to a dirt road intersecting the Goldsmith Road at a point 1.9 m. W of Route 3. The North Branch may be examined from this point to determine water levels. A minimum level for this section is no more

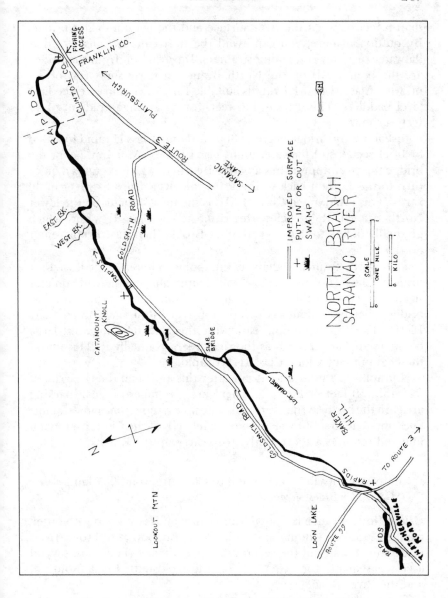

NORTH BRANCH
SARANAC RIVER

than 5 feet between the river surface and the bottom of this bridge. By putting in here, you can avoid the upstream sections of either flatwater or water containing strainers. Downstream from the bridge are the best rapids on the North Branch, a fairly short run of 3.4 m. with Class II and III rapids suitable for novice and intermediate level paddlers. The drop is 140 feet, for an average gradient of 41 feet per mile.

Just above the bridge begins a 300 yard long Class II rapid followed by brief sections of flatwater and Class I rapids. At 0.4 m. below the bridge the river approaches a boulder garden, which requires a quick turn to the L, then back to the R, as the river drops 6–8 feet in 30 yards. This rapid, rated Class II–III, is the most difficult on the lower North Branch. Right below this is 0.5 m. of Class II water, which gradually tapers to flatwater as West Brook, then East Brook, enter on the L.

The North Branch widens at this point. There are at least four distinct Class II rapids below this point, alternating with quieter stretches. At a notable turn to the R (about 2.5 m. below the last bridge) there is a double drop of 4–6 feet in 20 yards rated Class II–III. The rapids become easier for the next 0.25 m. until large boulders appear on the L as the river veers gradually R. This marks the beginning of a long Class II–III rapid.

No rapids of significance occur after this and soon the river comes to within 50 feet of Route 3. There are a number of small parking areas on the highway, marked by fishing access signs, that allow suitable take-out. The first of these is immediately NE of the Clinton-Franklin line and requires a short, fairly steep carry up the R bank.

Clinton County line on Route 3 to Clayburg, 6 m. (9.7 km.)
USGS: Alder Brook, Redford 7.5

The North Branch is a good fishing stream. It is stocked with brook trout in Franklin County and with brook, rainbow, and brown trout in Clinton County in the section described below. There are several access easements for fishermen on the Goldsmith Road, Route 3, and the River Road.

The gradient moderates in a 6-m. section beginning near the Clinton County line and ending at confluence with the main stem. The drop is a modest 55 feet, and the grade is remarkably steady. Rips and rapids are numerous but mild. There are no sharp pitches. The course is uncomplicated and in spring is good training for the practiced beginner on the threshold of intermediate skills. Two short segments reach Class II difficulty. Adequate depths are not assured after mid-May but may recur with fall rains.

Wherever the river widens much over 50 feet, it is quite shallow. Keep in the main current, which is moderately fast in spring.

The first mile and the last, where the river winds through hills too steep for pasture or cultivation, are scenic. The rest of the run is in farmland and small woodlots. Below Riverview the highway, farm buildings, and suburban homes are often in sight. Deep woods and solitude must be sought elsewhere. The main attraction is the almost effortless, bouncy coast with a few moments of excitement.

There are many put-in and take-out sites at bridges and state fishing-rights easements all the way from the Franklin-Clinton County line to Clayburg. The best upland access is an embankment 0.1 m. E of the clearly marked county line on Route 3 and about 1.4 m. W of Riverview (see the map on p. 232). Here the highway makes a close approach to the river. Though the river is not visible from a car, it is only a 40-yard drag down a steep slope. A DEC fishing-rights sign assures access for fishermen here. An alternative put-in for those without fishing license and tackle is the bridge in Riverview.

Above Riverview there are a few shoals in the cobbly riverbed where islands divide channels. These places may be scratchy for aluminum canoes with keels. The ideal craft for this situation is made of vinyl foam, a tough plastic just flexible enough to ripple over smooth stones. Aluminum, once stranded, seems to weld itself to rock.

In the 2 m. from the bridge in Riverview to the Route 3 bridge, the current is a little faster and rapids more numerous. Caution is needed at the bends to avoid fallen trees and snags. Just above the Route 3 bridge the stream is compressed into a chute of slick water at an old bridge crossing or broken-out dam; one enjoys a fast coast down the tongue into the pool below.

In the last lap of 2.2 m. to the bridge in Clayburg the scenery improves as the banks steepen and become heavily wooded. About 0.7 m. below the Route 3 bridge is a rocky rift of 0.15 m. culminating in a divided channel. The L channel is a go if entered between rocks at midstream. About 0.45 m. below this rapid the channel divides again around a large island of several acres. The R channel is the wider and more inviting. About halfway around, the channel narrows and turns turbulent in a ramp-like incline about 100 feet long. At medium-high water there are no rocks to dodge, but waves may splash into the canoe. There is a 40-yard carry on the R bank.

You can take out at the bridge on the Silver Lake Road in Clayburg or continue down the main stem of the Saranac from the confluence just below that bridge.

THE NORTH FLOW VOYAGEUR

The Raquette River, second longest in the state, is an obvious choice for the long-distance tripper. Its 102 m. from Blue Mountain Lake to the foot of Carry Falls Reservoir (or 116 m. to South Colton) lie wholly within the northwest watershed. An alternative trip, making possible a linkage of the two major drainage basins of North Flow, is a shuttle at Indian Carry to the Saranac system. Again, starting at Blue Mountain Lake, paddlers can descend the Raquette to the mouth of Stony Creek, go up the creek and its chain of three ponds, carry across the 1.1 m. divide, and proceed down the Saranac and its lakes to Saranac Lake Village (79 m.) or Union Falls (100 m.).

The purpose of this chapter is to outline four other paddle-and-camp trips of several days to a week in duration, each involving the waters of both North Flow drainage basins. Detailed descriptions are unnecessary because the components of these routes have been dealt with in other chapters, though sometimes in reverse order to that followed below. As of this writing, it appears possible that International Paper may allow a carry from Bog Lake to the railroad tracks connecting Sabbatis with Lake Lila. Such a development would open up another voyageur trip connecting the Bog River system with the Beaver River system via Rainer and Harrington Brooks.

Transit Trail: Piercefield to Union Falls, 68 m. (109.4 km.)
USGS: Tupper Lake, Long Lake, Saint Regis, Saranac Lake, Lake Placid 15; Alder Brook 7.5

This canoe trail crosses the lake region of the north central Adirondacks and ends in a pass through the main axis of elevation, almost in the shadow of Whiteface Mountain. Alternate starting points are the Route 3 bridge at Piercefield or the S end of Tupper Lake; either of these sites would make a trip of 68 m. The trail ascends the Raquette River to Stony Creek. ("Ascend" may be a misleading verb for a rise of 12 feet in 24 m., with one short carry at Setting Pole Dam.) The shuttle to the Saranac system of chain lakes and river is made at Indian Carry. There are five carries in all totaling 2.1 m. unless one chooses to make a sixth at Permanent Rapids (Class II) below Bloomingdale.

Pond-Hopping Trail: Lake Kushaqua to Saranac Lake Village, 55.2 m. (88.8 km.)
USGS: Loon Lake, Debar Mountain 7.5; Saranac Lake, Saint Regis 15

This is an intricate trail looping through 35 lakes and ponds at the headwaters of five rivers—North Branch of the Saranac, Osgood, Middle and West branches of the St. Regis, and main stem of the Saranac. It should please the enthusiast for pond-hopping marathons and the connoisseur of choice camping sites. Though it begins and ends in powerboat waters, its midsection invites lingering in the silence of that pocket-sized wilderness, the St. Regis Canoe Area, where all motors are banned. One warning. This trail calls for a strong back as well as enthusiasm. There are 20 carries totaling 7.6 m.

N end of Lake Kushaqua to S end of Rainbow Lake	7.0 m.
Carry to Jones Pond	.75
Jones Pond to Paul Smiths via outlet; Osgood, Little Osgood, and Church ponds	4.0
Carry at Paul Smiths	.3
Lower St. Regis, Spitfire, Upper St. Regis lakes	3.2
Carry to Bog Pond	.1
Bog Pond	.1
Carry to Bear Pond	.1
Bear Pond	.5
Carry to Little Long Pond	.2
Little Long Pond	1.0
Carry to Green Pond	.15
Green Pond	.15
Carry to St. Regis Pond	.1
St. Regis Pond	1.3
Carry to Ochre Pond	.7
Ochre Pond	.2
Carry to Fish Pond	1.1
Fish Pond	.65
Carry to Little Fish Pond	.05
Little Fish Pond	.25
Carry to Little Long Pond	.05
Little Long Pond	.25
Carry to Kit Fox Pond	.2
Kit Fox Pond	.15
Carry to Nellie Pond	.25
Nellie Pond	.25
Carry to Bessie Pond (round trip)	.25
Bessie Pond (along W shore)	.05
Carry to Long Pond	1.5
Long Pond	1.5
Carry to Floodwood Pond	.8
Floodwood Pond	1.0
Carry to Rollins Pond	.2

Rollins Pond	2.0
Carry to Whey Pond	.1
Whey Pond	.8
Carry to Copperas Pond	.3
Copperas Pond	.3
Fish Creek, Fish Creek Ponds, Fish Creek Bay	3.6
Upper Saranac Lake	4.6
Bartlett Carry	.4
Middle and Lower Saranac lakes, First and Second ponds, Saranac River, Oseetah Lake, Lake Flower to the dam in Saranac Lake Village	14.8

Bog River Flow-Oswegatchie to Inlet, 30 m. + (48.3 km. +)
USGS: Tupper Lake 15; Wolf Mountain, Five Ponds 7.5

Proceed up Bog River Flow to the W end of Lows Lake (pp 110-112). From here scouting parties in 1985 took three different routes to the Oswegatchie, all rigorous. The most direct (3.5 m.) is along the county line to Nicks Pond by way of Big Deer. Gary Koch made this trip in 1987 and reported that the trail was in reasonably good shape. It is apparently maintained by Boy Scouts from Lows Lake, as the state no longer maintains it. On approaching Nicks Pond, this trail detours a short distance N to cross a dip in the esker. The second route takes in the ponds N of the county line—Tamarack, Slender, and Clear—with trails most of the way. From Nicks Pond both routes continue W over a rough, often wet trail to Pine Ridge on the Oswegatchie. The third party paddled across Big Deer Pond; then struck out WSW, without trail, and climbed the esker S of Nicks Pond. They followed the crest most of the way to the Oswegatchie at a point 2.5 m. above Pine Ridge. Encountering much blowdown, they concluded that ground below the esker would be easier though less scenic. Thomas Brown, head of the DEC's regional Watertown office, who took this route, said of the entire trip: "It is one of the most exciting and adventurous canoe treks in the entire Adirondacks, if not in the Northeast." This third route was cleared and established as a formal carry by the DEC in 1988 and is now marked with DEC discs. It begins just N of the terminus of the Broadhead Gore trail and connects with two roads leading to Big Deer Pond. It picks up again on the W shore of Big Deer and proceeds S, following the E base of the esker. It finally crosses the esker and reaches the Oswegatchie at a site formerly known as Beaverdam.

See addendum for trip from Newton Falls to Meacham Lake.

AUSABLE RIVER

The Ausable shares with the Hudson the task of draining Mount Marcy and other lofty domes and gables at the rooftop of New York. The Hudson is by far the longest river in the state: 315 m. from Lake Tear to Battery Park. The Ausable is far short of the Hudson in length and volume. But in steepness it has only one rival, the Boquet, when its drop of nearly one mile from Mount Marcy to the 95-foot level of Lake Champlain is averaged over its modest length.

Standard gazetteers give the Ausable's length (East Branch and main stem) as 50 m.; that is only a little short if the outlet of Lower Ausable Lake is taken as the beginning. But the highest source is runnels off the dome of Marcy which feed the Marcy Brook of Panther Gorge. Measured thence, the length is about 67 m.—45 to Au Sable Forks and 22 from there to Lake Champlain. From the head of another Marcy Brook on the N side of the mountain, the West Branch is about 43 m. to the Forks. The two branches, their tributaries, and the main stem encompass the most rugged and magnificent scenery of the Adirondacks. Consider some of the names they string on the map: Indian Pass, Scott Pond, MacIntyre Mountains, Avalanche Pass, Indian Falls, Lake Placid, Wilmington Notch, High Falls, Whiteface Mountain, Ausable Lakes, Roaring Brook Falls, the Great Range, Rainbow Falls, Beaver Meadow Falls, Chapel Pond, Giant Mountain, Keene Valley, Cascade Lakes, and Ausable Chasm.

The Ausable, especially the East Branch, is subject to flash floods. They generally occur during snowmelt but may also result from heavy rainfall. Probably the most severe on record occurred in September 1856. Flood waters released by the breaking of the state dam at the foot of Lower Ausable Lake, combined with drenching rain, caused three drownings in Keene and extensive property damage all the way to Au Sable Forks. In the same valley in 1973 and 1976 winter thaws caused heavy flood and ice damage to property.

The third dimension figures prominently in Ausable country and exposes a limitation of the canoe. The streams and lakes alone are not enough. Keep a pair of sturdy hiking shoes in your waterproof bag, along with a copy of the Adirondack Mountain Club's *Guide to Adirondack Trails.*

Until recently there was a general impression that the Ausable is not a canoeing stream. The ranger in Jay, speaking of the East Branch and the main stem, told me in 1973 that he had seen very few canoes or kayaks. This may have been due to the fact that summer hikers see the river only when it looks like a cemetery for broken mountains. What the hikers and tourists may not see is the grand spring house-cleaning when floods of snowmelt rampage down from the heights, flush out billets and other loose stuff, and cushion most of the boulders. After the flood comes the moderately high water level of late April and early May which is most favorable to canoeing on this rocky stream. Similar conditions may exist briefly after heavy rains in summer and fall. Enjoy the day. It may be your last chance for months.

In Ausable waters there are short reaches of stream as well as lake that the novice can enjoy whenever the ice is out. But the whitewater stretches are usually runnable only in spring and call for intermediate or expert skills.

LAKE PLACID

Lake Placid is a remnant of the great postglacial lakes that once filled the valleys eastward from Tupper Lake through the High Peaks Region. If one had been around with a canoe at the time of South Meadow Lake (altitude 1,940 to 2,210 feet), he could have enjoyed a cruise from Ampersand Lake to Heart Lake, having floated over the sites of the Robert Louis Stevenson cottage, the APA and DEC complex at Ray Brook, the Center for the Arts, the Winter Olympics of '32 and '80, and John Brown's Grave and around the island of Mt. Jo. Later, when ice lobes had melted away to unplug several mountain passes, the canoeist on Lower Lake Newman (1,740–1,780 feet) would have enjoyed a still greater range, without a single carry: from Tupper Lake through the valleys of the Saranac, Ray Brook, the Chubb, and the West Branch of the Ausable into Wilmington Notch and on to Chapel Pond over a deeply flooded Keene Valley. Today opportunities are more limited. Lake Placid, seventh largest of Adirondack lakes, is an insignificant fragment of those great glacial lakes. However, its N end hints at what mountain views must have been like across the postglacial lacustrine foreground hiding all low relief around such a giant as Whiteface.

The most convenient public access to the lake is a DEC parking lot and boat ramp at the N end of Mirror Lake Drive, where a narrow ridge separates the two lakes (*Lake Placid* 15 or the 7.5 × 15-minute metric map of 1978). A circular tour of Lake Placid is recommended: from the launching site on East Lake through Sunset Strait and along the sheltered W shore of West Lake, around Moose and Hawk islands; and with a return in East Lake in the shelter of the islands and the Peninsula. Elaborate summer camps line much of the main shore and the islands. Motorboat traffic is heavy but thins out somewhat at the northern end of the lake, where summer camps are few.

A trail up Whiteface Mountain begins at Whiteface Landing in Barrel Bay. Canoeists intending to climb the mountain by this route often camp in a secluded cove at the N end of Moose Island, where two state lean-tos overlook the peak.

The outlet of Lake Placid is not navigable. It is a principal feeder of the Chubb River, which in turn feeds the West Branch of the Ausable.

CHUBB RIVER

The river is sometimes incorrectly spelled "Chub." According to Mary MacKenzie, historian of Lake Placid and North Elba, the name derives from one Joseph Chubb, an early settler in North Elba. He left the area in 1810 but bequeathed his name to the river.

The Chubb River drains the NW slopes of Street and Nye mountains and, below Wanika Falls, enters the pass through which the Northville-Lake Placid Trail runs. Three miles above its confluence with the West Branch of the Ausable it is augmented by the outlet of Lake Placid. There is a world of difference between this lower stretch, which skirts Lake Placid Village on the S, and the upper Chubb. The village has not been kindly to its river. It turns its cosmetic face, of resort and Olympic fame, to its two lakes on the heights. There, as early as 1920, before the face-lifting of two winter Olympics, the buildings overhanging the water of Mirror Lake suggested to Alfred Donaldson a Venetian scene, at least at night. No one could possibly liken the lower Chubb to a scene in Venice.

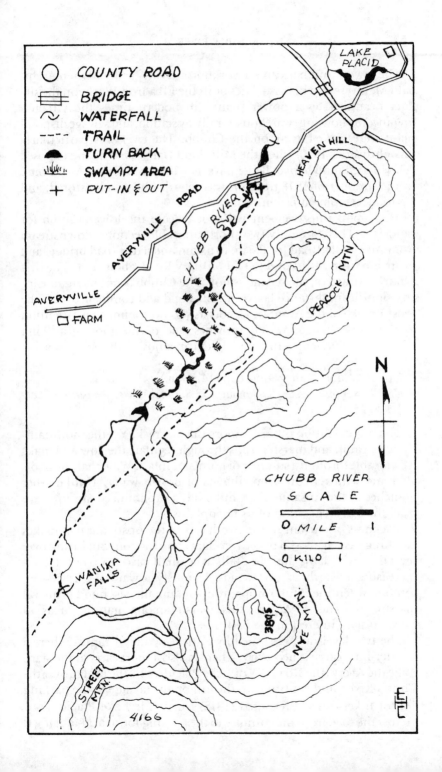

COUNTY ROAD
BRIDGE
WATERFALL
TRAIL
TURN BACK
SWAMPY AREA
PUT-IN & OUT

LAKE PLACID

HEAVEN HILL

AVERYVILLE ROAD

CHUBB RIVER

AVERYVILLE

FARM

PEACOCK MTN

N

CHUBB RIVER
SCALE

0 MILE 1

0 KILO 1

WANIKA FALLS

NYE MTN.

3895

STREET MTN.

4166

The lower Chubb became a workhorse as early as 1809 when Archibald McIntyre and his associates built the Elba Iron Works on the site later occupied by a power plant. In modern times the village's low-income housing, warehouses, railway station, and sewage disposal plant were tucked away on the Chubb. The river was particularly unsightly after 1970, when the Mill Pond Dam caved in and exposed debris-laden mud banks. Better days may lie ahead for the Mill Pond. In the summer of 1978 the dam was rebuilt, the pond restored, and a park development began.

This small improvement will not redeem the lower Chubb for canoeists. There are only two short canoeable sections: downstream from Averyville Road for 0.6 m. to a dam and a dirt road bridge, and upstream from Mill Pond to Old Military Road, about 1 m. The first is fairly attractive, the second is not. The Chubb is not navigable for any significant distance between Mill Pond and confluence with the West Branch of the Ausable. Canoeists should confine their attention to the upper reach, which provides one of the most gratifying wilderness experiences that a paddler can enjoy in the Adirondacks.

Upper Chubb, 9 m. round trip (14.5 km.)
USGS: Saranac Lake, Santanoni 15; Saranac Lake, Ampersand Lake 7.5 × 15

The upper Chubb is hardly more than a creek. Yet the mountain-ringed swamp and marsh it runs through regulate the flow and make it canoeable through a summer of normal rainfall. Wide shallow pools alternate with narrow deep ribbons of brown water. Unlike other branches of the Ausable, the Chubb has a pronounced tannin stain from the lush vegetation of its floodplains.

Slackness of current in the two levels of the upstream trip makes paddling easy. It also favors beaver-dam construction. But lifting over several beaver dams and deadfalls is a small price to pay for ever-increasing rewards as one winds deviously toward the 1,860-foot contour, where the Chubb drops ;from a mountain pass into a primeval marshland. The APA lists this marsh among natural areas of extraordinary interest in the park.

The two levels are separated by a short ravine of rapids where a quarter-mile carry is necessary. There is also a short carry at the start. Take the Averyville Road SW of Lake Placid, cross the bridge over the Chubb River, and continue up the hill on the far side to the parking lot for hikers on the rerouted (1978) Northville-Lake Placid Trail. Across the road from the entrance to the parking lot, at a 20-foot jog to the R, is a carry trail of about 120 yards to put-in on the Chubb in a pool above rapids. (An alternative, but longer and muddier, carry is the new northern terminus of the Northville-Lake Placid Trail on the E side of the bridge.)

The first level, 1.5 m. as the stream flows, is through a swamp. Low shores are lined with berry bushes backed by a dense conifer forest footed in spongy sphagnum. The tamaracks near the shores are especially fine in their spring-green dress of late May and the antique gold of late October. Wood sorrel blooms through most of the summer in the cool mosses of the spruce-fir swamp.

At 1 m. a private camp high on the R bank comes into view. Beyond this there are no man-made structures as the Forest Preserve of the High Peaks Wilderness Area closes in on both sides. Narrowing somewhat, the stream now enters a scenic corridor in which the R bank, then the L, gradually rise above flood level. In a narrow defile there is a quarter-mile carry on the L bank around rapids. About half way along the carry is a wooded terrace on the R beside the rapids. This makes an attractive camp site for those who have started the trip in mid-afternoon or are benighted on the return trip. Defense against insects is essential for those with low tolerance to bites.

Having crossed the 1840-foot contour in ascending the rapids, one puts in on the second and longer level of about 3 m. For the next 1.5 m. wooded shores restrict views on the L, but finally, at a wide eastward loop, one enters the Chubb River Marsh. Bold mountain vistas open up. Wildlife is frequently sighted. The marsh averages about a half mile in width. You snake through the middle or from side to side through low vegetation in several shades of green. Winding around the base of Peacock Mountain, you approach Nye and Street, two of the High Peaks, as every Forty-Sixer knows. The deep pass between them and Three Peaks looms ahead. Off the R bank is the Sawtooth Range. The sense of enclosure in a primitive world would be complete except for the plane or two liable to break the silence.

Feeders come in on the L and then the R as the Chubb narrows. Persistent beaver-dam find it navigable to the second feeder on the L, which drains Nye Mountain on the NW. Weaving through the marsh in an amphitheater of mountains is an unforgettable experience.

WEST BRANCH

The West Branch of the Ausable has several other feeders in the High Peaks Region besides Lake Placid and the Chubb. East of Adirondak Loj and Mount Jo the West Branch first becomes a name on the map below the confluence of MacIntyre and South Meadow brooks with Marcy Brook. Reckoned from this elevation of 2,050 feet, it is 36 m. long. But its ultimate sources are the rugged cirques and defiles of the highest peaks in the state. Marcy Brook picks up a feeder from Avalanche Pass; at the height of land in this pass, a little waterfall forms a pool whose waters flow into both the Hudson on the S and the Ausable on the N. Another such divide is Indian Pass, where, just N of the height of land, caves of ice slowly melt into August to feed Indian Pass Brook, which empties into the West Branch at North Meadow. Except for very short intervals, all of these brooks are too steep and rocky for canoeing, and the West Branch itself above the bridge on Route 73 is for paddlers with advanced skills.

From the vicinity of Heart Lake, the West Branch skirts Mt. Jo in a NNW direction. Reaching the base of the high arable plateau once known as the Plains of Abraham, where John Brown's farm and grave are located, the river veers toward the NE, a course it keeps to Au Sable Forks. The total drop in 35.7 m. is 1,510 feet. The APA study report on the river estimates that 44% is rapids, 27% moderate flow, and 29% stillwater. The steepest segment is in Wilmington Notch, a rugged pass between the Sentinel Range and Whiteface Mountain.

South Meadow Brook to Route 73, 8 m. (12.9 km.)
USGS: Keene Valley 7.5 × 15; Mount Marcy, Lake Placid 15

The uppermost section of the West Branch certainly rates as one of the most beautiful whitewater runs in the Adirondacks and also has more than its share of excitement. It can only be run at very high water levels. There is a new gauge on the SE span of the Route 73 bridge (upstream L side), replacing an older, faded one. A reading of 2.5 feet on the new gauge is minimal; 3.5 to 4.0 feet is ideal.

The highest access is reached by traveling up the Adirondak Loj Road for 5.7 m. and turning L on the South Meadow fire road. This dirt road tends to be very muddy in early spring during peak water levels. As of this writing, the dirt road remains open, but the DEC is considering plans to close it to motorized vehicles. Boaters wishing to paddle this section but unable to drive or unwilling to risk getting stuck in the mud may want to carry their boats up this road or consider the alternate put-in described below. At 0.8 m. up the fire road are parking spaces. Carry 200 yards on a trail on the R. Put-in is on South Meadow Brook, immediately past a gate across the trail.

South Meadow Brook is a very narrow stream requiring a close watch for bushes and trees. The brook gradually widens as a number of minor feeder streams merge. At 0.7 m. Marcy Brook merges to form the West Branch. The West Branch continues for an additional 0.8 m. until crossing under Adirondak Loj Road. Throughout this distance the river has dropped 25 feet, with a number of small class I-II rapids. The rapids are very small but require technical maneuvering because of the narrowness and shallowness of the brook.

At the Adirondak Loj Road bridge the West Branch's character changes drastically. In the next 2.7 m. to the confluence with Indian Pass Brook at Last Chance Ranch the river drops 185 feet for an average gradient of 70 feet per mile. This section requires advanced paddling skills and river-reading abilities. The bridge serves as a take-out point for those wishing to avoid the rapids below or, alternately, as a put-in for those desiring a shorter run.

The first 0.4 m. below the bridge consists of very technical Class II–III rapids. The river becomes increasingly congested and steep as the rapids become Class IV in difficulty at a bend to the R. The recommended course is on the L, on either side of a large boulder. Scouting is recommended to identify the proper course and the location of possible strainers. The bottom of the drop poses the potential for pins. Below, the river returns to Class III for the next 0.4 m., again presenting a relatively technical, congested course.

At a steep sandbank on the R the rapids settle down to mild Class I. At 1 m. below the bridge the river passes under a footbridge, where Class III-IV rapids begin alternating with Class II-III ones. Rapids revert to Class II to confluence with Indian Pass Brook at Last Chance Ranch. This confluence is an unusual sight: Indian Pass Brook meets the West Branch head on with the combined flow turning sharply out of view to the R. The result is an optical illusion of sorts in which it appears that the current has suddenly changed direction and is aiming right at you. The previous edition noted possible plans by the DEC to acquire Last Chance Ranch. As of this writing, no such plans are being pursued, and access at this site continues to be restricted.

Below the confluence with Indian Pass Brook the river widens noticeably and the water volume increases. The West Branch becomes less technical from here to Route 73. The drop in this section is 125 feet over 3.8 m. for an average gradient of 33 feet per mile. Two Class II rapids are met before North Meadow Branch joins the West Branch in 0.7 m. In another 0.5 m. the channel

divides, signalling the paddler to stay R. In 100 yards the West
Branch begins a long, sweeping 150-degree turn to the L with five
large boulders blocking the R channel. This marks the beginning
of a 200-yard Class III-IV rapids. Two more distinct rapids of
Class III difficulty follow this. In turn these are followed by 1.25
m. of nearly continuous Class III rapids. The technical difficulty is
less than in rapids encountered earlier, but waves are bigger. The
rapids gradually diminish as the 70 and 90-meter ski jumps come
into view. Take-out is below the right-hand bridge on the R Bank.

Route 73 to the Conservation Monument on Route 86, 8.0 m.
(12.9 km.)
USGS: Lake Placid 15 or 7.5 × 15

The best cruising reach of any length is along Riverside Drive E
of Lake Placid Village. This reach is 6.5, 7.5, or 8.0 m. depending
on the starting place. It is canoeable throughout summers of normal
rainfall (except perhaps the first 0.5 m.) but is most enjoyable in
May, when snows still blanket the crests of the High Peaks and the
current moves one along swiftly over well submerged boulders and
sandbars. Since 1955, Memorial Day canoe races have been held on
this stretch. The drop is about 40 feet. There is one carry around a
cascade and rapid near the end of the cruise. Otherwise, smooth
water is broken only by riffles at some of the bends.

Glimpses of Algonquin and neighboring peaks, of the rugged 8-
m. long Sentinel Range, and of Whiteface and its outlying nubbles
are a distinctive feature. My companion on a May 23rd, however,
was more interested in the activities of warblers and sandpipers. Besides spotted sandpipers, which nest in the area, we saw numbers of
solitary sandpipers, resting and feeding along the banks on their way
to the Canadian wilds.

A two-car shuttle is desirable; the alternative is a walk or bike ride
(the road is 2 m. shorter than the river) or a pickup back to the
starting place. The car at the end of the run is parked on a loop
road off Route 86 at the monument commemorating the fiftieth anniversary of the Conservation Law of 1885 creating the Forest Preserve.
This is 1.1 m. E of the West Branch bridge on Route 86. The other
car is driven back to this bridge and then L on Riverside Drive to

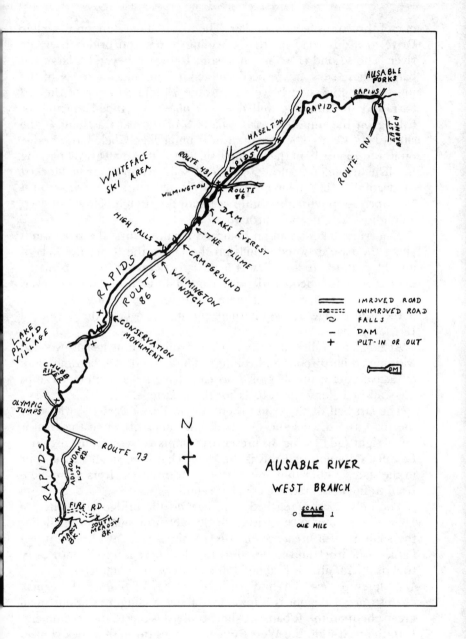

AUSABLE FORKS

RAPIDS

RAPIDS

HASELTON

EAST BRANCH

ROUTE ON

WHITEFACE SKI AREA

ROUTE 431

RAPIDS

WILMINGTON

ROUTE 86

DAM

LAKE EVEREST

HIGH FALLS

THE FLUME

CAMPGROUND

RAPIDS

ROUTE 86

WILMINGTON NOTCH

LAKE PLACID VILLAGE

CONSERVATION MONUMENT

CHUBB RIVER

OLYMPIC JUMPS

N

ROUTE 73

RAPIDS

ADIRONDAK LOJ RD.

FIRE RD.

MARCY BK.

SOUTH MEADOW BK.

IMPROVED ROAD
UNIMPROVED ROAD
FALLS
DAM
PUT-IN OR OUT

AUSABLE RIVER

WEST BRANCH

SCALE
0   1
ONE MILE

one of three possible put-in sites. The first is about 3 m. on Riverside Drive to a dirt road on the R leading to an iron bridge over the river. The second is 3.5 m. to a bank 100 yards beyond a large red barn. (These sites are respectively about 1 m. and 0.5 m. N of the junction of Riverside Drive with Route 73.) The owner of the red barn and surrounding land does not object to canoe-launching or fishing on the unposted grassy bank S of the barn as long as the site is kept clean. The third put-in is immediately below the bridge on Route 73 just W of the Olympic ski jumps at a small gravel parking lot. The first 0.5 m. below Route 73 is scratchy and may be blocked by deadfalls. The next mile below the red barn is a cruise on a V-shaped loop which is shallower than the stretch below but deep enough to float a canoe through most of May.

The cruise takes about an hour and a half. At first the river winds along the base of wooded hills on the L. On the R are the flats of an old pasture. In this first 1.5 m. it is necessary to keep in the main current for adequate depths. Around the bend of the V, however, the Chubb enters, and from here on depths are greater. At 1.5 m. is the iron bridge at the alternate put-in site, where the Memorial Day races begin.

At 2.5 m. the valley narrows and both banks become heavily wooded with mixed hardwoods and conifers. These woods will become more attractive after a number of dead elms have fallen. Summer camps are scattered along the R bank for the next mile.

The last half of the cruise is entirely in Forest Preserve with only the road as a distraction. One welcomes intervals when the road is out of sight and hearing. Its presence prompts a dissent from Lawrence Grinnell's opinion that this is the "most charming small stream tour in the state." Other tours on northern Adirondack rivers are remote from traffic noise and are equally scenic.

The only carry is reached 1 m. beyond the bridge on Route 86. Here the stream is constricted to 20 feet in a small gorge. Below the spillway of a breached dam is a white torrent twisting between flanks of bedrock and followed by rapids. There is a well-worn carry trail of 0.2 m. on the R about 100 feet above the cataract.

A close-up view of Whiteface over a fringe of pines is the climax of this tour. Take-out is a few yards above a gauging station (small green shed) on the R bank. A short trail leads out to the monument.

In the next 6 m. the West Branch plunges through a rock-choked gorge, dropping over 600 feet. Much of this section can be run by skilled paddlers at medium high to high water in spring. Others prefer to admire this stretch from turnouts along the highway. There are too many fishermen to observe an embarrassing crash or flip.

The fishermen are there because they have heard the often repeated remark that the West Branch of the Ausable is "the best trout stream east of the Rocky Mountains." Special regulations and limits apply to the 2.2 m. below the monument. In spite of these restrictions, the West Branch is one of the most heavily fished streams in the state and must be stocked each year with 125,000 yearlings (rainbow, speckled, and brown trout) to sustain its reputation.

Though some fishermen may be disappointed with "the best trout stream in the East," no one can question the grandeur of the next 6 m. of wild river. It is worthwhile to pull out of the rush of traffic on Route 86 now and then to view the architecture of eroded ledges, of huge monoliths dividing foaming waters, and of the gray walls of the narrow gorge. Wilmington Notch is a fault zone. Escarpments tower above the river, reaching a maximum of 700 feet on the S side and 1,700 on the N. High Falls is a private inholding developed for tourists, with restaurant and souvenir shop; admission is charged for use of stairway, trail, and bridge in the gorge. East of High Falls are a state campsite and the entrance to the Whiteface Mountain Ski Center. The chair lift is operated in summer as well as during the ski season. The West Branch makes one more spectacular plunge in the Flume (falls and gorge) before it crosses the 1,000-foot contour in quieter waters above Wilmington.

Conservation Monument on Route 86 to Lake Everest, 6.8 m. (11.0 km.)
USGA: Lake Placid 15; Lake Placid 7.5 x 15

This section of the West Branch ranks as one of the most challenging of North Flow waters. In the 6.8 m. between the Monument and Lake Everest, the West Branch drops 640 feet for an average gradient of 94 feet per mile. The gradient is far from evenly distributed, however. A blend of mild rapids, major rapids, unrunnable falls, and steep cliffs inspires awe. Those wishing to paddle this section should possess expert skills. There are numerous take-out sites along Route 86, which parallels much of the river. There is a gauge just above the Whiteface Ski Area road on the L bank. A reading of 1.7 is the minimum level for this run and 2.7 is optimal. Water levels for this section generally rise 8 to 14 hours after heavy rains.

Put in is immediately above or below the Conservation Monument. The first rapid is a Class III-IV flume with a drop of 6 to 8 feet. It can be approached very slowly because of slackwater above. A prominent roostertail is present at most levels and can be used to choose the proper course down the middle. The rapids gradually subside below this drop, and the river veers L away from the road for one of the two notable sections of flatwater. As the river once again approaches Route 86, Class III rapids begin and continue for 0.3 m. After a brief run of fast current a tributary enters from the R at 1.0 m., passing under a grade-level bridge on the highway. From here to the beginning of Wilmington Notch, a distance of 1.2 m., the West Branch drops 120 feet. The rapids in this section are fairly discrete and all are rated Class III-IV. The first two drops are especially technical and may require scouting from the R bank. There is then a second stretch of flatwater as the Notch becomes visible. Below this the rapids return to Class III-IV. There is a protected area for endangered wildlife on the L, and paddlers should periodically switch their focus from the river to its surroundings in the hope of seeing some of these animals. Just below a parking lot on the R, the river comes to within 15 feet of Route 86 where the R bank is supported by an extended wall of sandbags. This marks the beginning of the Wilmington Notch section, in which the West Branch drops 50 feet in 0.3 m. as it turns L and then R. This section, rated Class V-VI, should be considered very dangerous. Careful scouting is highly recommended and adequate safety precautions should be taken. Even so, this rapid should only be attempted by strong parties with advanced paddling skills. Take-out is on the R bank up the steep wall of sandbags or, preferably, at a parking area on the R bank 0.2 m. upstream. Use of this take-out will require advance knowledge of its location, which can be obtained by scouting the river from the highway during a shuttle run. At most water levels the main channels of the Notch are blocked by large boulders very difficult to avoid, given the steepness of the gradient and the speed of the current. The most difficult section is the sharp turn back to the R. Those who have run this section usually do so by staying very close to the R bank till they have negotiated the sharp R turn.

The next practical put-in below the Notch is the next parking area on the R bank. By this point the rapids have subsided to Class III. In the next 0.8 m. rapids are continuous but fade to Class I. Soon a parking lot appears on the R. Shortly below it is a footbridge used by those touring High Falls Gorge. Take out on the R at the parking lot and carry down Route 86 for 200 yards to a sign that reads "State Wilderness Area," just past the fence marking the property line for

High Falls Gorge. Turn L and follow the steep trail for 100 yards down to the river. The land around High Falls Gorge is privately owned and no legal (or practical) carry exists in the river corridor. High Falls is an impressive series of drops totaling about 120 feet, most of which can be seen from the put-in.

Between this put-in and the next the West Branch drops steadily and presents powerful, complex rapids. At least two carries are necessary and paddlers should possess advanced skills to complete the remaining rapids. Below High Falls is a major Class IV rapid that builds in power and complexity for 0.4 m. until it falls 20 feet in a complex Class V–VI maze. This drop may be carried on either bank. Below this is a short section of Class IV-V rapids, then another major series of falls dropping 60 feet in two distinct pitches. There is a 0.2 m. carry on the R bank around these falls and a short, boulder-infested gorge, rated Class VI. This carry passes through a state camping area, where one may park for a day-use fee, and terminates at the access bridge to the Whiteface Ski Area. As an alternative, the paddler can carry down a very steep hill on the L bank and put-in at a slackwater above the bridge. There is a short Class IV rapid just above this slackwater and a major Class IV-V drop just below the slackwater and above the bridge. This rapid may be run at favorable water levels, but a large hydraulic must be dealt with. One hundred yards below the bridge the river takes a sharp turn to the R. At high water this section is rated Class V. At lower water it can be run on the far L by expert paddlers.

The large rapids above and below the bridge can be avoided by carrying to the far end of the parking lot on the R bank. From the parking lot, walk to the river's edge, wade across a narrow channel to a small island, and put in on the far side of the island in one of several eddies in the main channel of the river. This put-in is just above a Class IV section of 200 yards. For the next 1.0 m. there are continuous Class II–III rapids until the river takes a sharp turn to the R at the Hungry Trout Restaurant. Take out on the L bank as soon as the bridge on Route 87 is visible. Bushwhack for 15 yards to a jeep trail and turn R. Proceed to a small parking lot in 50 yards. Starting just above the bridge is the Flume, a series of major drops totaling over 70 feet in about 200 yards. Those wishing to continue to Lake Everest should carry down the R side of the highway for 60 yards to a parking area and then down a fishing/hiking trail for 30 yards. Class IV rapids continue from the end of the Flume to the end of the first island, then Class II-III rapids for another 200 yards. Below this point the current gradually fades on approaching Lake Everest.

Lake Everest, 4 m. round trip (6.4 km.)
USGS: Lake Placid 15 or Wilmington 7.5 × 15

A backwater above the dam in Wilmington is locally known as Lake Everest. It is attractive to canoeists chiefly for its close-up views of Marble, Lookout, Esther, and Whiteface mountains on the outgoing trip and of the Stephenson Range on the return. Whiteface towers an impressive 3,870 feet above the water. Rugged spurs radiate outward from the pointed peak, enclosing bowl-like depressions plucked out by old glaciers.

A public put-in site is at the NW Corner of the bridge in Wilmington. There is ample parking space on a graded bank, which canoeists share with fishermen and village youngsters who in summer jump off the highway bridge into deep water and swim to a raft held in place by a guy line. The popularity of this stunt at the bridge contributes to the peace and quiet of a fine sandy public beach a little way up the river.

About 0.6 m. upstream is the brown-shingled building, on the R, of the Wilmington bathing beach. The lagoon above the lodge should not be mistaken for the main channel. A reef extending diagonally across the river from a sandbar should be skirted on the downstream side to the far L, where the main channel is visible only as you near it. Finally, "Lake Everest" tapers to a muscular little stream determined not to be further encroached on.

Wilmington Dam to Au Sable Forks, 11m. (17.7 km.)
USGS: Lake Placid, Au Sable Forks 15; Wilmington, Au Sable Forks 7.5 × 15

The lower 11 m. of the West Branch from below the dam at Wilmington to confluence with the East Branch at Au Sable Forks is a whitewater run for intermediate to advanced paddlers. The drop is 440 feet in Class II–III–IV waters. Water levels are most likely to be satisfactory in late April and early May.

Unlike the upper sections of the river, the lower West Branch is heavily posted and access is often difficult. Put-in is on the L bank immediately below a newly developed gravel parking area marked by an Olympic Region sign. Access to the river requires a short carry around a set of cables supporting a rusted metal retaining wall. Wade a narrow channel several feet wide to a small island just below the dam. The next put-in is a fishing-rights easement, marked by a yellow sign, on the L bank 1.6 m. NE of the four corners W of the river in

Wilmington. The road begins as blacktop and turns to gravel at a R fork. From the parking lot of the easement, there is a six-minute carry into a deep trough between wooded slopes. Rapids in the 2.2 m. from Wilmington to the bridge on Haselton Rd. are continuous and mostly Class II. These build briefly to Class III at 0.5 m. and 0.75 m. below the dam. The gradient in this section averages 50 feet per mile.

The highway bridge on the Haselton Road is posted at all four corners. You can, however, gain access to the river by staying within the allowed right-of-way and putting in underneath the bridge. Below the bridge Class II rapids quickly fade. The next stretch consists of swift water and some occasional Class I rapids. There are nice backward views of Whiteface and Esther Mtns. and the peaks of the Stephenson Range. Homes and camps dot the banks. The wide floodplain narrows as Black Brook enters from the L.

The next opportunity for put-in is 2 m. E of Haselton, just beyond a bridge over Black Brook. A jeep road which soon enters state land leads to the river bank in 0.3 m. This road is too wet and rutty for cars in spring; a carry is recommended. Below this put-in site the gradient steepens again to an average 40 feet per mile till the backwater of a high concrete dam is reached. Below Black Brook rapids are nearly continuous for the next 3.3 m. They begin as Class I and quickly escalate to Class II. These continue for the next 2 m. before escalating again. Class III rapids continue for another mile till just after a tight S-turn. Below this, rapids moderate and end at the head of a small gorge where the backwater begins. Paddlers not wishing to continue downstream can exit the river here on the R bank. Take out just past the first rocky point, carry up a steep piny ridge and intersect a jeep trail. Turn L and go 50 yds. to a small parking area 0.1 m. W of the abandoned mill site described below.

The backwater is about 200 yds. long and ends at the dam. Approach cautiously; there is no boom. On the L side is a wooden shed resting on a concrete platform. Exit from the river is on the far R, where a narrow V-shaped cove is flanked on the downstream side by the dam itself. From this take-out, a steep switchback trail ascends a cliff to a parking lot adjacent to a water tower. This take-out is about 250 yards from a blacktop road along the S side of the river through a small settlement known as "Rome." The road, known as Au Sable Drive, connects with West Church Street in Au Sable Forks.

Advanced paddlers may want to try the steep, bouldery staircase of 1.2 m. from the dam to the confluence with the East Branch. The drop in this section is over 100 feet. At present, a carry around the dam is very difficult over the treacherous chaotic rubble of an old pulp mill. There are two abandoned mills in fact, the upper one in topsy-turvy ruins and the lower one well on the way to ruin. Fortunately, for the paddler, enough attention is required to read the river that the unsightliness of the corridor can be overlooked. This is a shame since the corridor was surely beautiful in its natural state. Immediately below the dam the rapids are large Class IV for 100 yards, although access from the R bank is virtually impossible and entry eddies are extremely small and turbulent. Access is only slightly easier below this point. There is a proposal to use this site to develop hydroelectric power by "the run of the river." As proposed, there should be little impact on the rapids above and below the dam. A cleared-out carry trail and a boom upstream from the R side of the dam are part of the proposal. Bear L at the first washed-out bridge (actually an old pulp conveyor). Below this bridge the rapids subside to Class III until passing under an abandoned bridge near the end of West Church Street. From here on, the rapids gradually diminish to Class II until the bridge on Route 9N in Au Sable Forks. Take out is at the Forge Street bridge, described as the put-in for the Main Stem.

Black Brook, a feeder of the West Branch about 5 m. above Au Sable Forks, drains Taylor Pond, an 810-acre body of water N of Catamount Mountain. The 3-m. long pond, entirely surrounded by Forest Preserve, makes pleasant canoeing. There is a state campsite at its E end, accessible from the Silver Lake Road.

EAST BRANCH

Headwaters
USGS: Mount Marcy, Elizabethtown 15; Mount Marcy, Keene Valley 7.5 × 15

Mountaineers, poets, and painters have paid tribute to the mountain brooks that feed the East Branch on both sides of Keene Valley. Some people have a favorite. For Old Mountain Phelps, once sought-after guide of Keene Valley, it was "Mercy" Brook of Panther Gorge. He addressed it in shy ritual words when he came to it in the course of a random scoot. But choosing is not necessary. Follow almost any of these brooks upward into the lurking places of the mountains and you will find serial fantasies in running or falling water, rock, and greenery.

Most of the streams have the NE-SW orientation of the principal ridges and valleys of the High Peaks. But Keene Valley with its East Branch is an exception. It lies almost due S-N. The brooks therefore slide into the East Branch at an angle of 30–45 degrees. This lattice pattern is very pronounced on the W. Three parallel stream valleys are especially prominent on the *Mount Marcy* map: the Ausable Lakes with their outlet, Johns Brook, and the Cascade Lakes and outlet. These three dramatic clefts in the mountains, along with another parallel one N of Pitchoff Mountain, are probably fault zones.

A large glacial lake once filled Keene Valley to levels as high as the sand terraces on East Hill above the Mountain House. When Keene Lake was at those levels, the passes, including Chapel Pond on the S, were plugged with ice lobes. Chapel Pond and the Ausable Lakes are remnants of Keene Lake.

I. *Chapel Pond.* Since lakes and ponds are in short supply in the High Peaks, perhaps little Chapel Pond deserves the attention of canoeists. Only 0.5 m. long, it fills a basin in the shadows of the sheer cliffs of Round Mountain. If you scan those cliffs closely, you may see rock climbers inching their way up. There is a small swimming beach at the sandy mouth of the inlet at the S end. The outlet at the N end is a feeder of the East Branch.

The easiest access is by car over an obscure woods road 0.3 m. N of the Route 73 parking lot at the middle of the pond. The dirt road soon forks near a good tent site with a natural fireplace. Take the R fork to a put-in on a sand ramp at the N end of the pond. There is another small tent site here.

II. *Ausable Lakes.* The East Branch first gets recognition on the map as it drains the Ausable Lakes. Access to the lower of the twin lakes is a road and trails in the Adirondack Mountain Reserve (Ausable Club). The club has a public parking lot near its southern entrance on Route 73, a half mile from the club house. From here it is 4 m. to the Lower Lake by road, which the public can use on foot or, in July and August, by a bus operated hourly from the club house. A network of mountain trails off this road is open to the public (see the St. Huberts section of *Guide to Adirondack Trails*).

In a major acquisition in 1978 the state purchased 9,100 acres from the Adirondack Mountain Reserve, including the summits and upper slopes of 12 mountains over 4,000 feet high. All 46 of the High Peaks are now state owned. Along with the sale, the AMR gave the state a permanent scenic easement on its remaining land and permanent right of way for foot travel by the public over all trails except a few adjacent to the Upper Lake. Prohibited uses are about what they have been in the past. The public is not permitted to boat, camp, swim, hunt, bring pets, or bushwhack in the valley and the lower slopes up to the 2,500-foot level.

The East Branch from Marcy Swamp (above the Ausable Lakes) to St. Huberts is classified as a scenic river. Unfortunately, one of the finest lake and mountain views in the Adirondacks is not available to the public: this is the view of the Great Range and Sawteeth from a boat on Upper Ausable Lake; the view that Old Mountain Phelps warned his patrons not "ter hog down" but cherish in brief installments; the view that Noah Porter, president of Yale University, wanted to see one more time before he died. As consolation, you can, by a short hike from the foot of the Lower Lake, enjoy the view from Indian Head. The river below the lakes is best seen by a round trip hike from the Ausable Club over the East River Trail and the West River Trail, which are slower than the road but closer to the stream and more scenic. Beaver Meadow Falls and Rainbow Falls on tributary streams should not be missed.

While fishing along this stretch in the last century, Charles Dudley Warner got lost. The predicament of a man lost in this narrow cleft, with brooks and river to guide him out to civilization, is more comic than fearsome, and this friend and collaborator of Mark Twain makes the most of the comedy in a mock-serious parody of all "lost-in-the-woods" stories in his book about the Adirondacks, *In the Wilderness* (1876).

III. *Cascade Lakes.* These two lakes occupy a long narrow cleft between Cascade and Pitchoff mountains. There is a tradition that a single lake was separated into two by an avalanche. But a patent of 1812 shows that the two lakes existed then. Today the state-owned neck of land between them is a popular picnicking site. It is also a good place to launch canoes. Cars with trailers should not attempt to use the steep spur road to the picnic area, however. There is risk of getting stuck in loose gravel on leaving the site up the steep grade. I and several other people in cars were once marooned for over an hour in the picnic area while a tow truck came from Keene to pull a camper trailer up the grade.

The upper lake is 0.5 m. long, the lower 1 m. Cascade Mountain towers 2,060 feet above them, Pitchoff 1,450. The steep ravine between the two lakes is a sporting way to bushwhack up Cascade Mountain, with a descent by the trail.

East Branch in Keene Valley, 6 m. (9.7 km.)
USGS: Mount Marcy 15 or Keene Valley 7.5 × 15

From St. Huberts to Au Sable Forks the East Branch is classified as a recreational river. Highways parallel it for the whole distance and make access easy for canoeist and fisherman. They also attract commercial and residential development. Though the hamlets are small, the houses of summer and year-round residents appear in every mile of the corridor. The quality of water is high to Au Sable Forks, where pollution is first apparent. The East Branch is a noted fishing stream and is stocked with rainbow, speckled, and brown trout.

Timing is all important for the short but delightful run of 4 to 6 m. in Keene Valley. Adequate water levels are not assured after the middle of May, and in a dry spring not even that late. Rushing down mountain ravines, the East Branch and its tributaries carry a load of loose sand and gravel which, as the current slows in the valley, they deposit in the stream bed. Eroded banks give a compensating width to the stream to carry off floods of snowmelt in spring. Later in the season the river is relatively wide for its modest volume of water and hence quite shallow. Best conditions prevail in April and through the first week in May. The East Branch then is deep enough to insure a fast, exhilarating float without wading.

Difficulties do not exceed Class II at medium high water. But a warning is due on the cold water—and possibly the air too. These conditions were brought home to me by a flip in the stretch above the hamlet of Keene Valley. A wet suit is advisable on this stretch, which is swifter and has sharper bends than the stretch below the hamlet. The chief danger is being swept into "strainers" at bends. (A strainer is a fallen tree which blocks passage for canoe and paddlers while the water keeps moving. A flip is certain if occupants of the canoe lean upstream. Then there is danger of being swept under the blockage and perhaps trapped in a tangle of branches.)

Put-in for the upper stretch is, by road, about 1.5 m. S of the hamlet of Keene Valley at a bridge on a spur road off Route 73. As the river flows, the distance to the stone bridge in Keene Valley is 2 m. The drop is about 38 feet. Mild rapids are almost continuous and the current is fast.

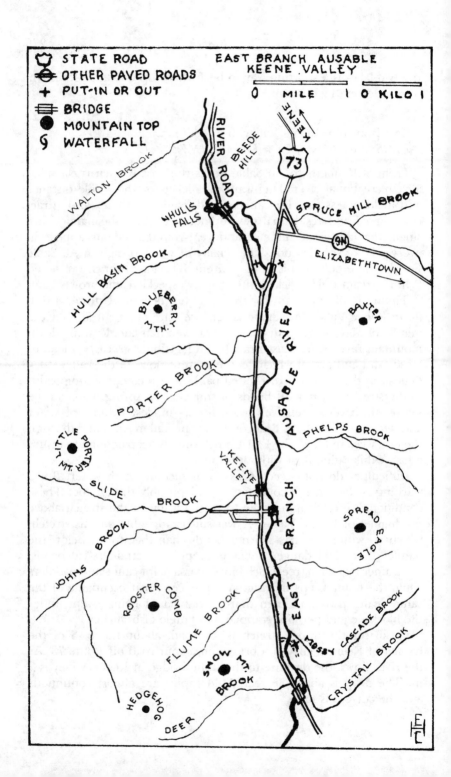

There is little risk of an upset in the 4 m. below Keene Valley. The gradient is less steep, averaging a steady 13 feet per mile; and the bends are wider. The chief concern is to stay in the main current where depths are adequate.

The stone bridge in Keene Valley is a convenient put-in site. To reach it, drive E at the four corners in the center of the hamlet on a tree-lined lane through a small park. There is a sand ramp at the SE corner of the bridge. The graceful single-arched structure was built in 1913 with the evident intention of erecting a man-made object worthy of the natural setting.

The highest waves (about a foot) are encountered in the first two rapids, both inside the hamlet. Several rapids follow these, but they are not complicated by crosscurrents or eddies. The only interruption is a fisheries dam (to form a plunge pool) below the Keene Highway Department barn. A short carry on the L is advisable here because of a reversal wave below the dam.

Houses, barns, and the highway are often in sight. But so too are splendid mountain vistas. The most impressive ones are usually behind, but Porter Mountain is off the bow across a meadow, and on the E side of the valley the stream washes the base of Baxter Mountain.

Take-out places are the bridge on Route 73 and the L bank 0.2 m. below the bridge where the stream loops close to the River Road. If the latter is used, the spot should be selected in advance. The current is swift here and good landings are few. Beyond this, the river draws away from the road in private land and crosses it next only to plunge over Hulls Falls.

Hulls Falls to Keene, 2 m. (3.2 km.)
USGS: Mount Marcy, Lake Placid 15; Keene Valley, Lake Placid 7.5 × 15

Below Hulls Falls the East Branch follows a zigzag postglacial channel in crushed, faulted rock. The preglacial channel, now blocked by a delta of sand, wound eastward around Beede Hill. In its present course W of the hill the river offers spectacular scenery and sections of whitewater suitable to advanced paddlers. In this short section the East Branch drops about 130 feet with most of the gradient occurring in a steep, dangerous section below the Old Grist Mill Road bridge (now closed to vehicular traffic). Several glimpses of the river are available from this and from Hulls Falls Road, both turning off Route 73 in the village of Keene. The first two drops below Hulls Falls should be scouted from the R bank; the section below the bridge on Old Grist Mill Road can be scouted from that road at various locations. Even expert paddlers should consider carrying the steepest section below the bridge during high water because of the risks involved. This portion of the East Branch is best run at high water levels although the steepest portions are runnable at lower levels as well; advanced scouting from the above-mentioned roads and bridges can determine if water levels are sufficient.

The pool below Hulls Falls is a popular spot frequented by swimmers and fishermen. Access to this area ia via a well-worn trail along the R bank. The shores are heavily posted, however, and the access trail extends beyond the allowed right-of-way. It is advisable to check with the landowner, even though this site is widely used by the public. The bridge on Old Grist Mill Road serves as an alternative access point.

Rapids begin immediately below the pool. In 50 yards there is a double drop of about 10 feet rated Class IV-V and in another 30 yds., at a turn to the L, a Class III-IV drop of about 6 ft. Class III rapids predominate for the next 0.3 m. and gradually subside to Class I by the time the river runs under the bridge on the Old Grist Mill Road bridge at 0.8 m.

Mild Class I rapids continue under the bridge past the confluence of Weston Brook on the L. The rapids then build to Class II and quickly to Class III-IV as a boulder garden is reached 0.4 m. below the bridge. Paddlers should exit on the L bank above the boulder garden, for the L bank adjacent to it is posted and a carry on the R (the Hulls Falls Road side) is impossible. Shortly below the boulder garden begins a series of precipitous drops known as Champagne Falls, rated Class V-VI for the first 150 yards and Class IV-V for the next 100 yards. In two places the drops are large enough (6 to 8 feet) to warrant being considered small falls and precise maneuvering is required. Carry or scout on the R. The presence of several large potholes attests to the power of the river as it flows through this small gorge. Below these drops is a small turnout on the Old Grist Mill Road. Paddlers who have carried around the drops can re-enter the river at this point. From here on, the East Branch is an extended boulder garden with a gradient substantially milder than that found above. Rapids are Class III until a washed-out dam is reached in 0.2 m. Class II rapids then continue to the bridge under Route 73. Take-out is below this bridge on the L bank at the Community Center.

Keene to Upper Jay Dam, 6.3 m. (10.1 km.)
USGS: Lake Placid 15 or 7.5 × 15

Given the opportune moment and skills of at least intermediate
class, this is one of the most enjoyable raceways in the northern Adiron-

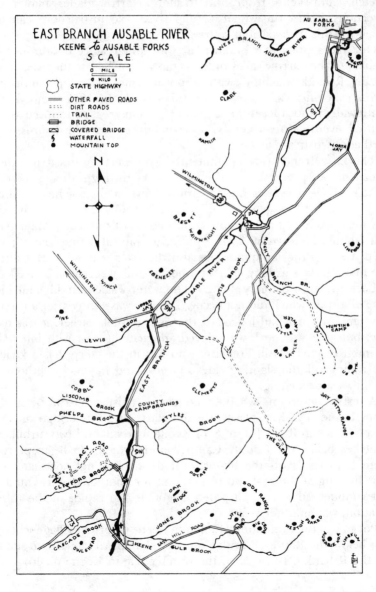

dacks. At medium high to high water levels, Class I–II–III rapids are very frequent in the first 5 m., which have an average gradient of 24 feet. The total drop from Keene to Upper Jay is 140 feet. Alert maneuvering is required. At one widening of the bed, boulders stretch helter-skelter from shore to shore. Narrow glades splay in all directions amidst the whitecaps and rocks. No instructions can be given for this tricky slalom course.

One races along at 8 m. an hour with little chance to admire the scenery of the narrow valley or to say more than "Hi" to the fishermen on the R bank watching, with skeptical grins, for a flip. Until the 1970s canoeing was a novelty on this stretch. In 1977, however, a whitewater canoe race from Keene to Upper Jay was introduced as an annual event. More recently, a second race was added, finishing further downstream at Jay.

The East Branch is temperamental. You must try to catch it in a genial mood, preferably as the sun breaks through after a torrent of rain. The river rises fast in spring thaws or during heavy rains, and it falls fast too, generally in cycles of 24 to 48 hours. Conditions are most likely to be favorable from mid-April into early May. Wet suits should be worn in April. I prefer to wait till spring thaws have crept well up the mountainsides and the river is less icy. But after the first ten days in May, luck or a persistently wet season is needed.

Luck was with us on a May 20. The water was endurably chilly in case of a spill, which did not occur. The day was sunny after a three-day rain. When I had looked at the river a week earlier, it was too low; but as it was now, we enjoyed an exciting coast with intervals of intense activity. Bill Frenette, who was in the stern, has a knack for rolling off the slanting sides of rocks and haystacks without a scrape or a drenching.

A test to determine whether the level is satisfactory can be made from Route 9N. Key places are the start, the iron bridge on the Lacey-Limekiln Road 1.5 m. N of Keene by road, and two turbulent stretches below the County Campgrounds which can be inspected from loop roads off the highway. If depths are not adequate for easy floating at the first two places, wait for another day. If you are not confident that you can safely negotiate the rapids in the third location, wait another year.

Put-in is at the Community Center in Keene (a former village school) just below the Route 73 bridge on the L bank. An alternative site is on the R bank 0.15 m. N of the traffic circle in Keene on Route 9

N, where a steep trail descends to the river.

The first 3.4 m. consist primarily of Class I and II rapids. The mouth of Styles Brook is then passed on the R, signaling the beginning of the most turbulent stretch. At a sweeping turn to the L is the beginning of Ark Rapids, much of which is visible from a loop road on the R. Ark Rapids is a complex boulder garden about 150 yards long and Class III in difficulty. Class II rapids continue below here and are fairly constant for the next mile and a half. The gradient lessens on the approach to Upper Jay. A fisheries dam is reached at 5.5 m. A calm above the dam (0.8 m. above Upper Jay) makes the take-out easy, on the R. The carry is 100 feet for those proceeding downstream. Those choosing to run the Class II drop over the dam should choose a small tongue approximately 15 feet from the R bank; scouting may be necessary to identify the proper course.

There is no state land touching the river between Keene and Au Sable Forks. But the town of Keene maintains a small picnic area for the public 3.2 m. N of Keene on 9N.

Upper Jay Dam to Jay, 5 m. (8 km.)
USGS: Lake Placid, Au Sable Forks 15; Lake Placid, Lewis 7.5 × 15

The river is quiet through Upper Jay. On the R bank the Land of Makebelieve was for 25 years a popular attraction for youngsters until a succession of damaging floods led to its closing in 1980. The gray cliffs and pines of shapely Ebenezer Mountain tower above the L bank. As the valley widens, the long ridges of the Jay Mountains come into view on the R. There is leisure now to rest on the paddle and dream of a second home in this pleasant intervale between the two Jays.

Calms and rapids of Class I and II alternate. Several shoals require medium high water for easy cruising. At that level a log deflector is hardly noticed as one floats over it.

About 0.7 m. above the bridge in Jay a loop in the river comes close to a parking lot and picnic area on the highway. (A take-out here avoids the rocky ravine and Jay Falls in the hamlet.) At medium high water most of the ravine is passable. It is approximately 100 yards long, with the most difficult section rated Class III. It is slightly easier to run this rapid on the R. An easy carry is available a little way up the R bank on an abandoned road parallel to the river. The last 0.2 m. above the falls is smooth water. Jay Falls is a potentially dangerous Class V drop in several sections. It can be run by expert paddlers at favorable water levels. The preferred course begins on the far L down a 12-foot slide. Immediately turn 90 degrees to the R and in 50 feet maneuver over an 8-foot drop. Finally, turn sharply back to the L and negotiate a series of Class IV ledges. For those choosing to carry, land on flat rock on the R and carry up the bank to a parking lot and picnic table overlooking the picturesque falls and bridge. One of the oldest covered bridges in New York State, it was built in 1856 and is still in use on the secondary road SE of the hamlet. (There are plans to convert the surrounding area into a public park in the hope of preserving the bridge.) Ice jams repeatedly threaten it, but so far it has proved sturdy enough to escape serious damage. Not so fortunate were residents of the valley in a January thaw of 1976. Floods and ice jams caused heavy damage and forced 25 families to leave their homes.

Jay Mountains. The massive range of the Jays dominates this part of the Ausable Valley. Seen from the river, the long bare ridge line is irresistible to mountaineers. Though most of the high land is Forest Preserve, the state does not maintain a trail. There are hunters' trails from the SW and the NW, both requiring a little bushwhacking at the steepest gradients. The former and better known starts from The Glen. But local people prefer what they call "the back way," and I believe they are right. A full day should be devoted to this enjoyable hike. The *Au Sable Forks* map and a compass are essential.

The route begins at the take-out just described, on the S side of the covered bridge. A car can be driven over the first 3 m. Bear R on a good blacktop road in a S and SSE direction. At a T, turn R on a wide bend and continue a little way past two white houses, one on each side of the road (about 1.5 m. from the covered bridge). In a meadow beyond the house on the L, turn L on a gravel road, which soon crosses a tributary of Rocky Branch Brook. Proceed on this road, parallel to the unseen Rocky Branch, 1.5 m. farther to a small meadow now much overgrown with saplings. Park here and proceed on foot 0.2 m. to a jeep road, which is not shown on the map. Follow the jeep road, R, on alternate steep and gentle slopes, till it ends at a hunter's camp (in land owned by a local lumber company but open to hikers). Above this is state land. There is a choice of two routes from this point on.

(1) Above the hunter's cabin, on the L, look for an old logging trace at the top of the steep bank of a brook which feeds the Rocky Branch. Follow this trace to an obscure brook crossing and look for a continuation on the other bank. When that too ends or pulls away from the brook, bushwhack S up steep grades and around cliffs just

W of Grassy Notch to "Jay Mt," as this 3,300-foot peak in the range is designated on the map. You now emerge on the open rock of an undulating ridge spread out in both directions in a great arc about 1.5 m. long. This crest was denuded in a forest fire and has remained bare. It provides the kind of skyline hiking one finds in the Presidential Range of the White Mountains but rarely in the Adirondacks for any great distance.

(2) The other route from the hunter's camp follows a roughly parallel course a little farther to the W. It is a faint trail that passes the woodpile of the hunting camp in a southerly direction and soon crosses a small brook. After climbing some distance, it joins a logging trace which skirts under the N spur of "Jay Mt" on the E side. When, looking up, you can see the rock crest, leave the logging trace and climb to the top. This route puts you at the NW end of the arc of open bedrock. You can take the skyline walk to the other end ("Jay, 3600"), all in the open except for a few brushy notches, and then return to Grassy Notch for a descent by the route described in (1).

Jay to Au Sable Forks, 7.2 m. (11.6 km.)
USGS: Au Sable Forks 15 or 7.5 × 15

The gradient averages 10 feet a mile in this stretch. There are numerous Class I and II rapids. Depths are normally adequate into early June in the first 4.7 m. to Stickney Bridge. Below that, the river is wider and shallower, and some wading may be necessary after-mid May. Pebbles, cobbles, and boulders strew the bottom in the shallow parts.

Mountain ranges are often in view over banks now wooded, now open. The water is clear except at flood stage or after heavy rains, when it may be clouded with sediment. Highway traffic is often in sight and hearing.

Put-in is at the SE corner of the covered bridge in Jay. A carry trail descends the bank between the bridge and a red barn. About 1.8 m. downstream one can float over a log deflector at medium high water.

Stickney Bridge, at 4.7 m., makes a pleasant lunch stop. On the R bank, 25 yards up the road to North Jay, is a cold spring. Drivers of cars cross the bridge, fill containers of various kinds at the spring, and turn around and drive back. The popularity of the spring is well deserved.

There are many reefs and rapids below Stickney Bridge. On a June 11 we were obliged to wade in several places.

For those not continuing down the main stem of the Ausable, the most convenient take-out is on the L bank at the second bridge in Au Sable Forks, just above the confluence of the two branches.

The percentage of runoff is high on relatively impervious mountain slopes. The East Branch therefore has the greatest spread between maximum recorded streamflow (20,100 cubic feet per second) and minimum (20 cfs) of all Adirondack rivers for which statistics are available. The average discharge at the gauging station in Au Sable Forks is 300 cfs. Because of these extreme variations, good canoeing is limited to the spring runoff season or brief 48-hour periods after heavy or prolonged rains.

MAIN STEM

The confluence of the East and West Branch at Au Sable Forks does not extend the canoeing season as much as might be supposed on the main stem. A steep, swift mountain river, the Ausable has carved out a wide bed, where not constricted by bedrock, to accommodate the spring runoff. The main stem averages over 100 feet wide. Several segments of it are boulder jungles which may be dangerous at very high water but in dry seasons are tedious to thread if not impassably shallow. Satisfactory depths normally prevail from April to mid-May. However, heavy rainfall in summer or fall can provide short intervals of adequate water.

It is convenient to describe the 22 miles of the main stem in three sections: (1) Au Sable Forks to Keeseville, 13.6 m.; (2) Keeseville to the northernmost Ausable River bridge on Route 9; (3) the same bridge to Lake Champlain, 2.5 m. The first and last are described below as canoe routes. The second section, with a total drop of 260 feet, is largely impractical. Although canoeists may be enticed by the opening series of Class II ledges, they quickly encounter a number of difficulties in this short section. Just below the motels north of Keeseville there is a 6–8 foot falls known locally as Indian Falls. This falls, rated Class III–IV, can only be run at favorable water levels. It is best negotiated on the far R, about 30 feet from the bank. About a quarter mile downstream is Alice Falls, a 40-foot drop. A hydroelectric dam has recently been built at this site, where once there was a mill. The impoundment behind this dam may, at some water levels, reduce the drop at Indian Falls. Take out on the L bank. Immediately below Alice Falls dam is another power dam, then the impressive Rainbow Falls, a double drop of 75 feet located at the head of Ausable Chasm. Ausable Chasm, one of the leading attractions of the East, is controlled by the Ausable Chasm Company, which does not allow paddlers to carry around the falls or rapids, citing insurance risks, so interested parties must visit as the tourists do, on foot through the upper part of the canyon and by guided boat tour in the lower. There is no legal access to the river between the head of the canyon and the northernmost bridge on Route 9.

Ausable Chasm expresses the genius of this mountain stream—its swiftness and, given time to work in, its cutting power. Another condition necessary to the structuring of the beautiful canyon is a thick bed of horizontal, stratified rock for the river to cross in what is probably a postglacial channel. Such a bed was laid down hundreds of millions of years ago when the Adirondack Mountains were an island in a surrounding sea. The bed is composed of sedimentary rock which was deposited in layers as sand washed down from the weathered rock of the mountains. The Potsdam sandstone of Ausable Chasm is softer than the crystalline rock of the mountains. Consequently, the Chasm is very different from the gorges of Hulls Falls on the East Branch and Wilmington Notch on the West Branch. The walls are more box-like: deeper and more nearly vertical or even overhanging. They are also layered, with projecting ledges. In the spring, when flood waters rise as much as 40 feet in the canyon, blocks are dislodged and swept downstream. The architecture is constantly changing as time and the river work away at the walls.

Low water would be no problem to a canoeist in the lower part of Ausable Chasm. In the Flume, for instance, where walls contract to 13 feet, the river is 60 feet deep at low stage. The upper part of the chasm, however, presents quite a different picture, even at low water levels. Horseshoe Falls, a drop of 12 feet, is unrunnable and is followed in turn by a series of discrete rapids ranging from Class IV to Class VI in difficulty. What makes these rapids particularly interesting to would-be paddlers is the fact that exit from most eddies is impossible due to the sheerness of the chasm's walls.

Prior to 1971 tourists in the Chasm used to ask the guides why the water was a murky pink or a murky green. If the right answer was forthcoming, it acknowledged the waste discharge from a paper mill on the West Branch above Au Sable Forks. The river below the Forks took on the color of the dye being used at the mill. But in the spring of 1971 the mill closed because it could not afford the expense of an anti-pollution system required by new laws directed at cleaning the waterways of the state. Tourists in the Chasm no longer ask embarrassing questions.

The main stem is classified as a recreational river throughout its length. The state has acquired fishing easements on it and stocks it with rainbow and brown trout. The lower part may benefit from a program to restore salmon in Lake Champlain.

Au Sable Forks to Keeseville, 13.6 m. (21.7 km.)
USGS: Au Sable Forks 15 or 7.5 × 15, Willsboro 15

Now that the Au Sable Forks mill is closed, fish are coming back and the water is regaining the transparency natural to a mountain stream. But other abuses are more apparent than ever. The people in the valley, having lost respect for their smelly, turbid river while the mill was operating, used it as both dump and sewer. Now that the water is no longer opaque, the history of these secondary abuses is written all over the river bottom, in and below Au Sable Forks, in a mosaic of colored plastic, oil drums, refrigerators, bed springs, bread tins, etc. The banks too are littered with trash from the Forks to a point below Clintonville where roads on the N and S mercifully pull away from the river. In Clintonville an auto-graveyard disfigures the L bank. Au Sable Forks, which in the past poured its raw sewage into the river, has taken steps to install a modern disposal plant. But cleaning the riverbed and banks is a Herculean task. The source of a possible labor supply is not apparent.

Consequently, a trip on this upper part of the main stem is a mixed pleasure. The trick is to keep eyes averted, wherever possible, from the trash underneath and at the sides and train them on the hills, where every prospect pleases. Nature had quite other intentions for this valley from what man has made of it.

The drop from Au Sable Forks to Keeseville is 140 feet in 13.6 m. Most of the difficulties, as well as the trash, come in the upper 6.2 m. to the bridge in Clintonville, where the gradient averages 15 feet a mile. There are several Class I–II rapids. The two chief danger spots are the Class II (III at high water) rapids above Rogers and an irregular reef of boulders below the Catholic Church in Clintonville. The latter pitch, though short, is severe. An open canoe is liable to ship water. Both stretches can readily be carried if skills are not adequate or water levels unfavorable.

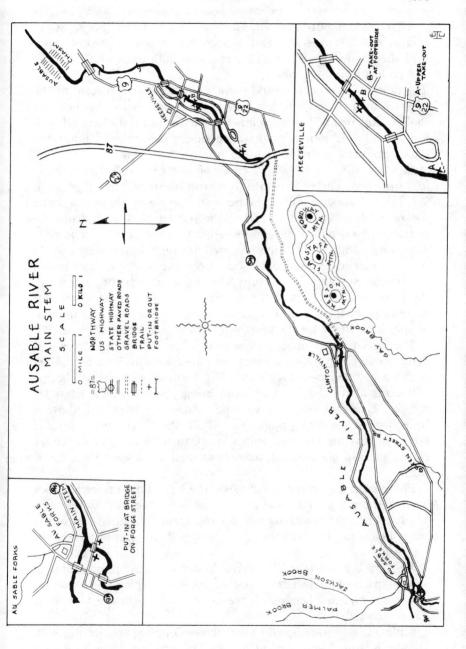

AUSABLE RIVER
MAIN STEM

SCALE

0 MILE 1
0 KILO 1

=87= NORTHWAY
US HIGHWAY
STATE HIGHWAY
OTHER PAVED ROADS
GRAVEL ROADS
BRIDGE
TRAIL
PUT-IN OR OUT
FOOTBRIDGE

KEESEVILLE

AUSABLE CHASM

B-TAKE-OUT AT FOOTBRIDGE
A-UPPER TAKE-OUT

NORDWAY MTN.
FLAGSTAFF MTN.
KEETON MTN.

GAY BROOK

CLINTONVILLE

AUSABLE RIVER

GREEN STREET BR.

JACKSON BROOK

AUSABLE FORKS

PALMER BROOK

AU SABLE FORKS

AUSABLE FORKS

MAIN STEM

PUT-IN AT BRIDGE ON FORGE STREET

A convenient put-in site in Au Sable Forks is the Forge Street bridge, which crosses the East Branch 0.1 m. above its confluence with the West. There is parking space at both ends of the bridge and paths down the banks.

A cautious approach should be made to the faster current of the West Branch. Below the junction is an island. Both channels are shallow and rocky. The R channel is narrow but less cluttered with junk than the L. Rapids gradually moderate below the island and at 0.6 m. give way to smoother water with a fast current.

At 3.4 m., where a dairy bar is visible on Route 9N, boulders multiply in a wide bed. The river begins to narrow, funneling into a gorge at a L bend. Canoeists not at home in rough water should examine the next 0.6 m. (to the W end of the hamlet of Rogers) from the nearby highway before deciding whether to run it or carry. The difficulty varies with water levels. At medium high water, waves up to two feet are encountered. A large rock outcrop on the L shore marks the narrowest part of the gorge. As you approach this, swerve to the L to avoid boulders in the center. Below this, where a low cliff appears on the R bank, the deepest channel, requiring the least maneuvering, is on the R for the remainder of the rough stretch.

The river is fairly quiet for the next 1.7 m. As it approaches a R bend above Clintonville, it cants onto another boulder patch. Most of this is easy to run at high water, but the midportion, which begins 150 yards above the Dugway Road bridge, is a technical Class III section. A reef of boulders stretches across the river just above a huge, jagged projecting boulder on the L shore. The best course is far L, toward the boulder, with a quick turn back to the R. Other routes are also possible but are best scouted in advance from the R bank.

There is an easy carry of 0.2 m. on the L, and the projecting rock on that shore is also a good place to examine the reef. Carry up a low bank to a terrace along which runs a truck trace parallel to the river. Below the big rock, the trace swings R to a put-in well below the reef.

The next 0.2 m. to the Clintonville bridge is an easy passage among widely spaced boulders. Be wary of boulders under the center of the bridge and just below it, however. A course near the L shore is less obstructed.

Riffles, Class I rapids, and fast current continue for 1.3 m., with knobby Keeton Mountain on the R. The gradient then lessens as the river rolls through meadow flats for the next 5 m. This is a serene, winding passage in somewhat slower current. The highway on the N is usually distant enough to deaden traffic noise, and a secondary road on the S also pulls away from the river. The banks are cleaner.

At 4.3 m. below Clintonville a hairpin bend washes the base of a steep bank below Route 9N, the last close approach to the highway above Keeseville. The river continues smooth as it swings SE under Fordway Mountain. Then comes a horseshoe bend (upper L corner of *Willsboro* map) from S to N, with a high embankment on the R and the flats of Ausable River Campsite (private) on the L. At the lower end of the campsite, the lofty bridge of the Northway crosses the river.

Smooth water continues for another 0.3 m. The river now begins to cant at the head of a series of step-like ledges separated by pools. These gradually build in intensity to Class II–III by the time the Ausable passes under the next bridge. The ledges continue to the footbridge in the center of Keeseville. At lower water levels it is often necessary to wade or line over these ledges.

There is a possible take-out near the head of the ledges. A pick-up should be arranged or a second car should be parked on the outskirts of Keeseville. To reach the place by car, drive S of the business section on combined routes 9 and 22 to Margaret Street, R. Follow the winding blacktop around the outer edge of a suburban development for another 0.4 m. to the second of two L bends. Park here on undeveloped ground on the R at the top of a steep embankment above the ravine of a brook feeding the Ausable. The river is not visible, but a trail drops down the bank to the mouth of the brook, about 250 yards.

To make connections with this carry from the river, pass through the first ledge below the Northway and then look for the small brook mouth (possibly dry in summer) on the R. It is about halfway between the first two ledges. The carry trail is on the lower side of the brook mouth and climbs on the crest of a high bank, with yellow blazes.

Those continuing downriver through the ledges (*Keeseville* map) pass under an auto bridge. Around the next L bend a high footbridge comes into view. Immediately below this footbridge are a breached dam and dangerous waterfall. Take-out is immediately below this footbridge at a small village park overlooking the waterfall. This waterfall, rated Class V, drops 18 feet in 50 yards and is best run on the far L. At higher water there is a substantial hydraulic.

Keeseville is an attractive village with several buildings of weathered stone along the waterfront. It has come a long way in sophistication

since William J. Stillman, artist and journalist, described it as the
"frontier town" where a carefully selected committee of citizens wel-
comed the most illustrious party of ten ever to visit the Adirondacks
for a camp-out. "Philosophers' Camp," the guides called it. At Keeseville "the whole community," wrote Stillman, "was on the *qui vive* to
see, not Emerson or Lowell, of whom they knew nothing [in 1858,
mind you], but Agassiz, who had become famous in the commonplace
world through having refused, not long before, an offer from the
Emperor of the French of the keepership of the Jardin des Plantes
and a senatorship if he would come to Paris and live." The welcoming
committee had brought an engraved portrait of Agassiz along to guard
against misdirecting their attentions. "The head of the deputation,
after having carefully compared Agassiz to the engraving, turned
gravely to his followers and said, 'Yes, it's him'; and they proceeded
with the same gravity to shake hands in their order, ignoring all the
other luminaries."

Ausable and Little Ausable Deltas, 4.7 m.+ (7.6 km.+)
USGS: Keeseville 7.5

The distance between the mouths of the Ausable and the Little
Ausable is short. But a half day can agreeably be spent in exploring
not only the river deltas but also the sloughs in wetlands where the
state maintains the Ausable Marsh Game Management Area. The
swift river finally slows down before emptying into Lake Champlain.
The river mouths are deep enough to float a canoe throughout summer.

Days of strong winds should be avoided. High waves on Lake Champlain can be troublesome in going from one mouth to another.

This is not a wilderness trip. Noise pollution is much in evidence.
Air Force jets roar overhead, flying low to and from the nearby Platts-
burgh base at short intervals throughout the day and into the night.
In summer the popular bathing beaches of Ausable Point and the
Upper Mouth ring with laughter and shouting.

An interesting circuit, if a gale is not blowing on the lake, starts
on or near the highway, Route 9, and combines the mouth of the
Little Ausable with the Upper Mouth of the Ausable. The Little Ausable is an entirely separate stream; cursory scouting indicates that it
affords no cruises of satisfactory length upstream. But its mouth,
through a waterfowl management area, is canoeable and attractive.

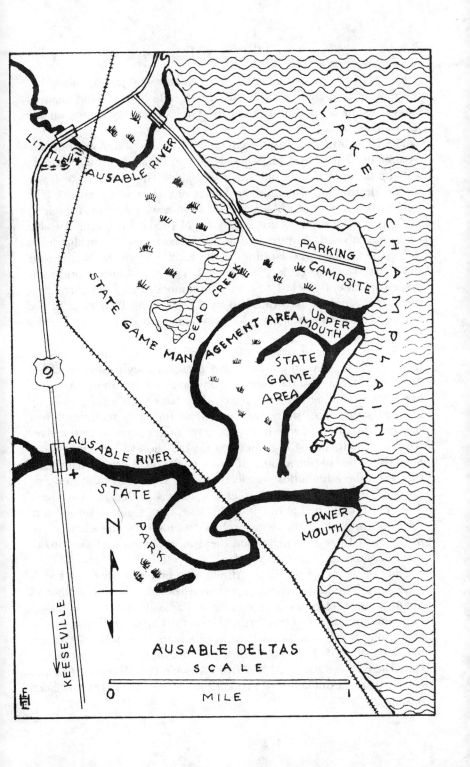

LAKE CHAMPLAIN

LITTLE AUSABLE RIVER

PARKING
CAMPSITE

STATE GAME MANAGEMENT AREA

DEAD CREEK

UPPER MOUTH

STATE
GAME
AREA

9

AUSABLE RIVER
STATE PARK

N

LOWER
MOUTH

KEESEVILLE

AUSABLE DELTAS
SCALE

0   MILE   1

(Users of the outdated *Plattsburgh 15* quadrangle should note that the mouth, as rechanneled, is now a half mile N of the old channel shown on the map. The present location is correctly shown on the *Keeseville 7.5* map.)

The Little Ausable-Ausable circuit is 4.7 m. by water without side excursions. Put-in and take-out are 1.4 m. apart by road, an easy walking distance if only one car is available. The direction of travel should depend on the wind, to which one is exposed on the lake portion of the trip. With a S or SW wind, a start on the Ausable at the green bridge on Route 9, 2.6 m. N of the bridge at Ausable Chasm, is advised. A spur road at the SE corner of the bridge leads to a parking place and landing. If the wind is from the N, the tour should start at the Little Ausable, either at the Route 9 bridge or more conveniently below it, over a hummocky dirt road through a game management area (marked by a DEC sign), 0.15 m. S of the bridge. This road goes E a little way and then turns down to the river bank.

There is a contrast between the two rivers. The Upper Mouth of the Ausable is wide and shallow and passes through a woods of big deciduous trees (willow and cottonwood are prominent), great branches extending over the water. The banks are levees, built up at flood stage here where the current of the swift mountain river slackens. Luxuriant ferns top these level ridges separating the river from its floodplains. Kingfishers patrol the shores. The clear water flows over a bed of ribbed sand. If it weren't for the Air Force overhead, this would be a limberlost—at least till one approaches the camping area at the mouth. A sandy reef, ideal for bathing as many have discovered, extends far out into the lake. The sandy riverbed and the long sandbar of the delta probably account for the name given to the river by the French when they were masters of Lake Champlain—*Rivière au Sable* or *aux Sables*.

The last 0.8 m. of the Little Ausable resembles an arm crooked at the elbow. The lower part is a rechannelization. There are signs of pollution in this stream. The water is murky, with occasional patches of green scum. But you can forget this on the narrow, intimate stream beautifully lined with swamp maples, poplars, and willows. Watery meadows of reeds and cattails obscure the mouth when approached from the lake. As you head NW from Ausable Point, your aim should be the boats at anchor in the small harbor just N of the concealed mouth.

The lake is shallow in the vicinity of the river deltas. Weeds reaching to the surface or near it help to moderate the waves on a breezy day, except in the deeper waters around Ausable Point, where wind and waves can sweep one into the rocky breakwater if it is not given ample clearance.

This area is unique and well worth a visit even if you have to plug your ears against those low-flying jets.

BOQUET RIVER

According to Winslow C. Watson, an Essex County historian of the 19th century, the first house erected by "civilized man" on the W shore of Lake Champlain between Crown Point and Canada was probably at Willsboro, 2.5 m. above the mouth of the Boquet River. The year was 1765, a very early date in Adirondack history. The builder was an enterprising Irishman, William Gilliland. By his early thirties Gilliland was a successful merchant in New York City. But he had dreams of a more brilliant destiny as lord of the manor with tenants and slaves. He realized this dream in the next ten years. Evidently believing that Lake Champlain, a bloody path of empire since 1609, was at last pacified by the British victory over the French in Canada, Gilliland chose to found his baronial estate of thousands of acres on the W shore between Split Rock and the Boquet River. Many families settled on his lands, paying him rent.

But Gilliland's efforts were premature. The Champlain Valley was to be a stage for two more wars. When the Revolutionary War broke out, his fortunes were at their height. Siding with the Colonies, he entertained at his own expense an entire American army on a disastrous retreat from Canada. But the war and its aftermath ruined him. His colony was ravaged by troops of both sides as well as by Indians. In 1777, when a force of British regulars, mercenaries, and Indians sailed up the lake to recapture Ticonderoga and attempt to split New England from New York, the army encamped for several days on the Boquet near Willsboro. The Indians with General John Burgoyne destroyed most of what was left of Gilliland's colony. Gilliland himself was falsely charged with treason. Most of his holdings were confiscated by the state. He spent six miserable years in debtor's prison in New York and was a broken man by the time of his release. While living with a son-in-law at Essex, a remnant of his old estate, he wandered off into the woods on a cold February day in 1796 and died of exposure.

Gilliland's journal for June 8, 1765, reads: "Arrived at the mouth of the Boquet, proceeded up the river to the falls [at Willsboro]." At that time the river already had its odd name. As with several other Adirondack rivers, the origin is uncertain. Was the river named for General Boquet, a British general in the French wars, who, however, never seems to have visited the Champlain Valley; for the abundance of flowers on its banks; or for its trough-like mouth (French *baquet*), the explanation preferred by Winslow Watson? Having discovered and named Lake Champlain, the French would seem to have a proprietary interest in naming its feeders too. P. Schuyler Miller suggests another plausible French origin. He believes that the river was named for a French Jesuit novitiate, Charles Boquet, who can be traced for 25 years in the mid-1600s through the pages of the *Jesuit Relations*. A good woodsman, he went on several missions to the Iroquois. Koert Burnham was so thoroughly convinced of the latter derivation that in 1982 he persuaded the U.S. Board of Geographical Names to abandon "Bouquet" and recognize "Boquet" as the official spelling. Two pronunciations are current locally: Bo-KET and Bo-KWET.

Like the Ausable, the Boquet is a swift mountain stream in its upper parts. From sources high on the slopes of Dix Mountain, sixth highest Adirondack peak, it drops more than 4,000 feet to Lake Champlain. The North Fork drains Hunters Pass; the S side of the same pass feeds the Hudson through the Schroon. The South Fork drains Dix on the SE and the slopes of the other peaks in the Dix Mountain Wilderness Area.

Both forks, with their bouldery beds and foaming cascades, are well known to mountaineers. (They were classified as scenic rivers in the Rivers Act of 1972.) They are too steep for canoeing. Most of the Boquet's drop comes in the first 9 m. (North Fork) to the confluence of the two forks at the 1,100-foot level. An additional 240 feet of drop occurs in the 2.4 m. from the forks to the top of Split Rock Falls, with continuous rapids throughout. Rapids are generally mild at spots where the river parallels the highway, but quickly become very difficult and congested as the river veers away. Rapids in these portions range from Class III to Class VI, with the first gorge being particularly dangerous. This section might be paddleable by experts at very favorable water levels, but is best avoided by everyone else. Seventy-five percent of the remaining 45 m., however, is of gentle gradient. People who see the Boquet only in summer do not realize that it is one of the most enjoyable canoeing streams in the Adirondacks in the spring of the year. Its combination of wild mountain and open meadow reminds one, especially in the reach between Split Rock Falls and Elizabethtown, of a vale in Switzerland.

The Boquet has "branches" as well as "forks." The Branch (also called Little Boquet), which drains Knob Lock and Hurricane mountains, enters the main stem in Elizabethtown. It is not canoeable for any length. The North Branch, heading in Trout Pond S of Clintonville, enters the main stem 3 m. above Willsboro. A stretch of about 3 m. in woods and meadows above and below Deerhead (*Au Sable Forks* map) appears to be canoeable at medium high water but is heavily posted at take-out on the Reber Road. Other important feeders are a creek misleadingly called Black River, draining Lincoln Pond, and Spruce Mill Brook.

Though a small river, seldom over 80 feet wide and often much less, the main stem is adapted to canoe cruising in the spring (and immediately after heavy rains in summer and fall) for a surprising 34 m. In addition, there are two whitewater reaches, one below Elizabethtown and the other below Boquet, for the intermediate canoeist. The main stem has been classified as "recreational." The DEC stocks it with rainbow, speckled, and brown trout.

Beaver Meadow Brook to Elizabethtown, 11 m. (17.7 km.)
USGS: Elizabethtown 15 or 7.5 × 15

We made this run on April 22 at medium high water; the month had been dry but snows were still melting in the mountains. With rainfall at or above seasonal norms, water levels should be satisfactory in this stretch till mid or late May. A start in New Russia, below the waterfall, should extend the season another week or two.

This part of the Boquet is narrow, intimate, and winding with a moderately fast current. One speeds along at 6 m. an hour. The drop is about 120 feet. The gradient is steepest in the upper part to the waterfall in New Russia. Here the narrowness of the stream and the need for maneuvering give an exciting impression of speed. But the incline is remarkably steady both above and below New Russia.

Except at flood, the water is clear. It runs smoothly over firm sand or ripples over beds of pebbles and cobbles. Boulders are comparatively few in this reach. Mild rapids are numerous. None exceeds Class II at medium high water, except for the fall in New Russia, where a short carry is necessary. But a degree of danger lurks in deadfalls and leaning trees, especially at sharp bends where the current undercuts the banks. The best evasive maneuver is a back-stroke ferry if executed in time. If broadside contact is made with a strainer (fallen tree), a flip can often be prevented by leaning strongly on the downstream side.

Near the confluence of the North Fork and the South, there is a fork in the highway, Route 9 heading NE down the valley of the Boquet. About 2.5 m. from the fork, Split Rock Falls, R, deserves a

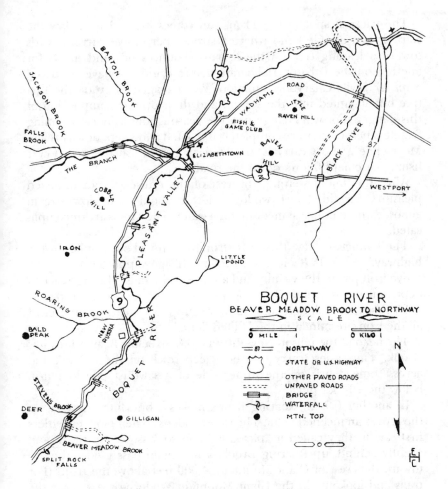

BOQUET RIVER
BEAVER MEADOW BROOK TO NORTHWAY
SCALE

0 MILE 1   0 KILO 1

=87= NORTHWAY

STATE OR U.S. HIGHWAY

OTHER PAVED ROADS
UNPAVED ROADS
BRIDGE
WATERFALL
MTN. TOP

N

visit. Its former owner, Richard W. Lawrence, Jr., who permitted
public access, has now conveyed the area to the state. In summer
the pool is a favorite swimming hole among local teenagers. The
river plunges through a narrow chasm of jagged rock in a fault zone.
Emerging from the gorge into a slowly broadening valley, the stream
quiets down in the next half mile.

The most convenient put-in site is a fishermen's parking lot near
a bridge on a side road which turns E and follows the ravine of
Beaver Meadow Brook. At frequent intervals along Route 9 are bridges
on side roads and fishing-rights easements where one can enter or
leave the river.

The trickiest spot in the 11-m. run comes just 0.2 m. below the start. It is a double bend where a strong, persuasive current swirls toward a leaning tree on the R bank, bounces off, and heads for another on the L bank. Deliberate malice could not have contrived a niftier Scylla-Charybdis situation. We managed to evade the first tree but slammed into the second and flipped. The composition of this danger spot will change in a few seasons, the leaners becoming strainers before they are completely uprooted and swept downstream. Meanwhile a short carry is indicated or a put-in at the next lower fishing easement 0.5 m. down the road.

After this initial wetting, the rest of the cruise was an unmixed pleasure. We glided over two log deflectors about a mile downstream almost without notice at medium high water. The rapids are uncomplicated.

The hamlet of New Russia is strung out for about a mile on the highway. In the 1870s it was a thriving village supported largely by active iron pits in the vicinity and a forge at the falls. Having reached depletion or unprofitability, the pits were abandoned in 1882. In 1880 Essex and Clinton counties were supplying nearly a quarter of all the iron ore mined in the United States.

The head of the falls in New Russia is 3.8 m. below Beaver Meadow Brook. The easiest carry is over a jeep track on the L bank and across some debris on the upper side of a sawdust pile to put-in below the 10-foot pitch.

In another 0.7 m. Roaring Brook makes a brawling entrance on the L over an inclined delta. The valley widens. When pioneer settlers first saw it, they called it "pleasant," and so it is. Off to the L and slightly behind, up Roaring Brook, a mountain pass guides the eye toward the crest of Giant Mountain, 4,000 feet above the river. (For trails and lookouts in the Giant Mountain Wilderness Area, see the ADK's *Guide to Adirondack Trails*.) After a fairly straight stretch of a half mile, the Boquet begins a series of meanders through meadow flats, once the bed of a glacial lake. Usually one side of the river or the other is at wood's edge, while on the open side one looks up at rugged mountain slopes.

Rapids are more widely separated in this lower reach, but the current is still strong. One short bouldery rapid at a bend kicks up the highest waves on the trip, but it is easy to read and negotiate.

Shapely Cobble Hill is much in view before the valley begins to contract and the woods to close in on both sides. Approaching Elizabethtown, the river flows darkly and smoothly in a trough between steep wooded slopes. Tall pines and hemlocks wall in the winding passage. Although the map indicates that village streets are only 200-300 yards away over the hills on the L, no buildings are visible from the river till the bridge on 9N is reached. All approaches to this fairest of Adirondack villages are pleasing, but the river approach is best of all. One wonders how these beautiful forested bluffs ever escaped development. Could it have been planned that way? Or are they simply too steep for a housing development?

Well, E-Town is not entirely blameless. As the banks lowered and some houses began to appear below the first bridge (Route 9N), we saw beer cans on the bank for the first time. In spite of several fishing-rights easements below Beaver Meadow Brook, we had seen no litter till now. Pleasant Valley is pleasant indeed.

The Branch now enters the main stem. A little way below its mouth is the second bridge, the one on the Wadhams Road. Take-out is at the lower R corner of this bridge. Or one can continue 0.8 m. to a fishermen's parking lot at a wide L bend where the river pulls away from the Wadhams Road at a fish and game club. In this section are two log deflectors and a low fisheries dam which should be examined from the road to make sure that, at the existing water level, the wave below each is not a reversal capable of trapping a canoe.

Wadhams Road Bridge to Northway, 6.6 m. (10.6 km.)
USGS: Elizabethtown 15 or 7.5 × 15; Port Henry 15

This section is not a cruising reach. It is best suited for novice to intermediate level whitewater paddlers. Though the first 3 m. are placid, the river then cants into a bouldery trough in the Steele Woods section. It is scratchy unless water levels are high. The first put-in for this section is on the R bank at a fishermen's parking area below the bridge on the Wadhams Road. An informal gauge for this section is the culvert next to the bridge. There should be no more than 2.5 feet of space between the bottom of the culvert and the surface of the river. Mild Class II rapids are encountered for the first 0.8 m. with the only problem the low fisheries dam referred to in the previous section. The drop below this dam results in a sizable hydraulic extending across most of the river. It should generally be avoided, although it is possible to run this drop on the R side after appropriate scouting. In the next 5.8 m. the river drops about 140 feet, with several extended sections of Class II rapids.

In 0.8 m. there is a fisherman's parking lot on the R which serves as an alternate put-in spot. The river assumes a meandering course as it alternates between flat water and mild Class I rapids until Cobble Hill comes into view at 2.5 m. The rapids accelerate slightly for the next 0.5 m., alternating between Class I and II rapids. At a group of islands the current begins to quicken and solid Class II rapids are encountered for the next 0.3 m. They end in a technical Class III drop in which the river goes sharply L, then back to the R, over a course of 30 yards.

Below this point there are nearly continuous Class II rapids for 0.75 m., picking up to Class II-III as Iron Mountain comes into view after a long turn to the R. Here the rapids return to Class I-II for another 0.4 m. until the Steele Woods Road becomes visible on the L. This sight signals a return to Class II-III rapids for several hundred yards before fading to Class I. Mild rapids continue under the Brainards Forge Road bridge at 5.2 m.

From this bridge the Boquet continues 1.4 m. to the Northway (I-87). Most of this water is flat or Class I until 200 yards above the Northway. Class II rapids start at this point and continue under the Northway overpass, where the river turns R into a Class II-III drop of 6 feet in 30 yards posing no major difficulties for intermediate to advanced paddlers. As the bottom portion of this rapid is difficult to see, less experienced paddlers should scout this drop from the R bank to determine the best course. Take-out is on the L just before this drop and involves a short carry up to the Lewis-Wadhams Road. Those who run the drop should then carry upstream on the R bank and ferry over to the L shore take-out just described. The previous edition described a fishing-rights easement 0.6 m. below the Northway on the L bank (0.3 m. by road). The DEC has indicated that this easement does not include canoeing access across the 0.1 m. of farmer's meadow between the river and the Lewis-Wadhams Road. Thus, this take-out (or put-in) should no longer be used.

Northway to Boquet, 16.6 m. (26.8 km.)
USGS: Willsboro, Port Henry 15

In 1972 the Blue Line was extended eastward into Lake Champlain to include the northern part of the town of Westport and the whole of the towns of Essex and Willsboro, former dominions of William Gilliland. This extension puts the entire course of the Boquet in the Adirondack Park.

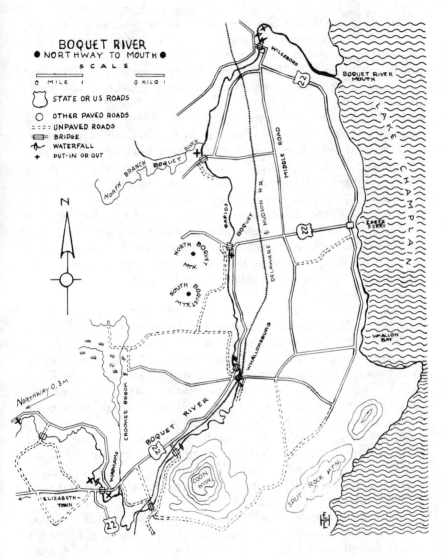

The country is more open on the lower part of the river. The mountains diminish to hills, conical, knob-like, or elongated. The river washes bedrock only at Wadhams, in the cleft under Coon Mountain, at Whallonsburg, and below Boquet. Between these places are quiet reaches in sand and sandy loam soils. The water, clear above the Northway, now shows some cloudiness as it passes through crop and pasture land. Banks are often deeply eroded. Cornices of turf, sliced off in the spring floods or broken off by grazing herds, hang loosely from moorings at the top of the banks. Before the dairy land becomes monotonous, however, the river winds into woods or along the base of a shapely hill. The alternation between wild and cultivated has appeal. No single mile is without some feature of novelty or natural beauty.

Having received important tributaries, the Boquet is a little deeper as well as wider than in the section above Elizabethtown—enough so to extend the canoeing season by another week or two into June if rainfall is normal or above. Three carries are necessary where ledges are encountered. A yoke is therefore advisable. The longer carries (0.3 m. and 0.5 m.) can be avoided by having a waiting car at Wadhams and Whallonsburg. Aside from the carrying places, all rapids are of I-II grade at moderately high water. The drop is about 125 feet in 16.6 m. There are long stretches of meandering flat water, such as the first 5.1 m. to Wadhams, suitable for family canoeing (see Betsy McCamic's "Canoeing the Bouquet" in the September-October 1978 issue of *Adirondack Life*).

The most scenic drive to the put-in is the Wadhams Road out of Elizabethtown. In 4.5 m. it descends into the valley of the creek known as Black River. Just W of the bridge, turn L on the gravel surfaced Brainards Forge Road, which crosses the Boquet on a cement bridge and soon reaches a junction with the hard-surfaced Lewis-Wadhams Road. Turn R here to a put-in beneath the Northway as described in the previous section. The Class II-III rapid immediately below the Northway may be carried or scouted on the R.

At 1.6 m. from put-in was a bridge, now out, on a gravel road. For the next 1.5 m. the river meanders between eroded banks past a large dairy farm and a weatherbeaten, bell-towered antique called the French School. At the second iron bridge, on a dead-end road, is another easement for public fishing.

At 3.6 m. the river heads straight for a picturesque gray cliff buttressing a hill and, on reaching it, makes an abrupt 90-degree L bend. It has hollowed out a small cavity in the rock. At 4.1 m. the channel draws close to the Lewis-Wadhams Road. After looping away from the road again, the river returns to it in the village. The head of Wadhams Falls is reached at 5.1 m.

The owner of land on both sides of the falls has kindly consented to a canoe carry on the R bank if it is understood that he is not liable for any accidents on his property. Appreciation of his cordiality can be shown by using the landing only as a carry and leaving no trace of your passage. Draw over to the R in quiet water, land on a shelving rock, and carry about 100 yards downgrade on a truck track to Route 22. Turn L on the highway, still downgrade; pass the Wadhams Free Library, cross the bridge, and take the first R turn on a dead-end street past a few houses, a cemetery, and a church. The road ends at the river bank in the churchyard. This carry is about 0.3 m. For those desiring to run the rapids below Wadhams Falls, proceed to the R bank 50 yards below the bridge on Route 22 and carry down to the river at a small gravel parking area.

Below Wadhams the river is a little wider, 50–70 feet, and often quite shallow over its bed of sand and gravel. It is probably not canoeable after early June (except following heavy rains) without considerable wading. In mid-May no wading was necessary. The water is clear here except when carrying the sediment washed into it by rainfall.

To Coon Mountain, this is a country of green meadows, rolling hills, and deciduous woods. A railroad bridge is reached at 2.2 m. and soon after, an auto bridge. After some extravagant loops, the stream straightens as it approaches a cleft at the base of Coon Mountain, a ridge which from the river looks like an elephant's back. There are Class I rapids in a cobbly bed. The Ferris Road on the R bank recrosses the river on a second auto bridge about 1.2 m. below the first (3.8 m. below Wadhams). The river narrows here and pours over a ledge. Class II rapids begin about 150 feet above the bridge. If depths are adequate for cruising, there is a narrow squeeze between rocks at the far L and another just R of center. In case a carry (or scouting) is decided on, the country road on the R is convenient. As it approaches the bridge, a short trail on the same bank leads down to a sandy cove where one can relaunch.

Rapids continue for the next 0.7 m. as the river winds around a N spur of Coon Mountain. With the exception of one sharp pitch (Little Falls), they are mild and easy to negotiate. But the bed is shallow in places, and it is necessary to stay in the main current.

About 0.2 m. below the bridge the river narrows to 30 feet in a small chasm and pitches over a V-shaped ledge with a drop of about 6-7 feet known as Little Falls. This drop is rated Class III-IV and is best run on the extreme L. The approach is a little tricky and successful negotiation requires the paddler to punch through the wave at the bottom of the drop and then turn L to go over a second smaller drop. There is a short carry trail on the L bank.

Below Little Falls, the river widens again and ripples over a cobbly bed with passages at the far L and center. As it bends E after rounding the spur of Coon Mountain, two islands divide the channel. The L channel around both makes a bouncy, winding raceway.

Below the islands smooth water of greater depth continues to the outskirts of Whallonsburg. A high eroded bank on the R is perforated by rows of cliff dwellings. The dipping and wheeling of bank swallows in pursuit of insects make a lively scene here in May.

It is 8 m. from Wadhams to Whallonsburg. In the latter hamlet the river drops about 15 feet in 100 yards in a winding, impressive staircase. This passage should be attempted only by skilled boaters and can be examined from the shore or from either of two road bridges in the center of the hamlet. This staircase is rated Class III-IV and requires a zigzag maneuver from L to R and back to L to avoid substantial hydraulics below each ledge. The current here is very fast and makes the required maneuvering very difficult. The rapids subside to Class II by the time the Boquet passes under the first bridge and fade to moving water as the second bridge is reached in 50 yards.

There are two possible carries, one of nearly a half mile and the other of 0.3 m. If a car is available to transport the canoe, the former is preferable. It begins at the railroad bridge at the head of rapids. Carry up the R bank and follow the tracks a little way till a road is seen on the R; take this downhill, turn L in the center of the hamlet, cross a bridge, and continue upgrade to a junction with Route 22. Turn R on the highway and cross the second bridge. Just beyond it, L, is the fire department barn. A bank behind it leads down to a fair landing on the river below the ledges. There is a better put-in behind a white trailer next to the fire house; ask permission of the owner.

The 3.2 m. from Whallonsburg to Boquet is winding smooth water, sometimes clouded with sediment from bordering farms. Traffic on parallel Route 22 is often heard. The E bank is subject to landslides at long intervals. A slide that occurred in June 1937 drew the interest of state geologists. They discovered about ten places where other slides had taken place. One is about 1.5 m. below Whallonsburg near Burt Cemetery, at the crescent-shaped slough (an abandoned channel of the river) which is shown on the 1956 survey map.

A little farther on, the twin peaks, South and North Boquet, come into view. The former, which rises nearly 1,000 feet above the river, restores wildness to the pastoral country in the last 1 m. to the bridge at Boquet. The riverbed is now lightly strewn with boulders. There are occasionaly riffles as a warning of what lies ahead.

Cruising waters end abruptly. Pass under the bridge below the hamlet of Boquet and take out on a ledge at the L. Below the bridge are complex ledges, cascades, and rapids.

Boquet to Willsboro, 6.1 m. (9.8 km.)
USGS: Willsboro 15

The first part of this trip is best reserved for paddlers with basic whitewater skills. The Boquet drops 40 feet in the next 2.5 m., and cruising paddlers who wish to avoid mild rapids may prefer to put in downriver at the next crossing, a concrete bridge on a secondary road. To reach this by car, drive E from Boquet on Route 22 for a little over a mile to a L turn; then N on the latter 1.8 m. to a second L turn, which goes W to the river. (From Willsboro take the West Road and turn R at a T to reach the same concrete bridge.) Put in at the lower W side of the bridge or upstream 0.3 m. from a gravel road on the W bank.

Paddlers who wish to run the upper section below Boquet should carefully scout the initial cascade. This is a Class IV chute dropping over a series of concentric ledges. A far R course is best, although the bedrock is barely covered in spots even at high water levels and there are sizable hydraulics below the bottom ledge. Paddlers wishing to run this may put in on a ledge on the L as described in the previous section. Those wishing to avoid the cascade should carry down a short access track on the W side and put in below the cascade. The next mile consists of predominantly Class I and II rapids with the trickiest section occurring at the first bend.

The rest of the run to Willsboro is alternating flat water and Class I rapids. At 3 m. (just beyond the concrete bridge) the North Branch of the Boquet enters the main stem. Of the last 3 m. Betsy McCamic writes: "This is a good stretch for the novice to practice whitewater technique—eddy turns, draw stroke, back paddling and ferrying." After the last rapid behind the Methodist Church in Willsboro, the stream turns smooth on the approach to the bridge on Route 22. Pass under the bridge (a dam is just 300 yards beyond it), pull to the R, and take out below the bandstand in front of the Willsboro Central School.

The Mouth, 4.4 m. round trip (7.1 km.)
USGS: Willsboro 15

Except for rapids just below the dam and waterfall in Willsboro,
the last 2.2-m. reach is flat water. It has gained in attractiveness since
the closing of a pulp mill in the village. Sludge has settled and the
water has cleared.

The mouth of the Boquet is notable as the site of the first settlement
of Gilliland's colony and General John Burgoyne's treaty with the
Indians in 1777. In the War of 1812 small boats of the British also
used the mouth.

An historic tour that begins and ends in a wasteland, however,
has shortcomings. Access is on the seamy side of an otherwise pleasant
village. One can drive downstream on either side of the river on
streets that soon turn into one-lane tracks below the dam. The track
on the W side passes walls and rubble of the abandoned Georgia-
Pacific pulp mill. The lane on the E skirts a large black cinder dump.
On either side, drive about 0.4 m. below the bridge in the business
section to a put-in at the foot of Willsboro Falls but above a short
rapid at a R bend; to reach flat water below the horseshoe bend,
drive 0.2 m. farther. The lane on the E turns R at a fork, swings
around the slag dump, and comes to a dead-end on the river.

The river is shallow and slow moving between wide wooded banks.
Herons and wood ducks are often sighted. A fish ladder at the dam
in Willsboro, completed in 1982, opened 14 m. of the main stem of
the Boquet and 10 m. of the North Branch to migrating salmon
from Lake Champlain. The river is now one of the leading salmon
fisheries of the state. The banks along the last mile of the river and
also the lakeshore are posted, but boaters use the sandbar inside the
mouth for picnics, fishing, and bathing. Across the lake is the impressive skyline of the Green Mountains. The mouth of the river frames
a magnificent view of the Camel's Hump. The privately owned L
bank is protected in perpetuity against development by a scenic easement held by the Nature Conservancy.

In 1984 the National Park Service completed a study of the Boquet
River, available on request.

LAKES CHAMPLAIN AND GEORGE

Although part of Lake Champlain and all of Lake George are in the southern half of the Adirondacks, they drain into the St. Lawrence through the Richelieu River. They are therefore part of the region's northward flow.

To deal with the two lakes comprehensively would require another volume (see, for instance, Frederic F. Van de Water's *Lake Champlain and Lake George*, 1946, 381 pp.). Their history is rich and complex. Written annals of the region begin in 1609 when Samuel de Champlain canoed up the St. Lawrence and Richelieu rivers into the lake bearing his name and set foot on Adirondack soil near Ticonderoga. The two lakes formed an opening through impenetrable forests that has been called the Path of Empire. Before and after 1609 it was the main route for war parties of the Iroquois of central New York and the Algonquins and Hurons of Canada in their quarrels over territory and the fur trade. The British and the French fought over possession of it for nearly a century. Then for 40 years longer the contestants were the British and the Americans. Many of the most savage and the most brilliant engagements in New World military history took place on the waters or shores of the two lakes. The rest of the Adirondacks was Couchsachrage, land of mystery, till nearly the middle of the 19th century. Time and history passed it by. It was indeed "our dark unstoried woods." But when Francis Parkman coined that phrase, he could not have had the Champlain-George Valley in mind. Hardly an island, a headland, or a bay is without its story.

The names associated with the valley belong to both history and romance, and the distinctions are blurred by the fact that the most romantic of historians and a romancer of historical bent wrote about them. Cooper's Hawkeye, Chingachgook, and Uncas are as real as the figures of Parkman's history of the French and English in the New World, which the author preferred to think of as a history of the American forest. Few corners of the world can yield a more colorful set of characters than Parkman's Champlain, Father Jogues, General Johnson, Hendrick, Duncan Campbell, Major Rogers, General Montcalm, and that model of military virtues, Lord Howe, who died in a chance encounter in "the blind intricacies of the forest" just as the fate of 15,000 troops depended on his leadership. Flawed heroes, most of them, but capable of gestures as splendid as the scenes they moved in. Later action in the valley lacked the benefit of Parkman's pen. But Ethan Allen, Benedict Arnold, and Commodore Thomas MacDonough did pretty well on their own.

To the paddler, the two lakes of the eastern perimeter are a little overpowering. The scale is too grand, in both space and time. Out there in your canoe, you feel like the one frail craft in a Hudson River School painting of Lake George: a dwarf in the immensity, an artist's foil. This is a drastic change from waters of the Adirondack interior. Their history, if any at all, is on a modest scale, and the shores are close enough to make a lone canoe a significant part of the landscape. On spacious George or Champlain, it takes a cabin cruiser, a steamboat, or better yet an armada to cut a figure.

Off Pilot Knob, a gale blowing at your back, waves cresting in foam around your 16-footer, you realize that General Abercrombie had a better idea of fitness in his massive progress down Lake George in 1,000 bateaux and barges. "From front to rear," writes Parkman, "the line was six miles long. The spectacle was superb: the brightness of the summer day; the romantic beauty of the scenery; the sheen and sparkle of those crystal waters; the countless islets, tufted with pine, birch, and fir; the bordering mountains with their green summits and sunny crags; the flash of oars and glitter of weapons; the banners, the varied uniforms, and the notes of bugle, trumpet, bagpipe, and drum, answered and prolonged by a hundred woodland echoes." Lake George deserves that kind of panoply.

To space and time, add weather. Even the Iroquois respected volatile Lake Champlain, sometimes taking a slower and harder route through the forest. To put the situation in the modern vernacular of a camp counselor on the W shore of the lake, "It's a different ballgame out there when the winds come up." This opinion was shared by a Vermonter, Horace Chittenden, writing in *Forest and Stream* in 1900 in answer to a query about canoeing on the lake. "I believe I know every part of its surface and most of its bottom. I have been very near its bottom many times, and very near staying there permanently more than once." The lake is "very tempestuous." According to Chittenden's reckoning, it is navigable for canoes about two days out of seven; the wind blows a gale three days from the S, moderates for two days, and blows two days from the N. As for a trip from Ticonderoga to Burlington or Plattsburgh, the scenery is glorious, the skies brilliant; "nothing will mar your pleasure but the confounded winds."

Two correspondents disputed these views in later issues of the periodical. They denied that winds blow a gale five days out of seven in the months of June, July, and August. One held that Champlain is fine for a sailing canoe, and the other asserted: "I spend one month of happiness every summer cruising and fishing in small boats on those tempest-tossed waters." Still, staying close to shore is a wise precaution against sudden, unannounced squalls that kick up waves capable of swamping an undecked canoe.

Sampling the two lakes piecemeal in favorable weather is probably more enjoyable and certainly less risky than pushing doggedly through the 32-m. length of Lake George or the 125 m. of Lake Champlain, come what may. There isn't enough kudos in it to outweigh the risk. The real long-distance tripper sets his sights on greater feats. For him, George and Champlain are only links in a continental chain of waters. Nathaniel Bishop made boating history when in 1874 he paddled, rowed, and sailed from Quebec City via the St. Lawrence, the Richelieu, Lake Champlain, and Lake George to Troy; thence by a new 15-foot paper canoe down the Hudson and through coastal waters to Florida. Eight years later, at the close of the American Canoe Association meet on Lake George, Charles Neidé set out from Canoe Islands in a Rushton canoe, *Aurora,* on a marathon journey from Lake George through the southern part of Champlain, the Champlain Canal, and the Hudson to Troy; thence by the Erie Canal to Buffalo; he then portaged 70 m. by rail to descend the Alleghany, the Ohio, and the Mississippi to New Orleans. Thence the little *Aurora,* with hoisted sail, continued in salt water along the Gulf coast to Pensacola.

Bishop and Neidé had a companion, but in a second canoe. Going tandem on a long trip risks psychological complications, as two young office workers, Sheldon Taylor and Geoffrey Pope, found in paddling a canoe from New York to Nome, Alaska, in 1936–7. In the first part of their trip, New York to Montreal, they got on each other's nerves, a state known among wilderness travelers as "bushed." One of them said later that the first lap between the two cities was the worst part of the trip. In Montreal they were on the point of abandoning the whole project till newspapers began playing it up and securing financial support. To save face, they completed their northwest passage of 7,000 m. in all. That record was broken on December 15, 1983, when Verlen Kruger and Steven Landick, in two canoes, completed at their home town of Lansing, Michigan, a three-and-a-half year, 28,000-m. marathon in and around North America. To them, who portaged a total of 523 m. and paddled or poled 6,700 m. upstream, the cruise down the Hudson and Lake Champlain was a snap.

A trip like the Taylor-Pope expedition justifies paddling the full length of Champlain. Even a one-season circuit of Northern New York might justify it, on the ground of demonstrating that the top of the state is in reality an island. Starting at Troy, one could take the Barge Canal W to the Oswego River; then paddle down Lake Ontario and the St. Lawrence River to Sorel; and up the Richelieu, Lake Champlain, and the Champlain Canal to the Hudson and back to Troy.

But the people who most enjoy the Champlain-George Valley are the canoe campers on island or mainland who wait out the squalls, take advantage of morning and evening calms, and plan a series of shore cruises in the shelter of bays and islands.

Lake Champlain South
USGS: Whitehall, Ticonderoga, Port Henry 15 (7.5-minute maps also available)

The southern third of Lake Champlain is a river-like narrows never more than 1 mi. wide and usually much less. Marshy shores loved by redwings taper off to pickerelweed beds and cattails in the shallows. The water is somewhat murky.

A DEC leaflet, "Canoe Trips," suggests a 90-m. tour beginning on the Champlain Canal at Fort Ann and ending at the beach in Lake George Village, with a portage between the lakes at Ticonderoga (described below). This might mean bucking the prevalent SW winds on Lake George, however. And the Champlain Canal, entered as far S as Fort Ann, can become monotonous unless enlivened with a little good fishing.

Putting in at Whitehall and continuing N on Lake Champlain to the public beach on Crown Point (37 m.) takes advantage of prevailing summer winds as well as of narrow, protected waters. (The trip can also be ended at the DEC boat launching site at Ft. Ticonderoga on Route 74.) There is no state land in this stretch. Camping is limited to narrow strips between the railroad tracks and the lake unless one obtains permission from private owners at more attractive sites.

Two convenient put-in sites are the northernmost bridge in the village of Whitehall and a DEC launching ramp and parking lot on Route 22. To reach the former, drive past the locks on the main shopping street in Whitehall, which fronts the canal on the L bank, to a small parking area on the N side of the bridge. A trail and concrete steps lead down to a landing. The DEC launching site, a spacious facility, is located 2 m. N on Route 22 across the highway bridge, R, on the W shore.

The latter site can also be used for a short round-trip tour of South Bay. This cleft in the mountains is one of the most beautiful parts of the lake. If two cars are available, a one-way cruise is possible by putting in near the head of the bay from a scenic, little-used road on the W shore. Where this road forks at 2.8 m., take the L fork, which descends to the shore. Stop at the Tracys', the first house, L, below the fork, and ask permission to use a landing near one of the camps owned by the Tracy family at the bottom of the hill, just before the blacktop ends. (A dirt road continues for a half mile farther, past camps, to a scenic waterfall on Day's Creek, which has a vertical drop of 100 feet or more.) Local people caution against landing at the head of the bay in the mouth of South Bay Creek. Rattlesnakes. The old saying that rattlesnakes do not advance (in elevation) beyond the oaks holds true of the Adirondacks. Both rattlers and oaks are found at the comparatively low elevations of the George-Champlain Valley but drop out above the 1,300-foot level. Most of the Adirondacks is free of poisonous snakes.

At Crown Point, the outer part of the peninsula near the Crown Point Bridge is public land, and the state maintains a campground at this historic place. The Crown Point Reservation Campsite is adjacent to the ruins of Fort St. Frederic, built by the French in 1731–36, and Fort Crown Point, built by the British in 1759. The walls of the latter are still standing. Near the forts are a museum and a bathing beach.

Lake Champlain North
USGS: Port Henry, Willsboro 15; Keeseville, Plattsburgh 7.5

For over two centuries Lake Champlain was a link in a chain of travel and transportation from New York City up the Hudson to Glens Falls, by road to Lake George, down the lake by boat, by portage to Lake Champlain at Ticonderoga, and on into Canada.

North of Crown Point, Lake Champlain widens, reaching a maximum of over 12 m. and becoming risky for small boats. The views are magnificent. On the E, across broad pasturelands, rises the wall of the Green Mountains. On the W, the rugged slopes of the Adirondacks rise abruptly from the shore in many places.

Short cruises in the sheltered bays of the W shore and out to nearby islands are suggested, especially in morning hours when winds are likely to be light.

Bullwaga Bay lies between the Crown Point peninsula and the mainland. Canoes can be launched either at Crown Point or at a public beach in Port Henry maintained by the village and the DEC. The flats around this bay provide little protection against wind, however, and are less attractive than other parts of the W shore.

The next prominent indentation is North West Bay. A public launching site is located in the village of Westport, below the Route 22 bridge over Hammond Brook. The cruise from here to Whallon Bay is perhaps the most scenic on the W shore. It is also hazardous on windy days. In the Narrows N of Rock Harbor elevations steepen into palisades under Split Rock Mountain that are dramatic to look at but afford few emergency landings. Even close to shore depths are great. The lake reaches its maximum depth of nearly 400 feet N of Split Rock Point. Taking advantage of good weather, however, camp groups paddle canoes almost every year from Westport around Split Rock Point to Essex or the mouth of the Boquet River, or reverse.

Whallon Bay affords shelter for an interesting short cruise through the split in Split Rock, which marked the boundary between British and French dominions in the New World established by the Treaty of Utrecht. The Essex Town Beach, 2.5 m. S of Essex on the shore road in the crook of the bay, is a convenient put-in site; indeed, the only one for public use. Private owners along the shore are not glad to see uninvited guests, though if an emergency landing is necessary and the owner is courteously approached, he will probably be helpful.

The mouth of the Boquet has already been described. Four-mile deep Willsboro Bay is one of the most scenic parts of the lake. Its E shore, Willsboro Point, is a park-like peninsula of summer homes, and the mainland is ruggedly mountainous. The entire perimeter of the bay is private land except for one small state-owned parcel on the E shore. This is located on the N side of a cove where the neck of the peninsula is narrowest. It is 2.5 m. N of the junction of the Willsboro Point Road (R fork) with Route 22. A L turn off the

Willsboro Point Road leads to a DEC boat ramp and paved parking lot. (There is also a marina in Indian Bay at the outer tip of the point.) Willsboro Bay is ideally suited to canoe cruising.

A public launching site in the hamlet of Port Douglass gives access to Corlear Bay. Schuyler Island, about 1 m. off shore and overlooking Trembleau Mountain, is the only state land in the vicinity. Still farther N are a large state game management area and a public campground near the deltas of the Ausable and Little Ausable rivers, previously described.

The northernmost reach of the Blue Line in Lake Champlain is Valcour Island, a commodious campground which has few rivals elsewhere in the Adirondacks. It is quieter and more isolated than Ausable Point Campsite. It is almost entirely state owned. To protect its wildlife and vegetation, it has been classified as a primitive area under the State Land Master Plan.

In 1972 the Blue Line was extended N and E to include a strip along the shore of Lake Champlain N of the Ausable River and also the whole of Valcour Island. Owners of motels and lodges on the mainland object to inclusion in the Adirondack Park because of restrictions on new building. But the addition of Valcour Island to the park was a major victory for conservationists.

Less than 1 m. from the mainland, the island is unique as a natural area and historic site. Here the British defeated a French fleet in 1759. In the strait between the island and the mainland the first naval engagement of the Revolutionary War took place on October 11, 1776. The makeshift American fleet put together by Benedict Arnold was defeated by the superior fire power of the British fleet in a gallant encounter. Arnold lost nearly two-thirds of his ships. But by holding off the invaders from the N for many months, he gained valuable time for the Colonies.

Valcour is a large island, oblong in shape, "standing green on its pedestal of wave-worn rock." Abundant white cedars grace its headlands and bays. The interior is mostly forest with some overgrown farmland. The climate differs from that of the mainland. In spring, because of the chilling effect of waters just released from ice, the trees are still bare a week or more after leaves emerge on the mainland. In fall a reverse, moderating effect is noted. The island is still in flaming color by the time trees on the mainland are mostly bare.

The mainland shore opposite the island is private and posted. However, there is a public dock, known as Peru Dock, across from the lighthouse on Bluff Point (7.5 m. N of the Ausable Chasm bridge on Route 9). One can also put in at the Route 9 bridge just above the mouth of the Salmon River.

There is no fee for camping, but permits are required at a limited number of prepared sites on the perimeter of the island. Most sites are small and isolated from one another, though on the W shore there is cluster camping at Indian Point and a picnic area in Butterfly Bay. Permits are obtained from a park ranger, who makes daily patrols. If you can't find him, select an unoccupied numbered site and he will issue a permit during his regular patrol. In off-seasons permits can be obtained from the forest ranger in Peru. The most secluded camping sites are on the E shore, which provides a buffer of woods against the roar of jets from the Plattsburgh Air Force base. In circumnavigating the island, beware of Mason's Reef, extending 200 feet from shore, at the N end. And don't pass by Smuggler Harbor on the E shore without a visit. A sickle-shaped point of gray limestone, beaten into odd shapes by wind and wave, encloses a fine natural beach.

The DEC has prepared a system of trails. The main one skirts the entire perimeter, and there are two cross trails, one from the picnic area in Butterfly Bay and the other from Indian Point.

Visitors to Valcour should first read an excellent illustrated article on the island by Anthony Tyrell in the September-October 1982 issue of the *Conservationist*, obtainable in most libraries in the state.

Lake George
USGS: Glens Falls, Bolton Landing, Whitehall, Ticonderoga 15 (or Lake George, Bolton Landing, Shelving Rock, Silver Bay, Putnam, Ticonderoga 7.5)

In appropriating Lake George, North Flow makes a deep incursion into the southern Adirondacks. This is sometimes misunderstood by downstaters. Oriented to the Hudson, they speak of going "up" Lakes George and Champlain when directed Canadaward. After all, the Hudson and its tributary the Schroon, only four to eight miles W of Lake George, are south-flowing streams. The lake is a geographical anomaly. Before the Ice Age the basin it fills was probably a gorge occupied by *two* rivers, one flowing S from the Narrows and the other flowing N. Faulting at some remote time widened the gap, and subsequently the glacier knocked out the divide at the Narrows and left deposits at the S end of the valley to create the present lake.

Lake George is less dangerous for canoe tripping than Lake Champlain. Its maximum width, off Montcalm Point, is 3 m., and its 225 islands, as well as lofty heights, give considerable shelter from winds. Indeed, the lake invites island hopping, and for this the canoe is an ideal craft. Over 150 of the islands are state owned, and of these a third are available for camping.

The largest body of water wholly within the Adirondack Park, Lake George occupies a cleft in the mountains 32 m. long from Lake George Village at the head to Ticonderoga at the foot. It is 319 feet above sea level. Its maximum depth, in a basin of rock and sand, is 187 feet. Fed mainly by springs, its waters are a crystal-clear blue-green.

Lake George has a shut-in appearance. Forested mountains with cliffs and ledges rise abruptly to 2,000 feet or more above the surface, heights unusual on the outer rim of the Adirondack uplift. They are most impressive at the Narrows, a six-mile corridor where the long ridge of Tongue Mountain confronts Shelving Rock, Erebus, and Black mountains. At this central part of the lake the state owns over 20,000 acres on both mainland shores. Here too is a matchless archipelago. Islands range from mere knobs of rock laced with ferns and moss to several acres of wild garden. Paradise Bay, below Erebus Mountain, has been called the loveliest niche of water, rock, and greenery in the world.

The natural beauty of the lake is enhanced by associations from history, legend, art, and literature. As a link in the natural highway through the forest from the Hudson to the St. Lawrence, Lake George once had strategic importance. The first white man of record to see it was the French Jesuit priest, Isaac Jogues, who visited it on Corpus Christi eve in 1646 and named it Lac du Saint Sacrement. During the English challenge to France in the New World (1690–1760) and during the American Revolution, Lake George changed hands several times. It was the scene of scouting expeditions by Rogers' Rangers, of countless skirmishes, and of two major battles. In 1755, after rechristening the lake in honor of his sovereign, George II, General William Johnson defeated the attacking French commander, Baron Dieskau, at the head of the lake. In 1757 Fort William Henry, which Johnson had built near the same site, was besieged and taken by Montcalm. Indian allies of the French commander got out of control and massacred many prisoners. This episode is the historical setting for Cooper's *Last of the Mohicans.*

War delayed settlement for two centuries. In the 1790s a few families cleared land on the gentle slopes between the head of the lake and

Bolton. Even here farming was cramped. Lumbering provided a better livelihood till the tall white pines and other marketable timber gave out. By then, however, tourists were coming in sufficient numbers to leave no doubt about Lake George's destiny as one of the world's principal resort centers.

Today the lake is part developed, part wild. Knowing that recreation is its one lasting source of wealth, local and state protective societies try to preserve its natural beauty as well as to enforce sanitary and navigation codes, stock the waters, and maintain bathing beaches, trails, and camping grounds. Campers on the islands are still able to use the AA-rated water for drinking as well as cooking. (There are springs or wells on a few of the islands.) Considering the heavy use made of the lake, these protective measures have been fairly successful.

On privately owned shores the developments of a prosperous year-round tourist resort and summer colony range from the modest to the elaborate and garish. As early as 1892 Francis Parkman became alarmed by this trend. He wanted to destroy all these works and restore "the most beautiful lake in America" to its primitive wildness. Others thought it was not developed enough. For them it was a country cousin to the elegance of Lake Como's palaces and garden terraces. Grounds for both of these views exist today. But most Americans seem content with the compromise as, on summer weekends, they throng up the Northway to Lake George Village or some of the quieter resort centers down the lake.

Lake George (Cooper's "Horicon") is the setting of the most exciting canoe chase in American literature. Skimming down the lake in a birchbark canoe during an early morning calm, Hawkeye and his party pursue the Indian captors of Cora and Alice. Approaching the Narrows, Hawkeye and Uncas notice a curl of black smoke edging the white mist that rises from the water behind an island. Versed in woodcraft, they know it for a dying campfire. Now they in turn are pursued; merciless foes in front of them and foes behind. Waiting till all seems hopeless, Hawkeye finally lets his rifle Killdeer speak with telling effect. For the moment his party is safe as it disembarks at the foot of the lake.

Lake George has become pacified in the two centuries since that famous chase in *The Last of the Mohicans*. The curl of dark smoke edging the mist now rises from the beaches of many islands in the Narrows. Campers from Brooklyn and the Bronx have replaced the scouts and Indians of other days. Yet you may find yourself working harder on the paddle and suppressing a shudder as you round Mohican, Uncas, or Horicon Island in early morning mists.

When the American Canoe Association was founded in 1880, there was little question about an appropriate place for the first congress. One of the founders who arrived early at Lake George wrote to another, "Everything here is simply perfect. It is the ideal paradise of the canoeist." They had a grand time that August week at the head of the lake, staging races for sailing and paddling canoes and clowning in a dump race. A few months later three of the founders purchased the group of islands known as the Three Sisters 5 m. below the head of the lake. Rechristened Canoe Islands, they became the site of the next two annual encampments. And in 1980 the ACA celebrated its first centennial at the head of the lake.

Today it would be misleading to call Lake George the ideal paradise of the canoeist. The internal combustion engine is now lord of the lake. Powerboats, from put-puts to speedboats, yachts, and excursion vessels, greatly outnumber canoes. The bigger the lake, the bigger the powerboats, the more numerous the water skiers, and the less tolerant they all are of the canoeist.

The powerboat nuisance is hard to escape on a two-day, full-length cruise of the lake in summer. It can be escaped, however, by choosing time and place carefully. In early morning the lake's surface is likely to be calm and powerboats few. The rest of the day can be spent exploring a group of islands, hiking on state trails on the mainland, or puttering about an island camp. In this way a full-length cruise can enjoyably be stretched to five days or a week. The DEC has provided excellent facilities to make camping and lingering agreeable. Canoes and camping equipment can be rented in village and hamlet at the head of the lake and along the W shore.

On the mainland are three large public campgrounds: Lake George Battleground Campsite at the head, adjacent to Battleground Park and the celebrated Million Dollar Beach; Hearthstone Point, 2 m. N on Route 9N; and Rogers Rock, 3 m. N of Hague near the foot of the lake. Most canoeists prefer to camp on the islands. Forty-eight of the state-owned islands are equipped for camping, with tent sites, fireplaces, and privies; another group is reserved exclusively for picnic parties. For a sketch map naming and locating the islands and for information about camping, write to the State Department of Environmental Conservation, Bureau of Forest Recreation, Albany, N.Y. 12233. Leaflets can also be picked up at the district office of the

DEC in Warrensburg. For trails in the Lake George region, see *Guide to Adirondack Trails: Eastern Region*, published by the Adirondack Mountain Club.

Briefly, there are three centers for island camping. Permits must be secured from caretakers (on duty from mid-May to mid-September) at each of these centers before tents can be erected. In the southern part of the lake, Long Island is the center; at the Narrows, Glen Island, where there are a store, a post office, and public telephones; and Narrow Island, near Huletts Landing.

The islands of the Narrows are closest to the trails in the Forest Preserve that extends for nearly 9 m. along both shores. A limited number of camping sites, accessible only by water, have also been developed on the mainland shore between Pearl Point and Red Rock Bay. The primitive conditions that Parkman first admired as a college sophomore and wanted to keep forever are best preserved at this part of the lake.

The two most convenient access points for cruising among islands of the Narrows are Rogers Memorial Park and Beach in Bolton Landing (reached by a lane on the S side of the Bolton Free Library) and a DEC launching site 6 m. N on 9N. From the former it is 2.5 m. to the Narrows group; from the latter, nearly 5 m. by way of Northwest Bay Brook, Northwest Bay, and Montcalm Point.

A rather complicated portage in Ticonderoga awaits the long-distance tripper shuttling from George to Champlain. The 3.5-m. outlet, La Chute River (referred to on some maps as Ticonderoga Creek), drops 224 feet over a series of dams and rapids in circling Mount Defiance. It empties into Lake Champlain near reconstructed Fort Ticonderoga and a museum commemorating the checkered history of the place under various flags. Here in 1775 Ethan Allen surprised the British commander with his pants down and demanded surrender "in the name of the Great Jehovah and the Continental Congress." An inspired banner for the nation aborning; cocky yet tentative, like the national character.

Virtually all of the 224-foot drop occurs in the initial 1.5 m., where there are six dams and whitewater sections. Several of the dams are breached and all but one (the third) require carries. Sections between the dams generally range from moving water to Class III ledges; the major exception is a brief Class IV drop between the first and second dams. A recently completed construction project by the DEC has diverted the existing flow into two penstocks, one of which is underground. A minimum flow of 30 cubic feet per second, barely a trickle, will continue down the existing channel. This will all but eliminate paddleable sections on this part of LaChute unless additional water is directed into the riverbed during periods of high water. Thus, this construction project has resulted in a virtual loss of meaning for the original Mohawk word for Ticonderoga. Murray Heller tells us that this word, Chigonderoga, means "the place where waters sing as they swiftly cascade over the rocks into the lake." River enthusiasts will now have to be satisfied with hiking along the riverbed and imagining what this river looked (and sounded) like in its original wild state. Nevertheless, the tailrace of the lower penstock enters the riverbed just below the last dam, where a falls is located. This should allow sufficent water for a cruising trip down the remaining 2 m. of river.

Although the upper part of LaChute River is steep and obstructed, the last 2 m. are navigable. Use of the public landing at Mossy Point would involve a carry of 2.4 m. through the village. This can be shortened by 1 m. by proceeding N in the outlet bay to the bridge on Alexandria Avenue. Take out just below the bridge or at the end of a gravel road, Tin Pan Alley. From here carry R to the village street that honors its origin by the name of The Portage, though it is lined now by houses instead of pine trees. Follow The Portage downhill into the business section and turn R on Montcalm Street to the Heritage Museum in a village park, once the site of an abandoned paper mill. Put in below the falls, at a covered bridge designed only for foot traffiic, for a flatwater float to Lake Champlain. At the mouth you are just below Fort Ticonderoga. No signs or gates deter paddlers from walking right up into the grounds. Visitors, friendly or hostile, are no longer expected from the water, as they were in the 18th century.

In 19th century art and letters Lake George was a symbol of the grandeur of the primitive American landscape. To see the lake as it was represented by Cooper and Parkman and by such painters as John F. Kensett and Asher B. Durand, time and place must be carefully chosen. Pick one of those magical sunny days in October when a calm settles over the waters and the glassy surface of the bays reflects the shore's crimsons and golds. The water skiers have gone. Cold nights have discouraged campers on the islands. Most of the retired people on leaf-watching tours are content with the view from motel terraces.

On such a day, paddle out from Bolton Landing. Once in the Narrows, among the islands, you may have the luck of experiencing the lake in its primitive silence and majesty.

CANOE CAMPING
by Robert N. Bliss

The enjoyment of the Forest Preserve need not be restricted to the backpacker, the bushwhacker, and the peak-collector. For many, an intimate view of the assets with which our wilderness areas abound can be attained in rather easy fashion by canoe. One starts with those lakes easily accessible from boat liveries; but the determined canoeist soon leaves the big lakes behind and explores the smaller lakes and ponds, the winding streams that connect them, and the inlets that drain the swampy areas, which are as characteristic of the Adirondacks as are its High Peaks.

The best canoe exploration is the one in which the pressure of time is not dominant. Imaginative planning for an extended trip allows for stopovers to permit the fisherman to try his skill, the photographer or artist to capture the activity at a beaver dam, the bird watcher to stalk the blue heron or the loon. Although an early morning start is often essential when the afternoon wind is a threat on a big lake, time should be set aside occasionally for a leisurely breakfast of piles of blueberry pancakes, preceded by a hot cupful of wild cranberry sauce. It pays to stop early enough in the afternoon to select your campsite for more than merely the essentials of tent space and clean water; you'll want to site the tent for a view of the dying fire, of the rising moon, or of the first rays of the morning sun. And with luck, you may find a cedar log to cut and split for a quick blaze and unforgettable smell.

We in the Adirondacks are fortunate that, up to now, provisions of the law and its administration by the DEC have allowed considerable freedom to both hiker and canoeist. Compare the situation in the Maine Woods and in the Pine Barrens of New Jersey, for instance, where fire danger has restricted available camping area to designated sites easily supervised. In Maine many trips may be taken only with a state-certified guide. In the Adirondacks the self-guided canoeist is free to select his own camp site on state land, provided that it is at least 150 feet removed from a road, trail, stream, spring or pond and is under 4,000 feet in elevation. With the exception of heavily used areas, no permit is necessary in the Forest Preserve for stays of up to three nights. On some water courses the state has erected lean-tos, with some fireplaces and pit privies. These too can be used for three nights without permit or fee.

Responsibility goes hand in hand with freedom. The next party appreciates a clean camp. Every canoeist should be a good ecologist. Cans, bottles, cartons, plastic bags and jugs are lighter after their contents have been emptied; they should all be carried out. So should foil and paper. Even biodegradable items like orange peels are offensive to those who follow soon after. Using the woods and streams as dumps is an abomination. The canoeist has even less excuse than the hiker for leaving any article behind him. Equipped with an easy way of floating trash out of the woods, he should cheerfully pick up after others as well as himself.

The supply of firewood is often short at lean-tos on popular routes such as the Saranac and the Raquette. According to regulations on the use of the Forest Preserve, only trees that are dead and down can be used for fires. Though a wood fire is a pleasant thing at close of day, sometimes it involves more labor than it is worth. A lightweight camp stove with fuel is quick and safe. Wood fires at undeveloped sites call for special precautions. In the top layer of forest soil a fire may smolder for days before it breaks into flame. A large flat rock is the best base for a wood fire. If none can be found, all inflammable material should be removed down to sand or clay. Fires should be allowed to burn out completely; the ash thoroughly wetted and then scattered to leave little or no trace.

Not so long ago one could drink Adirondack brook and spring water with confidence. That day has passed. It is wise to assume that local waters are unsafe. *Giardisias*, a parasite found in fresh water, represents the greatest concern. Known also as "Beaver Fever," *giardisias* has been reported with increasing frequency in the Adirondacks. Standard preventive measures are now called for, preferably bringing fluids from home. When this supply runs out, procure water from sources upstream from your camping site and boil all drinking water for at least three minutes.

Perhaps the greatest pleasures are made possible by the small group. A party using no more than four canoes is a safe, self-contained unit, can expect to find adequate campsites, and should be quiet and closely knit enough to see and hear all that the area has to offer.

Aluminum is a material used frequently in making canoes today. Once the almost exclusive choice of canoe liveries and wilderness outfitters, it is increasingly being replaced by other materials. Its primary advantages are its relatively low cost, its substantial carrying capacity, and the fact that it is practically unsinkable. It is noisy, however, and floats so high that it is a real problem in a wind. A fin keel is an aid to stability in lake travel but is a nuisance on rocky streams and in rough water, where quick maneuvering is necessary. An aluminum canoe intended for use primarily on streams should be fitted with a shoe keel.

Many trippers still prefer the canvas-covered wooden canoe, and a few purists even hold out for the all-wood craft. These are lovely objects in or out of water. But they are vulnerable, require a good deal of maintenance, and are relatively heavy.

The fiberglass canoe or kayak has now enjoyed many years of popularity. It compares favorably with aluminum in terms of weight and is durable and easy to repair. Cross bracing is not so essential as with aluminum or wood, and fewer thwarts leave more room for duffle and facilitate moving from one end to the other. Aesthetically, a canoe of this material can be a match for the wood-and-canvas one. Although most early kayaks and covered canoes were made of fiberglass, many newer models are constructed using plastic or Kevlar materials as described below.

A structural material known under the trade name of Royalex and described by one manufacturer as "vinyl/ABS/foam sandwich" came into wide use in the 1970s. It is tough, lightweight, more flexible than fiberglass, and buoyant, providing its own flotation. Due to these qualities, Royalex and similar plastic materials are often preferred by whitewater paddlers. Like fiberglass, it needs little cross bracing. When struck by a paddle, it gives off a dull, hollow sound like wood. Its quietness in the water is an advantage in observing wildlife. It needs little repair or upkeep.

A still newer synthetic fiber, Kevlar, is said to be five times stronger than steel pound for pound. It is so light that manufacturers are able to make boats up to 40 pounds lighter than aluminum or fiberglass ones. Its portability may offset the greater cost, especially on routes where there are many carries. Some manufacturers combine Kevlar with other materials to help keep costs down while continuing to provide boats with sleek designs and high performance capabilities.

A useful purchaser's guide has appeared each year in a fall or winter issue of the magazine *Canoe*. It lists the principal makers of canoes and kayaks and the models they offer, with construction material, weight, dimensions, carrying capacity, and price. The same magazine has a buyer's guide to canoe and kayak paddles, now offered in a bewildering variety of styles and materials. You must experiment to find the paddle best suited to you. Make sure that you have a spare one in each canoe in case of breakage.

In trips that push on regardless of weather, it is important to keep equipment dry. Each trip leader favors his own time- and trip-tested mode of packing, but all agree that it is important to place a few light poles in the bottom of the canoe to raise the cargo above the bilge water resulting from heavy rain or from waves shipped over the side. If, in addition, you pack all your food and personal gear in double plastic bags and cover the whole with a tarp or ground cloth, well tucked in, you should be in good shape to enjoy the bad weather when it comes. What is worse than a wet sleeping bag? And don't forget foul-weather gear for yourself as well; it's better to be sweaty and warm than shivering from a leaky raincoat or windbreaker. For early spring and late fall trips, many use skin divers' wet suits or even dry suits as a precaution against upset in cold water. State boating regulations require that a life saving device for each person be on board.

Anticipating and sharing the jobs that are an essential part of canoe camping are a must. The fun and the fellowship that are by-products of community cooking are worth all the work they involve. Keep menus simple. Encourage a rotation of the work schedule: men make good cooks and women are excellent wood gatherers. A folding saw and a sharp hatchet may be preferable to an axe. All should share in the various phases of clean-up preparatory to leaving a campsite. If you have packed your food intelligently, you will be carrying no extra weight in glass or metal containers which you must then pack out with you. Err on the side of cooking too little cereal or macaroni until you are aware of the varying appetites of your company. A hot fire can be used to burn excess food, but this is wasteful of both good material and the efforts of your cooking crew.

If you are primarily interested in the conveniences of civilization— replacement cartridges for your LP lantern, fresh eggs for breakfast, ice for your martini, and the six o'clock news report—these and many more are available through the expanding network of public campsites and boat liveries in New York and adjoining states. But to attain a feel for the wilderness and for the self-contained independence of the group that relies on its stomachs to tell the time and seeks to break away from schedules and bells, invest in a selection of topographic maps; spend time following dirt roads in your car; and put your canoe in a winding stream for a day of scouting. Don't forget to respect the "No Trespassing" sign of the private owner. Above all, expect to invest significant physical effort as a down payment for your isolation.

Adapted from *Adirondac*

SAFETY CODE OF THE AMERICAN WHITEWATER AFFILIATION

I. PERSONAL PREPAREDNESS AND RESPONSIBILITY

1. *Be a Competent Swimmer* with ability to handle yourself underwater.
2. *Wear a Lifejacket.*
3. *Keep Your Craft Under Control.* Control must be good enough at all times to stop or reach shore before you reach any danger. Do not enter a rapid unless you are reasonably sure you can safely navigate it or swim the entire rapid in event of capsize.
4. *Be Aware of River Hazards and Avoid Them.* Following are the most frequent *Killers:*
   A. HIGH WATER. The river's power and danger and the difficulty of rescue increase tremendously as the flow rate increases. It is often misleading to judge river level at the put-in. Look at a narrow, critical passage. Could a sudden rise from sun on a snow pack, rain, or a dam release occur on your trip?
   B. COLD. Cold quickly robs one's strength, along with one's will and ability to save oneself. Dress to protect yourself from cold water and weather extremes. When the water temperature is less than 50 degrees F., a diver's wetsuit is essential for safety in event of an upset. Next best is wool clothing under a windproof outer garment such as a splash-proof nylon shell; in this case one should also carry matches and a complete change of clothes in a waterproof package. If, after prolonged exposure, a person experiences uncontrollable shaking or has difficulty talking and moving, he must be warmed immediately by whatever means available.

    C. STRAINERS: Brush, fallen trees, bridge pilings, or anything else which allows river current to sweep through but pins boat and boater against the obstacle. The water pressure on anything trapped this way is overwhelming, and there may be little or no whitewater to warn of danger.

    D. WEIRS, REVERSALS, AND SOUSE HOLES. The water drops over an obstacle, then curls back on itself in a stationary wave, as is often seen at weirs and dams. The surface water is actually going UPSTREAM, and this action will trap any floating object between the drop and the wave. Once trapped, a swimmer's only hope is to dive below the surface where current is flowing downstream, or try to swim out the end of the wave.

5. *Boating Alone* is not recommended. The preferred minimum is three craft.

6. *Have a Frank Knowledge of Your Boating Ability.* Don't attempt waters beyond this ability. Learn paddling skills and teamwork, if in a multiple-manned craft, to match the river you plan to boat.

7. *Be in Good Physical Condition* consistent with the difficulties that may be expected.

8. *Be Practiced in Escape* from an overturned craft, in self rescue, in rescue, and in artificial respiration. Know first aid.

9. *The Eskimo Roll* should be mastered by kayakers and canoers planning to run large rivers and/or rivers with continuous rapids where a swimmer would have trouble reaching shore.

10. *Wear a Crash Helmet* where an upset is likely. This is essential in a kayak or covered canoe.

11. *Be Suitably Equipped.* Wear shoes that will protect your feet during a bad swim or a walk for help, yet will not interfere with swimming (tennis shoes recommended). Carry a knife and waterproof matches. If you need eyeglasses, tie them on and carry a spare pair. Do not wear bulky clothing that will interfere with your swimming when water-logged.

II. BOAT AND EQUIPMENT PREPAREDNESS

1. *Test New and Unfamiliar Equipment* before relying on it for difficult runs.

2. *Be Sure Craft is in Good Repair* before starting a trip. Eliminate sharp projections that could cause injury during a swim.

3. Inflatable craft should have *Multiple Air Chambers* and should be test-inflated before starting a trip.

4. *Have Strong, Adequately Sized Paddles or Oars* for controlling the craft and carry sufficient spares for the length of the trip.
5. *Install Flotation Devices* in non-inflatable craft, securely fixed, and designed to displace as much water from the craft as possible.
6. *Be Certain There is Absolutely Nothing to Cause Entanglement* when coming free from an upset craft; i.e., a spray skirt that won't release or tangles around legs; life jacket buckles, or clothing that might snag; canoe seats that lock on shoe heels; foot braces that fail or allow feet to jam under them; flexible decks that collapse on boater's legs when a kayak is trapped by water pressure; baggage that dangles in an upset; loose rope in the craft, or badly secured bow/stern lines.
7. *Provide Ropes to Allow You to Hold Onto Your Craft* in case of upset, and so that it may be rescued. Following are the recommended methods:
    A. KAYAKS AND COVERED CANOES should have 6 inch diameter grab loops of ¼ inch rope attached to bow and stern. A stern painter 7 or 8 feet long is optional and may be used if properly secured to prevent entanglement.
    B. OPEN CANOES should have bow and stern lines (painters) securely attached consisting of 8 to 10 feet of ¼ or ⅜ inch rope. These lines must be secured in such a way that they will not come loose accidentally and entangle the boaters during a swim, yet they must be ready for immediate use during an emergency. Attached balls, floats, and knots are *not* recommended.
    C. RAFTS AND DORIES should have taut perimeter grab lines threaded through the loops usually provided.
8. *Respect Rules for Craft Capacity* and know how these capacities should be reduced for whitewater use. (Life raft ratings must generally be halved.)
9. *Carry Appropriate Repair Materials:* tape (heating duct tape) for short trips, complete repair kit for wilderness trips.
10. *Car Top Racks Must Be Strong* and positively attached to the vehicle, and each boat must be tied to each rack. In addition, each end of each boat should be tied to car bumper. Suction cup racks are poor. The entire arrangement should be able to withstand all but the most violent vehicle accident.

III. LEADER'S PREPAREDNESS AND RESPONSIBILITY

1. *River Conditions.* Have a reasonable knowledge of the difficult parts of the run, or if an exploratory trip, examine maps to estimate the feasibility of the run. Be aware of possible rapid changes in river level, and how these changes can affect the difficulty of the run. If important, determine approximate flow rate or level. If trip involves important tidal currents, secure tide information.

2. *Participants.* Inform participants of expected river conditions and determine if the prospective boaters are qualified for the trip. All decisions should be based on group safety and comfort. Difficult decisions on the participation of marginal boaters must be based on total group strength.

3. *Equipment.* Plan so that all necessary group equipment is present on the trip; 50 to 100 foot throwing rope, first aid kit with fresh and adequate supplies, extra paddles, repair materials, and survival equipment if appropriate. Check equipment as necessary at the put-in, especially life jackets, boat flotation, and any items that could prevent complete escape from the boat in case of an upset.

4. *Organization.* Remind each member of individual responsibility in keeping group compact and intact between leader and sweep (capable rear boater). If group is too large, divide into smaller groups, each of appropriate boating strength, and designate leaders and sweeps.

5. *Float Plan.* If trip is into a wilderness area, or for an extended period, your plans should be filed with appropriate authorities, or left with someone who will contact them after a certain time. Establishment of checkpoints along the way at which civilization could be contacted if necessary should be considered. Knowing location of possible help could speed rescue in any case.

IV. IN CASE OF UPSET

1. *Evacuate Your Boat Immediately* if there is imminent danger of being trapped against logs, brush, or any other form of strainer.

2. *Recover With an Eskimo Roll if Possible.*

3. *If You Swim, Hold onto Your Craft.* It has much flotation and is easy for rescuers to spot. Get to the upstream end so craft cannot crush you against obstacles.

4. *Release Your Craft if This Improves Your Safety.* If rescue is not imminent and water is numbing cold, or if worse rapids follow, then strike out for the nearest shore.
5. *When Swimming Rocky Rapids, Use Backstroke with Legs Downstream and Feet Near the Surface.* If your foot wedges on the bottom, fast water will push you under and hold you there. Get to Slow or Very Shallow Water before Trying to Stand or Walk. Look Ahead. Avoid possible entrapment situations: rock wedges, fissures, strainers, brush, logs, weirs, reversals and souse holes. Watch for eddies and slack water so that you can be ready to use these when you approach. Use every opportunity to work your way toward shore.
6. If others spill, *Go After the Boaters.* Rescue boats and equipment only if this can be done safely.

INTERNATIONAL SCALE OF RIVER DIFFICULTY

(If rapids on a river generally fit into one of the following classifications, but the water temperature is below 50 degrees F., or if the trip is an extended one in a wilderness area, the river should be considered one class more difficult than normal.)

CLASS I. Moving water with a few riffles and small waves. Few or no obstructions.

CLASS II. Easy rapids with waves up to three feet and wide, clear channels that are obvious without scouting. Some maneuvering is required.

CLASS III. Rapids with high, irregular waves often capable of swamping an open canoe. Narrow passages that often require complex maneuvering. May require scouting from shore.

CLASS IV. Long, difficult rapids with constricted passages that often require precise maneuvering in very turbulent waters. Scouting from shore is often necessary, and conditions make rescue difficult. Generally not possible for open canoes. Boaters in covered canoes and kayaks should be able to Eskimo roll.

CLASS V. Extremely difficult, long, and very violent rapids with highly congested routes which nearly always must be scouted from shore. Rescue conditions are difficult and there is a significant hazard to life in event of a mishap. Ability to Eskimo roll is essential for kayaks and canoes.

CLASS VI. Difficulties of Class V carried to the extreme of navigability. Nearly impossible and very dangerous. For teams of experts only, after close study and with all precautions taken.

INDEX

Owls Head Mt. (Raquette R.), 72
Owls Head (pinnacle), 191-192
Oxbow, 82, 84

Pace University, 3
Palmer Brook, 80
Palmer Creek, 17
Palmer Hill, 62
Panther Gorge, 254, 270
Panther Mt., 208
Paradise Bay, 313
Parkman, Francis, 305-306, 314, 316-317
Parishville, 123
Parmenter Site, 95-96
Path of Empire, 305
Partlow Milldam, 20
Partlow Mt., 30-31
Pa's Falls, 109
Paul Smiths (post office), 125, 127, 132, 149-150, 158, 160, 207, 241, 252
Paul Smith's College, 89, 126-127, 153, 241-242, 349
Paul Smith's Hotel, 124, 153, 210
Peacock Mt., 259
Perkins, Terry, 30-31
Permanent Rapids, 229, 251
Pern, 312
Peterborough canoes, 24, 126
Pettis, Clifford, 153
Pettis Pond, 30
Phelps, Orson S. ("Old Mountain"), 61, 270, 272
Philosophers' Camp, 64, 228
Picketts Corners, 239
Picquet, Francois, 6
Piercefield, 65-66, 80, 86, 88, 95, 98, 251
Piercefield Dam, 88-89, 93
Piercefield Flow, 66, 88
Pier Rapids, 90
Pine Pond (Franklin Co.), 226-227
Pine Pond (St. Lawrence Co.), 50
Pine Ridge, 27-28, 253, 349
Pink Pond, 213
Pins Creek Trail, 12, 346
Pioneers' Crossing, 194
pioneers, 29, 72, 243
Pitchoff Mt., 271-272
Plains of Abraham, 260
Plains, The, 26-27
Plattsburgh, 203, 206, 240, 307
Plattsburgh Air Force Base, 288, 290, 312
Pleasant Valley, 296-297
Ploof Falls, 140
Plumadore Mt., 191

Plumley, John, 65
poling, xii, 23-24, 28, 52, 86, 230, 308
Polliwog Pond, 211-213
pollution, 40, 126, 131, 228, 273, 283-284, 288, 304, 319
Poncet, Joseph, 6
pond-hopping, 209, 252-253
Pond Road, 184-186, 191-192
Portage, The, 317
Port Douglas, 311
Porter Mt., 275
Porter, Noah, 272
Port Henry, 310
Port Kent, 206
Port Kent-Hopkinton Turnpike, 146
Port Kent Road, 141-142
posting, 2-3, 15, 33, 39, 46-47, 114, 133, 142, 144, 190, 193-194, 234, 245, 268-269, 276, 294
Post, Marjorie Meriweather, 126
potholes, 77
Potsdam, 44, 65, 96
Potsdam sandstone, 141, 205, 283
Power Project Road, 97
Precambrian rock, 57, 140-141
Presidential Range (White Mts.), 281
Preston Ponds, 99, 100
private preserves, 42, 71, 103, 113, 116, 123, 131, 192
Pulaski, 141, 181
Pulpmill Road, 141, 181

Quebec Brook, 132-133
Quebec Province, 1, 6, 193
Queen Victoria, 208

Radford, Harry V., 116
Rainbow Falls
  Ausable Lakes, 272
  Ausable R., 254, 282
  Grass S. Br., 47, 53, 57
  Osweg. M. Br., 17, 347
Rainbow Falls Reservoir, 97
Rainbow Inn, 243
Rainbow Lake, 126, 151, 207, 241, 243, 253
Rainbow Narrows, 241, 243-244
Randorf, Gary, 153
Rapids Trail, 32
Raquette Falls, 64-65, 77, 79
Raquette Lake, 63-64, 66-67, 70
Raquette Lake (hamlet), xii
Raquette Pond, 82, 85-86

ADDENDUM 1

Long Pond Road to Bryants Bridge, 22 miles (33.5 km.)
USGS: Number Four 15; Oswegatchie SW, Oswegatchie SE 7.5

Access to the headwaters is reached by taking the Long Pond
Road extension to the E, past an area known as Bergen's Clearing.
Town maintenance ends here and the road is gated during the off
season. Since 1986, the DEC has kept this stretch of dirt road open
during good weather, usually from mid-to-late May until conditions begin to deteriorate in the fall. The road is about 10 m. long
and requires 45 to 60 minutes to traverse one way. Four-wheel drive
is not needed, but vehicles should have medium to high clearance
for the numerous ledges, rocks, and culverts.

Just under 10 m. from the gate the road passes next to the river at
a point called High Landing, a quarter mile E of Buck Pond, the
headwater of the West Branch. This is the easiest put-in, down a
steep, 30 foot high bank. Just beyond this the road is again gated
and there is a small parking area for day and overnight users. Those
camping over three nights require a permit from the local ranger
stationed in Croghan. This ranger and staff from the Watertown
office may be contacted for information regarding water levels and
dates when the gate is open.

The put-in is located about 8.5 m. below Walker Lake, the
headwater of the Middle Branch. There is a short canoeable section
upstream from the put-in, at Moynihan Flow, although travel to
the Flow is very difficult. Below the put-in the Middle Branch is
classified as a wild river and drops 740 feet on its way to Bryants
Bridge. Much of the drop is concentrated in two sections of heavy
rapids. Paddlers wishing to attempt these sections of rapids should
possess intermediate to advanced skills and should check for
appropriate water levels. The best gauge is at the take-out at
Bryants Bridge. The water surface should be no more than 4-5
inches below the bottom of the drain pipe in the concrete base of the

bridge. At these levels the first extended stretch of rapids is still quite rocky. Paddlers should realize that they are unlikely to find higher water levels during those times when the Long Pond Road extension is ungated. This stretch is best run after periods of heavy rainfall in late spring or early fall.

At High Landing the Middle Branch flows NE. The first half-mile consists of shoals, tapering gradually to a sandy bottom and mild current as the river enters Alder Bed Flow. The Flow is simply beautiful. It begins very narrow, about 20 feet wide, with banks alternating between grass and trees. An esker lines the left bank. Gradually widening to about one-third of a mile, the corridor offers a pleasant vista of Alder Bed Mt. to the L and a high altitude marsh teeming with deer and waterfowl. The western boundary of the Totten and Crossfield Purchase crosses the Flow at about the halfway point. Tracing the 106-year-old blazes left by the original survey party, Colvin and his party in 1878 were impressed by the Flow: "We reached at length a broad branch of the little Oswe-gatchie, flowing through a large swamp; the stream abounded with speckled trout, and a handsome string was easily caught with coarse tackle from where we forded it."

At just under 5 m. below the put-in the Flow narrows and turns to the NW. Here the Middle Branch begins its first tumultuous descent of the upper plateau, with rapids beginning at the ruins of an old wooden bridge. In the next 2.6 m. the river drops a total of 180 feet. With the exception of three brief flat stretches, rapids are continuous. Several foot trails enter from the L, but are difficult to find from the river's edge.

The first half of the rapids requires constant maneuvering through a long, congested boulder garden requiring precise, technical maneuvering in the shallow water. These rapids are pre-dominately Class II and III, with two brief stretches of Class V. One is a steeper portion of the boulder garden where the route becomes highly congested and the other, a 10-foot vertical drop. Carries are short but require dragging boats through dense growth. In the second half of these rapids the boulder gardens tend to end in steeply sloping drops and ledges ranging from 3 to 8 feet. These drops are generally Class IV in difficulty, but one, at a sharp turn to the right, is Class V. Shortly before the end of the 2.6 m. stretch the river touches the boundary of St. Lawrence and Herkimer counties. This point is indicated by an old posting by Schuler Farms, the previous landowner before the property was acquired by the state.

One-third of a mile later Glasby Creek enters from the L and signals the end of the first extended stretch of rapids.

At this point the river begins to veer N. Rapids become less frequent and intense and are separated by delightful cruising sections. Shortly below Glasby Creek the river crosses into St. Lawrence County. There is a 10-foot high log dam flanked by the first of many pink granite ledges, followed by a half-mile long ravine where rapids gradually build to Class III. The next mile is a relaxing float, punctuated by several easy rapids. Bassets Creek enters from the R, shortly before encountering another half-mile stretch of Class II-III rapids.

Below this the Middle Branch flattens and the banks begin to be dominated by several varieties of softwoods, mostly spruce. The river also veers back to the NE as it begins to approach the Streeter Lake trail off the R bank. This area is a good spot to camp for those wishing to break the trip into two days. Below, the river turns sharply 120 degrees to the L and heads W, passing a second approach to the Streeter Lake trail. Soon, there is a second old posting by Schuler Farms on the R and, directly across from it, yellow blaze marks indicating an earlier boundary of the Forest Preserve.

In the next 3 m. the river drops 80 feet. Rapids are Class I and II, with one slightly more difficult stretch at the S-shaped opening of a small ravine. Pins Creek enters from the R, with the Pins Creek trail bordering the R bank for a short distance below. Toward the end of this 3 m. stretch the river again enters Herkimer County, marked by blue blazes, and private postings begin to appear. Wolf Creek enters from the left. In the next 1.2 m. rapids become somewhat more difficult, generally Class II and III. At the tail end of one rapid is an old camp on the L bank, signalling the beginning of a dramatic change in the river's character. In contrast to earlier stretches, the next several miles of rapids consist of fairly discrete drops and cascades which are very powerful. Many of the drops require carries by intermediate level paddlers and even advanced paddlers will need to scout the drops very carefully.

Rapids above the camp are Class II and build quickly to Class IV as the camp is reached at the head of a scenic mini-gorge flanked by pink granite ledges. At the top of the gorge, the river drops 10 feet in 20 yards. Immediately below is a Class V rapid consisting of three successive drops of 5 to 8 feet, the last one just after a 90 degree turn to the R. Rapids taper past a second camp on the L upon entering a short flatwater stretch called Mullins Flow. Below Mullins Flow is a washed-out bridge and then another Class III ravine. Mild rapids continue below here to a concrete bridge. While in these rapids the river crosses into Lewis County, marked by the first postings of a second game club. The county line represents the beginning of the canoe easement from Lassiter. Lassiter allows car travel on the 4-m. length of gravel road connecting Bryants Bridge and the concrete bridge, but only for the purpose of subsequent canoe travel; passage is not allowed for hiking or other purposes. The concrete bridge serves as take-out for those wishing to avoid the next several miles of river or, alternately, as a put-in for those wishing to paddle only the 4-m. stretch to Bryants Bridge. As is the case with Long Pond Road extension, this road is gated during the off season. Paddlers considering use of this road are advised to check with Lassiter or the Watertown office of the DEC prior to their trip to confirm that the road is open.

Below here, rapids are consistently difficult and require intermediate to expert skills. The total drop is 300 feet. In 0.75 m. the river turns 90 degrees to the R at the head of a deep ravine. Major rapids run continuously for the entire length of the ravine, about 100 yards, beginning with a series of Class IV pitches and ending in a dangerous but potentially runnable Class V-VI drop of 10 feet. The carry is tough and involves lowering boats down steep vertical ridges. Lady's slippers are in abundance here in early June and allow a pleasant diversion from the grueling carry.

Class I-III rapids are found to the head of the next ravine in about 0.5 m. At this constriction the river drops 12 feet, turns sharply right, and drops another 18 feet over a protruding ledge. This cascade is unrunnable and must be carried. Class III-IV rapids predominate in the next quarter mile before gradually tapering to Class II-III and then a short section of flatwater. The next drop is a Class V sloping ledge with an 18 foot drop in 15 yards, reminiscent of some others on the East Branch of the Oswegatchie between Fine and South Edwards. Next is a twisting, corkscrew-shaped drop of about 15 feet, rated Class V-VI. Mild water ensues for the next 0.3 m. upon approaching Rainbow Falls. This dramatic falls drops about 85 feet in two fairly distinct pitches of 35 and 50 feet. Between these two pitches is a rather abrupt 90 degree turn to the L. The carry on the L takes advantage of the shortened distance as well as several existing foot trails. A number of camping sites can be found at the top of the ridge and are very inviting. Rainbow Falls must surely rank with any other Adirondack waterfall in majesty and beauty. Spend some time here, well off the beaten path, to enjoy a rare vista. Camping becomes restricted at a point 500 feet below the falls.

From the top of the ridge, carry 0.1 miles to a convenient entry point and negotiate 0.5 m. of Class II-III rapids. These end in a Class IV-V flume dropping 12 feet in two pitches followed quickly by a slightly easier flume dropping 8 feet. From here to Bryants Bridge, about 0.5 m., rapids are predominately Class II-III, with one more Class IV pitch of 8 feet thrown in at the midpoint.

A single-day trip takes a minimum of 8 hours on the river and another 4 for the longest and slowest of Adirondack shuttles proportionate to the 22 miles of river travel. Those choosing a single day paddle will find it a most tiring experience, as did my partner, Chip Jenkins, and I (DM). Others wanting to try this same stretch in one day are advised to get an early start, take few breaks, and hope for no misfortunes along the way. Draft a friend if you can—someone with a phobia for river running but a spirit of adventure for the road—to drive you from Bryants Bridge to the headwaters. Of course, the trip can easily be stretched to two or three days, allowing a chance to relax and explore the surrounding terrain. The drawback, however, is that parties with camping gear are going to have to line or carry many of the rapids. Like the upper Cold, perhaps the best compromise is to paddle this stretch in lightweight boats unencumbered by camping gear and arrange to meet friends at a midway point.

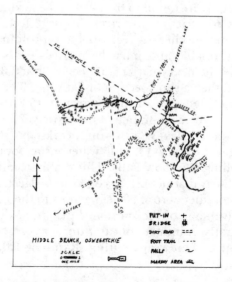

MIDDLE BRANCH, OSWEGATCHIE

ADDENDUM 2

Newton Falls to Meacham Lake, 131 m. (211.3 km.)
USGS: Newton Falls, Cranberry Lake, Five Ponds, Wolf Mountain, Meacham Lake 7.5; Long Lake 15; Tupper Lake 15 or 7.5 x 15; Upper Saranac Lake, Saint Regis Mtn. 7.5 x 15; Saint Regis, Saranac 15

This trail connects the Oswegatchie and Osgood systems and was scouted by Ron Canter. It begins with the East Branch of the Oswegatchie at Newton Falls and continues upstream to Pine Ridge. Here it traverses the county line trail described on page 253 to Nicks Pond, Big Deer Pond, and the W end of Lows Lake. Proceed down the Bog River to Tupper Lake, up the Raquette to Stony Creek, and over Indian Carry to Upper Saranac Lake. From the launching site at the N end of the latter, carry 1.7 m. to Little Green Pond and proceed over the route of the Seven Carries (see index) to Paul Smith's College. Carry N across the campus to Church Pond and paddle through the chain of ponds to Osgood. At the NW corner of Osgood Pond look for an old logging road and follow it out to Route 30. Carry on Route 30 to a trail on the L to Barnum Pond (0.8 m.). Paddle to the N end of Barnum Pond and then take Route 30 again to the access road on the R to Mountain Pond, 0.7 m. Paddle from the S to the N end of the latter. Take out at a campsite on the L and carry N 0.7 m. to the Osgood River by road, passing around a gate over a state fire truck road. Paddle down the Osgood into Meacham Lake, cross the S end of that lake into its outlet (E Branch of the St. Regis), and take out at the Route 30 launching site.